W9-COL-659

THE INTERNATIONAL NOMADS

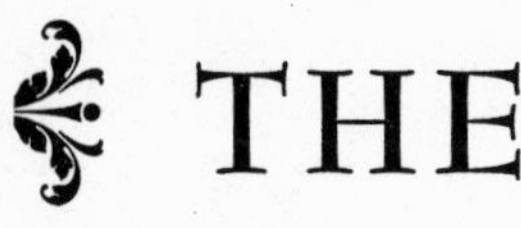

THE INTERNATIONAL NOMADS

by Lanfranco Rasponi

G. P. PUTNAM'S SONS

NEW YORK

© 1966 *by* LANFRANCO RASPONI

All rights reserved. This book, or parts thereof, must not be reproduced in any form without permission.

Published simultaneously in the Dominion of Canada by Longmans Canada Limited, Toronto.

Library of Congress Catalog Card Number: 66-15588

PRINTED IN THE UNITED STATES OF AMERICA

To My Mother

The nomadic instinct is a human instinct. . . . It has a charm, which once tasted, a man will yearn to taste again.

—Mark Twain in *The Innocents Abroad*

Contents

Illustrations will be found
at page 128

Introduction

In order to obtain the necessary information for this volume, I became a wayfarer myself for one year and followed as many members of the migrant set as possible during their various displacements. Since then the problem with which I have been confronted has been an overabundance of material. At the time I first became conscious of the growing impact that this new, vast society had on our times, I lived in New York City where I ran a public relations firm. It was, however, only when I actually joined these wanderers and studied them at close range that I realized how profound the ramifications involving this new way of life are, along with the deep psychological consequences.

I chose Paris as my headquarters to write about this roving species for two reasons. First of all, the components of this new breed of population pass through the French capital several times a year on their numerous professional assignments and pleasurable pursuits, and secondly, the phenomenon of globe trotting is new to the French, among the most conservative of races. This appeared, therefore, as a worthwhile observation post. It did not take me long to discover that the Ritz Hotel bar is no longer the place to feel the throbbing pulse of people in motion, but Orly Airport. There, in the space of an hour, one runs into numerous members of this shifting society, either arriving or departing.

It is impossible to evaluate so revolutionary a period of transition until much later. But it is safe to predict that the astonishing restlessness which has taken over so large a group of humanity must eventually somewhat subside. As yet, people are still fascinated by the fact that new means of transportation have annihilated distances, and they cannot take this speed in their stride.

This constant uprooting, the main basis for nomadism, is not only a form of escape but a purveyor of various processes in which dehumanization plays a leading role. The pendulum must eventually swing back, and some persons are bound to realize that while a Caravelle is a most satisfactory method of conveyance, it does not provide a cozy permanent home.

The tapestry facing me has been exceedingly wide, and the difficulty in keeping up with the changes in the lives of the persons mentioned in the forthcoming pages has been considerable. Every time I came to a new paragraph, news reached me of a divorce, remarriage, a house sold or bought, a suicide, a tragic car accident, or a fatal heart attack. As I write this short preface, I am well aware of the inevitable modifications which will have occurred by the time the book appears in print. To write about the contemporary scene is becoming increasingly tricky for today the river of life no longer flows but rushes by at gigantic speed.

No malice has been intended, but humor, yes, as every society has its humorous aspects and none as many as this ever-growing number of men and women poised for flight. Unfortunately, people in a tearing hurry have less time to laugh, particularly at themselves. The greatest sadness confronting today's nomads is that spinning in orbit augments their nervous tension, allowing them less and less opportunity to stop and take stock of their foibles.

During my wanderings to study nomadic habits the most unusual member of this species I ran into was a very old professional beggar who always stood at the same street corner in Tangiers. He attracted my attention because every time I went by him, I heard the sound of music. One day I stopped to inquire where it came from and he showed me a small transistor radio he kept in a pocket of his long, flowing, tattered robe. The magic box kept him company, he explained, during the long, lonely hours of the exercise of his trade.

I also discovered that he was a nomad, too, spending the winter in Marrakesh, the spring and summer in Tangiers, and the fall in Rabat. He followed the tourist trade. Usually he traveled by bus, but on one occasion a wealthy Moroccan had given him a lift in his private plane. "It was very exciting," he said, "but the time went by too fast. A great part of the pleasure of travel to me is the realization that certain distances must be covered. Aladdin's wondrous carpet has made the world smaller, but has it made life any better?"

I am indebted to him for these wise words, as I am to all the many friends and acquaintances who have assisted me generously in helping me gather the material. I am grateful to Nancy Mitford for inventing the status of U members as against the non-U, Julia McCarthy for the designation "chic chat" she sometimes uses in her Nancy Randolph column in the *Daily News,* and *Vogue* magazine for the very eloquent term "youthquake." The initials N.S., which run through the book, are a short cut to Nomadic Society, an expression I have coined for this new group of persons in constant motion. C.C., on the other hand, stands for a certain elite which I describe as the Chic Club.

Lanfranco Rasponi
Paris, August 1965

1

The Roots of Today's Nomadism

A rapidly increasing new group of people has emerged, after the Second World War, molding a new way of life—the nomadic one. Ever on the move, these persons have created a veritable revolution in the social structure of all classes with far-reaching consequences which as yet cannot be properly and completely evaluated.

Throughout time immemorial in certain sections of Asia, the Middle East, and the Dark Continent, today as two thousand years ago, certain tribes have followed a migrant existence, from birth to death, without ever knowing any permanent home. With their roots deeply implanted in their ancestral clans, these men and women were capable of recreating a community every few weeks in a new locality. Their choice was usually determined by where, at a given time of the year, the best grazing land could be located for their animals. With their easily transportable tents, the only semblance of a hearth, these people limited their possessions to a minimum, since for many, the only means of transportation was walking.

The new Western nomads have little in common with their Oriental and African counterparts except ideologically, since they are too in a continual search for greener pastures. On a practical basis, they are confronted with far more varied difficulties and their peregrinations are infinitely more complex. For millions the motive is business or work, for some a tax situation, and for others a combination of restlessness and the pursuit of pleasure. While the latter are, numerically, the most insignificant, they are the most easily recognizable and therefore the most discussed and publicized.

Today's nomads are always engaging in skirmishes along several fronts in their peripatetic lives. The barriers of language, diet, and climate are profound, but the hardest to pierce is also the most subtle: understanding the psychology of the people and country they happen to be visiting. Although the citizens of the world in the upper strata tend to do away more and more with their particular customs, there is still a long way to go before their racial and national characteristics, imbued with centuries of traditions, are totally erased.

Travel has become a huge business today, with such far-reaching consequences that even the Ecumenical Council of 1964 took it up at length during some of its sessions in Vatican City. In a very short space of time, traveling has changed from an occupation of the rich or near rich to an overall concern of the masses.

In her genial tome *A Winter in Mallorca,* Aurore Dudevant (who wrote under the pen name of George Sand), makes the following statement: "All of us, when we have a little leisure and money, travel, or rather we escape, for the question is not so much to travel but to escape. Is there anyone among us who has no sorrow to distract or yoke to shake? No one." These words, which she formulated in Nohant in 1855, ring today as those of a prophetess.

Little could this extraordinary woman have imagined that her journey to Mallorca, in the exalted company of Frédéric

Chopin, would usher in a new conception of mobile living. People moved around, of course, in her day, but with the exception of explorers and diplomats, always along some conventional itineraries. This lady did not just go to the remote Balearic island—getting there a century ago presented untold complications—for an outing, but to settle down in order to get away from the wear and tear of the French capital. She rented a drafty apartment in a former convent and lived there for several months. So completely startling was this action of hers, in thought and execution, that the dazzled Parisians spoke of little else that season.

Since Palma, on Mallorca, is today less than a two-hour hop from the French capital, many are those who fly there for the weekend. All over the Parisian metro are plastered announcements of cottages for sale there, another proof of the evolution which has taken place in the one hundred and ten years since George Sand put this part of the world on the map. Mallorca today is run-of-the-mill, and the waterfront of Palma, similar to the silhouette of Manhattan, is thick with skyscraping hotels.

As vital as pleasure travel has become in the contemporary design for living, with many millions every year becoming globe-trotters, trade travel is even more significant, affecting countless families in numerous nations throughout the year. Even a moderately successful businessman inevitably spreads his activities on an international level and his interests keep him on the go.

Immigrants were, until a short time ago, citizens who pulled up their stakes at home to settle in another country for the rest of their lives. This is rarely true today. Laborers nowadays take on temporary jobs, often moving from one state to the other, fulfilling certain commitments on a contractual basis and bargaining for a better one elsewhere. Over a million and a half Italians are now employed in Germany, France, Switzerland, Holland, Belgium, and England, with Spaniards, Portuguese, Greeks, North Africans, and more recently Turks, being brought in by huge airlifts. Latest figures reveal, among others, that Germany has well over one million foreign workers and Switzerland in excess of seven hundred thousand. The result of this constant shifting of populations is that hundreds of thousands of people flow yearly within the European boundaries—not to speak of all those who take off for Australia, Canada, and South Africa. Their wives and children follow them, tearing up their roots and necessitating no end of adjustments. Never have embassies and consulates been snowed under by so many pressing needs to solve and so many new responsibilities.

The invasion of the Negro is also a fascinating new occurrence. More and more Africans who come to attend schools and universities find jobs, marry European girls, and never go home. Despite the collapse of both the British and French colonial empires, the bond appears to be still very strong. London is jammed with East Africans and West Indians, with the large English cities following suit. Paris and the industrial French centers are heavily accented with West Africans and natives from Martinique and Guadeloupe. As far as the North Africans are concerned, with unemployment rising constantly in their countries, a conservative estimate is that one hundred thousand are coming into France each year.

With the exception of the United States, the need for technicians, mechanics, masons, electricians, plumbers, and blacksmiths is so pressing that every facility is supplied to encourage this mass migration and render it as painless as possible. In the Swiss cities it is calculated that one out of three inhabitants is a foreigner, and in the streets of Geneva, Lausanne, Bern, and Zurich far more Italian and Spanish is heard than French or German. As in New York City, where several motion-picture houses show only Spanish-language films, there are many European cities in which certain theaters give exclusively Italian and Spanish features. There recently have been regular campaigns in the Swiss press against the growing proportion of marriages between the local girls and the foreign workers, but the government has not felt it could interfere in this matrimonial merry-go-round. Where would Switzerland be at present were it not for this imported population? Who would build the badly needed highways, work in the hospitals and hotels? Many would have to close down. But as the standard of living keeps rising everywhere, one wonders where laborers will be found.

The business interests of the United States all over the world have become so gigantic that it is estimated that well over two million Americans are currently living out of the country. This number can only increase with the continuing new investments large American corporations are making in foreign lands.

Among the greatest nomads today are the Heads of State, who are perpetually paying official visits to their colleagues and issuing endless communiqués on their beliefs of the brotherhood of man and democracy. The various capitals are greatly inconvenienced by these frequent arrivals and departures, with the main avenues and streets closed to normal traffic, forbidden for parking, and all sorts of other restrictions enforced.

These state visits represent a tremendous expense on all sides. These dignitaries bring with them large retinues of aides, hangers-on and political appointees, along with a vast crew of secret service men. Their transportation usually consists of costly jets or Caravelles chartered for the occasion. The host, anxious to put his best foot forward, organizes as good a show as possible, entertaining at immense receptions where guests queue up for ages, dinners, banquets, theatrical spectacles, military reviews, and parades during which heaps of medals pass hands. Everyone decorates everyone else. First ladies are sent on a tour of hospitals and orphan homes, and official photographs are taken showing them holding some child in their arms. These festivities never fail to disrupt the existence of many officials who must drop other important assignments in order to map out the details of the forthcoming stay of the distinguished (*distinguished,* that is the word always used to describe them) guests.

Each government appears to control the press sufficiently to have it publish glowing accounts of how new industrial areas are rising out of some jungle a few weeks before the forthcoming visit of the President of an obscure African country (hard to find on a map, since only a short time ago it did not exist) or a minor South American republic. This is done in a routine attempt to try to stir up some enthusiasm in the local population which could not be more apathetic to these foreign Heads of State with whom it has absolutely no interest in common.

What everyone agrees upon is that these journeys are very effective publicity in promoting government chiefs at home and abroad. The journalists find far more to write about General de Gaulle shaking hands with the colorful Peruvian Indians than with the bourgeois folks in Arcachon and about the Pope blessing the wretched Hindu pariahs in Bombay than the usual pilgrims at the Vatican.

It is now an accepted dogma that in order to be better known one must be in orbit much of the time. The Kennedy administration understood this so well that the late President paid several official visits abroad, enhancing his prestige among his countrymen and around the world, and his photogenic consort went on trips of her own which received daily front-page headlines in every country. Photographs of the First Lady riding an elephant in India and on nautical skis in the bay of Amalfi are among the many which have remained in the memory. All the European newsreels gave tremendous coverage to Senator Robert Kennedy's Polish visit.

The Pope, who has come out of the ivory tower of his predecessors, has taken to jets and helicopters like a pro. His recent excursions to Jordan, India, and the United States are but the beginning of his travels. Symbolically enough, he spent his sixty-eighth birthday among gypsies from all over the world at Pomezia, near Rome, and called them "beloved nomads." What Paul VI has lost and gained by so doing will be undoubtedly discussed for many years to come. The only two Heads of State who remain in their respective countries are Generalissimo Franco of Spain and Doctor António Salazar of Portugal.

In mid-November 1964, as the King and Queen of the Belgians boarded the airplane for Teheran to be the guests of the Shah of Iran, a weary communiqué from Laeken Palace was issued stating that this would be the last trip of state Their Majesties would undertake for the rest of the calendar year. This simply meant that since their stay in the Middle East was to last fifteen days, they actually would not go off, officially, during the month of December.

Royal visits are much coveted, even by republics, for their publicity value. Fabiola of Belgium learning how to go through the tea ceremonies in Japan; Fabiola comforting the lepers in India; Fabiola praying along the various stations of the cross in Jordanian Jerusalem, this is the stuff of which newspaper dreams are made. And the graceful Spanish lady, who has proved to be a superb Queen, is helpless and must play along as if she were a movie actress. Publicity is vital in the lives of royalty and, willing or unwilling, they must learn to accept it.

The following story is an indication of how paramount promotion is today among the royal families. The Grand Duchess Charlotte of Luxembourg, who recently abdicated in favor of her son Jean after a rule which stretched for more than four decades, has always been shy and somewhat retiring. When, shortly before her resignation from public office, she went on a state visit to France, gossip has it that some members of General de Gaulle's entourage felt that, since she only ruled over 370,000 people and since, because of her aversion to publicity, she was in no way a world figure, a few of the expensive items on the usual program for Heads of State could be cut out.

No, the General is reported to have replied, the Grand Duchess may not be a great attraction for the press, but she is a very fine lady who behaved magnificently during the last World War, and she shall have every honor and privilege. Needless to say, what the General wants he gets, and the Grand Duchess was treated the way her sturdy qualities merited.

All Cabinet Ministers, for one reason or the other, are ever in the air, and close on their heels are the countless officers of NATO, SHAPE, the UN, EURATON, UNESCO, FAO, UNICEF, the European Economic Commission, the Common Market, and a myriad of other organizations. Senators and congressmen of many nations are constantly on the go, sometimes with their wives and children, attending some international conference. In the name of culture, thousands travel every year with all expenses paid. Exhibits of all kinds, artistic or industrial, ramble here, there, everywhere, with officials in charge. The inanimate precious cargoes usually have leading personages following them around. When Leonardo's "La Gioconda," Whistler's "Mother," the "Venus de Milo," Michelangelo's "Pietà," go on a journey, all types of experts are on hand. Every sort of entertainment unit is sent on long propaganda tours and in rapid succession the people of Seattle, Bordeaux, or Santiago are exposed to the Japanese Kabukis, a German Chamber Orchestra, the Mexican National Ballet, the Soviet Choir of Leningrad, or a troupe of Balinese dancers.

With the rising standards of living everywhere, the growing attitude of spending and not saving, the "Travel Now, Pay Later" arrangements, the vacation periods getting longer, the vast number of men and women who retire at an earlier age, travel is not only within everyone's reach but a feverish state of mind shared by all. Everywhere one is confronted with some advertisement for a holiday. The "Relax and Unbend" industry has become a veritable monster with infinite commercial overtones. The correct wearing apparel plays a big role, along with the means of transportation which is resolved, in some cases, by trailers. The latter, which have reached such a staggering number in the United States, are also on the increase in Europe, but are not used so much as permanent homes.

This travel convulsion is all the more fascinating in what have been, up until a short time ago, the sedentary races, especially the French. Suddenly, inexplicably, they are all over the place, and between June and September in 1964 it was calculated that seven million Frenchmen spent their francs in Spain. The United States, which had never been properly aware of its tourist potentialities except among its own citizens, is now devoting time and energy to attract foreign tourists. The American Commerce Department reported that during 1964 there were close to one million business and pleasure visitors to the U.S.A.

Although it is not the concern of this volume to discuss or enter the many interesting phases of mass tourism, an indication of the rabid importance governments assign to the cut-throat competition which has arisen as a result merits a short parenthesis, particularly because of its humorous aspects.

Italian newspapers and magazines, all through 1964, bemoaned and decried the diminution of tourism in their country. The statistics of the Ministry of Tourism had indicated that twenty-one million tourists had come to Italy during 1962, a decrease from the preceding years. The real shock came when it was learned that this was not a general malady but a local one, since Greece had increased her tourist industry by 20 percent and Spain by 15. In the overwhelming mass of recriminations—it must be remembered that tourism is the greatest source of foreign exchange in Italy—several causes were adduced, such as a general increase in prices, the appalling noise made by the motorscooters which prevented guests from sleeping at night, the frightening lack of discipline of the Italian motorists, the defilement of the beaches by the petrol and sewage, and the growing presence of thieves in hotels and pensions. But since the Italians always have their minds on sex, the directors of the Ministry of Tourism concluded that many women tourists had been scared away by the *pappagalli* (parrots), the name given to importuning males in search of companionship. Therefore it was decided to form special police battalions to be on the lookout for these disturbers of the peace.

"They should have their heads examined," a hotelkeeper declared to me in Ischia. "These hypocritical Christian Democrats are now really going to drive tourism into the ground. This is the final straw. The main reason foreign ladies come to Italy is simply because of the Italian male. They absolutely adore being molested and get very upset when no attention is paid to them. Don't these idiots know that in Greece and Spain the males also assault and besiege the girls? What do you think all these Swiss, German, and Scandinavian members of the fair sex have been coming to Italy for? Just to look at the ruins and visit the churches? Let me tell you differently, and I have been in the hotel business over thirty years. After those long, cold winters in their northern countries with their well-behaved men, they want some excitement, and we Italians provide it for them." This opinion is shared by many in the hotel trade and it will be most enlightening to see if this point of view is correct and if the *Squadre del Buon Costume* (literally, the Squads of Good Habits) will affect tourism even more adversely.

The theory advanced by some of the hotelkeepers is not disproved by certain facts, for if there has been marked tendency of northern women to go to the Mediterranean countries without male escorts, there has been an equally marked tendency for dark, swarthy men to invade the northern countries in the summer months. Anyone who has been to Norway, Sweden, Denmark, Germany, and Holland at this time of the year can attest to it. The coldness of these waters and beaches has suddenly become a great magnet for Italian, Greek, and Spanish males, as well as for the North Africans and Negroes settled in Europe. A Moroccan student at the Sorbonne, who headed a group of five in a rented car to tour the Scandinavian countries, thus summed up the situation to me: "Girls in France are not in the least difficult," he said, "but one must discuss Balzac, Proust, and Simone de Beauvoir for at least three hours before reaching the evaluation of the pleasures sung so effectively by Ovid. In the northern lands, girls are sensible enough to want to recite the erotic poems of Ovid almost immediately after the first meeting."

To travel for free is a spreading tendency for more and more individuals. The most fantastic reasons keep coming to the fore, but the word "mission" is rarely missing. Scholarships are ever expanding and so are all sorts of grants for esoteric research. One is apt to meet someone who has been sent by a foundation to make a study around South America of streaked blue and yellow butterflies, or to investigate the use of pink shells among primitive races, or write a report on the different string instruments employed by Polynesians. No country is better equipped with foundations than the United States—a direct consequences of the tax system. And there are all types of Americans, rambling all over the cosmos, who are enjoying this setup from which they draw, quite rightly, every possible advantage.

Scientific expeditions are spreading in all directions, paid for by foundations, with men intent on destroying every bit of mystery left in nature and his fellow creature. Universities seemingly afford all sorts of treks for chemists, geologists, physicists, biologists, ornithologists, zoologists and archaeologists. The last swarm over Turkey, Greece, Egypt, southern Italy, North Africa, the Kenya and Tanganyika coasts, Mexico, and many other sites, digging happily away. Since every country is thirsty for tourists, these archaeological discoveries are seemingly profitable. Excavations, according to government officials, are costly but in the long run pay back their investment when the locality becomes a mecca for visitors.

All over the world, cities, universities, and colleges have their own sports aggregations which are on the move both at home and abroad. The rugby squads of Europe and South America have become so immensely rich that they can afford to buy players at astronomical sums from their competitors. Therefore, a provincial team in Italy is apt to have a Brazilian Negro, an Englishman, and a Cypriot if these men are necessary to provide the right kind of shot in the arm. Athletes of all sorts, both men and women, professional and amateur, are forever catching a plane to make another personal appearance somewhere.

Conventions, which grow larger and more numerous daily, have become economically so desirable for a city or resort that the mayors, the hotel managers and the airline executives turn somersaults in order to obtain their patronage. As companies increase their revenues and their employees receive better salaries, more and more of these gigantic get-togethers take place abroad. It is naturally more exciting for the druggists of Portland, Maine, and Davenport, Iowa, to assemble for their annual meeting in Mexico City than in Denver. The same is true for the Central American dentists, who would much prefer to gather in Trinidad at Carnival time than in Panama City.

International congresses, also leaping forward in number, are another reason for all sorts of executives being aboard planes. Certain industrial shows are again a cause of travel. Let anyone try to find a free bed in Paris at the time of the Automobile Show in the early fall. There isn't one available as throngs pour in from all sides.

With taxes steadily, inexorably, rising everywhere, and socialism no longer on the march but on the double, individuals are understandably doing what they can to defend their interests against these all-enveloping octopi. With the glaring examples of what can happen suddenly (Egypt, Cuba, Algeria, Tunisia, and all the way down the line) when private property is either confiscated or paid close to nothing, the public is more and more inclined to distribute its investments high and wide. With the wind of agrarian reform blowing on all the continents (except in the United States), the form of rural wealth, which for centuries was the most dependable, is not only finished but condemned to oblivion. It is a strange paradox indeed that just as the governments are expropriating land from the owners to distribute to the unwilling peasants, the latter are fleeing farms by the thousands to go and live in crowded dwellings in large cities and work in industries. The future of agriculture is so dreary at the moment that no one is buying land anywhere except for building purposes.

Despite the general collapse of the agricultural fabric of the economy, real estate booms are surging. Wherever investors have reason to believe that socialism is advancing at a slower pace (areas like the Caribbean islands, Greece, Portugal, Spain), a veritable rush is on to acquire every available plot of land. Because of recent developments, the North African countries, with the exception of Morocco, which some consider less risky, have been eliminated completely from the blueprints of speculators.

The tax system, which is so designed everywhere that it affects the middle incomes more than the high ones, is responsible for the remarkable crescendo of nomads who simply cannot afford to be residents anywhere. They must keep on the move, stay less than six months here, fewer than three there. One hears all the time that it is cheaper for persons of a certain income to keep roving than to stay still, and absurd as it may seem, if one investigates this matter, it is absolutely true. If they stay beyond a certain period, they automatically become residents, and then the internal revenue agents pounce on them like lions on helpless zebras.

International lawyers and accountants are multiplying everywhere, daily, hourly, and rule over the lives of these individuals, keeping abreast of all the changing rules and regulations which, in the over-all name of democracy, tie up the citizen in invisible cords of silk. The abrupt love for tiny islands, mountain villages, or minute principalities which so many men and women affect nowadays is a form of deep gratitude they feel for the place which temporarily affords them protections from some tax. New corporations are born yearly by the thousands in Panama, Liberia, Monaco, Lichtenstein, the Bahamas, or anywhere in the world that is favorable to these special setups. People increasingly avoid having properties in their own names and place everything they own under that of some company.

Universities all over Europe and the Americas are swarming with students from Asia, Africa, and the Near East. They live in lodging homes and fraternities, creating an incredible impact on all the youths with whom they come in contact and fostering desires to journey to distant countries. In the space of six weeks, while driving around Europe, I ran into some Jordanian students in Seville, who had learned Spanish well enough to be able to follow the courses at the university there and prepare for graduation, various Iranians who were following courses in Portuguese at the celebrated University of Coimbra and a group of Nigerians studying medicine in Munich. These thousands of students often do not go home for the holidays, preferring to travel.

The impact of youth in this second half of the twentieth century is like a flood which breaks down all the dikes. There is no stopping this rising generation. At a very early age they are utterly independent from their kin, manage to roam on very little, often pick up jobs as they go along, stay in ever-expanding youth hostels or in extensive tent towns which now meet the eye all over the world in the warm months. Some of these camps, to which even older members are admitted, are the last word in comfort, with the Club Méditerranée leading them all. Rothschild financing has been most advantageous in acquiring some of the finest stretches of beach in existence for this corporation. It has now extended its activities as far as Tahiti and a charter flight from Paris, with a three-week stay in the Pacific paradise, costs around one thousand dollars. Alluring tents or straw huts for sleeping quarters can be found in Polynesia, Sardinia, Sicily, Greece, or on the Spanish coast, the food is reputed to be most satisfactory, and there are up-to-date shower facilities with hot and cold running water. In the Alps in winter time this club is also forging ahead with a growing number of accommodations in huts and cabins which are in demand because of their low rates.

American youngsters have invaded Europe, North Africa, and Central America. By the thousands, they arrive on freighters or charter flights, their luggage often consisting of a knapsack. They hitch rides for their excursions or buy broken-down automobiles and scooters. Some of them are real beatniks—the men with stringy hair and beard and the girls wearing shapeless tunics—who often form choral units to the accompaniment of guitars and ukuleles, making the rounds of cafés in the evening and passing the plate. The artists do large chalk drawings on the sidewalks and then sheepishly suggest to the passerby that he drop a coin. Many of them settle down abroad, and Tangiers is full of them. I have heard them referred to in Europe as "The American Flea Market."

There are no greater wayfarers than the members of the entertainment guilds. It is rare indeed that a film today is made in only one place, and, when it is, there are usually some very strong publicity reasons. Tennessee Williams' play *The Night of the Iguana* could easily have been shot in a studio, since most of the action takes place in a rundown tropical hotel. However, John Huston wisely had the set built at Mismaloya, a remote location on the Pacific coast which can only be reached by boat from Puerto Vallarta (which is connected with the rest of Mexico only by air). The expense must have been considerable, since even all the cottages for the stars had to be constructed, but the publicity value of his plan to isolate in the jungle these strong personalities was absolutely brilliant. The space given in the newspapers and publications to the making of this motion picture will remain memorable in the annals of drum-beating.

A great many screen projects are currently international and actors, directors, producers, and technicians from several countries are forced to be mobile because of their commitments, their tax situation, or the prizes they must go in person to receive. A galaxy of awards is handed out at each and every film festival all over the globe (there is a new one every five minutes) and at countless resorts (in Italy there are many more than days in the year), which have instituted these ceremonies in order to attract personalities and photographers at least once every twelve months. Wearily, the stars rush from Taormina to San Sebastian, from Beirut to Acapulco, in order to publicize their latest film effort.

Theatrical directors used to do their chores in theaters where their own language was spoken. This is no longer true. A short time ago Jacques Charon of Paris' *Comédie française* directed plays of Feydeau both in London and Rome; and Parisian audiences recently saw the play *The Vicar* written by a German, directed by a Britisher, Peter Brook, and the American play *Who's Afraid of Virginia Woolf*, directed by Franco Zeffirelli, an Italian. Another similar blending took place when Arthur Miller's *After the Fall* received its French *première* under the guidance of Luchino Visconti.

Actors are becoming so proficient in different languages that they now take on leading roles on a variety of international stages. Ingrid Bergman, who is a Swede, has appeared in the United States, Italy, and France in taxing roles, knowing well, therefore, three tongues which are not her own.

Mannequins and cameramen are forever traveling. Clothes have become so dull that they are again and again no longer photographed in a studio but against the Inca ruins of Macchu Picchu in Peru, the teeming bazaars of Marrakesh, the fishing nets of some village in the Algarve, or wherever the enterprising fashion editor has succeeded in making a useful deal with the tourist officials of the country where these shots will be taken.

Domestic help in most European cities today is strictly nomadic. Most of the servants are foreign and move from country to country, town to town, according to a better offer or the wanderlust of which they are also victims. A short time ago there was a sketch in the Parisian musical comedy *Sacré Léonard* which told of the tribulations of a gentleman who ends by hiring an interpreter for his household in order to remove the language barriers among the members of his personnel. There are relatively few houses in Great Britain or Central Europe today where a maid or a butler can take a proper message on the telephone because of their inability to understand. Again another great Parisian hit, Félicien Marceau's *La Preuve à Quatre* has a delectable scene in which the Italian maid does not even recognize the voice of her employer on the telephone and repeats to him, like a parrot, the one French sentence she has learned, "The Master is out and will not return until tonight."

At the Spanish church in the rue de la Pompe in the French capital there are queues daily of ladies filling out papers in the hope that on some recent train a new domestic has landed from the Iberian peninsula. How many times friends of mine have told me that they were taking accelerated courses in Spanish, Portuguese, or Italian in order to communicate with their help. "Will you come to a Sénégalese dinner I am having on Thursday?" is the sort of invitation one receives in Brussels. This does not, in the least, signify that the hostess is an original who believes in impressing her guests with an exotic menu. Not at all; it simply means that she has been able to latch on to a cook from Senegal.

In Geneva, a diplomat and his wife who invited me to a dinner, told the guests before entering the dining room not to speak English. "We have a brand-new butler," they explained, "a very nice Jamaican drummer out of a job. Whenever we speak English, he invariably joins into the conversation, and we don't dare to tell him not do it. He might get offended and leave us."

Where are the great chefs and why are they so hard to locate? The answer is that the demand for cooks far exceeds the supply because of the colossal number of new hotels and clubs which are willing to pay the kind of wages not even a very rich family can afford.

At Frenchman's Creek, which is not only advertised as the most expensive hotel in Jamaica but in the entire world, I talked to a German chef. As if it were the most natural thing imaginable, he told me that at the end of March he would fly for a three-month engagement in a hotel in Durban, South Africa, followed by another stretch in a Swiss resort for twelve weeks during the summer. "I have some very tempting bids for the fall season," he said to me, just as a tenor would talk about the offers from prominent Opera Houses, "but I enjoy taking a breather in the fall, settling down in some good hotel in Paris and taking in the new shows." Accomplished barmen, maîtres d'hotel and the like are booked solidly months and years in advance, and their air passages are paid with return fare for relatively short periods of time.

Spending weekends in the country, until the end of the Second World War, was strictly a habit of the British and Americans. It is now widespread globally, and the exodus today of people, be it in Madrid, Buenos Aires, Frankfurt, or Teheran, is simply staggering, with the highways bogging down under the heavy traffic and radio newsmen giving breathless, frantic advice as to which side road is slightly less crowded. This, also, means that most of these weekenders have houses in the country to which they retire from the cities for thirty-six or forty-eight hours a week.

This is true of diversified classes of people and not only the more privileged ones. Those who remain in town over the weekend feel impelled to explain and excuse themselves, since they are convinced it is a loss of face to admit either not owning a rustic hideaway somewhere, or what is even worse, not having been invited by someone who does. This mass migration from the cities has caused bazaars, fairs, and theaters to protest that weekending has cut down immensely on their business, claiming that those who come from the provinces on Saturdays and Sundays do not make up for all the others who are absent the year around.

The status seekers, of whom Vance Packard has written so adroitly, no longer feel that two residences, one in town and one in the country, suffice. In the last few years there has developed an impelling urge to own a cottage by the sea and also a boat to operate excursions in along the immediate coastline. Since many do not have the cash to spend on these extravagances, they borrow money from the banks, and it is no wonder that today banking and real estate have such close connections. The result is that every inch of the European littorals is rapidly going, going, gone. It is perfectly safe to assume that if this craze continues at its current speed, with the speculators blind to the havoc they are creating, there will not be a patch of earth on the shore between Gibraltar and Messina which will not be occupied by an apartment house, a skyscraper, or bungalow. This is already true of the once magnificent Riviera between Marseilles and La Spezia where building after building rises, with the pine trees and the shrubs decreasing visibly every year to make room for new blocks of concrete.

The same, unfortunately, is happening in all the Mediterranean islands, with Mallorca, Ibiza, Corfu, Sardinia, and Corsica the hardest hit. Every European newspaper carries big advertisements inviting readers to buy, on the installment plan, apartments in various localities of the Costa Brava, the Costa del Sol, and the Balearic Isles. Every available islet, consisting of a few rocks and trees, is being bought up by agents or rich industrialists. The boom in the Caribbean is also frightening to all those who loved its quiet coves and beaches and the lack of sophistication of its towns and natives. All this is changing with dizzying rapidity, with the bulldozer at work everywhere tearing up secular roots, and hideous hotels and cottages emerging out of palm groves, accompanied by golf courses, tennis courts, and swimming pools.

The Alps, a little less quickly, are receiving the same treatment. Some of the status seekers feel they must also own a chalet where they can spend a few weeks during the skiing season. St. Moritz, Gstaad, Klosters, Megeve, Chamonix, Zermatt, Kitzbühel, St. Anton, Cortina d'Ampezzo, are all bursting with construction fever, and acres of forests are being chopped down to accommodate the new residents. Many plans are also afoot to develop the potentials of winter stations in the Pyrenees and in the Sierra Nevada in southern Spain.

Since publicity today is the center around which the universe spins, many people are allowed to travel for free provided they are glamorous enough to shed some light on some not so luminous undertaking. The opening of a hotel, for instance, is a much repeated case in point. The company, which has spent several millions in building it, wishes to waste no time in launching it swiftly on a cosmopolitan footing. Therefore it hires a jet and offers a free trip, room and board, to those personalities who will lend a certain glitter and renown to the occasion, and most essential of all, who will be acceptable to the reporters and photographers invited from different countries.

This presents complications for the persons, who are known everywhere and need not be explained in the accompanying captions, are only a few hundred. Since top motion-picture and theater stars are rarely available—they are always tied up to some contract or the other—the next best are the less active, slightly fading actors and actresses who still evoke pleasant memories but who are no longer, sadly enough, front-page news. Not infrequent are cruises on ocean liners, which, in order to attract a greater number of passengers, advertise through the columns that certain celebrities (who are naturally invited) will be on board.

Any public relations executive who has gone through the agony of assembling such a group of notables learns soon that he must invite a far larger quantity than is wanted or needed, for at least half of those who have accepted drop by the wayside at the last minute. For one reason or the other—sometimes there is none which is valid—these renowned men and women cancel, leaving the P.R. executive holding the bag vis-à-vis his client. They usually never want to come alone and insist on bringing some unexciting member of their entourage.

Even very affluent people are often delighted to accept such a bid for they adore getting something for nothing. I have been utterly astonished at times that certain persons who are financially independent would want to become involved in such glaring commercialism, but they don't mind at all. So whether it is at Baron Edmond de Rothschild's in Mégève or at one of Conrad Hilton's new hotels halfway around the globe, there are throngs who are only too gratified to accept the hospitality of a host on whom they have never laid their eyes before. This freeloading has become so integral an item of today's living that it surprises only the pure in heart (and there are very few of them left).

If the journey consists of a charter flight, then the guests must return on the same plane, but if the round trip is on a commercial jet, they often extend their ticket and stay on or stop elsewhere on their own steam.

This same kind of publicity and promotion hits every business, and many are those who admit frankly that the reason they want to be well known is to be able to live, as much as possible, for free. Many of the dressmakers give clothes, or at least reduce their rates drastically, to certain women who are considered so chic that it is useful to be identified with them. In France this habit is called *en exclusivité.*

Not too long ago, at a dinner dance on the Costa del Sol, a Spanish couturier was bragging to a colleague of his and to me about certain ladies who, that evening, were wearing his clothes. Later, referring to this conversation, the other designer said to me, "He must be very rich if he can afford to dress all those ladies he mentioned. I know them all and I doubt if any of them even own half a checkbook between them. I am only interested in the sort of clients who pay."

Real estate operators are tremendously conscious that in order to make their particular areas desirable to the public, they must circulate the news that certain glamorous persons have acquired some land and are in the process of building a house on it. In most cases, they make a gift of the acreage, total or partial, and extend every facility for the construction of the cottage. In return, those on the receiving end agree to go along with all facets of the promotion and allow their nest to be photographed from every angle.

Promoters soon learn who will play this game and who will not, but as time goes on this bizarre transaction—material rewards in exchange for the prestige of a name—is spreading like wildfire. How long it will last is debatable, for in the long run all those who accept this kind of bargain eventually lose their value when the news of their availability for exploitation is bruited around.

Everyone, in theory, whether in nomadic society or on the fringes of it, agrees that the most precious luxury today is privacy. The more opulent certain people are, the more they cry and protest how difficult it is to maintain it. But, ordinarily, these persons are those who expose themselves to lots of publicity. They would like to be famous and newsworthy and at the same time place the key in the door of their private lives, locking it at their own convenience. This has become impossible today. In order to have seclusion it is essential to keep out of the public eye, and this many refuse to do.

Where does privacy begin and anonymity end? The two are very closely interrelated. The average person is anonymous and in consequence enjoys a certain degree of privacy. The farmer, mountaineer, and citizen of a small community can still manage to preserve it, but anyone who lives in a large city cannot. He inhabits a beehive home, rides on a bus or subway teeming with humanity to and from work, sits in a crowded office all day, and lunches in a jammed restaurant. Wherever he goes for recreation on Friday night he stands in line. If he leaves town for the weekend he is haunted by bumper-to-bumper traffic on the highways, and so on. The rich have ways of avoiding these inconveniences but they complain that their lives are always under scrutiny and that their freedom is limited.

Many are the women in the United States and Europe who allow their houses to be photographed, including their bedrooms, bathrooms, closets and kitchens, for a variety of publications. What is so astonishing is that they are well-married, wealthy, and do not have a career to project. How numerous are those who blissfully pose for fashion magazines or newspapers, year in and out, in a borrowed dress, shoes, jewelry, and every possible type of accessory! They also agree to a credit for a makeup concern and hairdresser. Naturally, what interests these publications is to pay back editorially the advertising space which represents their bread and butter. In certain cases, husbands rush back from their offices at three o'clock in the afternoon, change to dinner jackets, and pose happily with their wives.

When the day comes for plastic surgeons to advertise their operations in the magazines, it is easy to foresee that these publications will be forced to give them editorial space. Therefore we shall see the photograph of a not-so-young matron looking absolutely splendid and among the credits in the caption we shall read, "the reconstruction of her face was performed by Doctor Scalpel Bisturi."

Is not all of this an invasion of one's privacy, a surrender of one's ivory tower? The answer is that the mentality has so rapidly changed today that what was considered self-glorification a short time ago is now called prestige. Members of the French burnt crust, as the aristocracy is called in the Fifth Republic, are either way ahead of the time or way behind. (I cannot quite make up my mind.) They show their friendliness to the various art magazines (*Connaissance des Arts,* in particular, which is considered the most influential in certain avenues) by allowing them to photograph their beautiful mansions in town or in the country. But there is a *but.* The condition they impose is a very fine one; under no circumstances can their name be mentioned. Therefore these treasure-filled residences appear, but the owners are always referred to as Monsieur X or Madame X.

In other countries, the privacy they grumble about is obviously far less fundamental to them than the consecration they receive by being constantly in the public eye. Until two decades ago, on a local basis, those who fulfilled leading parts of one sort or the other in the community knew one another by everyday exposure. Now the cities have become so immense that these same people often do not have the opportunity of meeting and only read about one another in the papers.

Nomadic existence plays an even more commanding role in this drum-beating picture for it curtails to a great extent the identity process. Publicity does today, in a certain strange and somewhat whimsical way, what the *Almanac de Gotha* or the *Social Register* (before so many leading American families ceased to be in it) used to do. It assigns a certain background to a person and acts as a kind of passport.

If a leading magazine—or several of them—singles out a certain lady, then the average person is impressed and concludes she must be worth knowing. As an illustration of this, *Vogue* recently gave four pages to the Marchesa Sieuwke Bisleti who operates, with her husband, a farm in the highlands of Kenya. Many of us have never heard of her, and the magazine, unfortunately, gives little personal information. Obviously the Marchese must be Italian, but what nationality is she with a name like Sieuwke? From the enchanting photographs she looks more Nordic than Latin, but what matters is that anyone, going to Kenya, will certainly want to meet her, for she sounds highly original and entertaining with her collection of wild animals wandering freely all over her house. What results these pages have brought to the life of the charming Marchesa would be interesting to learn. It would be, for instance, conceivable indeed that some publisher, struck by this lady's great familiarity with leopards, cheetahs, and lions, would ask her to write a book like Joy Adamson's best-seller *Born Free.*

Not all publicized women are, unfortunately, as thrilling as the Marchesa. In opening an issue of a leading society magazine at random, I ran across a delightful photograph of a woman, all done up in loaned regalia. The caption tells us where to buy both the fur coat and the earrings she is wearing. Again, I have never had the pleasure of meeting this lovely creature, but should I run into her, there is a great deal I now know about her and conversation should prove easy. The magazine informs us what she does in her spare time (but no clue as to what, if anything, she does professionally), what her aesthetic tastes are and the kind of dinner party she gives. She sounds like a very nice girl all the way around. What is so fascinating about this write-up is that obviously international society must be interested in knowing all these not very epoch-making preferences in her life or such a sophisticated magazine would not print them. While the Marchesa Bisleti was photographed on the premises of her estate and wearing her own outfits, this woman compromised all the way. Not only is everything she wears in the picture an advertisement for the stores but the locale where she posed is not even her own apartment (which would have been far more interesting) but a New York nightspot.

There are some glaring examples, on the reverse side of the picture, of important people, whose weight internationally is a heavy one, but whose names never appear anywhere. The reason is very simple: they know how to take their precautions in order to avoid receiving attention. A couple which comes to mind is Mr. and Mrs. De Witt Wallace, the originators of the *Reader's Digest* and its indefatigable architects. With one of the most far-reaching publishing empires in existence (the magazine is printed in so many countries and languages it is impossible to list them all), their influence is colossal. Yet they prefer to remain in the background. When they travel—and they are constantly in orbit—I understand that usually even the American Embassy is unaware of their presence in a capital.

Some years ago I gave a luncheon in New York City for Oliver Messel before the opening of his entrancing exhibit at the Sagittarius Gallery. I asked this gifted British stage designer (who happens to be the uncle of the Earl of Snowdon, the husband of Princess Margaret) whom he wished me to invite and he gave me a list of important members of the arts and society. There was one person I did not know, however, Mrs. De Witt Wallace. He suggested I go ahead and invite her anyhow, which I did with an explanatory letter. To my surprise she accepted and came, a highly intelligent, extraordinary, self-effacing person. As I introduced her around to the other guests, no one knew her, and yet she could have put each and every one of them in her pocket in more ways than one. If we were to meet again I might not recognize her, for there was nothing in her appearance which stood out, nor have I ever seen a photograph of her anywhere to refresh the memory. But I have not forgotten her uncommon mental agility.

There are also many cases of persons who decided, after

receiving their share of publicity, that they had had enough of it and have since managed to keep out of the limelight. Doris Duke is one of them. Her comings and goings in her various houses in Newport, New York, New Jersey, Beverly Hills, and Honolulu or her many trips are hardly ever mentioned any more. The Doris Duke foundation does valuable work in several fields but it is handled most discreetly. Gloria Baker, half-sister of Alfred Vanderbilt, is another example. One of the most written-up and discussed young women of her generation, before and after her marriage to Henry J. Topping, she has faded into oblivion since she became the wife of Brigadier General Edward Alexander. But only because she made up her mind that she preferred it that way.

Some of them, like movie stars, cannot resist making a come-back. Brenda Frazier, one of the most bewitching and best publicized debutantes of all time, retired to a quiet life in Massachusetts, after many vicissitudes, with her second husband Robert Chatfield Taylor. She has now separated, but she felt compelled to bare her soul to millions of readers of *Life* magazine in the fall of 1963. This public confession, as in the days of the Inquisition, would, according to her psychiatric mentor, help her find her peace of mind again. To wash the harm done by one sort of publicity with the soap of some even more sensational publicity is the leitmotiv one is confronted with along the jet-set trail.

To make a real dent in any kind of society, unless one is born to it, has always been an arduous task. But as difficult as it was in the past, the limitations and standards imposed by a certain clique were well-defined and one knew what one was up against. Today, in the gigantic cosmopolitan cauldron, the boundaries of the different societies are vague and the yardstick nonexistent. There is no longer a restricted social system, but snobbism, infinitely more rampant than ever, dominates, confusing the issues at different levels.

Any local staid society has always had the advantage of

presenting each person within a definite frame, be it old or new. International society is so fluid that none of its components can be contained within a definite ornamental border. To many of the uninitiated it presents, at first, the same problems of incomprehensibility that a large abstract painting does.

The common malady, which affects many members of society today, is the inferiority complex. Psychologists and psychiatrists believe that the connection between feelings of inferiority, which make them richer by the half hour, and wayfaring is a very strong one. In the shifting and nondefined conventions of today's society, knowing no longer to what echelon they belong, many persons become unsure of themselves. They are in search of status symbols which they deem compulsory in whatever milieu or town they are in.

The amenities of life have been greatly disturbed by nomadism, and none has suffered more than friendship and manners. In order to be thoughtful, the essential basis of operation for the well-educated, the element of time is paramount, but this is a necessity which has become rare and precious. A telephone call to find out how someone is or to express appreciation for some extended courtesy, to write a thank-you note for a party one has attended, or for some thoughtfulness of which one has been the object, to cut out a clipping from a newspaper or magazine one thinks would be of interest, to convey congratulations for some anniversary or condolences for the death of a relative or close friend—none of these can be accomplished while operating under continuous pressure. One must be able to have the peace of mind necessary to organize one's thoughts, and more significant, give vent to one's heart.

It is the latter around which friendship revolves, and the ability to place ourselves in the shoes of those of whom we are fond. Consideration is a prime element which one's nomadic friends are apt to ignore. These globe-trotters rarely are thoughtful enough to announce their impending arrival and length of stay. This would facilitate matters no end, for it would give the time, in the midst of one's busy schedule, to plan something properly for them. They telephone instead, disclosing their presence for a very limited period, and one can sense their disappointment when circumstances are such that it is impossible to organize some special entertainment. If they do write in advance, it is in most cases because they need some hard-to-obtain hotel or theater reservations which they often want to cancel at the eleventh hour, leaving one with the nerve-wracking assignment of doing this ungrateful job.

One of the most obvious ramifications of nomadism is the convenient absence of responsibility. If a person never stays long in the same place, his obligations to the community and his friends are far less strenuous. Absence is a convincing excuse which cancels all sorts of duties.

In N.S. death is a great inconvenience and must be ignored as much as possible. It gets in the way of those who are spinning around and who have their plans made for weeks and months, sometimes years, in advance. As nomadic life dehumanizes its members more and more, uprooting affections and traditions, death is an unwelcome interruption into their completely set program. Mourning is considered not only superfluous but ridiculous. Some persons go to the extent of explaining how the dead relative had often said that he wanted life to go straight on, after his passing, without any interruption. A stock phrase one also hears is "He (or she) simply hated black. He (or she) would be so unhappy if I wore it."

With the new peripatetic system of life, the number of acquaintances grows daily and the number of friends diminishes. Friendship has become in certain circles a tenuous relation, superficial and inconsequential. There are few human beings in this here-today-there-tomorrow existence who are capable of giving enough of themselves to irrigate the plants and flowers of friendship. The French have devised a word, *copain*, to denote this kind of relationship which exists between people. Its meaning is close to pal and chum, but it indicates more explicitly a sort of membership in a group which boasts a common interest.

Family connections, out of necessity, are weakening on all fronts. It was inconceivable some years ago for children to be separated from their parents at Christmas, New Year, or Easter time. Certain holidays were considered sacred, had to be shared, and one never could envisage them away from home except out of necessity. Today, even in the most conservative European clans, it is accepted that youngsters take off for skiing or some other reason.

First and second cousins used to be as close as brothers and sisters and they were thrown together constantly because of kindred ties. Nowadays the custom of spending the summer in a large country house under the same roof is vanishing, and the restlessness of the young, who are always taking off for some other destination, is separating clans more and more. There is no doubt that this independence, which characterizes the young, brings with it a more manifest emotional indifference not only to blood relationships but also to feelings of sentiment.

Time is a commodity jet-setters do not possess. "I did not have the time," is the sentence which pops up the most often in the conversation of migrants. This is used in connection with everything, ranging from the reading of the morning's paper to telephoning the hospital for news of a sick friend, from going to see a play or an exhibit to signing a check for something bought long ago.

Letters of introduction, employed until recently to introduce wayfaring friends, have gone out of style. It is a pity, for they were enlightening, containing details on the person in question. Today, the nomads suddenly turn up and telephone, introducing themselves. One is, therefore, caught unaware, with no criteria about the identity or interests of the person in question. After one has entertained these friends of friends, they usually disappear without ever penning a word of gratitude. The English are the last letter-writing survivors, but even in Great

Britain in the younger set this delightful habit, so rewarding and attractive, is ebbing away. The Duchess of Bedford, abreast of the times, has had signs put up in all the bedrooms of Woburn Abbey telling her guests it is not necessary to write a bread-and-butter note. "They all so hate doing it," she explained to me, "so why not dispense with it?"

All correspondence is coming rapidly to a stop. The only way to get an answer is to telephone. Upon writing, one does not hear for weeks or months, and when the hurried reply eventually comes, it always bears the same message: "I have not been able to reply before because I have been so terribly busy."

The excitement of the discovery of some remote place, which friends used to share with one by letter, has ceased. Now one receives postal cards which are usually scribbled so rapidly it is difficult to figure out whom they are from. The lost gift of writing is tied to the inability of self-expression. Faced with the necessity of putting one's impressions down in black and white helped one enormously to catch an image lastingly. This is also true of one's emotions. People rarely write love letters any more—they telephone instead—and by doing so they are no longer blessed with those welcome hours of learning how to examine and evaluate their feelings. Any kind of a written message has a permanence which the spoken word over the telephone can never capture.

Two-thirds of our knowledge of the past has come down to us through letters. Of our era, all that will remain will be the reporting in the press, radio, and television, filed away in tape form. Archives of families will be strangely empty except for the bills and bank statements, and future Stendhals will find nothing of interest.

In every capital, large city or resort, there are certain beehives which are more tuned to N.S. than others. As nomads, basically, all belong to one vast international tribe, they are all, at least by hearsay, known to one another. Often they are related by family, marriage ties, or business connections. Since so many members of this enormous club are always in passage, the various branches are obliged to fortify themselves by constantly adding new members to their ranks.

There are also, in every city, those who stay put, with whom the nomads check regularly upon arrival to learn who is in town at that particular moment. These people, who are forced to live in one place because of some unfortunate job which does not involve much moving around, enjoy knowing all their wonderful friends in orbit.

Upon being telephoned, she (or he) will say "Gloria and Loel are here until Monday, and Luis and Aline until Tuesday (these names are easy, it can only mean the Guinnesses and the Romanones-Quintanillas). Cristina (which Cristina?) arrives tomorrow on her way to Mexico (this gives no clue), Dolly is off to Nassau today but returns at the end of the week (must be Mrs. Nicholas Goulandris, since she is building a house there). Teddy should have come in yesterday but I have checked the hotel and there is no news (it could be Baron van Zuylen), Jaynie is coming from Florida just for thirty-six hours to look at a wonderful Louis XV mirror which has come on the market (this must be Mrs. Charles Wrightsman) and Whitney, the darling, is due Saturday from London but he is booked every minute. He is only staying thirty-six hours and then must rush back to the ranch (what a marvelous clue, this can only be Whitney Warren who has a farm near San Francisco and a lovely house in town), but forgive me, I must ring off and talk to you later. My other phone is ringing and it is probably Clé-Clé (this can only be the Countess de Maillé) checking in. She is expected this morning." This list, generously shared with a delicious quiver in her voice, could be the subject of a conversation in New York, Paris, Rome, London, or Madrid. Name the city and it is yours. It's so exciting, the person implies, to have all these marvelous people coming and going, so many parties to look forward to, such delicious perturbation and dislocation.

For some reason or other, between half or two-thirds of any group one rings up upon arriving in a city is never there. A convention, a congress, a business appointment halfway around the world, a holiday, a *première* of a new play or opera, a graduation, a birthday, a shopping expedition, a sports event —any of these may be the cause for their absence.

Twenty years ago if someone who traveled knew well ten persons in a city, he could be sure of having a jolly time. Now he must be able to call up at least thirty. Half of those he talks to are so sorry they cannot see him because they are departing the next day. A friend of mine, who lived in Madrid for several years, returned there to spend ten days recently and she could not believe the change which had taken place in the somewhat tranquil habits of the Spaniards of all classes. She started to telephone her old friends and found that most of them were away. A duke and duchess were visiting in Ibiza, a marquesa was shooting big game in Mozambique, a count was on a temporary diplomatic assignment to Bonn, a viscountess was on the Costa del Sol supervising a house she was erecting there. My friend, thinking this was the new design of living for the aristocrats, began telephoning the nonpatricians and discovered there was no difference. A university professor was on a lecture tour in the Philippines, a doctor was attending a medical congress in Puerto Rico, an architect was in Tenerife drawing plans for a hotel, an actress was making a film in the Argentine, a decorator was in Estoril finishing work on a new restaurant, a textile manufacturer was on a business trip to northern Italy, and a painter had been sent on a cultural mission to Costa Rica.

As these experiences hit every jet-setter today, the fever of adding new acquaintances to the address book has become an epidemic. Even those with high standards at home are willing to let go of most of them when in orbit, seeing the sort of people they would never consent to mix with at their base. Drama ensues when the latter turn up eventually and accounts must be squared, particularly when the intention is to return to that certain country and place where they have been ever so useful. "I am putting you next to Geranium," a hostess is apt to say gently. "She is no ball of fire, but when you go to Bangkok, she will make your stay memorable." Or a desperate call comes from someone in distress. "The friends with whom I always stay in Molokai have arrived. I am so indebted to them and I have had such wonderful times on their heavenly ranch. Please come and help me entertain them. You would simply adore them." And then, in subdued tones, "He is a little deaf, but such a dear. She drinks too much, but is so kind."

Today's nomads dine in New Delhi with the Maharajah and Maharanee of Jaipur or some other high-ranking Indian but do not have the time to see Fatehpur Sikri; they lunch with Sir Desmond and Lady Cochrane in Beirut, and their social schedule is so full there they do not have the opportunity to go visit nearby Byblos; they have drinks with Salvador and Galarina Dali at Port Llegat but it would take too long to inspect the neighboring fabulous Monastery of San Pedro de Roda.

Until a few years ago a visitor to India, Japan, or some other distant outpost tried to see as much as he could since he knew the chances of returning within a lifetime were limited. But this is no longer true. One hears in Tokyo, "I skipped Nikko because I must save something for when I come back next year," or in Bombay, "I did not go to see the caves of Ajanta for I shall be spending a month in India next spring."

Since trends and styles always have started at the top and will continue to do so, this volume deals mainly with the glamorous nomads. It is they who are blazing the trail, and already there are many obvious patterns of imitation on the part of their roving followers. Since, in the hop-and-stop set, the whereabouts of those who have a tent is vital, close attention has been paid to some of the local tribal chieftains who attract those in orbit. After staying put for a while, lending phosphorescence to a certain oasis, it is their turn to move on and be the guests of their colleagues elsewhere.

The most curious aspect of this entire picture is that, for a growing multitude, it is no longer the site of the encampment that counts but what sort of caravans stop there. In an era where the term democracy is mentioned constantly, the struggle on the part of certain groups to keep the "undesirables" from joining them has gained tremendous momentum and is complicated to follow since the location of the battlegrounds keeps shifting. When too many enemies have entrenched themselves somewhere, the others move out in a flash and begin their camping elsewhere. In the process, too, one meets with surprises, for some of the foes are nimble and elastic enough to learn the ABC's of their idols and therefore join them on a footing which becomes increasingly equitable.

2

The Tribal Customs

In the current continuous shifting of nomadic society, being "in" is capricious and frail. This status is frequently affected by many circumstances. A lasting position, of which certain persons could be sure in the past because of birth or marriage, does not exist in N.S. In order to be a member of the upper echelons of the international milieus, there is no choice but to be always going somewhere.

Since wealth and a well-publicized name are prerequisites (but, as explained elsewhere, not the only ones) for this continued station, any change in these two particular conditions can bring about radical alterations. At times, a wife or a husband is happy to follow the exhausting jet-set trail as a member of a team, but when left to his own devices, the impetus and the wish to continue cease. In reverse, someone who was never in the jet-set stream, because of an unwilling and uninitiated mate, suddenly, upon being remarried to one who is "in," immediately becomes a vital part of it. Alimony plays a leading role in the circumstances of the divorced person, as does the capacity of latching onto another mate who is either "in" or has the wherewithal to become a member in good standing.

A typical example of this fragile image was the Fashion Institute's decision to drop from its 1965 best-dressed list the hauntingly beautiful Fiona Campbell Walter. Although there was no mention of the reason, some experts claimed it was not difficult to detect. Her divorce from the enormously wealthy and very U Baron Heinie Thyssen-Bornemisza had been allotted much space in the world press, but as yet, no mention had been made of the alimony figure. It goes without saying that the latter always plays a definite and intrinsic role in a woman's ability to continue purchasing exorbitantly priced Parisian gowns.

In the opinion of eminently qualified members of top N.S., the Baroness was as well dressed after the news broke of the cessation of the marriage as before. But she was eliminated, lock, stock, and barrel. The voters must have had a good hunch as to what sort of settlement she would receive, since soon after they removed her from her position as a leading clothes horse the figures were made public. While they were not negligible, they were hardly impressive. Although it is doubtful that the Baroness will be able to indulge in quite the same wardrobe as before, I do not think she has any reason to worry. Her beauty is so radiant that it will be discussed long after the counting of the ballots is forgotten. I shall always remember her riding at the Sevilla Fair shortly before her divorce, sitting stupendously erect on her horse, in a stunning Flamenco outfit, her copper hair giving out intermittent fires ignited by the brilliant Andalusian sunshine. It was a vision all those voters would have treasured for many years to come.

As generously as Baron Edmond de Rothschild has provided bank accounts for his former Bulgarian wife, Lina, her position has, nevertheless, changed. Although she has many friends, it was her ex-husband's varied and exciting interests which drew her into a meteoric orbit.

At the time that Herbert May was the much-wed husband of Marjorie Merriweather Post-Close-Hutton-Davies, he was "in." He acted as the very accomplished host at all those marvelous parties his wife gave in her resplendent homes in Palm Beach, Washington, and her camp in the Adirondacks, but the part he played was one of reflected light. Now he is taking a nice rest.

On the other hand, when the attractive Hélène Tourtois (a French-American beauty) parted company from one Brazilian Croesus, Walter Moreira Sales, and married another, Ermelino Matarazzo, her situation both in the Amazon River country and globally did not change one iota. The only difference was that had she remained married to No. 1, she would have been the wife of the former Brazilian Minister of Finance and the former Ambassador to the United States. Her "in" status has remained, however, positively glowing.

Before her total and complete estrangement from Vermouth tycoon (Martini and Rossi) Count Theo Rossi, his wife, Lady Moira Forbes, was very much in orbit. She could not have been born to a more noble and wealthy Anglo-American heritage. Her brother is the ninth Earl of Granard and her mother is the sister of the late Ogden Mills (he had been U.S. Secretary of the Treasury) and of Palm Beach's reigning dowager, Mrs. Henry Carnegie Phipps. But, obviously, it was her husband who generated the motion. She now leads a quiet existence in Turin and Rapallo. The dashing Count, instead, is still constantly on the go, with two excellent headquarters: a fascinating chalet in St. Moritz for the winter, where he skis to his heart's content, and a delightful yacht in summer. In the fall months he participates in various marvelous shoots.

Anne Ford, instead, is far more of a dazzling nomad today than when she was Mrs. Henry Ford, for she is now free to come and go as she pleases. She is no longer saddled with the duties she discharged so well in and out of Grosse Pointe, Detroit, and the vast Ford empire. With the imposing settlement she received, she can now lead a most attractive cosmopolitan life, and does.

The same is true of Anne Ford's ex-uncle, Ernest Kanzler (his late wife was Henry Ford's aunt), who used to lead a conservative existence in Grosse Pointe, with a winter house at Hobe Sound and a summer residence in Maine. All this was before his second marriage to the spirited Swiss-born widow of his good friend, Frederick Weicker. Because of her untiring energy he is right in the midst of the swinging aero-turbine set and having a wonderful time. He has added two more houses in Europe to his three American ones, a magnificent new cottage in St. Moritz, and a large mansion at Saint Jean, Cap Ferrat.

Another one who has joined the international set through marriage is London's Tom Meyer, who, until he slipped the third gold band on Fleur Fenton's finger, was known mainly in the lumber business. The enormous vitality of his American mate will keep him "in," for few women have ever been endowed with more tenacity, will power, and discipline. Blessed with a singular ego which must find recurrent satisfaction, she has proved that she could think up and organize, even if only for a brief period, the imaginative magazine *Flair;* become a good authoress (she wrote an excellent biography of Salvador Dali); and also be a talented painter. Using England as a base (with two houses there, one in London and one in the country), she is frequently on the move with husband No. 3 accompanying her. Professionally, however, she insists on using the name of her second divorced husband, Gardner Cowles, and the lumber tycoon has graciously accepted her point of view. What's in a name anyhow?

The death of a mate can bring about a transformation when the one who survives never really made much of an effort and was carried along despite a state of inertia.

Margaret Strong, whose mother was a sister of the late John D. Rockefeller, was constantly in the public eye while her husband, the infinitely personable ballet Maecenas, Marquis Georges de Cuevas, was alive. But it was he who enjoyed society and kept open house wherever he was. She never cared much for it and did not wish, after his death, to continue with the complicated chores of running the always-in-the-news ballet company, which she dissolved. She still wanders around, occupying her various houses in the United States and abroad, but few people see her.

There was no more feted or welcome couple in international society than Grace Moore, the Tennessee songbird, and her handsome, affable Spanish husband, Valentino Parara. Tragedy struck suddenly when the soprano lost her life, along with the Crown Prince of Sweden and others, in an airplane crash in Denmark. Parara, in due time, remarried and vanished from the turbine-propelled milieus. He has returned to live in Spain and follows a less hectic schedule.

Membership in N.S. can be lost, too, understandably enough, by those who have enjoyed the privileges, and then, for some inexplicable reason, do not appear to remember them. An example that illustrates this point is the recent case of Richard Avedon. No one could have been more appreciated in high ranks of international society than he, and everyone raved about his boyish, pixie charm and his magnificent ability in taking such wonderfully glamorous photographs. But when his book of pictures *Nothing Personal* appeared, along with a sharp commentary by his former schoolmate, James Baldwin, there was a cry of anguish on all sides. His lens, this time, had been without warning infinitely cruel, and his portraits were no longer flattering but, as *Time* magazine reported, "a chilling, engrossing display of ferocity."

A change in job affects the status of a person enormously. All over the world, a quick identification tag is a necessity. The attractiveness of a person has become almost secondary to what he does. Being the new assistant in a film production of Stanley Donen, the art editor of the *Etruscan Tombs Gazette,* or the public relations director of one of the international branches of the *Cosmopolitan Hotel* chain immediately establishes a certain solid frame to someone's portrait. Because a certain individual is the director of some wonderfully exclusive new club in Tobago, the decorator of a new group of intercontinental department stores, or has been assigned to a prominent desk at *Newsweek* magazine, he is likely to be accepted in N.S. provided he is capable of those social amenities that a sophisticated group requires. Actually, it is his work that makes him useful in all sorts of ways, be it an invitation to a junket, the business he can send in their direction, or the press promotion he can exert in their behalf. But if and when the job ends, much of the enchantment is gone, unless the person has, in the meantime, revealed such sturdy "in" membership qualities that he can stand on his own two feet of charm and wit alone.

This change in status is particularly noticeable in the case of many ex-ambassadors and their wives. Not only, in many instances, is their varnish, in consequence of their retirement, far less glossy, but their finances have shrunk. The transition from a large embassy residence, with masses of servants and continuous open house, to far less spacious surroundings attended by a skeleton staff is never an easy one. Every hostess is anxious for an ambassador to bring lustre to her gatherings, but an ex-ambassador often becomes the cause of seating complications. Former editors and columnists are far less in demand than before and their standing in the changeable N.S. is affected. I recall Carmel Snow, for several decades an illustrious magazine editor, telling me with that dry Irish humor which characterized her, how, after her return to private life, in certain restaurants she was no longer assigned the usual central table. In order to be in the right place at the correct time smart nomads develop a special compass which is needed nowadays since seasons no longer last several months or weeks. They are now, in most cases, restricted to a few days in capitals as well as resorts, with the dates mysteriously varying from year to year. How to keep abreast of all these alterations in schedule is perplexing and a gigantic effort is required, along with payment of a huge telephone bill.

Naples never is a mecca in the late summer, but if the Duke and Duchess Serra di Cassano open up their magnificent palace for a ball in early September, then Naples is *the* place to be in just at this moment. Nor is Brussels usually a magnet in early June, but when the thrillingly rich Baron Leon Lambert inaugurates his huge penthouse, built on top of his bank, with a ball, every hotel in the Belgian capital is jammed. Paris suffers from the worst doldrums in February, but when it is announced that Maria Callas will sing *Tosca* at the Opera, all the ski resorts are suddenly emptied and everyone rushes to the *ville lumiere* to attend the opening night, no matter what it costs.

The state of Virginia is hardly bait for internationalites during the very warm, sticky June weather, but when, in a marvelously distinguished lack of publicity drums, invitations were received for the bow to American society of Eliza Lloyd, the stepdaughter of Paul Mellon, everyone had a hunch this would be the most unforgettable party ever. And, apparently, it was. The appetite to see the young lady was considerable, but even stronger was the wish to see "Oak Spring," near Upperville, one of the most ravishing estates in America, and the only private one the present Queen of England honored with her regal presence during her state visit to the President of the United States.

Seville in the hot months is as dead as it is alive at Holy Week or dashing Feria time. But if a corrida by El Cordobes is scheduled for the middle of August, the constituents of the inner N.S. circles arrive in droves from everywhere, since the bullfighter, who has no pretense at being stylish himself, is idolized by them. Rio de Janeiro's society flees the city in winter time, retiring to Persepolis or Cabo Frio, since it is too hot and noisy, but when it becomes known that the Princesses Peggy d'Arenberg and Honeychile Hohenlohe are heading a well-known group of cosmopolites for the Carnival, then it becomes suddenly smart for the native elite to stay in town at that time.

The desirable status of either owning a yacht or renting a good-sized one is still at its peak, but looking carefully one can begin to detect here and there a few signs of its tapering off. All the yacht basins are so jammed that it has now become imperative to reserve space a long time ahead, and therefore, that wonderful freedom of last-minute decisions of where to go and where to stop is a thing of the past. While for a few years people would seek hospitality on any yacht, so anxious they were to participate in this sport, now they are beginning to be far more particular and want to know just what sort of a boat it is, what is its speed, how many there are in the crew, and who the other guests will be on board. These questions, naturally, are never asked of such celebrated yacht owners as Antenor Patiño, the Aga Khan, Loel Guinness, Baron Edmond de Rothschild, Sam Spiegel, Henry Ford, Earl Beatty, the Count of Barcelona, Lowell Weicker, or Julius "Junky" Fleischman.

But, undoubtedly, the invitations members of the C.C. long for the most are those of Stavros Niarchos and Aristotle Onassis, whose cold war continues in far more muted tones than when they used to be brothers-in-law. Niarchos' *Creole*, now past its twelfth year in his faithful service, is a 190-foot schooner which is considered in every nautical community as the most splendid of its sort in existence. Needless to say, it is provided with a powerful motor if and when the wind is weak. With a crew of thirty, it affords the V.I.P.s on board every luxurious comfort. Until recently it was filled with memorable Impressionist paintings which were removed because of the harmful dampness of the sea.

The *Christina*, named for Onassis' daughter, is reputed to be the most alluring floating palace in private hands. Among its treasures are reported to be a painting by El Greco, a map of the Aegean sea in lapis lazuli, a swimming pool which magically becomes a dance floor covered by a mosaic representing a Cretan bull game and a priceless jade Buddha. The water closets vary from a pink decor to a blue one and the nine guest rooms are so cozy the guests never want to leave them. The private aircraft of the owner is also on board, ready to take off for any destination.

While Onassis has always specialized in flamboyant guests, ranging from the late Sir Winston Churchill and Mrs. Jacqueline Kennedy to Greta Garbo, not to speak of Maria Callas, a permanent fixture of the vessel, Niarchos has gone in for the more U members of *Debrett's Peerage* and the Greek Royal Family.

In the last few years the yachts of opulent Italian industrial leaders have acquired a desirable mark of distinction. It is, therefore, at the moment a bright feather in a nomad's diary to be asked on a cruise by Giorgio Varvaro on his *Taitu,* textile magnate Count Gaetano Marzotto on his *Trenora,* Annibale Scotti on his *Moonbeam,* publishing tycoon Angelo Rizzoli on *il Sereno,* Vermouth's Count Theo Rossi on *La Tritona,* Mrs. Enrico Piaggio on *Shyrara,* and the Duke and Duchess Serra di Cassano (she is of the important business family Parodi Delfino) on their *Sylvia.* The latter is sometimes leased to Gianni and Marella Agnelli since their 90-foot GA-30 is not large enough for long journeys.

There are so many thousands of yachts for charter all over the globe—some at exceedingly reasonable rates—that everyone is yachting today. The American wife of a Belgian industrialist told me how delighted she had been to spot her pedicurist at a *trattoria* in Portofino. Since her feet needed attention, she immediately asked him for an appointment. "Oh, no," he replied. "I am having a holiday on my boat and I depart this evening with my guests for Corsica." She later noticed, when he left the restaurant, that he was wearing a regular captain's cap.

At the moment a small private jet is still the quintessence of sophistication, because, after all the counting is done, there are not too many of them around. In New York someone will say "I am flying to Florida tomorrow with Joe and Louise. It is so adorable of them to give me a lift." The voice is so smooth, almost flat, and yet the casual way this bit of information about the Pulitzer private company aircraft is thrown into the chic chat invariably hits the target.

In Mexico City a friend telephones to cancel a luncheon appointment two days hence. "Merle and Bruno are nipping down to Acapulco in their little bird to spend a few days in their new house there, and I have decided to go with them just to spend forty-eight hours in the sun. Can we change our date from Tuesday to Thursday?" Again there is in the tone the obvious satisfaction of being asked by the charming screen actress Miss Oberon and her industrialist husband, Bruno Pagliai, to partake in this exclusive flight.

In St. Moritz, in the lobby of the Palace Hotel, running into a British peer and his wife at ten o'clock in the morning, in order to make conversation one asks them why it is that they are not in their skiing outfits but in city attire. "We are about to take off for Milan on a few hours' excursion to do some shopping on the Via Montenapoleone. Don't you think it has some of the finest shops in the world?" they reply and then, after a pause, "It is so jolly nice of Stavros to fly us down. We understand one just brushes over those Alpine peaks and it is a question of half an hour." The British always understate their feelings, but one can sense that they are indeed grateful to Niarchos for this sign of his benevolence in lending them his baby jet. A few steps farther on one meets another couple, resplendent in the latest winter sports regalia, who are joining the well-organized Niarchos in his helicopter to do some skiing in the higher valleys.

On the French Riviera I heard people talking about Vittorio and Chantal. I admitted my ignorance and asked who they were. "Haven't they crossed your path yet?" a friend inquired. "Perhaps a year ago you could afford not to know them, but today you simply cannot. They fly everywhere in their two darling jets, and they both are fully licensed pilots." It took me about forty-eight hours to piece the various scraps of information together—there were ever so many to sort out. These revealed that Vittorio de Nora is Italian born and his pretty wife is a Swiss, whose father used to be Consul General in Milan. They collect houses—a magnificent one at Saint Jean Cap Ferrat, a penthouse in Milan, a villa in Positano, a residence in Mexico, and a new one in the making in Rome—and never stay put for more than a few days at a time. In fact, I never did catch up with them. But everyone is impressed with her jewels, a red mink coat, a white Rolls Royce (in use on the Riviera), a black one (in Milan), and above all, those wonderful jets. No one was sure what were his business interests that made this cornucopia possible, and no one was really very interested. Some said it was Kuwait petrol; others, atomic energy.

Although racing, in itself, is currently accepted as fashionable, there are too many races for all of them to be considered such. There are some, however, that the internationalities cannot afford to miss. There is not much point, however, for the nomad to attend the Grand Prix in Paris the last Sunday in June unless he is invited to the huge dinner dance the young Aga Khan gives yearly, that same night, at the Pre' Catalan in the Bois de Boulogne, following the tradition established by his popular father, Prince Aly Khan. Since the Aga is a serious sportsman—in the winter he takes his skiing training strictly to heart—his appearances in society are erratic. The opportunities, therefore, to meet him and be invited, unless one is in the racing world, or on one of the old lists of his father, are few and far between. Many are those who feel sadly that they have not, as yet, registered with him sufficiently. Since he is currently greatly interested in his vast Sardinian real estate project—he heads a large corporation—he does spend a considerable amount of time there in the summer and people have caught on to the fact that by staying a few days at his Hotel "Cala di Volpe" there they have a chance of meeting him.

It is less embarrassing for the jet-setters who are seen at the eminently desirable Dublin Derby, also in June, not to be asked to the splendid ball Aileen Guinness, ex Mrs. Valerian Rybar, hosts at Lustrellstown Castle. The affair is always held the following night, and therefore there is always the handy excuse that one could not remain for it.

Ascot week (also in June) is an absolute must for most internationalites—and the United States Ambassador to England and his wife go crazy trying to keep all their friends happy, since there is a deluge of Americans frantically demanding tickets. The importance of Ascot is well illustrated by the following story. Despite the great interest she has shown in every possible way in the Spoleto Festival of the Two Worlds, Mrs. H. J. Heinz was horrified one year when she discovered that Gian Carlo Menotti, unknowingly, had picked out the same date for the first night of his musical fete as the opening day of Ascot. Even with jet travel, it was impossible for Mrs. Heinz to divide her loyalties in two, and it was the horses that won, not the music.

The Arc de Triomphe in Paris, in early October, is also a must race with tremendous coverage. Few of the nomads who attended a recent one remember who won it, but everyone recalls the sensation produced when the Marchioness of Blandford (Tina Livanos ex-Onassis), who had flown over from England, and the Baroness Marie Helene de Rothschild wore the exact copy of a suit by Chanel. They received more attention than when Elizabeth Taylor and Gina Lollobrigida arrived at the same party in Moscow in exactly the same dress. But, as we explain elsewhere, this is the era of social vedettes.

A rapid status is earned by the nomad who has succeeded in seeing or doing something ahead of the others. Therefore it is a source of superiority for a Canadian to arrive in Paris at the moment when his friends are discussing the merits of a play by Edward Albee which has just opened there. He appears interested until he hears the title. "I would rather remain," he says, with contrived sadness in his voice, "with the memory of the production in New York. I saw it there last year, and it was so beautifully acted." The Argentinian who breezes into New York where people are talking about a certain adaptation of a play by André Roussin will declare, "I would not mind seeing it again. It must be at least seven years since I attended the *première* in Paris. I would be interested to see how much it has aged since then."

Another unmistakable clue to "in" status is to know, in whatever city you are going, the producer, the author, or the actor who will get you the best seats without the humiliation of using the ordinary system of going through an agency. So, just at the height of the impossibility to obtain a ticket for *Funny Girl,* the Swedish Countess who flew into New York and said, "Barbra is getting me the house seats," meant she was friendly with Barbra Streisand, a big new star. Or the Beverly Hills matron who arrived in London at the time when every stall was taken for *Maggie May* and stated, "I am such an intimate friend of Rachel and Rex, I have no reason to worry," spelled out she was "in" with Rachel Roberts, who starred in the musical, and her husband Rex Harrison. It was impressive because this couple picks and chooses carefully among the invitations that pour in on them, and it is not easy to know them that well.

In Madrid, the grandees do not usually worry about the theater unless it is a play directed by Luis Escobar. Then, because of this brilliant gentleman's international reputation (he has even been called by La Scala of Milan to lend his hand to a production there of Mozart's *Don Giovanni*), everyone eagerly attends. It goes without saying that professionally he does not use his title, which is one of the most delightful in all of the Iberian peninsula, Marquess de las Marismas (of the marshes) del Guadalquivir.

In Milan and Rome the theater is considered ordinary by the U locals and therefore by the cosmopolitan ones, too. The exceptions are the productions of Luchino Visconti or his ex-pupil and current arch rival, Franco Zeffirelli. For their opening nights members of top nomadic echelons arrive from everywhere even when they have already seen the play in some other capital. Their fidelity is exemplary because, for instance, although Arthur Miller's *After the Fall* was, in the opinion of many of the jet-setters, heavy going, they were all in Rome at the opening in the Zeffirelli version and a short time later in Paris when Visconti's French edition was presented. "I just hope," one of these nomads said to me, letting her hair down, "that Luis Escobar will not direct it in Madrid. I think that is one time I will say to hell with chicness and not turn up for it." The theater in Germany and Austria is among the best anywhere, but the internationalites have not discovered it as yet and therefore ignore it.

By far the most passionate—often because their interests are more genuine, and consequently more opinionated—in this "I-was-ahead-of-you" business are the wayfaring musical connoisseurs. I asked a cultivated English music lover, who had just returned from New York, what he had heard of interest at the Metropolitan Opera. "You would not believe how provincial it all seemed to me," he said with infinite disdain. "They were all so excited about Schwarzkopf's Marshallin. Can you imagine? In Europe we have been hearing her sing this part ever since we were children." There was no argument with him there, for it is indeed shocking that the Metropolitan Opera waited until 1964 to sign this distinguished singer, when she was no longer at the supreme height of her vocal resources.

Oddly enough, the only other musical figure, besides Maria

Callas, to whom each and every nomad, including those who are notoriously unmusical, are supremely loyal is Herbert von Karajan. This is an amusing development in the career of the superb Maestro and for which his third wife Eliette, a former French mannequin, is greatly responsible. Young and pretty, she has become an intimate friend of many leading jet-setters. Often wearing her long, flowing blonde hair down her back, she is photographed as much as her husband, having become a personality on her own.

Wherever and whenever Karajan conducts today, all the internationalites turn up, dressed to the hilt. When he appeared with the Berlin Philharmonic in Paris, there was much yawning and napping in the boxes during his magnificent rendition of the interminable Eighth Symphony of Bruckner.

Salzburg never used to be on the beat of musically stone deaf globe-trotters, but now they too put in one or two appearances at one of his performances during the Festival. In 1965 they were able to kill two birds with one trip when they took in Karajan's interpretation of *Boris Godunov* along with the big ball, hosted in the Maestro's honor, by Demetrios Pappas. This rotund-looking gentleman is the Greek Consul General in the baroque town, and what is more economically sound, the representative of Mercedes Benz. With the priceless assistance of Baron Erwein Geumen-Waldek, the immensely diplomatic secretary of St. Moritz's Corviglia Club, he corralled many outstanding names.

When the Maestro broke the news that he was planning an extra Festival in Salzburg, independent of the other, to perform Wagner's *Ring* and *Tristan and Isolde* along with concerts dedicated to Bach and Bruckner, some of the tone-deaf members of the smart set had a fit. "How can Herbert do this to me?" one of them cried. "I can take it when he directs Richard Strauss's *Elektra,* for it lasts less than two hours. But *Siegfried, Götterdämmerung,* and the rest are going to kill me." There was no indication, however, that she had any intention of escaping this martyrdom. For the sake of Eliette and Herbert, she and many others will suffer this and other sacrifices.

The dedicated musical snob will do everything in his power to have a preview of some event to which none of his colleagues have entree. In the midst of a heat wave in a deserted Rome during the month of August one runs into a New Yorker who usually at this time shuttles among the Bayreuth, Munich, and Salzburg music festivals. "I am here," he explains quickly, "to sit in on the recording session of *La Forza del Destino.* Leontyne is such an angel and has made arrangements for me to be present every day. It's absolute bliss and she is in glorious voice." This indicates that he is "in" with Leontyne Price, one of the current leading sopranos, and is getting a special insight into the opera taping world.

In the summer of 1965, in the bar of the Grande Bretagne in Athens, the literary snob has just arrived from cruising in Turkish waters and has run into the yacht, rented by Gianni and Marella Agnelli, on which Truman Capote was also a guest. She does not come out and say that she has read some pages from Capote's eagerly awaited and then forthcoming book *In Cold Blood* but suggests that she has. "It is divine, much the finest thing he has ever written," she states enthusiastically, hinting that she is "in" with the eminent author.

At a luncheon given by Martha Kennedy in Honolulu a guest, who is on her way home to Tokyo from a visit in New York, announces that she had recently drawn Cleveland Amory as a dinner partner. "He is too clever for words," she recounts, "and he had enough confidence in me to tell me all about the new book he is writing. It's going to be fascinating." But she refuses to divulge its content, asserting once more how ahead she is in the "in" game.

At Duarte Pinto Coelho's cocktail party in Madrid everyone is discussing a feature which has just appeared in *Time* magazine's section entitled "Modern Living" on certain aspects of life in Washington's society. "I have known about it for months," a globe-trotter asserts. "Douglas Auchincloss, who is a great friend of mine, sent a researcher to see me when I stopped in New York for a few days on my way back from Lima." Many of those present are impressed by this American who is "in" with such a formidable publication and one of its much-quoted editors.

Every possible excuse is adduced to avoid funerals unless they are historically significant or glamorous. Then they become a must and are discussed like the first gala performance of a production directed by Sir John Gielgud or Peter Brook. Funerals of such personages as King Paul of Greece in Athens or Sir Winston Churchill in London are events and spectacles one must not miss.

What interests the nomads is not so much, for instance, whether Mrs. Harold Wilson's face was tearstained during the ceremony (Queen Juliana's of the Netherlands was) but how did the protocol officials handle the delicate situation of Aristotle Onassis and the Marchioness of Blandford. Onassis had given hospitality over and over again to the late great statesman both on his yacht and in Monte Carlo. As a matter of fact Churchill participated in the famous cruise that first brought into focus Maria Callas as a yachtswoman. On the other hand, Onassis' ex-wife is now a close member of the Churchill family. Was there any contact between them? How far apart were they seated? Apparently, even down to these details, the funeral was a masterpiece of tactics and the two were well apart.

Weddings vary enormously in their attractions to the jetsetters according to who the bride and the groom are. When Princess Alexandra of Kent became the wife of Angus Ogilvy, a son of the Earl of Airlie—a marriage that provided all the ideal elements because of the social prestige of the members of the team, their good looks, and royal solemnity—not one nomad who received an invitation declined. The internationalites flew in from everywhere to attend the magnificent ball the Queen gave to honor her cousin at Windsor Castle, and then the nuptials at Westminster Abbey. For instance, Pittsburgh's Jack Heinz, whose fifty-seven varieties are enjoying great prosperity in Great Britain, flew over with his dynamic wife Drue, for forty-eight hours, and then immediately returned home to his flourishing business.

Much the same happened when Loel Guinness' daughter (Be)Linda became the Marchioness of Dufferin and Ava, also at the Abbey, a rare privilege for nonroyalty, with Caravelle-loads of scintillating people arriving from everywhere. Curiosity about the mechanics of this wedding was at a high pitch because of all the ex-wives, husbands, stepbrothers, and sisters in the immediate family tree of the youthful pair, which caused relatively nightmarish seating complications. Present, in fact, were the two ex-wives of Loel Guinness—Princess Joan Aga Khan, with her son the Aga, and Lady Isabel Throckmorton (mother of the bride), with her current husband, Sir Robert—along with the third and current wife, Gloria.

Since the royal Abbey had been graciously loaned for the occasion, it was assumed that the entire royal clan would be present, but as it turned out, disappointingly enough, only Princess Margaret and Princess Alexandra came. The most titillating question of all, however, was whether Margaret, Duchess of Argyll, mother of the Duchess of Rutland (who is, by marriage, an aunt of the bride), would attend, since she had not been making social appearances after her much-discussed divorce, and her relations with the groom's mother were known to be not in the least cordial. She was not seen, and her absence was, to the gossips, of far greater interest than what either the sweet bride or her best-dressed stepmother (who occupies an eternal chair now in the Fashion Institute's Hall of Fame) was wearing.

The nuptials of Sir Laurence Olivier's son, Tarquin, to Ridelle Gibson in St. Mary's Church in London, on the other hand, were gratifying to the press, but not too many nomads came to them. At the time that Sir Laurence was married to Vivien

Leigh, their "in" status was glittering and everyone would have begged for an invitation. Since his third marriage to the talented Joan Plowright, the stature of the English actor has never been as resplendent—the extraordinary excitement that any social appearance with Vivien Leigh at his side produced has subsided. Whatever attraction this wedding had was due not so much to the gentle-looking bride and her learned mate-to-be (an ethnologist of merit) but to the fact that Sir Laurence was ever so gracious and considerate to wife No. 1, Jill Esmond (mother of the groom), and No. 2 (Vivien Leigh), and that No. 3 chose to remain absent from the ceremony. Since Miss Plowright is much younger, chic chat was divided into two opposing factions. Her friends said that she had abstained thoughtfully to give the two veteran actresses a field day, and her not-so-good friends intimated that she had feared that the glamor of the other two would overshadow her.

When Peggy Hitchcock, a member of the Mellon dynasty, married Dr. Luis Scarrone in Manhattan, the planes were busy transporting all sorts of U's across the ocean. It was the old-fashioned type of American wedding with bridesmaids and ushers—Princess Peggy d'Arenberg flew in from her Parisian headquarters for forty-eight hours to be one of the matrons of honor—and there were several fetes to entertain the nomads who had jetted in for the royal event.

For the semiroyal wedding of Olympia Torlonia to Paul-Annik Weiller in Rome, numerous wayfarers left the great ball of Baron and Baroness Guy de Rothschild at the Castle of Ferrières at dawn, drove straight to Orly Airport, and caught a Caravelle in time to arrive for the ceremony and the immense reception. They all flew back early the next morning to attend the Grand Prix at Longchamps and then the Aga Khan's dinner dance for four hundred and fifty guests.

There are nuptials which should be of *non plus ultra* interest to N.S., but because of certain unforeseen developments, are not. Under normal circumstances the wedding of Princess Irene of the Netherlands to Prince Hugues of Bourbon-Parme would have whetted the appetite of the most blasé nomad. However, the prodigious bloom and scent of orange blossoms suddenly withered with the announcement that the Protestant Queen of Holland, forced to take the step by irate Dutch public opinion at the groom's sudden pretensions to the Spanish crown (it would take 500,000 words to explain how and why he has now become the Carlist pretender), would not be present at the Catholic rites in Rome. This was not all. With the exception of a few relations of Prince Hugues (his aunt, the former Empress Zita of Austria, was one of them), all royal clans sent their regrets. They refused to do anything to displease either the Netherlands or hurt the susceptibility of the recognized and acknowledged pretender to the Spanish throne, Don Juan Carlos, whose wife Sophie is the sister of the King of Greece.

The partial debacle of the ceremony in Rome does not mean, however, that the status of Irene and Hugues has been affected, except perforce in Madrid (where only the aristocrats from Navarre, the region which backs his claims, pay court to them) and Holland. Everywhere else their glamour is much in demand. They have, as a matter of fact, become great international vedettes because of their much-commented-upon marriage. Since they are immensely publicity conscious, one is aware of their actions almost daily in the press.

At a performance of the second International Dance Festival, held at the Theatre des Champs Elysées, under the patronage of the Minister of Culture, I had proof of the singular attraction this couple has, even for the most sophisticated Parisians. Both the invitation—there were no tickets sold that evening—and the program revealed that the performance would be graced by the presence of Their Royal Highnesses Hugues and Irene. The singularity of this announcement was widely commented upon. Their position is in no way official, since she had to renounce the rights of the Dutch throne to marry "the man I love" and his family is not a reigning one. And yet, here they were being singled out in a very special way.

The French know how to put over this sort of a show superbly, and the evening could not have been more splendid. One had the impression that this was a ruling family to which every honor was due. Not only did Princess Irene wear, throughout the evening, a most attractive smile but a spectacular tiara perched atop her upswept coiffure. Her charming sisters-in-law—Princess Françoise Lobkowicz, Princess Mary of the Snows (Marie des Neiges) and Princess Cecile Bourbon-Parme—and a cousin, the stunning Countess Brenda Bourbon-Bousset (a branch descending straight from St. Louis), all followed her example, looking absolutely superb with their bejeweled heads expertly combed by Monsieur Alexandre to boost their diadems. When this sparkling assembly walked in, it was no wonder that the public and all the various ambassadors and their wives sprang to their feet to greet them and the photographers went wild with joy, snapping away like crazy.

In the case of a *mésalliance,* when either the girl or the young man marries outside of his exalted class, then the marriage is definitely not worth flying to.

It is always difficult to gauge the dash of those ceremonies uniting persons who are not exchanging rings for the first time. The U trend has been, until recently, not to overplay the rounds after the initial entry. But there are signs that all this may change. While those who were present at the wedding of Barbara Hutton to Porfirio Rubirosa (her fifth husband) in New York were not impressed with the *mise en scène,* the guests at her more recent nuptials to Prince Raymond de Champossak (her seventh) at her estate near Cuernavaca, in Mexico, agree unanimously that it was like a dream out of the Arabian nights. Consequently, all those who did not attend were absolutely sick about it. The bride, more beautiful and radiant than ever, looked exquisite in her Indochinese robes, and the gigantic seven-layer cake was mistaken by those present as signifying the seven marriages of this enchanting lady. They jumped to the wrong conclusion, for instead they represented the seven symbols of the groom's mandarin nobility or something equally and adorably Asiatic.

In the pre-jet-set era, it was judged poor manners to be late for a social engagement. Lateness was considered eccentric, never stylish. The only occasion, where it was reputed "a must" to arrive with a certain delay, was a performance at the Opera. Therefore, guests gathered for the dinner which preceded on time, but every effort was made to arrive at the theater and occupy the box long after the curtain had gone up. I recall one night dining at Mrs. Cornelius Vanderbilt's Fifth Avenue mansion before *Aida,* when Countess Marie Mercati, a genuine music enthusiast, realized that the opera would soon begin. She asked permission to leave before coffee was served in order not to miss Giovanni Martinelli's rendition of "Celeste Aida." "Now, Marie," a sophisticated guest said, "surely Verdi did not have a great opinion of this aria if he placed it at the beginning of the first act."

Today in New York (but not in Paris or London) boxholders are still late at the Metropolitan on Monday nights (the only dressy night in the entire week) or for some gala benefit. Opening night has become so overly commercial that the international set keeps away. The same thing has happened at La Scala in Milan but for a different reason. Some time ago, when it became known that the Italian Treasury Department would have spies in the audience to report which ladies were wearing expensive gowns and jewels, the enchantment was over. None of the familiar chic faces have shown up since.

Those who have the habit of being late are usually either very rich or prominent. They are far more inclined to express the courage of their habits and conveniences, particularly since they know that hosts and hostesses are more lenient with them.

It is an old axiom that the poor are to be endured but rarely forgiven.

Millicent Rogers, one of the most bewitching creatures ever to grace society between the two World Wars, was perpetually way behind schedule. Had she not been a Standard Oil heiress, she would have been condoned anyhow, for she was that rare person who lighted a room upon entering it. Although she adored going to the theater, she never saw the first act of any show. One evening after we had attended *The King and I*, we had supper with Yul Brynner. Quite seriously she said to him, "I have a marvelous idea for you. The number of people, like myself, who cannot avoid being late is such a large one that twice a month you should advertise the inversion of the two acts. All of us would return to see the initial act and then you could eliminate performing the second one, for during the first half, the theater would be empty."

Why is lateness considered part of the smart game in certain milieus? The most obvious answer would be to say that many of the leading international vedettes—Princess Maria Gabriella of Italy, Princess "Sunny" Auersperg (Martha Crawford), Sita Maharanee of Baroda, Mrs. Hugo Gouthier, Mrs. Howard Oxenberg, Mrs. Rodman de Heeren, Dolores Sherwood Ruspoli, Micheline Lerner—to name only a very few—are invariably late and that the others are copycats. But there are many other factors that cause this new-spreading practice.

The ever-increasing daily necessity of a hairdresser in a fashionable woman's life is often responsible for these delays. The majority of the prominent social vedettes would not dream of going out to dinner unless their hairdresser has come in the evening to give a *coup de peigne*. In a resort, his job is usually easier, for the distances are not so marked and the traffic is usually less intense. But in large cities, these arbiters of chic heads must rush from one apartment house to another, fighting their way through bottlenecks of automobiles that advance at a snail's pace. It must also be pointed out that some of these ladies no longer have personal maids traveling with them, which prolongs their dressing. Then, naturally enough, the jet-setter prefers to come into a room already filled with colleagues, for she enjoys making an entrance and being admired. Formidable competition may arise to see who can outdo the other and be the last to arrive. People also exist who have been running behind schedule ever since they first came into the world, and these simply cannot help themselves.

None of these N.S. exponents ever stay long enough anywhere to equip their homes with a steady staff. When planning a dinner, therefore, they are forced to hire caterers to attend to most of the details. They are consequently no longer aware of the turmoil their lateness creates in the regular kitchen staffs of their more rooted friends. The effect hoped to be achieved by these ladies is more momentous to them than the quality of the food, since they all eat so sparsely today anyhow.

A certain radar guides them, however, and most of them know pretty well where their delays will be accepted and forgiven and where they will not. Since they enjoy being entertained in some of the great houses, where a timetable still functions, they comply in these specific cases. No one dares, for instance, to be late for one of the magnificent dinners of Princess Isabelle Colonna, the gracious and firm ruler of Roman society. On the other hand, in many other circles their philosophy is: do to your hostess what she has done to you.

Sometimes these antennae fail. I remember attending a formal dinner given by the fabulous American-born Baroness Lo Monaco (Lilian Goldsol of Cleveland) shortly before her death —she was in her nineties—in her palatial Roman flat. The top conservative members of the Italian capital's society had gathered very punctually. The Baroness confided in me that she had invited a young American couple, described to her as attractive and jet-settish, sent to her with an introduction. But despite their acceptance there was no sign of them. After a short wait, she decided to delay no longer and dinner was served. There were two empty seats, and as it happened, one of them was next to mine. At the meat course, as the pair sailed in, all conversation came to a standstill. One could have heard a pin drop.

Despite their sophisticated looks, it was evident that they were embarrassed by their lateness, having quickly got the message that this was no "Dolce Vita" setup. Invariably equal to any situation, and always kind, the Baroness sprang up from her chair and loudly said in greeting them, "How wonderful for that nice director to stop the shooting of the film in time for you to come and at least have part of dinner with us."

"What film are you making?" I eventually asked the lovely creature who had come to occupy the seat near mine. "Do not tell anyone, please," she informed me in a whisper, "but neither of us are movie actors. At first I thought the old lady was balmy, but then I understood her sweetness in saying this to cover up our tardiness in front of all her guests. Everyone knows how film people are never on time. Actually, the reason for our delay is that at two other parties we have gone to in Rome everyone was one hour late."

American components of N.S. are more inclined to be late than Europeans. Dinners in New York, except in a few very special instances, get more and more delayed with the drinking period sometimes lasting anywhere between one hour and one hour and a half.

It is difficult, at times, to be able to predict whether a certain precedent will be imitated and followed by the masses. The world press was full of a soirée held in the Kanaki tavern in the village of Lipessi (which is near Athens) by a dashing group headed by Aristotle Onassis, Melina Mercouri, and Jules Dassin. Maria Callas, however, was absent from the exciting proceedings and missed out on tons of publicity. The shipping tycoon, the actress, and the film director suddenly felt in the mood to break everything within reach, and did. Plates, glasses, bottles, all were smashed, with the other customers following merrily in the destruction. The owners, Mr. and Mrs. Costas Zambetas, were delighted, for with the check they received they were able to go out and restock their restaurant from top to bottom. The attention this event merited was immensely appreciated and for the next few weeks the *taverna* was jammed to the rafters. Of course, nothing is new and this custom, reintroduced in Kanaki, was merely following the practice of the Czarist officers in Imperial Russia. Currently, several restaurant owners are asking themselves whether these three celebrities have re-established this breaking habit as a pastime.

Strangely enough, a custom which is the rage in St. Moritz at the moment, and in the same vein, has not been commented on by the press. The early slapstick movies of Charles Chaplin, Harold Lloyd, Fatty Arbuckle, and Buster Keaton are haunting the rich in this skiing resort. Those who are not old enough to have seen them may not know that most of the laughs were provoked by the throwing of food, ranging from soup to pies, and the very messy results which ensued. Jet-setters are currently going through this phase in this dignified Swiss village and there is no telling when this pastime will begin or end, early in the evening or late. So far it has not spread to the private chalets and it's the restaurants and clubs which have been exposed to these pranks which require much mopping up and make the dry cleaning establishments all the busier and richer.

In a few isolated instances there has also been a certain amount of breaking up of the furniture. Caviar, potatoes, and ice cream are, according to witnesses, the favorite ammunition, and as the bombardment proceeds, landing on dinner jackets and evening dresses, the waiters watch the amusement of the millionaires with inscrutable faces. A chic friend of mine told me that on her return to Paris she had to send each one of her dresses to be cleaned and that her embarrassed maid had decided, in order to avoid unfavorable comments, to take them to different establishments. Another one confessed to me that she had left the resort much earlier than planned since she felt that there must be a less expensive kindergarten elsewhere, in case she longed to join one.

The interesting thing about it is that in a minor key it fits into the general pattern of violence all over the world. It would be absurd to compare it to the throwing of stones at embassies or libraries, the amazing increase in murders, rapes, and vandalism in subways, streetcars, and on the streets, and yet what is this compelling desire to display some sort of physical violence? Is it a reaction to a form of life which daily becomes more abstract? Or is it a subconscious desire to throw away something, food in this instance, which their recent ancestors found difficult to come by? In most cases it is those who recently acquired their fortunes who release their energy in this, goodness knows, harmless but unappetizing way.

When "Taki" Theodoracopoulos, one of the Greeks most in orbit and a fine tennis player, started such a prank in Gstaad's Eagle Club a few years ago he was reprimanded, and his membership was revoked until the following year. Now, of course, he is considered an imaginative pioneer and a missionary of a new trend which is spreading to other resorts including Val d'Isere and the St. Tropez area.

It is becoming desirable for women who have reached a certain age not only to have their faces lifted but to discuss this somewhat innocent pastime with all their friends, both men and women. The choice of the plastic surgeon is of the utmost interest, accompanied by endless discussions pointing out the various pros and cons. A foreign doctor is generally more appreciated than the one near home, since this provides another good excuse to get on a jet and be off.

I was present when two ladies were discussing their experiences in Baden Baden and comparing, note by note, all the various stages of their respective surgeries. The American, who had the job done in London, was ecstatic over the handsomeness and sensitivity of her specialist. "He was so thoughtful," she explained, "that he even asked me who my favorite composer was. When I told him that it was Mozart, he had the most lovely excerpts from *La Finta Giardiniera* and the *Coronation Mass* played on the Hi-Fi while he was performing the operation." "It's the chicest thing I have ever heard," her friend replied. "I wish I could go to him right away, but I am not due for another lift until a year from next fall. I shall make a reservation in his clinic immediately."

But the overwhelming revolution in N.S. is the sudden, gigantic impact of youth. Up until a short time ago young people formed their own world, which was of no special interest to outsiders. Today all that the young do, think, and wear, has become of tremendous importance to all other age groups, and it is they who, in the last ten years, have pioneered many of the leading styles and points of view which have been adopted by their elders. What the Teddy Boys or the *Blousons Noirs* are wearing today or what singer they are about to applaud tomorrow become vital trends six months from now. No party today in N.S. is considered successful unless many juniors are present. It is they who contribute the elements of freshness and spontaneity, that offbeat quality which is now reputed "a must" for a sophisticated evening. Everywhere, in New York, London, Munich, or Stockholm, hostesses want to meet as many youths as they can for they know that, currently, a party without their presence is *démodé* and tame.

The Bostella suddenly became fashionable in Paris' left bank discoteques, and within a few weeks, it spread like wildfire, along with the Bostella coiffure and pants sporting leather-patched knees and bottoms. It is the teenagers who have started this craze, as they did with the Twist, Madison and Surf before. Any *à la page* hostess, while the Bostella lasts, knows her "at home" will be considered antiquated unless she can produce this hectic music and those who can do those acrobatic gyrations on the floor, which consist mainly of clapping one's hands and wiggling while lying down. She also is very aware that her soirée will be much more fun if she does not hire professionals—they always create a commercial touch—but can produce some young people on a guest level. She therefore frantically telephones everyone she knows to try and latch onto some of them and rushes to Castel's—the *boîte* where this dance gained impetus—to mix with the youngsters there and have the opportunity to invite them.

If the Olympia, the Palladium, the Teatro Sistina, or the Palace is jammed with middle-aged men and women to hear Hugues Aufray, the Beatles, Gigliola Cinquetti, Adamo, or Joan Baez whisper or belt out their songs, it is the teenagers who have caused it. It is their vociferous acclaim and hysterical fanaticism which, in a few months time, can transform an average career into a meteoric one.

A few years ago when Vladimir Nabokov's *Lolita* was published, most readers were unaware that this beautifully written, somewhat piquant tale, dealing with the exchange of interests between a mature man and a teenager, following a nomadic trail, was far more than just a novel. Many people saw this story as an isolated incident, played out in terms of the depraved lust a complex-ridden male feels for the bloom of adolescence. But actually the author went much further, having divined the ever-increasing, often subconscious, need of the aging generation to recapture, by some contact with youth, a spark of enthusiasm which the barrenness and disenchantment of the modern way of life has produced in them. The phenomenon may be sexual, in some instances, but this is by no means its main motivating force. The blasé satiety which affects a growing number of men and women—too much, too soon, what next—is still capable of receiving an electric shock from youth which is heading in the same direction but in delayed action.

Youth does not stay enthusiastic long before that wonderfully incandescent, tender innocence of puberty is going, gone.

Today it is considered useless, passé, and a waste of time, with parents doing nothing to encourage it. The prevailing theory is that teenagers should learn the answers early in order to be tough and self-sufficient and, impervious, stand on their own legs. Few questions are asked by the families and these youngsters travel long distances, invading cities and resorts during the summer and winter holidays, with no one quite knowing how the bills get paid. While their enthusiasm is vivid for a while, it does not survive long. The element of surprise soon ceases as the disenchantment of their elders reaches and envelopes them. We have all sorts of examples in such relatively youthful writers as Shelagh Delaney, Arthur Kopit, Arnold Wesker, Leroy Jones, Harold Pinter, and Edward Albee. They are all immensely vital, but where is the gaiety, the facetiousness, and the tomfoolery of youth?

Aristotle Onassis' wealth explains, only in part, why his son Alexander, a teenager, rushes around the French Riviera in a Ferrari sports car. He has a more expensive and striking automobile than most, but many contemporaries of his have a car of sorts. Should I have asked my parents for an automobile at their age, my request would have been interpreted as a misplaced joke.

When the dress house of Castillo in Paris engaged sixteen-year-old Christina Eustrateades as its star mannequin there was hardly a ripple of surprise. It is the youthful look which dominates more and more fashion, and many women wish to look like little girls. The consensus in fashion circles is that the huge success Michele Rosier (the daughter of Pierre and Helene Lazareff) has made in the ready-to-wear line comes from the fact that she is so young herself that she knows just how to make the female feel youthful-looking.

The fashion magazines are promoting this teenage crusade every inch of the way—one calls it a "youthquake"—lending a helping hand in creating the adolescent chic image. Recently American *Vogue* assigned full pages to Pilar Crespi, the thirteen-year-old daughter of Rudi and Consuelo O'Connor Crespi, whose caption informs the reader thrillingly that she "adores being a girl"; Cathy Hart, a daughter of the late playwright Moss Hart and Kitty Carlisle, aged fourteen, whose joys are numerous, but among them "the new dances Bird, Monkey, Surf, in order named"; and fifteen-year-old Stella Astor, whose parents are the British John Jacob Astors. "Everything delights her," the write-up tells us, "people, life, laughing." These girls, along with legions of others, will be real veterans of glamor when they eventually make their bows to society. But coming-out parties have become only a vague, nonfocused symbol, for little girls, aged twelve, now go to dances in evening dresses.

Along the avenues of companionship, older men have always sought the partnership of younger women who have returned their attentions with alacrity. There has never been any element of surprise in this sort of setup which, since time immemorial, has been accepted as a most natural occurrence. But not since the eighteenth century had the reverse been true and older women taken on very, very young men as their permanent companions.

In the eighteenth century in Italy a boy who preferred the company of mature ladies was called "cicisbeo" or "cavalier servente." Today, the Italians no longer have a name for him, but the French do and it is "minet." There seems to have been no other contemporary word coined to describe this type, and internationalites use this Gallic expression all the time. A "Minet," however—I have heard this subject discussed at length by authorities on the French language—should not only be young in age but also have a babyish face. However, since the jet-setters usually are not acquainted with the language of Bossuet and Voltaire to that extent, they refer to a youngster who escorts women, baby-face or not, as a "minet."

In rapid succession, one after the other, four of the most-in-view ladies in N.S. began this trend a short time ago, and it has caught on with the same ease scarlet fever does in a school.

Not only is there no embarrassment on their part but obvious pride and joy in showing off these boys, who are, usually, their sons' contemporaries, and sometimes their best friends.

The revival of this quaint custom reminds me of a captivating story told about Ninon de Lenclos. Not only was this witty woman a *grande amoureuse,* but her Parisian salon was the meeting place of the wits and brains of her day. Time marched on, but Ninon's charms, according to the chroniclers, remained undimmed. A young abbot, who courted her with ardor, was finally invited to dine with her alone by candlelight. But when, after the delicious food had been served, he approached her to come to terms with his passion, she asked him to wait until the nearby church bells would strike midnight. He complied and then spent an unforgettable night with her. When, very discreetly, he took his leave at dawn, he asked her to explain to him the reason for the tantalizing delay the night before. "Because," Ninon replied calmly, "at twelve o'clock I began to celebrate my eightieth birthday. I decided you were so attractive I could not find a better way to start this historical date in my life than acceding to your first embrace. I hope this is only the beginning of a long lasting romance between us."

On Long Island, a tempestuous affair was in progress between a lady in her middle forties and a young man. At a dinner I attended, people were discussing the difference in their ages, and someone insisted that the youngster was barely eighteen. "Now, let us be fair," said the hostess, coming to the defense of the lady in question. "She is not that much of a cradle-snatcher and I can prove to you that you are wrong." She quickly went into the library, pulled out a scrapbook and showed a photograph of this matron's wedding. Pointing with her long, immaculately manicured red fingernail to a page boy, holding the bride's train, she said, "He must have been at least four or five years old, wouldn't you think? And the marriage was exactly sixteen years ago."

Along the matrimonial avenues, there are all sorts of indications that there is a definite return to the times when the age difference, either way, was unimportant. It appears at the moment stylish for men and women of different generations to march to the altar and contribute to one another the advantages of their age groups. The woods are so full—in the United States, Europe, the Orient, Africa, and South America—of older celebrated pigeons who have in recent years wed young doves and made a success of it that one does not know where to start. In the interminable list, at random, one recalls Viscount Astor and his third bride Bronwen Pugh; Earl Beatty with his fourth choice, Diane Blundell; and the Duke of Rutland with his second, Frances Sweeny; Alfred Vanderbilt, Huntington Hartford, and Pat de Cicco, who all have reached the third marriage stage; Maestro Herbert von Karajan and his third Eliette Mouret; the Shah of Iran and his third Empress, Farah Diba; Harry Karl and Debbie Reynolds; the Duke of Cadaval, in his early fifties, and his twenty-one-year-old second bride, Claudine Pritz; Prince Christian of Hanover (brother of the Queen Mother of Greece, Frederica) and his recent bride, Mireille Dutry, well over twenty years his junior. In Africa this is true, too. Kenya's Prime Minister and strong man, Jomo Kenyatta, is thirty years older than his fourth wife, Ngina.

In the international sweepstakes of marriage, among some of the many recent wedding bells one remembers are those of fifty-one-year-old Stewart Granger, the British veteran actor, and Belgian Beauty Queen Caroline Lecerf, twenty-one-years his junior; Joe Hyams, the entertaining forty-year-old American journalist, to twenty-four-year-old German actress Elke Sommer; Stirling Moss, the thirty-four-year-old British car racer, to Elaine Barbarino, a New Yorker, ten years younger; the fifty-two-year-old columnist John Crosby to twenty-six-year-old British fashion editor Katharine Wood; forty-year-old British businessman John Ambler to Princess Margaretha of Sweden, eleven years his junior, and Cary Grant to Diane Cannon, twenty-seven years his junior.

The actor, Ugo Tognazzi, picked out as his partner a girl many years his junior, Margrete Robsam (it is the thing now among the Mediterranean men to bring home a Scandinavian wife). These Italian-Norwegian nuptials took place in the Mexican Consulate in Lugano, Switzerland.

Dr. James Murphy, a member of the Rockefeller University is, instead, a sturdy American who sticks to girls of his own nationality. He married Victoria Thompson, sixteen years younger, while his former wife, Margaretta (Happy) who was only four years his junior, is now the wife of Nelson Rockefeller, eighteen years her senior. From their second choices, one might conclude that in their instances they both needed a far greater disparity in age in their mates, for oddly enough, the differential in their second try is—year wise—almost identical but at opposite extremes.

Stavros Niarchos, who in the postwar years created the lasting image of the millionaire who has everything, established no new trend when he took as a bride, Charlotte Ford, reputedly thirty-three years his junior. But the manner in which he achieved this new matrimonial status has left even the most sophisticated members of N.S. gasping for breath.

Not even his intimate friends had any clue that he was in the process of divorcing his third wife, Eugenie Livanos, until the zero hour just before he emplaned for Juarez, Mexico, for the ring ceremony, minus the wedding bells. The latter were not in order either for the bride or the groom since the Catholic religion, to which she belongs, does not admit divorce and the Orthodox, in which he was born, allows only three marriages in church, an allotment he had seemingly used up. A motel, therefore, had to serve instead of a chapel.

If the announcement of the marriage came as a devastating surprise, the news of their honeymoon provided even more of a shock to a shockproof society. To where did the aging Midas fly his Michigan-bred nymph twenty-four hours later? Straight to St. Moritz where the discarded consort and the various children she had given him were waiting to welcome the newlyweds with open arms. Not even Noel Coward in his heyday was able to conceive a more advanced and civilized design for contemporary living. Mr. Niarchos now symbolizes to rich and poor alike the rare phenomenon of a man who knows how to enjoy both the old cake and the new.

Another trend, which is coming back strongly, is of greater interest. Any student of history can indicate innumerable cases of exalted historical figures of men who took to the altar, out of political expedience or love, women who were their elders. In the middle ages those two extraordinary Holy Roman Emperors, Henry VI and his son Frederick II, come to mind right away. Their consorts were exactly ten years older than they (and in those days, this meant far more in appearance than today). Later there was Josephine Tascher de la Pagerie, whom Napoleon made his first Empress. Although she was already seven years of age in Martinique when the future Emperor was born in Corsica, these two islanders defied their age in every possible way, including the divergence in their birth registers.

Of late, the press has been full of the great love match between the eldest daughter of the Count of Paris, Princess Isabelle of France, and the handsome Austrian Count Carl Federic Schoenborn. All the articles underlined the fact that she was six years older than he.

In Mexico, the imperishable Dolores del Rio, whose beauty is still so magical that she creates the impression that time has forgotten her existence, is happily married to Lewis Riley, an El Greco-ish looking Californian several years her junior. From the look of things, this third matrimonial venture for both of them is the best yet.

There is no more adorable creature than Janet Gaynor, who has retained a wonderfully youthful figure, and what is more essential, point of view. After several years' widowhood (her first husband was the unforgettable costume designer Gilbert

Adrian), she married the theatrical and film producer Paul Gregory. When they walk into a room they both so beam with happiness that the twelve years' age difference between them is not in the least noticeable. The same year interval applies to the ex-wife of Richard Burton, Sybil, who, at thirty-six, took on as her mate Jordan Christopher, twenty-four. Her decision was all the more significant since she had to renounce a sizable alimony.

Another movie actress, June Allyson, wedded a men's hair stylist, Glen Maxwell, nine years her junior, and the well-liked former social secretary to Mrs. John F. Kennedy, Laetitia "Tish" Baldridge, exchanged vows with Chicago real estate executive Robert Hollensteiner, who is also several years younger.

Along the Palm Beach, Long Island, and Chicago circuits, we have another marvelous example in the recent union of redheaded Molly Bragno, who has found much bliss with her youthful husband Albert Bostwick, Jr. Since neither of them is royal (although his family is among the most aristocratic in the United States), there is no way to look up in the *Gotha* what their birth dates are, but their friends claim that they are far apart.

This habit is also catching up in rarefied beatnik milieus, as the nuptials in Scotland of Michael Chaplin, the eldest son of the marriage of Charles Chaplin to Oona O'Neill, to Patricia John would indicate. She is six years his senior.

The story of Doris Duke's nuptial tie to dark, suave, sexy pianist Joe Castro, fifteen years her junior, is filled with mystery. When he asked for a divorce not long ago, no one, including the bride, had known they were ever wed. She has denied vehemently the ring-on-the-finger ceremony, but what is certain is that they both tinkled four hands strongly on the same piano for a long time.

Of course—as the nomads know only too well, trying to keep up with all the divorces of their friends and remarriages—

many are the unions which end before a judge, with or without a difference in age. One marriage, which lasted for a valiant period of fifteen years, is that of Time Inc.'s Board Chairman Andrew Heiskell to British actress Madeleine Carroll. It survived by five years the age span which separated them, and he is now married, for the third time, to the charming Marian Sulzberger Dryfoos of the *New York Times* dynasty.

Forty-one-year-old Gregg Sherwood Dodge, widow of the automobile Croesus, recently became the wife of Daniel D. Moran. Twelve years younger than she, this very good-looking chap, now a real estate agent in Florida, used to be a cop on the New York Police Force.

The time has certainly come when it is indeed impossible to assume what relationship exists between men and women who answer to the same surname but whose disparity in age is apparent. Until not long ago, one was safe in guessing in most instances that it was a mother-son or father-daughter connection. Today it is wise to say nothing until one can ascertain exactly what the case may be.

The most revealing story about this new development in relative age between the two sexes was told me by a friend. With her husband, she decided to go to a discothèque in London where youth congregated and performed all the latest dances. Since they found no accommodation, they were in the process of leaving when a young man leaped from his table and offered to make a place for them. Thanking him but not recalling where she had seen him before, she asked him if he was a schoolmate of her son at Oxford. "No, but I know him well," he replied. "In the last few months he and my mother have become quite inseparable." My friend admitted she gladly accepted his suggestion to sit down since she felt a little faint upon learning this bit of news. The only comment her husband made, on their way home, was that he had been unable to reply. "I was so stunned, my vocal chords were paralyzed," he told his wife.

3

Entertaining in Nomadic Society

Through the centuries society everywhere has resembled a game of some hide and many seek. Today, as in the past, while those born to it follow the regulations easily and naturally, others must learn the complexities of this sport one by one, having to depend more on their acquired knowledge than on innate instinct. The test comes when a delicate circumstance forces a decision for which the book of rules does not offer a solution.

To participate in the society game on a global basis and win some of the rounds (it is impossible to score one hundred percent) takes an enormous memory, a tremendous stamina and an elastic willingness to compromise on many levels. For many this play is necessitated by business reasons, but for others it is a challenge to their egos and vanities. Whatever the cause, it is understandable that anyone who enters this international frolic usually is motivated by enough personal pride to want to play it as well as possible. Since no overall volume of cosmopolitan protocol and etiquette exists, international skating often takes place on thin ice.

One of the toughest hurdles the nomad faces in his continuous wanderings is meeting new people and having to place them, quickly and knowingly, in their right frames and surroundings. He must, in the first stages, tread lightly in his new environment and avoid being either enthusiastic or impulsive. He must remember that the closets of his new acquaintances are full of all sorts of ghosts and he must take the time to sort them out to avoid committing blunders which are hard to repair for nomadic sensitivity is ever coming to the fore.

Nowadays the circle of so-called society in a large city, be it a capital or not, is so immense that it is nigh impossible to follow closely more than a few of the deeply entangled personal relations existing among members of one's own family, friends, and acquaintances. Society columnists are helpful in pointing out the eruption of some sudden violent new feud, but there are many buried ones which no longer haunt the memory. Unfortunately, when people kiss and make up, there is never any beating of the drums, since it is war that makes news, not peace.

When one enters the immense field of international society, these various situations are multiplied along so many tangents that it takes all sorts of barometers and compasses to know who is speaking to whom and who is temporarily congenial and *persona grata*. Marriages, divorces, remarriages, follow each other so closely on the world stage that a new expression has crept into N.S. conversation. "Two husbands ago" or "three wives ago" is currently and appropriately used to distinguish the various phases of a life.

Actually, a legitimate divorce usually leaves fewer scars than a broken promise of marriage or a disrupted liaison. It is far less of a *gaffe* if a hostess, unknowingly, places side by side a couple who used to be married, than a man and a woman, one of whom at a certain point has thrown the other overboard for someone else. The atmosphere, in such cases, has a tendency to become tense and strained.

At a large dinner I attended in St. Moritz, there were several such mix-ups both on the wedded and nonwedded level. A witty Frenchwoman, far better informed than our hosts, who had stepped unknowingly into many international hornets' nests, asked me whether I had read *Twenty Years Later*. "This party reminds me of that novel," she said, "with the difference that Alexandre Dumas wrote better plots about more interesting characters."

It does not take long for anyone to realize that the upper crust of nomadic society resembles a gigantic golden carrousel. Its thousands of eminently sophisticated riders rarely look for new racehorses, much preferring to stick to those belonging to well-known stables. Those relatively few brand new mares and stallions who step on the merry-go-round every year must quickly prove their value or get dropped again into less glamorous pastures where they are soon forgotten. As in Arthur Schnitzler's novel *La Ronde,* sooner or later weddings and romances are always enacted by the same leading men who copartner the same ladies. This intermarriage in the nomadic set is fascinating and it recreates a small town on a spherical scale.

Is it insecurity which prompts it, or indolence? This lack of spirit of adventure on the part of the N.S. is all the more arresting, since in the middle class milieus it is far from the case. On the contrary, intermarriage among persons of different nationalities, races, creeds, colors, and professions in vast numbers all over the world is the order of the day. Their spontaneity is far greater, not to mention their courage, in taking such a gamble on their mates.

One of the inescapable labyrinths nomads have to contend with are titles. To know the real from the false is a prime necessity. The greatest *faux pas* that can be committed in any society is to give precedence to a self-appointed patrician. The true nobleman values his title, since he feels that in the general leveling of all classes it has an historical significance. His contempt, therefore, for the invented artistocrat knows no bounds, resembling the scorn a legitimate doctor feels for a quack or a thoroughbred for a mule.

At times this disdain becomes so perverse that the real patrician accepts the hospitality of the false one only in order to make fun of him. At other times the invitation is accepted because it is financially profitable and his presence receives a remuneration of sorts. However, I have also heard the point of view expressed that the false nobility contributes much to the luster of the old one. "When people will no longer invent titles," a wise old Italian Count said to me, "this will mean that the aristocracy is finished. It is the same with fake jewels, which cause much of the glitter of the real gems. Should merchants cease manufacturing imitation diamonds, emeralds, and rubies, it will signify that the precious stones are no longer valuable." The last word was had recently by the Infanta Maria Cristina of Spain, wife of Vermouth industrialist Count Enrico Marone Cinzano. One of the most intelligent and attractive components of royalty, she is wit personified. When a certain well-known couple turned up in Geneva, where she lives, with a newer and more glowingly invented title, continuing the ascent on their self-created aristocratic ladder, she supposedly said, "If these nice people continue in this direction, they will end up, like so many royalties, in exile."

Impostors have always existed, and the world has never ceased to be amused by them (Giuseppe Balsamo appointed himself Count di Cagliostro and in between jail sentences was the darling of eighteenth-century European society), but to take them seriously is an unpardonable social error. As more and more nomads entertain an increasingly mixed bag of persons, they are compelled to learn how to separate the false coronets from the real, and consequently, what precedence prevails among the latter.

In the countries where a monarchy still functions, the titles are found to be legitimate. It is inconceivable that some Britisher in his right mind would take on a Baronetcy, an Earldom, or a Dukedom without having a right to it. No one would undertake such a masquerade with *Debrett's Peerage*, in its bright red binding, so casually evident in every British house. In England, seating the peers is not involved, for, with few exceptions, the rule is that those who received their titles first get served accordingly.

In the opinion of Nancy Mitford, the only surviving aristocracy in the world is the British, since it still exerts a political power in the House of Lords. With her inimitable humor, she compares the nobility which has survived in a republic to a chicken whose head has been cut off. The fact that it is still running around does not mean that it is not dead. There is a certain truth in what she says. Nevertheless, the historical significance of titles cannot but survive. In every period of history, the past always provides more glamor than the present.

In England only a very few titles can be inherited by women, but their husbands can never assume them, thus remaining what they were. For instance, when the Duke of Sutherland died in 1963, his titles split. Since he had no children of his own, the Dukedom, which could not be inherited by a female descendant, went to his closest male kinsman, the Earl of Ellesmere, but the earldom was assumed by his niece, Elizabeth Sutherland. The status of her husband, Charles Noël Janson, did not change and any invitation addressed to them reads "The Countess of Sutherland and Mr. Janson." In any seating, she always takes precedence for she is a peeress and he is not a peer. Another famous peeress in her own right is the Countess of Seafield, one of the wealthiest ladies in the British Commonwealth.

Spanish nobility differs from all the others. When there is no direct male heir, in the greatest number of cases the title is assumed by the female descendant. She, in turn, has the right to invest her husband with it in the quality of consort. Whoever inherits the titles (every important family has several) can distribute them to their children, brothers, sisters, and nephews. As deaths occur, these titles change hands, enabling some people to move a few steps up the aristocratic ladder. When an earldom or a marquesate is older and more historically significant than a Dukedom, the former is utilized.

The delightful wife of the present Spanish Ambassador to London is a case in point. Although she is the Duchess of San Carlos (this title dates from 1784) in her own right, she prefers to be known as the Marquesa de Santa Cruz (this one was granted in 1569), and the Ambassador, in the quality of his consort, follows suit. The Duke of Sueca, for instance, outranks some of his equals not on account of his duchy, which is only a little over one hundred and fifty years old, but because he is the eighteenth Count of Chinchon, an exceedingly old and eminent designation.

There are some families which have titles in more than one country. In N.S. one runs into the erudite and congenial Alfonso Falco, who in Spain is the Marquess de Castel-Rodrigo—his palace in Madrid was for several years the residence of the American Ambassador—and in Italy Prince Pio. Since his wife is Sveva Colonna, sister of Prince Aspreno Colonna, whose hereditary position of Assistant to the throne of the Pope automatically gives him the rank of a Cardinal, this couple has seating priority up and down the international circuit.

Just to confuse the newcomer to the Spanish jungle of titles, there is also the Duke of Ciudad Rodrigo, but this is the city and the other the Castle. He and the Duke of Wellington are the same person. In fact, should you meet the Duke of Wellington during one of his stays in Spain (where he spends several months a year in the property given to his glorious ancestor in gratitude for chasing Napoleon's armies from the Iberian Peninsula), he will be introduced as Duke of Ciudad Rodrigo. On the other hand, in Portugal he is presented as the Duke da Victoria, and in Holland as Prince of Waterloo.

A similar case in England is that of Viscount Bridport, who descends from Lord Nelson and therefore is also the Duke of Bronte in Italy. His ancestor was also given, along with the title, a fief in Sicily, the Castle of Maniace in the province of Catania. The Viscount-Duke, in fact, spends most of his time in Rome and Port' Ercole with his Dutch-born wife.

Above all, what counts in Spain is whether the *grandeza* (the ancient privilege permitting one to keep his hat on in the presence of the King) accompanies the title and if so, in what year it was granted. Thus a Count, with an old *grandeza,* passes ahead of a Duke with a more recent one. All Dukes are automatically Grandees but there are many Marquesses, Counts, and Viscounts who are not.

Every Spanish title must be reconfirmed by a formidable organization, Deputacion y Consejo de la Grandeza, of which the eighteenth Duke of Infantado, eight times a Grandee, is President, and certain dues must be paid. The assignment of a title to a member of the family must also be approved officially (it usually is) and many are the South Americans, whose ancestors at one time or the other had a title, who hire experts to comb the archives in the hope of discovering one they can lay claim to. Spain is a monarchy *de jure,* even if not as yet *de facto,* and Generalissimo Franco has continued to dispense titles, enabling a new aristocracy to arise since the end of the civil war. Grandezas have also been assigned, although there is no Sovereign in whose presence these gentlemen can remain hatted.

Any foreigner who undertakes to entertain formally in Spain is in for rough sailing on a stormy sea. I speak from experience. I shall never forget a luncheon I gave for twenty in Madrid at the Jockey Club. Cognizant of the perils of such an undertaking, what with royalty, diplomats, grandees, and future grandees (who pass ahead of those who will never be) on my guest list, I sent the names to the protocol experts of the Pardo Palace, who were kind enough to work out the seating in all its details. It seemed absolute perfection and I was very very much intrigued by the fact that I, the host, was placed at the end of the table.

Just as I was about to proceed to the door on the street to receive the former King of Italy, Umberto, a Duchess came up and, with a ravishing smile, informed me that there had been a mistake about the seat she had been assigned. She should not be on His Majesty's left, but on his right. "But what happens to the American Ambassadress?" I asked, whom the experts had placed on the King's right. "She must preside and sit opposite the King," she informed me. "But according to etiquette everywhere," I protested, "no lady can preside with a King or ex-King except a Queen or former Queen." In the midst of this unnerving discussion, His Majesty arrived and I had to apologize for not having received him, as protocol demands, at the street door. His aide de camp advised me to keep the seating as was and the attractive Duchess sat, unwillingly, on the King's left.

The final answer is that in Spain one either entertains in a big way at several tables, asking key figures to be hosts and preside, or one must be guided by those who know just who can be asked together, for there is a continuous conflict among the grandees, the diplomats, the government officials, about who is entitled to precedence.

In Germany, with the exception of a few false Barons, there is not too much feeling around. The Germans are very correct people, who are not too inclined to flights of fancy in the coats of arms department. In France and Italy, however, the anarchy is complete. Since France became a republic close to one hundred years ago, people suddenly take on titles which they have no right to. Although the elite knows—and the concierges, always the best-informed people in the French republic—in the confusion of today's N.S. some globe-trotters don't catch on and get scalded. The situation is complicated enough among the real aristocrats—the ancient ones of the Bourbons and the more recent ones of the Bonapartes, who are still at odds with one another. Some counts of the old regime actually think they should go ahead of the dukes, made during the Empire, and the only guiding light in this difficult maze is that those dukes who are Peers of the Realm go ahead of everybody.

On the French Riviera I overheard a group discussing the placement at a forthcoming gala for a certain couple. She is a member of one of the most respected clans, but no one is satisfied that his pompous title is genuine. "I cannot help you," replied a well-known Paris hostess, "I simply adore them but I only invite them to my buffet dinners."

In Italy, following the fall of the monarchy soon after the Second World War, false titles have been sprouting like mushrooms after the rain (some of them, one hears, are now registered in the tiny republic of San Marino which makes a tidy profit from this nebulous commerce). The various telephone books in Italian cities burst with marvelously imaginative invented knighthoods. In Italy there is also the riddle, nonexistent in France, of many persons having the surname of some of the princely families. While in France one rarely finds a Faucigny-Lucinge, Caraman, de Noailles, Descazes, La Rochefoucauld, or Levis Mirepoix outside the inner circle, south of the Alps there are plenty of Colonnas, Orsinis, Corsinis, Pallavicinis, Dorias, who have no connection whatsoever with the illustrious ones.

In Paris recently such a mistake happened, creating talk for weeks. A very well-born couple, much in the swim, gave a large dinner with an impressive list of guests including a former king, who naturally ranked No. 1. To the astonishment of many of those present, sitting next to the royal personage was a signora with the same surname as one of Italy's leading principessas but who did not hold the coronet and was not even remotely related. The many ladies who ranked ahead of her were amazed, stunned, and shocked until someone pointed out that even the great Marivaux wrote some of his best plays around cases of mistaken identity. This ray of sunshine in the stormy plight brought the party to a successful end.

Italy's real aristocracy, even in the more orderly days of the monarchy, presented all sorts of difficulties. Until 1870 the Italian peninsula was divided into different states, kingdoms, and principalities. Therefore, the blazons through the centuries had been assigned by the Pope and many different rulers (Spanish, French, Austrian, German, etcetera). One can, in the majority of cases, bank on a prince being either Roman (a Vatican assignation) or Neapolitan-Sicilian (the Spanish Bourbons were exceedingly lavish in the apportioning of princedoms), and as for Dukes, save for a cluster of them in the south, they are few and far between. Added perplexity comes from the old Italian custom of addressing a member of a princely clan as Prince even when, officially, he only has the right to be called Don.

A spellbinding number of amusing cases has emerged recently whereby title-hungry persons have acquired a highly debatable title by getting themselves adopted by a patrician (he must have no children of his own by law) in exchange for a financial remuneration. The trick consists in the fact that since the Italian republic does not *de jure* recognize titles (although it does *de facto*) the person who has been legally adopted takes the surname of his new father and with it the title. This would not have been possible at the time of the monarchy. One of the most hilarious and celebrated cases is that which involves an actor and his popular wife, who hails from a fine princely family. When she soon discovered that being plain *Signora* was not to her liking, she arranged for a Prince in need of funds to adopt her French husband so that she could go on wearing the same coronet she had been forced to give up on the day of her wedding. In the meantime she and her husband have separated and no one is quite sure, at this point, whether this delicious play is still being enacted or not.

On the French Riviera one sometimes meets Prince Marc of Hohenzollern and, unless one is aware of his background, it is easy to be baffled by the fact that anyone with such a splendid German name is French. Digging a little, it turns out that he was an actor, Marc Favrat, who was befriended and later adopted by the late Queen Elizabeth of Greece, who was born of the Roumanian branch of the Hohenzollern (her mother was the famous Queen Marie).

The most spectacular bouquet of false titles to blossom suddenly out of nowhere was the one which emerged among the exiles who fled the Russian Revolution. With extraordinary assurance and remarkable cheek, they invented coronets and denominations for themselves which today, particularly in the United States, are accepted as completely real and have been very helpful in earning a living.

I was present one day when a Long Island dowager asked a gentleman, in whose veins ran the bluest of Czarist blood, about a "delightful" Russian Prince she had met of late. "Is it a very old title?" she asked. "No," replied the poker-faced St. Petersburger. "It's one of those created by Lenin."

Conflict between the old aristocracy and the legitimate new one exists too, but in muted tones, and if properly handled, need never get in anyone's path. But those nomads who don't bother to find out, and give first place to the recent coats of arms, are like inexperienced cooks who cannot tell the young chicken from the old. The main course never turns out to be quite right.

A good anecdote, real or invented, to illustrate this long-seated *status quo* is one told about Isabelle II, Queen of Spain. When, because of political expediency, she created one of her subjects a Duke, some of her equerries and ladies-in-waiting were up in arms, since they did not consider the man in question worthy of this exalted rank. "His becoming a Duke," the Queen replied with the wisdom of centuries of rule, "does not mean that he is suddenly also a gentleman. But it is my sincerest hope that his descendants will learn to be what their ancestor was not." Of course the Queen was right. The Duke's heirs, much in evidence today, have lived up to Her Majesty's trust and aspirations.

A big hurdle in N.S. is how to address a divorced woman and what seat to assign her at luncheon or dinner. In the United States this problem is fortunately nonexistent. There, the lady in question is allowed to do exactly what she pleases, often keeping the surname of her former husband and exchanging his Christian name with her own maiden family one. Occasionally, there are women who prefer to return to the surname of a previous deceased husband. Thus, as an example, Janet Newbold, one of the great beauties of New York society, after an unsuccessful marriage in St. Louis, has reverted to the exact appellation by which she was known at the time of her second marriage to the late William Rhinelander Stewart. On the other hand, her daughter has resumed in full her maiden name after a brief marriage and is addressed, by her own wish, as Miss Serena Stewart. Since Americans are rarely concerned about seating, one often finds that a divorced woman (particularly if she is very rich) is seated ahead of one currently married.

But with Europeans this matter is fraught with all sorts of lurking perils. In France, by law, the woman must take back her maiden name in full, and if she does not the ex-husband and his relations frequently go to court about it. There are few exceptions where legally the divorced lady has not only kept her husband's name but the title. We have such examples in the Rothschild family with the former wives of the Barons Guy and Edmond who are addressed, respectively, as the Baroness Alix and the Baroness Lina de Rothschild.

On the other hand, Lina Rodriguez, a member of a well-known Colombian family, after divorcing her second French husband, Serge Eonnet, has reverted to calling herself Princess Lina Schoenburg-Hartenstein, the name and title belonging to her at the time of her marriage to her first, German, husband, Prince Peter. Since her rank is hard to define, she presents quite a problem about where she is to be seated at official dinners.

There are, invariably, those who on all official documents sign their maiden name but prefer to be addressed with the title and name of their former husbands, which is more important than that with which they are born. Friends, in order to be agreeable, comply, but when it comes to seating these charming ladies they must always take into consideration this artifice. It is here that the unknowing foreigner can walk right into a trap and seat a princess or a duchess, who is called so out of courtesy, ahead of a titled married woman. God help those who do, for they will never hear the end of it.

In Italy and Spain the only way out of matrimony is an annulment of the marriage which must be issued by the Vatican's *Sacra Rota* before it is recognized by the civil courts. If and when this is granted, the woman must return to her maiden surname, since the wedlock has not only ceased but in a sense never existed. Since annulments are hard to get and the waiting period is endless, one meets with countless ladies who are legally separated from their mates but who, to all effects, are married to them. Their surname, therefore, remains unchanged and whatever privileges of protocol go with it.

The real complication begins when the titled or high-ranking husband, tired of waiting for annulment, with or without the consent of his wife, manages to get a divorce in some other country and remarries. His divorce is, naturally, not recognized at home, and as far as his country of origin is concerned, he is still married to No. 1. She could, should she want to, sue him for bigamy. This happens rarely, for usually there has been some agreement between them. The situation, however, of the two wives remains anomalous, and in terms of protocol the seating of No. 2 in the home country or in any Catholic milieu is fraught with difficulties. The use of the title is also a complicated problem to resolve on an official level, for in Catholic society only No. 1 has a right to it.

In Spain, in the case of an annulment of the marriage of a woman who has her own title, the phenomenon is inverted. There it is the male who must relinquish the coronet which had been bestowed upon him by his wife the day of their wedding.

In England, a woman has a claim to hold on to the title of her divorced husband by placing her Christian name before the appellation. Therefore, Margaret Whigham, for instance, whose divorce from the Duke of Argyll has become a *cause célèbre,* can rightfully call herself, until she remarries, Margaret Duchess of Argyll. How or why she would want to continue, after all the sordid mud-slinging, is something else again. However, in terms of protocol her situation has changed. When she was the Duke's consort, because of his various hereditary positions such as Master of Her Majesty's Household in Scotland and Keeper of the Great Seal of Scotland, she ranked higher at certain functions than some of the other Duchesses.

The nonintroduced foreigner is prone to be thoroughly confused by a group of ladies who go on using titles which actually are no longer theirs. There are, in fact, some women in the British Isles who hang on to the titles of their late husbands despite their remarriages.

One of the famous virtuosas of this title-holding marathon is the beguiling Maureen Guinness, who continues to call herself Maureen the Marchioness of Dufferin and Ava, explaining that her late husband, the Marquess, would have wanted it that way. In the meantime, since his death, she married and divorced Major Harry Buchanan and is currently the happy wife of an important Judge, John Maude. Her sister, Oonagh, who recently divorced her third mate, Cuban dress designer Miguel Ferreras, has also confused her friends. She has reverted to calling herself Oonagh, Lady Oranmore and Browne, which is the appellation she used following her second divorce. A third sister, Aileen, is playing their same tune. Upon shedding her second consort, Valerian Rybar, she has taken back the surname Plunkett of her first marriage, which also ended in divorce.

Constance Cornwallis West divorced the late Duke of Westminster way back in 1919 and remarried Fitzpatrick Lewis, but she is still known as Constance Duchess of Westminster. Another source of perplexity is that of Audrey Pointing, who became the wife of Major Ernest Rowat after the death of her husband, the third Lord Doverdale, but goes on calling herself Lady Doverdale, along with the American-born widow of the second Lord Doverdale.

The most understandable of all is the instance of Marigold Lubbock, who, following the demise of her husband, the fourth Earl of Londesborough, was married for four years to a dashing Pole, Zygmund de Lubicz-Bakanowski. Upon divorcing him, in order to make life easier for her friends, she renounced the exotic name of her second mate and returned to the more Anglo-Saxon one of her first.

The how-you-were-born routine for women is of the utmost importance in Europe. From morning to night the expression "Née," "Nascida," "Nata," "Geborn," "Born," comes up regularly like an endless refrain to underline the social status of the female before her marriage. Undoubtedly the emphasis is greater today than ever before because of the continuous *més-alliance* which girls make by marrying outside of their class, prompted sometimes by love and often by money. It is frequent, indeed, for a woman to have her maiden name printed on her calling card with the approval of her husband, who is immensely proud of her heritage and constantly refers to it. The opposite never happens, for girls who are not born to an important name are not particularly anxious to advertise it.

In N.S. not to know a woman's birth can lead those who

entertain into serious mistakes in assigning precedence at a party. Among the many cases which come to mind are Mrs. Howard Oxenberg, the former Princess Elizabeth of Yugoslavia, a niece of Princess Marina Duchess of Kent; Mrs. André Spitz Jordan, who was Princess Monica of Lichtenstein, a member of the ruling family of the small principality, and Senhora Ernesto Martorell, who in reality is Princess Maria Theresa of Orleans-Bragança, sister of the Countess of Paris and one of the pretenders to the Brazilian throne, Don Pedro. These ladies, being born royal, go ahead of many other titled ones but their mates, respectively, an American, a Pole, and a Portuguese, have no rank. Most royal princesses who marry commoners for love rarely forget the privilege attached to their births, and eventually their friends and acquaintances discover that informality may amuse them from time to time—but not all of the time.

These problems continue even when the royal princesses marry aristocrats. Hostesses know that the handsome Prince of Civitella Cesi (whose mother, the late Elsie Moore, was an American), husband of the Infanta Beatriz of Spain (a sister of Maria Cristina), is very particular where he sits and that it is a mistake to have someone who outranks him at the same dinner. Less difficult to seat is the Taliani ménage, since he is a former Italian Ambassador and also a Marquess. His wife, the former Archduchess Margaret of Habsburg, does not outrank him too much.

Many hosts and hostesses who adore having a potpourri of royalty, members of the government, and diplomats to decorate their parties are forever in hot soup. An ambassador who is accredited to the country in which the party is given should go ahead of everyone, including a royal highness, but often the latter subscribes to this rule sheepishly. In most capitals, protocol also rules that a member of the Cabinet precedes a duke, but the latter (in Paris it becomes a Chinese torture when the duke happens also to be a Peer of the Realm) sometimes objects strenuously. Therefore the best advice to nomads is not to overdecorate their table and to limit the list of guests to those who can be seated according to a private book of protocol and not the official one.

To illustrate some of these fine points, here are some recent incidents which have been a source of gossip in N.S.

A prominent Ambassador in Paris gave a large dinner to which he had the temerity to invite several Cabinet Ministers and a prominent duke, who happened to be the president of an important club. I say temerity because, however he managed the seating, he was bound to offend either a minister or the duke. Having chosen the latter, he did not realize, however, how far the *gaffe* had gone. After dinner he asked the gentleman in question what he must do in order to become a permanent member of the club as a private citizen and not in his official capacity as envoy. "I am so sorry that I cannot help you," the Duke is reported to have answered. "I have a very bad cold." Only a French Duke, you must agree, could so quickly think up such a marvelously inconsistent reply, which has become, in a short time, a classic.

At another formal dinner in Paris, as is always the custom, the seating plan was prominently displayed in the hall. After consulting it, a high-ranking lady rushed up to the host and hostess and asked that her place be changed, since she was not on speaking terms with an official she had drawn as her partner. The poor hosts had to leave the receiving line in which they were standing to greet their guests and rush into the dining room to make some last-minute changes that defied protocol. Dinner was necessarily delayed, the incident immediately circulated among those present, finally reaching the formidable Princess Edwige de Bourbon-Parme, who, through her late husband, is related to every royal clan in Europe and, because of her late father, Duke de La Rochefoucauld, to every leading one in France. "I had a similar experience not long ago," she related with that wonderful authority which characterizes her, "but my choice was not to be a burden to my friends who were so kindly entertaining me." She then told the story of how, upon finding herself placed next to a gentleman she had not spoken to for years, she turned to him and said, "Monseigneur, because of these circumstances beyond my control, I shall declare a two-hour armistice tonight and talk to you."

Donina Gnecchi, who is one of the most adorable members of the French Riviera on-and-off colony, has a delightful villa in the hills above Beaulieu. She has taste, charm, and her own brand of style, as American buyers of her Val di Tevere *tissues* well know. Donina decided to give a luncheon in honor of Their Serene Highnesses Prince Rainier and Princess Grace of Monaco and assembled as glamorous a group as the Côte d'Azur can offer in July. Among those present were Sita Maharanee of Baroda and her son "Princie," Maria Callas, Baron de Rede, Jack and Drue Heinz, the Duchess of Acquarone, Count and Countess Amaury de Riencourt, David and Hjordis Niven, and many French patricians with their wives. Naturally, since such a luncheon, cozily arranged at many small tables, is not easy to seat, much thought had gone into it. Unfortunately the hostess simply did not know that the celebrated lawyer, Jean Michard-Péllissier, who was one of the guests, had been recently appointed to the Constitutional Council of France, which gave him an official position. She placed him at the Maharanee's table knowing he was a friend of hers, but did not single him out.

Michard-Péllissier was so upset he barely ate his food, refused to drink the coffee, and left. Within a matter of minutes, the entire Riviera was aware of this incident which assumed such proportions that it was obvious that nothing else of interest was going on. But the gossip, which was absolutely untrue, was that Their Serene Highnesses had given orders to the hostess not to place Péllissier at their table because they had resented the role he had played on the French side (very natural since he is French) in the skirmishes which had upset the harmony between Monaco and the Fifth Republic for a while. Donina Gnecchi, who was honest enough to confess her ignorance, which was shared by a great many other people, took the storm in her stride, and her luncheon became the most discussed event of the entire season on the Riviera.

Peter Glenville is a frequent visitor to Venice as the house guest of the delightful Countess Anna Maria Cicogna. Apart from being one of the outstanding stage and screen directors of today, he is also handsome, entertaining, a marvelous raconteur, and a loyal friend. No sponger, he wants to pay back those who entertain him in the various cities and resorts to which his jobs or holidays take him. As he discovered at vast expense, it does not always pay.

How nice it would be, he thought, to give a fête in return for the magnificent hospitality he had received in the beautiful palazzos as a member of his hostess's house party. After several discussions as to where and when the party should be held, it was decided to have a supper following the opening performance of *Romeo and Juliet* directed by Franco Zeffirelli at the Teatro della Fenice. The locale chosen appeared ideal for not only is the Taverna Fenice one of the finest restaurants in the world but is located right next to the theater, thereby doing away with the struggle the guests would have had finding gondolas or motorboats to go elsewhere.

Glenville enlisted the help of the Countess's daughter, Marina, one of the supernomads, in making the arrangements. She put such enthusiasm into this assignment that the host found himself saddled with forty-six guests. "What do we do about seating them?" he asked her. "It's not necessary," she retorted. "Informal parties are so much more fun, and people will sit just anywhere they please."

In one of the intermissions at the theater, Marina rushed up to Glenville and announced some news which she was sure would please him. She had just run into Prince Albert of

Belgium, the King's brother, and his beautiful wife Paola, and it was just so wonderful, they had no engagement after the performance and she had asked them and they had accepted. "Of course," said Marina, "one cannot place royalty anywhere. You must take Princess Paola on your right and I will take the Prince on mine."

After watching Romeo and Juliet die, Glenville rushed over to the Taverna Fenice to have two seats added, and it was not long before Their Royal Highnesses appeared. Other guests arrived and Marina made the introductions. Since Count and Countess Brando Brandolini had not come with their large house party, supper was served with everyone sitting, royalty excluded, catch as catch can.

When the Brandolinis swept in with their very glamorous group—reported to include Gaston Palewski, the then French Ambassador to Rome, currently a Cabinet Minister, the Duke and Duchess of Alba, and Cecil Beaton—one of the tables, which had, because of the presence of the Belgian Royalty and the host, become the principal one, was filled to the brim. The Countess, who is a sister of Gianni Agnelli and ever so chic and rich, took one look and marched out, followed by her companions. Everything had happened so fast there had been no time to explain anything or introduce Their Royal Highnesses. In the midst of what might have been described as Operation Withdrawal, those present heard a ringing voice exclaim, "It is a veritable scandal." The poor host was absolutely crestfallen and was grateful when the party ended.

By noon the Lido beach was a beehive of people discussing the activities of the night before. Never was such a marvelous time had by so many persons. The news of Glenville's party had traveled like wildfire on a windy night and camps had already been formed. Since the Countess Brandolini is not popular with some people, who claim that she forgets to recognize them, they took her over the coals, not so much for walking out on Glenville, but on the royal couple. Her loyal friends, instead, came strongly to her defense, saying that she had no choice, since she had been with an Ambassador and the Spanish Grandees, who should have been treated according to their exalted ranks. Glenville, as he arrived on the beach for his daily swim, found himself the undivided center of attention and treated like the great celebrity he is in theatrical and film circles.

But in true Shakesperian tradition, all is well that ends well. The Countess is far too civilized to hold a grudge for long. Having proven her point the night before, she extended the olive branch immediately by inviting him to go out to sea with her on one of those wonderful rubber mats. Glenville, who is very fond of her, accepted, breathing a sigh of relief. But since someone had to be blamed, who could be more ideally suited than Marina Cicogna? She is strong and can take that sort of thing in her stride. Actually she proved to be so stupendously cool about the entire matter that everyone was very impressed. The wits who sit for hours on end at the Caffé Florian in the Piazza San Marco were heard to say that she could afford a little abuse since she had not paid the considerable bill for supper at the Taverna Fenice.

British aristocrats are also very aware of where they sit as a well known couple discovered at one of the stately dinners they gave in their magnificent Palm Beach house. Among their guests were the Earl of Dudley and Cecil Beaton. As fabulous a personage as the latter is—photographer, playwright, actor, decorator, writer, painter, stage and costume designer—and such good company, he is younger than Dudley and not a member of *Debrett's Peerage*. He was given precedence, however, and placed on the hostess's right. The Earl, who knows the right from the left, took his leave immediately after coffee and by breakfast time all of Palm Beach was discussing the thrilling event. This anecdote would be just another in the endless series of incorrect seatings, which plague nomads wherever they go, were it not for the truly inspired explanation the host is supposed to have handed out. His wife had been sitting next to the Earl, he said, at so many parties, and Beaton, who is such an interesting person, had just arrived and there was so much to discuss with him. This of course showed basic common sense but not much knowledge of the intricate ways of international society.

Another famous story concerns the Prince de Ligne. This great patrician was asked to a dinner in Paris at which he was not assigned the precedence he should have received. He said nothing but at the end of the meal he went up to the hostess, thanked her and indicated he was departing. "Are you already leaving?" she asked, much concerned. "Yes," he replied, "I am since you so conveniently seated me next to the exit."

Another problem that must not be overlooked in entertaining in N.S. is that in high echelons many bastards come to the fore. People usually keep quiet about certain transgressions which originated in their mothers' or grandmothers' alcoves, but in upper international society the reverse takes place. Some persons are immensely proud that it was not their legal father who sired them but some king, prince, or great artist and personality. They never stop hinting at it in all sorts of ways and of course, in some cases, the resemblance is so striking that it helps to put this point across. In seating parties, sophisticated hosts are careful to remember these *sub rosa* blood relationships since it proves very embarrassing, let us say (it happens more often than you would think), to place a gentleman next to a charming lady who is actually his daughter, with the legal father at the same table. They all know and, being so very civilized, take it all in their stride, but there is no point in reminding everyone of the situation, apart from the fact that fathers don't want to sit next to their children at parties.

The perils of entertaining in N.S., not on a protocol level but on a personal or snobbish one, can be illustrated by a few incidents which have come to my attention during my wanderings. Many, of course, spring from the fact that, in the overwhelming hurry everyone is in today, the old and very satisfactory system of getting information about certain people who suddenly, for some reason or other, enter one's path, has been dispensed with altogether.

One used discreetly to write one's friends or acquaintances in whatever city the stranger emanated from or said he did, to get some kind of a line-up. Now all that matters is that a person be amusing, and whether his background is an honorable one or not is relatively unimportant.

A certain type of hostess, who would never dream of receiving, let us say, the son of a local butcher, is indifferent to entertaining one of another nationality under her roof, provided he is good looking, rich, or good company. She will laugh about his father's trade and say what fun it is or *très rigolo* or *molto divertente,* depending what language she is using. The fact that her daughter may eventually marry him amuses her less, but by then he is no longer called the butcher's son but a specialist in cattle. A *mésalliance* is far more embarrassing on a local level than on an international one, for the cosmopolitan other-side-of-the-tracks somehow always disconcerts persons infinitely less than their own.

In Estoril, at a party given by an attractive American couple, an English peeress was placed next to a handsome middle-aged bridge expert. Knowing how fond their British friend was of the game, they thought she would find him an interesting person to talk to. But to their distress, they noticed that she not only never addressed a word to him but managed to turn her back on him as far as possible at a table. Since they had known her a long time and had always been impressed by her exquisite manners, they simply could not figure out what had happened. When they had talked to her on the telephone they had mentioned the name of the man in question and she had said clearly that she did not know him. What could have happened?

The host and hostess discovered later the reason for this behavior. The dinner partner they had so thoughtfully provided Her Ladyship with had been the valet, over two decades ago, of her brother and had often served her at meals and at weekends in the country. The rise of the former servant was due, apparently, to the enthusiasm he had created in a Mexican admirer who had adopted him, leaving him at his death not only his name but also a vast fortune. The Americans, who had met him recently, had never realized that he was a Britisher and concluded he was a Mexican educated in England, but at neither Oxford nor Cambridge.

"I recognized him the minute he came to escort me in to dinner," the peeress told her hosts, "and naturally I thought he was your butler who, because of old times, was kind enough to show me to my seat. Never did I ever envisage the possibility he might be a guest. But I realized the ghastly reality when he sat down next to me, and then, when he opened the conversation by asking whether I still played bridge and how high were my stakes, something in me snapped and I lost my control. I replied by asking him whether he was still a valet and what were his wages."

In Tangiers, an elegant and independent South American lady had refused, following a dinner, to play canasta with a very beautiful woman whose title carries much weight in Europe. "I am sorry," she said to her host, "but she used to be my manicurist in London a few years ago. Surely it would embarrass her to see the fingers she used to care for so ably deal out the cards." True enough, but what the South American did not say was that the former manicurist had at one point threatened in no uncertain way her marriage, since her husband had fallen very much under her spell.

Speaking about hands, at a luncheon on the French Riviera, there was a crisis when an Italian-born wife of a Belgian industrialist refused to sit next to an athletic and sexy looking young Italian, married to the daughter of an Oriental rajah. "I am sorry to make difficulties," she told her hosts, "but he used to be my masseur, and a very good one, too, in Rome. Although he is terribly nice, the sight of his hands would spoil my appetite, for I can still smell the talcum on them."

In Ischia at a supper a Swedish couple gave in a restaurant, I noticed there was much whispering going on between a local resident and the hostess, which resulted in some of the place cards being changed. I later heard that a pretty and clever Scandinavian authoress had been placed next to a German automobile czar and that his Mexican-born wife had one of those fits only Latin women can have. It seems that the novelist had already, in the short space of fifteen years, broken up two of her marriages, and it was therefore perfectly understandable that she was terrified that once again another husband would find her irresistible.

In Antigua, at a small luncheon, there was much embarrassment when a prominent American social leader refused to shake hands with a very rich Greek shipping heir. She had, it appears, rented his yacht for a cruise in the Greek islands and not only had the captain proved a drunk, the steward a victim of epileptic fits, the sheets of cotton instead of linen (as promised), but an engine had exploded, ruining the deck furniture for the rest of the trip. Despite his efforts at atonement the Greek had been refused forgiveness. He claimed that it was all due to the presence on board of a British duke and duchess whom the hostess wanted to impress.

In Acapulco hostesses were in an absolute dither. One of the most fascinating grandees of Spain, who had come on a week's visit, refused to attend any party to which a local resident, an immensely rich Panamanian sugar baron, had also been invited. And it goes without saying that he had been asked to all of the entertainments in honor of the Spaniard and had accepted. The Grandee would not speak to him or wish to be in the same room with him because there was some question whether one of his race horses had been drugged by a groom working in the Panamanian's stables. It was a well-known story in Ireland, where both these men had breeding farms, but in the Pacific resort no one had heard about it. The result was that an epidemic of flu broke out among the hostesses and one by one every party was canceled. "The honor of my fillies," the Grandee is supposed to have said, "is more important to me than these ladies' list of badly chosen guests."

I remember the very witty, American-born Lady Cunard, who had the most wonderful knack for entertaining, used to say that she could always tell in an American house who were the richest people present since they always sat on the right of the host and hostess. Although this was a slight exaggeration, it is often true, for American aristocracy is a financial one. It also happens to be a fact that some of the richest families are also the oldest. But the rule, which for generations has dominated American society, is that, no matter who else is present, a guest of honor always goes ahead of everyone else.

In Europe parties are often given in honor of someone, but this never means that he can be singled out and assigned any kind of precedence unless his rank happens to warrant it.

There is the wonderful story of the American-born Countess di Frasso (she was Dorothy Taylor) who was an important force in Roman social circles between the two World Wars and presided over the fabulously beautiful Villa Madama. The Countess had remained enough of an American to want to give the first place to a guest of honor and yet she was cognizant enough of European etiquette to know she could not afford to forget it. At a large dinner she gave for the late William Randolph Hearst, she enthusiastically invited two Cabinet members and the flower of Roman aristocracy. The latter she could temporarily ignore for she received as an Italian and therefore could give precedence to a distinguished foreigner. But the Cabinet Ministers remained. After many consultations with the experts at Palazzo Chigi, it was worked out that one of the Ministers would be on her right and the other would sit opposite her and preside with her as host. This put Hearst on her left.

When dinner was announced, the Countess took Hearst under her arm and announced, "I am following to the letter the ancient Roman protocol. One of the Roman Emperors, I forget which, was left-handed and ever since, through the centuries, the place of honor in Rome has been on the left. Mr. Hearst found this ancient custom delightful but, since he left the Italian capital next morning, he probably never had a chance to learn what an exuberantly inventive mind the Countess had.

It is inevitable that the ivory tower, in which for so many decades American hosts have been withdrawing with their guests of honor, will crumble away because of the strong wind blowing from N.S. Although Americans are way ahead in establishing so many new trend-setting ideas which the nomads take up, they are at the same time losing their battle against protocol. It is the unavoidable consequence of being increasingly exposed to the importance it has outside of the United States and to the mounting globe-trotting of government officials and ambassadors, who increase by leaps and bounds (every year there are at least two new countries exploding on the surface of the earth). One of the real trail blazers has been the ex-French Ambassador to Washington, Hervé Alphand, who consistently refused to accept second placement—guest of honor included—unless he was outranked (which happened rarely).

In New York City, there have been many envoys to the United Nations who have freely discussed this subject and made it clear that they need not be invited, but if they are, they must be given the proper consideration, not for their own sake but for the nation they represent. What with the enormous number of delegates the various countries now have at the United Nations, with ambassadors and ministers, plus the many consul generals with rank of minister (one step below an ambassador), Manhattan society has had to become protocol wary. They are all learning that between an Ambassador representing his nation in Washington and his colleague at the UN it is the former who goes ahead, with the exception of the Secretary General who takes precedence over all ambassadors, both in the American capital and at the UN. As far as those in any capital are concerned, precedence is assigned according to the date of the presentation of their credentials to the government.

Therefore, if a hostess in Kansas City is saddled, let us say, with entertaining the Ambassadors of Chile and Peru at the time they come to her city to inaugurate a South American trade fair, she must find out who has been the longer in Washington. If she makes a mistake she will regret it, for there really is never any fun in knowing that the guests feel slighted. Although it should not need to be explained that anyone who commits an error of protocol does so out of ignorance and never out of malice, the offended person is invariably incapable of using logic and reacts purely on an emotional basis. Among some of the most sensitive persons are former ambassadors and officials who are wretched and miserable if they don't get the kind of consideration to which they think themselves entitled. They are swarming all over the place in N.S., and they create their own brand of very sensitivity.

There is no doubt that Americans are the most wonderfully hospitable people in the world. The main reason nomads like going to the United States is the exceedingly friendly and warm atmosphere of more or less permanent open arms. Americans adore parties and every occasion is used—an arrival, a departure, a marriage, a divorce, an anniversary, a house warming, a *première,* a last performance, etcetera—to throw one.

The English are hospitable too, but in a cozier, more personal and informal way. There never appears any effort in their form of entertainment, and everything is made to appear immensely casual and unprepared. English houses still seem lived in and don't have that look, which is sweeping the world, of a residence occupied only in an impermanent manner. The magazines are up-to-date, the flowers are real, the fire crackles in the chimneys.

The French, under the impact of globe trotting, are slowly opening their houses even to nomads. But the French aristocracy remains the hardest to crack in the world. The upper crust (*le gratin*) may marry into the middle and lower crust, thereby elevating some of its members, but they rarely receive them otherwise. Having survived the Revolution, they instinctively know they can survive anything and everything, and one feels this extraordinary strength in them.

The French race is wonderfully intelligent, and so is their aristocracy, whose standards have remained high. As in past centuries, the best passport to enter its portal is *l'esprit,* that very difficult to translate state of mind which encompasses wit and culture. The art of conversation is still alive in the French upper crust, and the choice of words with which the members express themselves rich and varied. This reticence of the old nobility to accept newcomers irritates the nomads, who retaliate by calling the *gratin* square and musty. Whether in orbit or not, the French aristocrats maintain excellent manners. They are never late for their appointments and they don't chuck engagements. Since French society is, on the whole, despite a sizable increase of isolated cases in the last few years, a somewhat airtight unit, the circles N.S. move in in the French capital are mainly still foreign. Paris is the only capital I know where many parties are given at which the natives are in the minority.

A Parisian jet-set hostess, the chic Madame Jacqueline Delubac, who adorned the theater for several decades and had the good luck to be one of the wives of the charming Sacha Guitry, complained to me that in these last few years her friends from the artistic and industrial milieus were away all the time. "I tried to give a dinner of ten this winter," she told me, "and made over one hundred calls. They were all away, some of them halfway around the world. It is no longer a question of can you come two weeks from today but will you still be in town."

Paris social life is tremendously affected by its traffic. Cocktail parties don't begin until seven-thirty or eight o'clock in the evening, for until then the streets are hopelessly bottled up. Unless a cocktail and a dinner happen to take place in the same section of the city, it is absolutely impossible to accept both the same day. While in London and New York people belonging to the smart set are apt to live in the same section, making party going infinitely easier, in Paris people reside in vast areas. All Mediterranean races are hospitable, and Italians, Spaniards, and Greeks either make a big effort or appear to do so. They'll all share a contagious enthusiasm which makes the nomad feel at home and wanted.

In these last few years people have been discovering how hospitable the Belgians are and that their culinary standards are the highest in Europe. There are many wonderfully rich families equipped with fine city houses and country estates who keep open house. The vast number of diplomats or persons who, because of the Common Market and many other international organizations which have their headquarters in Brussels, come and go all the time, feel welcome. More and more nomads too are suddenly aware of the charms of Belgian social life which is never jazzy but always very agreeable.

Society has traditionally accepted certain liaisons, particularly if the protagonists were important, but it demanded that they not be flaunted. The lover used to leave with the other guests and then return to his mistress's house—or vice versa—a few minutes later in order to protect her and save appearances. Today in N.S. no one can be bothered to play this kind of comedy. Unmarried couples travel together and are accepted. No attempt by either of them is made to keep their intimacy in *sourdine*. Many times their friends are aware of their attachment, but because of a certain reticence or friendship for one of the discarded mates, do not wish to have it written out in red ink. But when one telephones the hotel where they are stopping, invariably it is the one not asked for who answers, making it clear that they share the same bedroom.

Some high-class kept women were always received in upper echelons but in limited numbers. Today any kept woman who is attractive and amusing is welcome in N.S. Sometimes, if the man is unmarried, she borrows his name for a while and people are perfectly willing to play along with this make-believe. There are cases where people assume that two persons are married, and great is their amusement when they receive an invitation to their wedding.

In *The Italians* Luigi Barzini discusses this *impasse* with wisdom. "The illegal couples are no longer left alone, like lepers, to live a solitary and almost clandestine life. They are not considered outcasts, like Anna Karenina and Vronsky. They are accepted, invited everywhere, looked upon with compassion and commiseration, encouraged as the innocent victims of a cruel and medieval legislation. The lady is usually called by the name of her lover, out of courtesy. By means of legal tricks of various sorts their children are also illegally given the man's family's name. Such liaisons are now almost entirely respectable, so respectable and solid that many of these unmarried ladies and gentlemen begin to have love affairs on the side."

All sorts of ways have been devised to make certain liaisons appear more legal. There is, for instance, an English peer whose wife refuses to give him a divorce and who has, consequently, remedied his girl friend's awkward situation by having her legally change her surname and take his. Therefore, socially, they answer to the same appellation, and there are many people outside of Great Britain who are unaware that they are not married.

An interesting theory I have heard discussed by some ultra-sophisticated, knowledgeable nomads about why so many kept women (and men) are received today is that the percentage of their eventual marriages is much higher than it used to be.

After having an impressive number of such cases pointed out, I had to agree that being kept today does seem indeed a right step in the altar's direction. With sex so easy nowadays, and free, a kept woman (or man) provides much more than just sexual gratification to the employer. She keeps him amused (or he, her) and, of course, all sorts of interesting parallels can be drawn between today's western kept woman and the old-fashioned type of geisha. It is the amusement provided by these fun-loving employees which their bored partners eventually find irresistible.

In a more conventional era a kept woman who managed to marry was more than willing to let bygones be bygones and gratefully accepted the slow-coming hospitality of those who had previously ignored her. Today, instead, these ladies take their sweet revenge on those who had turned their backs on her. The men, it appears, are even more vindictive. They immediately start to give the most wonderfully entertaining parties and refuse to include any of the people who had not been anxious for their friendship in those days when the finger had not sported a golden band. So it follows that anxious, party-going nomads (they are legion) cannot afford to be squeamish about who pays the bills for whom.

More and more frequently people discover that some dinner they attended was not paid for by the person who had invited them but by someone else. Coordination is often missing and the cat is let out of the bag by those who have footed the bill. They are invariably unable to resist telling the truth, either because they feel they did not get enough out of it in terms of prestige and contacts or simply because they cannot help bragging.

Recently a large dinner was given at Maxim's in Paris by a most attractive couple very much in the swing and constantly on the go. Since they have always been frank about being plagued by a limited bank account, the many guests were fascinated by this lavish party. Anyone who has entertained at this restaurant is in for a traumatic shock when the bill is presented and therefore it was obvious that someone must be paying for this extravagance. But who? Up and down the various tables the guessing game went on all evening and the choice narrowed down to three persons who were known to be rich and who could not be considered by any means an addition to the evening.

One of the guests flew to Germany the next day and in the airport was cornered by a man who greeted him effusively and asked him whether he had enjoyed his party the night before. "But I think there must be a mistake," he said. "I went to a dinner at Maxim's last night." "That was my party," the man replied. "I paid for it." The guest thanked him, but recalled distinctly never being introduced to him.

I would have thought that this kind of socializing accomplished very little for the person in question but I am told by experts in this game that a series of such events helps in establishing the newcomers. They are seen here and there and although some people may suspect that it is they who are footing the bill, if they have the good sense to keep their mouths shut, no one is ever quite sure whether this rumor is true or not. In the meantime, they begin meeting more and more persons, begin inviting them on their own steam, and eventually get asked back by some. This is much easier, of course, in N.S., for no one ever stays long enough anywhere to see the finagling in all its details. Since photographers now appear everywhere, no one takes much notice when his photograph gets snapped. It often is in the company of some stranger standing nearby. This picture will never appear in the city where it was taken, but in the newspapers of the city where the stranger lives and where it will help enormously in establishing his local prestige.

Not long ago I was surprised to go to a flamenco party in Madrid given by a businessman and find some of the best names of Spain present. I concluded, wrongly, that he was very much in with them. "Not at all," a friend of mine explained. "They accept his invitations because he has the best gypsy dancers in the capital, but it would never occur to them to invite him back." "But why does he take all this trouble?" I asked. "It's all done for window dressing," came the reply. "He had some topnotch industrialists from Venezuela and Argentina to impress tonight. They meet all the Grandees, and like you, naturally assume that he is their best friend."

All over the world, but in New York in particular, one receives invitations to a party honoring somebody one knows well, although the name of the host or hostess means nothing. Sometimes it is a perfectly genuine, well-meant affair which a kind, thoughtful friend of the honoree is nice enough to invite one to. But how often it turns out that the poor guest of honor has been trapped into a publicity stunt of some kind or the other to the advantage and glory of a party-giver he hardly knows.

Not too long ago Mrs. Vincente Minnelli was on her way from California to Paris to accompany her husband who was going to direct a film there with Elizabeth Taylor and Richard Burton. A New York couple called her long distance from New York and suggested giving a party in her honor, during her brief stay in New York. Mrs. Minnelli gratefully accepted such thoughtfulness. A few days later, a horrified call came from a friend who had just received in the morning mail, a few minutes before, an engraved invitation to the party honoring her which read at the bottom twelve dollars and fifty cents per person. Mrs. Minnelli was naturally upset and never attended the party. The couple apologized profusely, explaining that it had all been a most unfortunate clerical error, which undoubtedly it was. But that it could have happened is indicative of the commercialism in which we live.

With rare exceptions, entertaining per se has become a chore everywhere today. With the servant problem becoming increasingly acute, one must organize outside help and, in order to do this, one must get started way ahead. Good butlers, maids, or caterers are very busy, and their calendar is chock full. Because they make excellent wages, they can take long vacations. There is a very popular caterer in New York who is so musically minded that he takes off every summer to attend all the festivals abroad.

Even for an intimate dinner one wishes to give for N.S. members passing through, the choice of days is very limited. At any time of the year, three-fourths of one's friends, wherever one lives, go away for weekends. This means that Friday, Saturday, and Sunday are out since those who don't go away usually stay in town for some specific reason and are already engaged. It's either the wedding of a relative or friend, a christening, a confirmation, a birthday party, the homecoming of a child from school, or the lecture of a business associate. Thursday is usually out too because it is the day the servants have free. So the choice is limited to Monday, Tuesday, and Wednesday.

After making a list of the persons the hostess thinks would be congenial and suited to the particular occasion, she begins to telephone. Seventy-five percent of the people she calls are away on some nomadic trail or other. The servant, who invariably speaks with a thick coat of accent, never has any idea where his employers are or when they will return. In those cases where an answering service functions, one never is lucky enough to speak to the operator who knows anything. "Out of town," is the monotonous phrase a slightly irritated voice wearily repeats. After exhausting attempts, she finally reaches the homes of friends who are not out of town. But they are either asleep and cannot be disturbed or they are already out and will not be back until evening. Leaving a message with a servant who speaks a pidgin language is a hopeless undertaking, particularly since the message is never a simple one.

If and when the friends call the hostess back, she is out and at least forty-eight hours pass before connections are made.

Then, in many instances, there is never an immediate reply. "I must check with my husband," the friend says. "He has so many business dinners." Or "I see a question mark in my calendar, for that night" or "Some great pals are arriving that day and I am keeping myself free until I hear further" or "I may have to leave town but I should know definitely in a couple of days." She makes the fatal mistake of agreeing to the postponement of the reply, and three days go by and she hears nothing. Then she starts the rounds again, and again runs into the same complications in order to talk to them.

Or the hostess has the idea of calling the executive in his office. Often the secretary tells her that he (or she) is in conference. "It's a busy schedule today," she says brightly, "every second is taken." "There is an opening between three-fifty-five and four. Could you call back then? Or could we call you? Where will you be?"

Invariably, at that particular moment she will not be available. "Perhaps I could take the message?" the secretary asks helpfully. The hostess who is an expert at the game never falls into this well-meaning trap, but others do. Twenty-four hours go by and the secretary has not called back. So she rings up again. "I am so terribly sorry," the secretary says, "I did mention your kind invitation but then we were interrupted and I was unable to receive a reply." And so it goes on and on. When the secretary does ring up to accept, there is often another message the next day saying it had been a mistake and no definite answer can be given for another three days. "He should be getting back from Hong Kong that morning, but the space has not been confirmed as yet," she says, or "He has a board meeting in Montreal that morning, and whether he can skip the luncheon after and catch the one o'clock jet has to be cleared."

Dinners along the jet trail are suspenseful from beginning to end. The day of the wretched party finally comes and the hostess receives a phone call from one of the guests or a secretary. "We have just received a cable from the So-and-so's who are coming to stay. They were going to arrive tomorrow, but now, because of Ireland being closed in by fog, they are skipping their one-day stop there and are coming directly. Could you be an angel and let us bring them?" She quickly figures out how she can squeeze in two more and says yes. The cook rushes out to get more food and after much switching around of who is to sit next to whom, the telephone rings again. "So sorry. The plane is delayed three hours. And, of course, it would be so rude of us not to go to the airport to meet them." The fact that they are being rude to their hosts, whose invitation they accepted three weeks ahead, never occurs to them. Their house guests are important to them for one reason or the other, either for prestige or for business, and they come first. In the meantime, four chairs are taken out of the dining room and the seating goes to hell.

The So-and-so's send a telegram or cable or telephone that they are arriving on a certain date, which, of course, means they expect to be entertained. A date is chosen and agreed upon and everything is set. The day before the party, or the same day, the guest of honor calls. "It's too awful, I am so very sorry," the voice, which does not in the least sound anguished, says. "The most terrible thing has happened. The only time Dr. Snooks—you do know he is the best in the world—can peel my face is at five o'clock and I could not possibly show myself right after. If you want him still, I shall send my husband" or "My husband's partner assumed we were free and has arranged a dinner. I am simply heartbroken, but it is business. You are so understanding and he is not. Your dinner will be so much more fun, I know that." Business always comes first, naturally. Everybody understands that, but in the meantime much effort and expense has gone into the dinner which never would have been started in the first place.

There are many other and more marvelous reasons why the guests of honor cannot come. "I could not be more distressed," the chic nomad telephones in. "When we ran into Marie and Johnny in Papeete two weeks ago we told them we would be coming, and they asked us to keep the sixteenth open. 'Where can we confirm it?' they said, and we gave them our address in Mexico City. But then we were having such a glorious time in Honolulu that we never went to Mexico, and we forgot, both of us, honestly, that they were to let us know. Well, they cabled to Mexico and naturally we never received it. It's too awful, really it is, but they have hired Watusi dancers, a stripteaser, and a band from Trinidad. They have gone to so much trouble, and we did accept their invitation first. I am sure you will understand." You don't understand, but then there is nothing you can do about it at the ninth hour.

Or the telephone trills just as the first guests are arriving. "I am desperately sorry to do this to you. I know you want to kill me, my darling," the voice quavers, "but my hair is such a mess. Monsieur Jacques had promised he would be here by eight at the latest to give me a *coup de peigne* but I cannot imagine what has happened. There is no sign of him. The shop is closed, and idiot that I am, I don't have his phone number at home and I cannot look it up in the book since I don't know what his surname is. It's absolutely hopeless, I simply could not show myself like this. I do usually travel with a wig or two, but this time that moron of a maid forgot to pack them. I could kill her. I am so indecent, I cannot begin to tell you. Should he turn up, I will come after dinner. Do give them all my tenderest love."

It may sound to some like a conversation in a silly play, but believe me, anyone who is exposed to N.S. knows this happens all the time. "I am tired, my sweetie," is another typical telephone call. "All my pals have been so adorable, they have put me on a stretcher. You don't want me in this condition, I know that. I am so tired, I could start weeping any minute. I must collapse in bed tonight with a glass of milk and a Miltown, but, I probably cannot even fall asleep."

Sometimes they just don't turn up, either having neglected to write the engagement down in their calendar or having mixed up their dates and flown off to some other city, oblivious of all the engagements they have made. "My dear, you do understand," a cheery voice says to one. "I simply forgot all about it. I have no excuse, absolutely none. It was the one party I was so looking forward to." "But I did send you a reminder." "Did you really? I am afraid I am several days behind reading my mail. Simply haven't had a minute. I have been so rushed I cannot begin to tell you."

Recently I happened to talk to a secretary as she struggled valiantly with a forthcoming dinner of her employer which was suffering several setbacks. "Out in Montana," she said, "the cowboys have a much easier time lassoing wild broncoes than a social secretary has corraling these ladies and gentlemen."

Undoubtedly the most unusual development today is that those hosts who want to make their parties truly cosmopolitan—and most of them do—ask someone they know in each capital or important city to send in a list of the most attractive residents. The invitations are then sent out to these persons who often don't even know the hosts in question but are only too delighted to accept since the party is another excuse to be on the move once again.

The people arrive in the city for the event, call up their best friends and discover that they have not been asked. It goes without saying that if a private dance is planned for five hundred guests and one-third or half of this number comes from the outside, the local list must be drastically cut. It happens, therefore, that a Washingtonian has a better chance to be asked to a ball in Manhattan and a Roman to one in Paris than in his own home town. With the explosion of N.S., hosts increasingly feel that they must add the international touch to their parties or they will not be successful.

4

The Decline and Rise of Chic Connotations

Webster's Dictionary informs us that the two synonyms of the expression "chic" are smart and stylish. It does not give, however, the most-in-use French meaning of this word which is kind and polite. If, on a Parisian streetcar, a man yields his seat to a woman who is without one, she may say in thanking him, "It is very chic of you." There is no greater compliment that a bourgeois can bestow than to describe someone as *un chic type.* In France there has always been an identification between well-cut clothes and good manners. In the past the two went together, and the same vocable was used for both. In the Fifth Republic it is still chic for a child to let his elders go by first, for a person to hold a swinging door for the next one and for a shop clerk to thank, each and every time, the customer for his patronage.

In English and other languages, unfortunately, the word has only the meaning the dictionary passes on to us. While in Webster's times this term referred to a great extent to one's wearing apparel and appearance, today it also serves to describe a way of life and state of mind. With the burial of the old staid society, new goals have emerged. It is the ambition of many today to belong to a vast organization, the Chic Club, or C.C., which affords an entree in New Delhi as well as in New York, in Honolulu as in Gstaad, in Sevilla or in Buenos Aires.

Not all nomads are chic, by a long shot, but the majority of them wish to take on the connotation of this status, which serves as a sort of universal passport. The C.C. stamp is very valuable.

At first one does not distinguish the many commercial aspects of this large, at times invisible net, but after a while one realizes that tremendous business interests are at stake. In fact chicness is a gigantic industry, an octopus with a few obvious and many subtle tentacles. It enriches merchants, artists, and speculators by billions of dollars yearly.

This chic status is expensive to achieve and becomes more so every year. In order to be a valid member of the C.C. it is necessary to own several houses, preferably not in the same country since the stress is upon the international motif, and always to be in the process of planning another one in some new, wonderfully exciting "in" resort. Each one must be complete with swimming pool, several automobiles, signed eighteenth-century furniture, impressionists pictures, recent Portuguese rugs copied from the old (it is a good excuse to go to Portugal to order them), Sèvres or Nymphenburg china (it is preferable to have both), a Fabergé collection of boxes and objects, wardrobes which will fit different climates and occasions, several dogs with superb pedigrees, and a racing stable. Each residence by the sea must be equipped with several motorboats for the house guests and at least one sailboat. The super C.C. members must also have an estate, where shooting parties can take place, a baby jet, and a helicopter.

There must be within flying distance an architect, a decorator, a contractor, a tax consultant, a lawyer, a doctor, a dentist, a chiropractor, and a hairdresser. An international staff of servants is a must. While at first it seemed distressing to communicate with these domestics in so many different languages, this necessity has now been cleverly turned into an asset. It is considered pedestrian and provincial to have a cook, chauffeur, maid, butler, and gardener traveling on the same-colored passport, for it is necessary to fit into the general cosmopolitan pattern. All this paraphernalia is not expected from every woman or man who wants to join the C.C., but some, who cannot manage on charm alone, must comply. To have the tenacity, the necessary funds, an identifiable background, an entertainment value, and an ability to make a quick impression are the assets needed to become satellites along the C.C.'s Milky Way.

Chic no longer means best-dressed. It is, in fact, far easier today to belong to the C.C. with a relatively unimportant wardrobe than it was a decade ago. The growing informality of life plays an important part in this, along with the constant shifting from one place to the other. When people stayed in the same city for six months straight and attended many parties, it was more awkward to appear in the same outfits.

Because of the growing uniformity of fashions, women are turning more and more to other symbols. Day clothes have taken a secondary place, particularly among the younger matrons, who devote only a passing interest to them even when they are financially equipped to go to the name couturiers. "I cannot be bothered," I have heard so many of them say over and over again. "It all takes too long, and anyhow, the pompous way of dressing is over."

Should you happen to go to the Luxembourg Gardens in Paris during one of those rare weeks when she is in town and not in orbit, you may meet Mrs. Jean Claude Abreu (she was Deedee Ladd of New York) airing her children. Her beauty, which is outstanding, is unaided by any makeup; she is wearing a sweater and pants, and her lovely blonde hair is covered by an unprepossessing handkerchief. On the Rue du Faubourg

Francis Goodman

The Duke and Duchess of Windsor at the eighteenth-century costume ball of Countess Sheila de Rochambeau at St. Brice near Paris. This was an event which all the nomads attended.

IN SEVILLE

Rasponi

Princess Peggy d'Arenberg, Orson Welles, and Mrs. Nancy Holmes at the Feria in Seville. The two ladies are wearing the traditional Andalusian costume

Rasponi

Fiona Campbell-Walter, recently divorced from Baron Thyssen-Bornemisza, riding to the Feria in Seville with Juan Manuel Urquijo.

Rasponi

The Marquess of Aracena, Mrs. Graham Mattison, and Antenor Pati at the Feria in Seville.

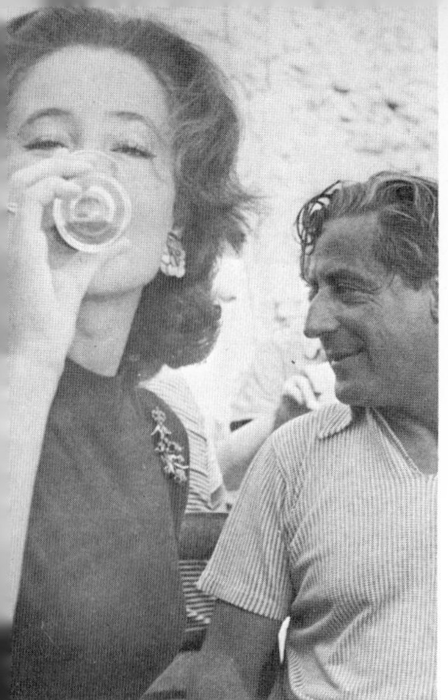

The Vicomtesse de Ribes quenching her thirst during a cruise in the Greek isles with Stavros Niarchos.

Rasponi

IN GREECE

Rasponi

Princess Ruprecht Löwenstein, Baron de Rede, and one of the mule attendants on the Grecian isle of Amorgos.

IN ST. MORITZ

Rasponi

Princess Ira Fürstenberg and Baron Erwein Gečmen-Waldek, who runs the Corviglia Club, on the terrace of the Palace Hotel in St. Moritz.

Herbert von Karajan, Count Theo Rossi, who acted as godfather, Mrs. Karajan and the Princess Theresa Fürstenberg, the godmother, right after the baptism of the Karajans' daughter, Arabel, at the Souvretta Chapel in St. Moritz.

Rasponi

Rasponi

Merle Oberon Pagliai by the swimming pool of her home in Mexico City with her two adopted children Francesca and Bruno, Jr.

Lady Sassoon, widow of Sir Victor Sassoon, and her house guests, Mrs. Elizabeth Graham (Elizabeth Arden) and Princess Stefanella Sciarra, in the garden of her house in Nassau.

Bahamas News Bureau

Raspo

Senator Jacob Javits and his wife Mari during a holiday in Acapulco on t terrace of the villa of Miguel Alema

IN THE TROPICS

Mr. and Mrs. Carl Holmes and M Charles Munroe getting ready for game of golf at Lyford Cay in Nassa

Raspo

Frank & Glo Mair

The Duke of Marlborough joins Jane Pickens Langley in a duet at the Hanover Charity Ball on the island of Jamaica.

Rasponi

Mrs. Warren Pershing and Mrs. J. Kingman Douglas (Adele Astaire) at Round Hill in Jamaica where they both own cottages.

IN THE TROPICS

Mrs. Oscar Hammerstein with the coiffeur Enrico Caruso at a luncheon given by Mrs. Warren Pershing in her cottage at Round Hill, Jamaica.

Rasponi

Tom Hustler

All the nomads flew to London for the wedding of the Marquess of Dufferin and Ava to "Lindy" Guinness.

Daily Expres

Not so many came for the wedding o Tarquin Olivier, the son of Sir Laurenc Olivier, to Riddelle Gibson.

Douglas and Mary Lee Fairbanks, two of the best American goodwill ambassadors in orbit, in front of their home in the Boltons in London.

Tom Blau

IN LONDON

Mrs. Stanley Donen, one of the mos appreciated American hostesses in Lon don, with Mrs. Barry Sainsbury.

Daily Expres

ON THE FRENCH RIVIERA

Rasponi

The designer Marquess Emilio Pucci and Mrs. H. J. Heinz after a luncheon hosted by Donina Gnecchi at Beaulieu on the French Riviera.

Rasponi

H.S.H. Princess Grace of Monaco and the Maharanee of Baroda sitting by the swimming pool of the Villa La Treille in Beaulieu.

Marella and Gianni Agnelli by the swimming pool of the Villa La Leopolda in Beaulieu which they recently sold to Mrs. Walton Killam.

Rasponi

Raspon

Countess Mona Bismarck, armed with her baskets, is on her way to start her favorite occupation, gardening, on her property Il Fortino on the island of Capri.

IN ITALY

IN SPAIN

Mr. and Mrs. Gilbert Miller, who are celebrated hosts in New York, London, and Mallorca, where they recently built a house at Costa de los Pinos.

Gyenes

Former Ambassador and Congressma John Lodge and his wife Francesca the Guadalmina Club in Marbella.

Raspo

St. Honoré, one is likely to run into Madame Anne Marie François-Poncet, makeup-less and with the profile of the Goddess Diana, or the mercurial Afdera Fonda, with not a trace of rouge or lipstick and wearing flat shoes and a country plaid coat. In New York one has the same experience with slim, finespun looking Mrs. Frederick Eberstadt, one of *Women's Wear*'s all-time darlings, taking her brood to Central Park, or, on Madison Avenue, with Miss Maria Cooper or Mrs. Alice Topping. I have mentioned, at random, these ladies because they are all young, ravishing, prominent, well-off, and outstanding members of N.S.'s C.C.

Five years ago it would have been unthinkable, but today these charmers, who are leading the path into the future, do not care how informal they look before evening time. Many of these women, who express boredom at long sessions at the dressmaker, spend hours instead browsing in antique shops, going to auctions, talking to their decorators about what changes they can make in their homes, or planning a new hairdo. Although they spend very little time in their houses, jet-setters have been mesmerized by the ingenious decorating industry. In France alone there are fourteen eminently successful furnishing magazines sold on the stands. It is the decorators and the hairdressers, as we shall discuss farther on, who hold the fair sex's time, attention, and purse strings today.

Mrs. Reginald Fellowes, a fashion empress for forty years, used to say that any woman with taste could be well-dressed, provided that, in lieu of ordering many clothes, she took enough time to be fitted over and over again.

Maisons de Couture claim that the decrease in their current business is due not only to the spiraling, vertiginous increase in their prices but to the frantic schedules that the majority of women keep. Even the richest women, ever on the move, no longer find the necessary time or inclination for suitable fittings.

The average customer today must often be cajoled, practically begged, to come to a salon for fittings. The decision about what clothes to purchase is influenced in great part by the rapid travel these ladies are subjected to, for they all know that pressing in hotels and private houses has become a vanishing art.

The supernomadic Queen Bee, the Princess Charles d'Arenberg, never travels with a personal maid. When her plane to Sevilla for the Duchess of Medinaceli's ball, which opened the Feria, was late, she changed very rapidly into an evening dress she barely had time to unpack. Noticing our amazement at her being able to get ready so quickly, she said, "I have learned to pick out clothes that need the least ironing possible."

As genial and pleasing as Emilio Pucci's sportswear is—so easy to pack and press—when it is duplicated on the backs of literally thousands of women, one can only reach the conclusion that the Western nomadic woman is adopting a uniform in the manner of her tribal sisters in Asia and Africa.

In an effort to offset this standardization in the use of pants, skirts, and blouses, a frenzied search is on for the exotic and bizarre. Whether it is the shawl of the fisherman's wife in Nazaré, or the baggy pantaloons of the blue-veiled men of the Sahara, or the tunic in which the stunning Indians in the neighboring villages of San Cristóbal de las Casas wrap themselves, it matters little. All are duplicated in a modified design and made available. This tendency to seek elegance among the underprivileged of the world is nothing new. The great arbiter of delicate and exquisite taste, Marie Antoinette, did not even search far from Versailles for her inspiration. At the Hameau or the Petit Trianon she and her ladies-in-waiting used to dress up like the local shepherdesses.

How much longer can these esoteric sources continue? Local color is disappearing everywhere. Blue jeans are gathering momentum daily, bringing the two sexes to the same common denominator. In St. Tropez or similar resorts, where the youth of the world congregates, one becomes aware of the leveling of the female and male species. In the dimly lit cafés and bistros along the French Riviera, the visual distinction between the two sexes has ceased. The same fringes on the foreheads appear on both girls and boys, along with the identical shirts, pants, and sandals. Despite their box-office success, the super-feminine shapes of Gina Lollobrigida or Anita Ekberg are considered madly unchic by our current standards.

While there is no doubt that Monte Carlo is losing ground and that it depicts in people's minds a bygone era of plush stateliness, a gala there at the Sporting d'Eté is still an aesthetic treat. It may no longer answer the current ideals and trends but the women, wearing long evening dresses, do achieve an identification of their own and are unmistakable, one by one. The unique birdlike appearance of Marella Agnelli, so very aristocratic and diaphanous, stands out when she is in a ball gown like a black pearl among white ones. The opulent, sensuous pulchritude of Mrs. David Niven, in a pink frock with décolleté, calls to mind one of the lush roses in the garden of her villa at Cap Ferrat. But should you see these two ladies the following night, dining in one of those crowded al fresco bistros on the wharf of St. Tropez (which are considered infinitely more fun), sitting at a long narrow table and wearing today's favorite uniform of pants and blouse, the special identity which characterized them the evening before is gone.

Exactly the same experience hits the visitor of those two competing island resorts, Nassau and Jamaica. Many prefer the latter for the atmosphere is more casual and people dress up only on specific occasions in the evening. I have heard several persons say "I hate Nassau because it is becoming more and more like Palm Beach. All the dinners are dressy there." If this is partially true, it is also incontestable that most parties in Nassau bring out the grace and femininity of women, and those in Jamaica do not. A formal candlelight dinner given by the Earl and Countess of Dudley in their adorable colonial house in Nassau is far more harmonious to the eye than the one the

Earl's son, Viscount Ednam, and his pretty wife may give the next day at Round Hill, Jamaica, where the feminine guests hide their forms in trousers and shirts.

When the Lido in Paris inaugurated its new show in the late fall of 1964, Georges Cravenne, the organizer, had the clever idea of ordering all the stars of society, screen, and stage, to come in dressy pantaloons or pyjamas. Publicity-wise, this trick was sensational and the result was that there were almost more photographers to record the unprecedented event than there were guests. There was a strong sense of competition, which is getting rare nowadays among members of the fair sex, and there was electricity in the air as each vedette made her entrance. The two who received the most attention and space were Elizabeth Taylor and Maria Callas, who, having defied the orders, came in evening dresses. Although neither of them has ever been considered best-dressed, they looked infinitely more glamorous than all the regular clothes horses present. Such resplendent international figures as Ira Fürstenberg, Mrs. Porfirio Rubirosa, and Jacqueline de Ribes looked as if they wished that they, too, had disobeyed the rules. It is undeniable that trousers manage to blur the prestige of feminine grace everywhere. During the course of the Lido evening, a Frenchman summed up the situation by saying, "These dressmakers apparently have forgotten that women were made to put pants on in harems so that they would not excite the hard to arouse eunuchs who took care of them. This is definitely an anti-sex crusade. The designers obviously think the world is full of jealous husbands who don't want their wives to awaken the interest of other men. But who, I ask you, obliges the single woman to wear them?"

What makes a best-dressed woman? What are the elements necessary to create this effect?

For many years there has been much understandable confusion in the minds of millions of readers, in the United States and elsewhere, about the best-dressed list which is released regularly every January first. It is distributed to the international press by an American organization entitled the Fashion Institute. The Institute explains that the choice is made after counting two thousand ballots filled out by people who are acknowledged to be well-versed in fashion leadership.

One can only guess just how commercial it is, but there is no doubt that a certain percentage of these votes are in the hands of the cloak and suit industry. It is, therefore, not surprising to discover that over the years it is the very rich who are voted in, for they are equipped with the money to keep the expensive dressmakers in business.

While it is not easy for the uninitiated to see it, some fascinating facts do transpire. The most riveting is the realization that the screen and theater no longer have any impact on fashion or society. Apart from Dina Merrill in the 1965 list, not one single name appears from the entertainment world, and certainly she is no criterion. She is well-born, one of the rare actresses in the New York social register (she is listed under her married name, Mrs. Stanley Rumbough, Jr.), wealthy in her own right (her mother is Mrs. Marjorie Merriweather Post-Close-Hutton-Davies May), and she is a cousin of Barbara Hutton. Although she is kept occupied with television and film assignments, one cannot say that her fashion silhouette is copied by women in Melbourne, Australia, or in Atlanta. Some of us can still remember the tremendous influence of Clara Bow, Carole Lombard, Marlene Dietrich, or Katharine Hepburn, to name a few actresses, on the fair sex across the world.

With a few exceptions, such as Audrey Hepburn, her husband Mel Ferrer, and George Hamilton, the new generation of screen stars rarely makes incursions into nomadic society. All those who do adorn the cosmopolitan party circuit—the Gish sisters, Rosalind Russell, Joan Fontaine, Merle Oberon, Claudette Colbert, Yul Brynner, Douglas Fairbanks, Jr., Danny Kaye, Dolores del Rio, and several others—are old-timers who maintain the habits and customs which existed at their entry into the film world.

One day while discussing this extraordinary change with me, Paulette Goddard, whom Jean Cocteau described as one of the most articulate women he had ever met, was eloquent on the subject. "We used to enjoy going to parties," she explained, "because they were a relaxation from our hard work. But today society tends to become more and more commercial. Almost every affair one goes to has some business connotation. Society folks, who have been publicized and tasted the sweet ambrosia of fame, compete with the stars, and in some cases, receive even more coverage. The social vedette today is the rage, and Ira Fürstenberg is the subject of much more attention than many a splendid young actress. The latter, therefore, feels, 'Why should I make the effort?' Can one blame her? It is also true that being social is expensive. Prewar stars were plagued infinitely less by the Internal Revenue boys, and consequently had far more cash to spend on life's amenities."

Therefore, according to the Institute, it is society which establishes the image, on a global scale, of the best-dressed. The decline and fall of the movie actress has been attested to recently by several screen magazines which have placed Mrs. John F. Kennedy on the cover instead of the customary star or starlet. If the good taste of these publications, in assigning star's status to the bereaved widow of a President, can be very seriously questioned, the Fashion Institute's poll reveals that the two thousand voters are equally insensitive—perhaps even more so. On the 1965 list, Mrs. Kennedy occupied second place and her mother-in-law, Mrs. Joseph Kennedy, third place. It is an amazing choice, indeed, when one stops to consider that at the time the ballots went out these two ladies were still in deep mourning in the wake of the appalling tragedy which had hit them. The implication would be that both had been deeply fashion conscious during this period, particularly since the mother of the late President had never appeared on the list before. Nothing could be further from the truth, but it does make one read this list with caution.

Granted that both Mrs. Paul Mellon and Mrs. William McCormick Blair, Jr., are well-dressed and that their wealth (Mrs. Mellon has the reputation of being Balenciaga's most important customer) permits them to refurbish and replenish their wardrobes at will, why were these rarely seen ladies singled out by these two thousand voters? It would be enlightening to have the answer.

Mrs. Mellon, who leads a secluded life in her many residences, loathes publicity. The average customer of the Italian Pavilion restaurant in New York would never know or recognize this lady, who frequently lunches there in a far-off corner, a lady in the true sense of the word, but shy and retiring. A brief flash of publicity occurred recently when she and her husband showed their justly celebrated collection of English pictures in London and were received by the Queen, but this could hardly be the reason.

Mrs. Blair is the comely wife of the American Ambassador to the Philippines, and one can only guess that many of these voters went to Manila during 1964 to reach their conclusion. If Mrs. Blair walked into Harry's Bar in Venice, the Claridge Grill in London, or Moustache in Paris, she would not cause a ripple of recognition among most of the clients. The 1965 selections indicated a significant trend that stunned Europeans. With the exception of the Queen of Siam, it would seem that the best-dressed Europeans—and there are many—either must go to New York to lunch a few times in a secluded corner of the Italian Pavilion or spend a few weeks in Manila in order to get on the world's best-dressed list.

Where does chicness end and elegance in N.S. begin? The chic woman, in order to be *à la page*, will sacrifice her personality and seek to adapt herself to the most recent temporary dictum. If she is handicapped by a large posterior, she will bravely wear the pants of Courreges or Irene Galitzine anyhow. If she is very tall, she will insist on an upswept hairdo, risking resembling a giantess in order to be in tune with her colleagues. Or she will use a certain shade of red which is "in," although it clashes with her complexion and hair tint. She will go barefoot, as the dictum in Palm Beach recently imposed, even if her feet are big and ungraceful.

An elegant woman never blindly obeys the latest dictates of fashion, but develops her own image and stays with it. What Honoré de Balzac wrote in 1830 in his treatise on elegance is just as true today as it was then: "The Constitutional principle of elegance is unity." Therefore the truly elegant person modifies the most recent musts to his own style, but this process requires thought, effort, time, and courage, all elements which are on a precipitous decline nowadays because of the frantic schedules people keep. It is easier, consequently, to follow the herd and let it go at that.

Mrs. Winston Guest, whose appearance and clothes change only imperceptibly from year to year, has developed a far subtler aura of elegance than another American, Consuelo Crespi, who changes her identity, fashions, and hairdos all the time. Countess Crespi works for a leading fashion magazine and is the wife of a social and industrial promoter. While the portrait of Mrs. Guest is a simple, translucent, and lasting one, that of Countess Crespi is ever changing. One day she wears the spit curls of a Spanish gypsy and the next a Gibson girl coiffure, with an accompanying change of outfit. Although Mrs. Guest is very much a member of the contemporary scene, she is never frantic and establishes a serene sense of permanence. She is, in my opinion, truly elegant, while Countess Crespi is merely chic.

The Vicomtesse de Ribes, an outstanding member of nomadic society, is a special case worth examining. Tall, with a fine figure, a somewhat long face, an aristocratic nose and small eyes, she manages to create at all times the illusion of beauty, which is infinitely more remarkable than actually being beautiful. Until she was elevated into the permanent Hall of Fame, she was voted regularly by Americans on the best-dressed list. In 1965 in France she was demoted from first to second place, losing the crown to the perfume empress, Madame Rochas. The sophisticated Parisians now are saying that the Vicomtesse has decided that she prefers being *bien costumée* to being *bien habillée*. In fact, her marvelous fashion sense has become more and more theatrical and she is one of the unique women of her generation who possesses that vanishing trait called allure. Hers is the capacity of doing the unexpected but in the limits of taste.

In the early summer of 1964 there were three much-discussed balls in the space of a week: the Baron de Rede's at the Palais Lambert in Paris, the Alfonso Fierros' in Madrid, and Le Bal des Petits Lits Blancs at the Beit El Din palace near Beirut. The Vicomtesse went to all of them, and as is her custom, made her entrance very late when some guests were already departing. The Vicomtesse is no Duchess of Alba (who claimed that she had only two evening dresses in her closets) and her wardrobe is one of the most resplendent imaginable. Great, therefore, was the amazement of all those who had turned up at the three affairs to see her appear at each event in the same costume.

There is no question that the Vicomtesse will duplicate this trick for she never repeats herself. But even if she did choose to show herself in three different countries in the same incarnation, no one could agree what she represented. Peter Glenville thought she looked like Lady Macbeth in her sleep-walking scene, some said that it was her own version of Maria Callas in the last act of Bellini's *La Sonnambula* and others a reevocation of Poppaea, Nero's consort. She was swathed in a long, abundantly flowered peplum of chiffon, her hair down her back in a cascade of waves. Hers is the uncanny ability to turn every event into a masked ball, and since she is not on the stage—not yet, anyhow—she uses the drawing rooms and gardens of her friends to express her superlative flair as a performer.

Her long hair lends itself to infinite inventions and none is overlooked: down, up, girlish, matronly, Grecian, Roman, Medieval, Baroque, Belle Epoque, everything one can wish for. It is no wonder that Monsieur Alexandre drools when her name is mentioned. "She is my masterpiece," he asserts proudly. At a gala for the handicapped in Paris' Odeon Theatre, she wore a pea-green floating gown and a gigantic headdress copied after a seventeenth century Nipponese Empress. She was such an eccentric sight that not even Sophia Loren received any attention. It was the Vicomtesse's evening from start to finish. Intelligent and daring, she is also sensitive and knows how far she can go and no further. Hers is a peculiar sort of melodramatic elegance no one could possibly imitate. Elegance is often a hard-to-define incantation, sometimes of the heart, at other times of the intellect. The wonderful thing about it is that it can never be faked.

Virgil, in his Aeneid, says, "The Goddess revealed herself by her bearing." The same applies to the Hudson River Valley's musical Egeria, Mrs. Lytle Hull, who with her beguiling reticence and swanlike figure, makes the chicest women in a concert hall in Manhattan, Vienna, or Milan seem slightly impermanent. Born with a class that is as distinctive as the tulle or lace ensemble in which she is dressed, she achieves a regal aspect which is the quintessence of elegance. Ever in orbit, Princess Cora Caetani, who runs Jansen's Boutique with such flair, wears neither unusual clothes nor hairdos, but when she enters a room something happens. All the youthful beauties, superbly decked out, who have until that moment seemed so captivating, suddenly appear a trifle artificial and their youth almost a handicap. Without the slightest bit of effort, her carriage is so splendid that she achieves a magic which is another form of elegance. Again, it is impossible to imitate, and

Solon's wise words come to mind, "Do not act the Prince until you have learned to be one."

Another to whom this phrase applies is Rome's Princess Clemente Aldobrandini, who is such a *grande dame* in her manner, such a thoroughbred, that she unconsciously dominates any group that she joins. One never recalls what she wore, simply because her deportment is far more significant than any frock could be. These last three mentioned ladies—an American, Italian (with an American mother), and a German-Chilean married to an Italian—have different backgrounds, lives, and interests. But the recurrent theme, tinkling on their keyboards, equally projected in their thinking and silhouette, is a sense of quality and discrimination. It is their transcendent breeding which gives them such authority, another definite form of elegance.

Greta Garbo's slouched hats, flat shoes, and trench coats are as much a topic of conversation today as they were thirty years ago. Many have tried to copy that almost sloppy look of hers, but no one has succeeded. It is her innate radiance that has made all the difference in creating her own offbeat and uncopyable brand of style.

The Vicomtesse de Noailles, or Marie Laure, as she signs her delightful oils, is short, thick of frame, with a long face dominated by small beady eyes. When one first sees her at a Parisian opening, it is evident that she is a personage to be reckoned with. Only impressed by wit, culture, and brains, she has enough of her own to maintain relations on an impressive footing with the leading writers and artists of her time.

Her originality is unquestionable. When recently the Baron and Baroness Alain de Rothschild hosted a party to unveil to their friends a portrait of the Baroness just completed by Balthus, Marie Laure, who has kept every single dress she has ever owned, appeared in the one in which Balthus painted her in 1925. She sat on a chair during the entire reception, in exactly the same position in which the famous artist had represented her. At Madame Rochas' enchanting ball in the Bois de Boulogne, on the theme of *My Fair Lady,* amidst all the women sporting tremendously high coiffures bedecked with aigrettes and paradise plumes, the Vicomtesse humorously came as an English nanny of the period and stole the show.

She has always enjoyed playing Pygmalion to young artists, and the story is told that many years ago she had one in tow when she attended Marie Louise Bousquet's Parisian reception for Thornton Wilder at the time of his triumph with *The Bridge of San Luis Rey*. On the stairs, going up to the apartment, she was heard instructing her protégé in what to say in English upon meeting the guest of honor. But the young man got thoroughly confused, and at the time of his introduction to the American author, was heard to say "My congratulations, Sir, for building that wonderful bridge in St. Louis."

The Vicomtesse's background is intriguing. In her veins runs the blood of the illustrious Belgian bankers, Bischoffsheim, the very respectable Andover, Massachusetts, clan of the Paynes, and also that of the Marquis de Sade, in whose honor the word *sadism* was coined. The Vicomtesse's elegance is entirely of the intellect, and her name figures prominently in any history of Parisian highbrow circles of the last four decades. Her husband, the Vicomte Charles, whose late mother, the Princess de Poix, was also partly American, is one of the last true gentlemen in Europe. His great interest is gardening and he is an authority in this field. A close friend of the Queen Mother of England, it is he who always arranges for her yearly sojourns in various provinces of France with a full sightseeing program of chateaux and, naturally, their gardens.

One of the most remarkable women to have maintained her own form of elegance is Diana Vreeland. It must not have been easy for her during all the years she was such a great influence at *Harper's Bazaar*, and recently even in a more exalted post as editor-in-chief of *Vogue* magazine, to resist the temptation to follow the fashion dicta she so successfully understands and dispenses to the public.

In the quarter century I have known her she has never modified her style. The hair is still combed back, shining and glossy, the eyelids slightly moist with ointment, the lips strongly made up, the fingernails long and round, the suits she continues to wear impeccably cut, the enthusiasm as keen and vital in everything and everyone. Her weight, I feel sure, has not changed one ounce either; and the firm, graceful, undulating walk, calling to mind a leopard, is exactly the same as when I was first introduced to her on a beach in Bermuda. She has always been a powerhouse, and every time I talk to her I feel charged with some new, vital, dynamic current. Hers is a unique duality. She has developed for herself a special image which, because of its utter timelessness, is not only never at odds but always in harmony with what the chic women whom she advises wear.

Elegance can also manifest itself in the way the very rich spend their money. In millionaire's row Mrs. William Hale Harkness (after her recent divorce from Dr. Ben Kean, she resumed the name of her previous, deceased husband) certainly stands out for her dash and imagination. A woman of indomitable will, she has achieved, with the fortune Harkness left her, much of interest. Apart from the many marvelous medical accomplishments, made possible by one of the foundations, this dynamic lady has now formed her own ballet company, assigned it headquarters in both Manhattan and Watch Hill, Rhode Island, commissioned scores from leading composers, sets from young artists, and given work to numerous dancers. She accompanies her troupe everywhere (it has appeared in offbeat places such as Kabul and Bucharest), takes daily ballet lessons herself to understand better the problems of her performers, and continues to study composition, a hobby which has kept her occupied for a long time.

Man's elegance, also timeless, usually transcends the style of his wardrobe. Artur Rubinstein is impeccably dressed, but the scintillating elegance he asserts is due to his prodigious vitality and remarkable wit. The latter is often a manifestation of polish and grace, and one of its leading practitioners is Harold Acton. His mind is so agile and his opinions so arresting that the fact this British author is well-dressed is of secondary importance. The moment Cecil Beaton enters a room one knows it. The sparks this prodigiously gifted artist sends in every direction are stimulating and elegant.

Elegance can be expressed by a way of life, and among the younger men none is a finer spokesman for it than Prince Sadri Khan. A dedicated man who works around the clock—he is doing a superb job as the United Nations Deputy High Commissioner for Refugees—and travels incessantly, he shuns publicity, drawing a curtain over his private life. His divorce from Nina Dyer, following an unhappy marriage, was for some time a secret, but when she committed suicide he was one of the few mourners at her burial service. Count Lorenzo Attolico, an officer of NATO, is as elegant a host as he is a rider. He combines a marvelous tailored look with a sense of discrimination rare in today's younger set.

Despite their peregrinations to sell their wares, Parisian designers do little to give *haute couture* a hypo and lift it out of the doldrums. Not only has Parisian enthusiasm seemingly disappeared but many of its practitioners appear to have retired to their cells to await judgment day. Instead of going out in N.S. and attempting to create some excitement, many withdraw. They appear professionally, and no more.

Between the two wars, and briefly after the second one, couturiers in Paris played a leading part in international society. They all had splendid houses, entertained constantly, often in an original way, and were very much in the general picture. Coco Chanel (who is now back in business but well beyond her eightieth birthday), Lucien Lelong, Elsa Schiaparelli, the Marquise M. Blanche de Polignac (born Lanvin), and later, Christian Dior, and Jacques Fath were all sharp personalities, excellent company, and enthusiastic champions of many causes. Today, no one has followed in their social footsteps with the exception of three who are non-French and are leading jet-set members on their own steam. All of them inherited topnotch social positions, are bright and personable, and were "in" long before they entered dressmaking professionally.

Simonetta, who recently moved her business from Rome to Paris, is the daughter of the late Duke Colonna di Cesaro, and at birth, the doors were open to her in all the patrician households in Europe. Emilio Pucci, a Marquess in his own right, stems from a family with a distinguished past in Tuscany, and the street on which his palace is situated has been Via dei Pucci for a long time. Irene Galitzine is a white Russian, educated in Rome, and anyone who knows his Russian *Gotha* is cognizant of the position her family had in Imperial Russia. Oddly enough, both Simonetta and Pucci had Russian grandmothers.

The successful entry into the world fashion market of these three non-Parisian-trained designers is easily explained. Being themselves among the first members of the brand-new rocket society, at the very moment of its inception, they became immediately aware of the changing wind in fashions. They all recognized, in their own individual way, the new order that nomadic life imposed on the sorts of garments women could pack and unpack with facility.

Interestingly enough, close to "Il Fortino," the estate of Count and Countess Bismarck on the island of Capri, are two houses, so close to one another that they appear much like two eggs in the same basket. In the summer they are occupied respectively by Simonetta and her husband, Alberto Fabiani, and by Irene Galitzine and her Italo-Brazilian mate, Silvio Medici. One would naturally assume that the reason these designers have chosen to live in such great proximity to each other is that they are intimate friends. Nothing could be further from the truth at this particular time, for they do not speak to each other. No one knows the real reason, and everyone remembers well when they used to be on cordial terms. In the Piazza of Capri, where one hears so many different things, the gossip which circulated was that Irene Galitzine said that Simonetta had betrayed Italian couture by going to settle in Paris. Others, more acid, claimed that she was sorry she had not taken the lead in making the move herself. While this freeze between these two attractive women complicates the social life of the island, since it is difficult to invite them both to a small party, restaurant owners are delighted because it means that those who entertain outside their houses have two dinners in lieu of one, in order to honor both of them.

Irene Galitzine Medici is stunning, with her dark complexion, a marvelous set of teeth, and luscious eyes. She has acquired a splendid group of big-name clients, especially in the department of her imaginative "at-homes," usually consisting of robes combined with pants, somewhat Oriental in feeling. Among her patronesses are Princess Paola of Belgium, Anne Ford and her daughters, Eugenie Niarchos, "Babe" Paley, Cyd Charisse, Mrs. David Niven, and Mrs. Jackie Kennedy. In fact, she is such a friend of the latter that she even went cruising with her when Aristotle Onassis placed at her disposal the *Cristina* for two weeks. Irene is a regular yachtswoman, and every summer many are her departures from Capri for various expeditions.

Simonetta is a bird of different plumage. While Irene is expansive, gregarious, and elastic in her mode of life, Simonetta is less so and is unable to compromise. Never does she "make" charm, or go after a possible client. A citadel of strength, she is splendid the way a Renaissance tower is, and so secure in her vigor that sometimes this is mistaken for arrogance. Particularly in the evening, she reminds one of those forceful, blooming beauties of the Medici family painted so unforgettably by Bronzino.

First wed to Count Gaio Visconti, and bored with leading merely a social life, she divorced him, launched herself in couture and became the wife of talented and good-natured Alberto Fabiani. At one point rivals in their field, they later combined forces only to split again. Their marriage, however, has survived, but while Paris is the basis of her operations, his is Rome. A regular beaver, Simonetta lives for her work, and everything plays second fiddle to it. Not particularly interested in big-name patronesses, she goes in for the solid sort who do not make headlines but pay their bills on time.

In Paris, where she is now settled cozily, she intrigued the French by her courage in having preferred to join their designers on an equal level rather than remain the big fish in the Italian dressmaking pond. Whether she will be able, in the end, to leave a real imprint on her times will have to be seen, but if she does not, it will not be for lack of discipline or will power. Parisian society, in which their own designers no longer play a lead role, has been happy to accept her, and she adorns all the parties.

Emilio Pucci's headquarters are in the Florentine palace from which he daily commutes to a villa he owns in the Tuscan hills nearby. The Renaissance mood of his homes and many of the prints and material he uses in his creations are perfectly in keeping with the Donatello identification of his young, delicately chiseled wife Cristina. But Pucci's home is the world, for more than any other designer, his influence in sports clothes is global, and he personally oversees his vast network of operations on five continents. A Member of Parliament and the Vice-President of the Italian National Chamber of Fashion, he finds time to relax by skiing, shooting, or chartering a yacht in the summer to roam around the Greek islands.

Pucci's genius never would have reached such a widespread audience had it not been matched by his energy. It is staggering, and I, who have known him always (we went to school together), can recall vividly in childhood his immense restlessness, charm, leadership faculties, and ego, all mixed together in a fantastic bouillabaisse. It is to his enormous credit that he was able, at a given point, not only to make some order out of all this but to utilize each and every one of these qualities by tying them together in masterly fashion.

But, in the meantime, whatever happened to the French? They exist, but none has come up with the beaming personality which at this stage of the nomadic picture French couture so desperately needs. Coco Chanel did return to the fold, invading the earth with her simple, expensive suits that every woman now wears with the same ineluctable fatality that a bullfighter has when he dons his matador apparel. But the "Grande Demoiselle," as Parisians call her, well in her eighties, can hardly be expected to become the life of parties. Balenciaga is usually blamed for establishing the monklike habits most of the other designers follow today. To couture, what Garbo was to the film industry in the thirties, this seventy-year-old Spaniard is rarely seen even by his most devoted clients. But while he can afford to stay isolated because of his aura and unique creativeness, the others should cure themselves of this Balenciaga-itis, which is not helping their trade.

The only real excitement of recent collections has been put into motion by Courreges, who came onto the scene in his own atelier after a long period of apprenticeship with the master, Balenciaga. He has had something new to express, and as difficult to put on as some women find his highly original, youthful-looking outfits, he is definitely a new star rising.

When the King of Jordan recently paid a state visit to France, President de Gaulle honored him with a ballet gala at the Theatre de l'Opéra, by invitation only. All the ladies present wore spectacular coiffures and some, tiaras. The King's consort, English-born Princess Muna, was the leading subject of chicchat at intermission time, and people wondered why, since nature had bestowed on her so much more height than on the King, she had allowed the hairdresser to create such a high pompadour. She looked well next to the French President, who is such a tall, imposing figure, but she dwarfed her husband completely. Since Madame de Gaulle, instead, tactfully wore a very low hairdo, spectators were commenting on her consideration for the guest of honor. I was intrigued, however, by the recurrent conversational theme which centered on the hair instead of the dress. So I asked what house had been responsible for the Princess Muna's dignified gown. "It must be Pierre Balmain," the Vicomtesse de Noailles said. "He seems to have cornered the royal market."

If Balmain has succeeded in hitching his wagon to the royal star, it is because he alone among the French couturiers does not suffer from Balenciaga-itis. Of this there can be no doubt when one watches him march into a drawing room, with much the same authority as a colonel heading a brigade of Grenadiers. A huge, bulky bachelor, he looks as if, minus the flowing moustaches, he had posed for many of those military portraits of the Second Empire. Royalty would naturally understand his positive assurance. My first and only professional contact with Balmain came a decade ago when the Marquis de Cuevas engaged my services to help him organize a large eighteenth-century costume ball in Biarritz to promote tourism in that region. Because of a general strike that paralyzed France, we were working in the most appalling chaos, totally cut off from the rest of the world. Balmain arrived in plenty of time, by car, since neither trains nor airplanes were functioning, having already rehearsed in Paris, down to the most infinitesimal detail, the brilliant entrance and the "tableau" of his group. It consisted of various ladies and gentlemen, representing the French planters in the Caribbean isles, all wearing entrancing costumes he had designed. Not one of them failed him, and there was never a moment of hysteria, indecision, or temperament. It was absolute perfection, and he led them with the assurance with which a shepherd steers his flock.

Since he dresses the majority of European Royal Princesses,

he also designs their wedding gowns. This alone keeps him on the move much of the year, for the number of princely marriages is enormous. Bangkok sees him often, since he must go there to consult his most enchanting and best-paying client, Queen Sirikit of Siam, who wears his creations exclusively when she dresses in western style. He is also one of the rare couturiers who entertain nowadays, mainly on the island of Elba where he holds house parties in a modern villa he has built there.

Ready-to-wear fashions, whose roots are so firmly entrenched in the United States, have now invaded Europe and along with the decline of the large Maisons de Couture, the little dressmakers and seamstresses around the corner are going out of business. The American Fashion Institute, which used to depend so much on European inspiration, is increasingly proving its independence and the number of Seventh Avenue buyers is shrinking yearly in Paris, Rome, and other centers.

The youthquake in the ready-made departments and the emergence of prominent youthful society designers is creating a stir on both sides of the ocean. In Palm Beach, for example, the story of talented Lilly Pulitzer's rise to success with her designs, the "Lilly" dresses, is already a legend. In Europe, redheaded Michele Rosier, the daughter of Pierre and Helene Lazareff, is another young and socially prominent member of N.S. who has achieved fame in fashion. Among other styles, she introduced the successful white vinyl raincoats.

The one French designer who shares his creative attention between women's and men's apparel is a young man, Pierre Cardin, whose narrow, long, fleshless, Gothic aspect might have served as a model for one of Niccolò Pisano's statues. Some fashion authorities predict that his creations are many years ahead of his time and speak of him as a prophet. In Europe, he receives most of his publicity because of Jeanne Moreau, whom he not only dresses, both in private and on the screen, but also escorts everywhere. Recently, he produced a considerable stir by going to England and announcing that he was so upset by the decline and imminent fall of the British male attire that he would undertake to prepare an entire line of men's fashions for Anglo-Saxon consumption.

Shortly before he made this statement, I was invited to watch a show of his feminine and masculine designs which I assumed incorrectly must have been created for a beatnik musical. They were, on the contrary, all for sale. The men's outfits, modeled by starved-looking youngsters, appeared so cramped and uncomfortable that one feared they might split should the models sit down. One also wondered how they could ever struggle out of those lean, slender-hipped, tightly cuffed trousers in time to put on the next costume. I can only hope that Cardin's revolutionary ideas will not sweep men's tailoring too fast and that Bond Street will survive a few more years without Cardinitis. But, apart from Monsieur Cardin's entries, there is no doubt that men's chicness in nomadic society is undergoing a transformation.

Often what made the widely traveled Anglo-Saxon male outstanding was his superbly cut English suit, but he too, like his women, is tending more and more to buy the manufactured one. This is not so much because of expense (men's tailors are, comparatively speaking, still fairly reasonable) but because of the constant rush he is in with an accompanying lack of time for his sessions with his tailor. The Latin, who is immensely vain and takes infinite trouble with his general appearance, will go without his lunch or game of golf to be properly fitted. The result is that, in most instances, the average Latin today is ahead in the best-dressed race. In a barber chair, the American, Britisher, or German man reads a magazine or newspaper and cannot wait to get out. In a Latin country, a client does not miss the slightest movement of the scissors in the mirror and directs operations with the same gestures a conductor uses to lead an orchestra.

Hairdressers have almost completely elbowed out milliners

and gathered momentum at astronaut's pace in the nomadic way of life. When women's wardrobes became so simplified, something drastic had to happen to transfer the attention elsewhere. Hair was it. As a result, the hairdresser has become the supreme arbiter of women today in all classes. He has found again the place he had won, and subsequently lost, in the eighteenth century when Joseph Addison wrote, "There is nothing so variable in nature as a woman's headdress."

It is very chic for women today to travel with their coiffeur. Farah Diba, the Empress of Iran, Princess Margaret, and Barbara Hutton usually do, but this does not prevent them from having "consultations" (this is what they are called) with leading hair specialists. At the Rio de Janeiro Carnival, Hollywood actress Marilyn Maxwell arrived with her West Coast coiffeuse who was included in all the invitations. Uncertain as to what sort of hair stylist they might unearth in Sevilla, at Feria time, Fiona Thyssen, Nancy Holmes and Kit Talbot brought Serge from Guillaume's in Paris, sharing in the expense.

When the *Cristina* sailed on the historical cruise starring Mrs. Kennedy and her sister Princess Radziwill, the host, Aristotle Onassis, provided the half-dozen ladies on board with not one but two hairdressers. Nothing is considered more nifty than having this service on a yacht for it means women can plunge into the sea and swim without a cap. The hair can then be dried, followed by the reassuring comb's stroke.

The sophisticated magazines speak of coiffeurs nowadays in such glowing terms that it comes as no surprise that, along with operatic tenors, they are among the most egomaniacal members of the artistic set. A young English hairdresser, Vidal Sassoon, was thus written up in *Harper's Bazaar:* "His work possesses a new architectural clarity and instead of muddying the planes of the face as some 'busier' bobs do, the Sassoon scissors throw them into striking relief." And further: "Vidal Sassoon is an unconventionally attractive, extraordinarily untemperamental lad who seems actually to dance as he swings the scissors (which perhaps encourages the swing he cuts into the hair)." This "lad" would indeed be a rare animal if he were to remain "untemperamental" after such lofty prose.

With the relentless advance of the hairdressers' momentum, a new class of professionals has arisen. Not even at the height of the eighteenth century, when its various Monsieur Beaucaires became future subjects for literature, had these men aspired to the social echelons they do today. Their ambitions have been, in the majority of instances, more than fulfilled in the last few years.

One runs into Mr. Kenneth at the parties of Mr. and Mrs. Denniston Slater and Mr. and Mrs. H. J. Heinz in Manhattan. Before her marriage to Thomas Bancroft, Jr., Melissa Weston was often seen out in public places with him. At the wedding of Amanda Mortimer to Carter Burden, Jr., he was one of the few celebrities present mentioned by *Time* magazine. Elizabeth Arden's Monsieur Roger dines with Barbara Hutton, and Madame Maria Carita attends all the Paris openings, glamorous in sweeping fur coats, and acclaimed like the great celebrity that she is.

At a Sunday brunch in the splendid residence of Charles and Jane Engelhard in New Jersey, I found myself talking to a young South African who turned out to be a coiffeur. In Round Hill, Jamaica, at a lunch given by Mrs. Warren Pershing, green-eyed Mrs. Oscar Hammerstein, the delightful Australian widow of the composer, insisted on being seated next to Enrico Caruso, no relation to the tenor, a hairdresser from Manhattan. He is that rare exception who uses a surname, for most coiffeurs are only known by their Christian names.

In Europe the No. 1 vedette in the hair-dressing elite is Monsieur Alexandre, although, on a competitive level, the two Carita sisters are not far behind. In the United States it is definitely, at the present time, Mister Kenneth who holds the scepter.

The stamina of Alexandre, who comes from St. Tropez of Italian parents (according to *Adam* magazine, his genealogy is impressive), is superhuman to meet the demands of a legion of such glorious ladies as the Countess of Paris (who is the only customer in the Salon who has the right to be addressed as "Madame," the way the Queen of France used to be); Princess Edwige de Bourbon-Parme and her innumerable royal nieces; and the Duchess of Windsor, who discovered him in Cannes shortly after the war when he was employed at Antoine's. "She not only has been my shining star," Alexandre explains, "but my mascotte. I have the greatest respect for her and owe an immense debt of gratitude to her as well as to the Begum. It was at the wedding of the former Yvette Labrousse to the Aga that my bejeweled headdress for her attracted world attention."

He has come a long way from those days, but he is responsible for the greatest impact a coiffeur has had since Monsieur Leonard, who was in charge of Marie Antoinette's hair styles and became a person to be reckoned with at the court of Versailles. Pierre Daninos in his amusing book, *Snobissimo,* claims that Alexandre's salon is the most exclusive ladies' club in all of Europe.

Short, wiry, bearded in the Henry IV manner, Alexandre has established a large empire. He reigns over many salons in Biarritz, Deauville, Le Touquet, St. Moritz, Milan, Brussels, and Beirut, with new ones in the planning stage in London, New York, and Rome. His crammed headquarters in Paris on the Rue du Faubourg St. Honoré employs an army of people, including thirty master hairdressers with one assistant each. Anywhere between two hundred and fifty and three hundred women pass through these portals daily and many of them come every single day. An average of forty-five permanents is given every twenty-four hours.

His secretaries have become adept at knowing the most intricate secrets of N.S. in order never to book at the same time the mistresses of certain gentlemen and their wives who are in the know and might create scenes. There is the added complication today of rich men having two mistresses simultaneously, and they too must never be taken at the same hour. Some dramatic incidents have occurred in the past, but with a system of following every scrap of gossip, the fireworks can now be avoided. Alexandre himself manages to give about thirty consultations a day. His hairdressers are all young and must, according to the master's rules, wear a romantic haircut, a dark suit, and a white shirt. He himself wears no jacket but a vest and a large knotless tie, held together by a diamond pin. All his suits are designed by Pierre Cardin. When Alexandre left Carita less than a decade ago, this professional divorce was one of the most advertised and emotional possible. Everyone cried copious tears, and the newspapers gave it more space than Xavier Cugat's break from Abbe Lane or Henry Ford's from Anne McDonnell. Some of the clients have not yet recovered from the shock, so divided are they in their loyalties to these two hair leaders.

"Between the hair stylist and the woman," Alexandre stated to me, in a most articulate manner, caressing ever so softly his beard, "a complete communion is necessarily like in church. In order to reach this relationship there must be a full confession of the client to the man she trusts with one of her most precious possessions: her locks. My task has been to re-educate the fair sex and build up its confidence. The right hairdo can make an ugly female beautiful, but in order to reach this stage, one must know the woman well, be aware of each and every mood and problem. One cannot be successful with a stranger. It just does not work in that manner."

Alexandre is of the opinion that the couturier has lost out to the hairdresser because women no longer have any contact with the designer. Most of the younger women buy ready-made clothes, which is a cut-and-dried performance. With her coiffeur, she has, day in and day out, a warm human contact, and he becomes her confidant, confessor, and friend.

Few men are more in orbit than Alexandre. He is always flying off, both to inspect the provinces of his shaggy kingdom and on assignments. Like Balmain, he is present at every royal marriage and his name lends prestige to the ceremony. At the wedding of the King of Greece to Anne Marie of Denmark, among the heads he coiffed were those of Grace of Monaco, former Queen Farida of Egypt, the young Duchesses of Aosta and Würtemberg, ex-Queen Marie José of Italy and her daughters Maria Gabriella and Beatrice, and the Queen of Siam. The latter is such a personal friend of his that he often flies to Bangkok to visit her and the King and offers a few pointers to her ladies-in-waiting about how to keep the moonlight beams in her hair. For the nuptial knot of Tatiana of Wittgenstein to Maurice of Hesse in a castle near Frankfurt, he went to place the tiara on the locks of Countess Mona Bismarck. When Richard Burton opened in *Hamlet* in New York, he flew there to set Elizabeth Taylor's curls, but Burton is his client too. In case Audrey Hepburn has to be photographed in her Swiss chalet by the magazines, he rushes there to make sure that she looks the way he thinks she should.

In his Parisian flat, where among his treasures is a porcelain tambouret from the *jardin d'hiver* of Marie Antoinette (all hairdressers are obsessed with her), and in his reconverted mill near the French capital, he entertains *les amis* which include Romy Schneider (*Je l'adore,* he says), Françoise Sagan, the Jean-Louis Barraults, Juliette Greco, and many others. He is seen everywhere; at Blenheim Palace's Ball of the Duke of Marlborough, at the famous annual Munich Carnival Ball of the Franz Burdas (they are the Sam Newhouses of Germany) and at various Rothschild cocktail parties (he has three baronesses as his clients, the wives of Alain, Elie, and Edmond) in Paris.

The Carita sisters' salon in Paris is a short distance from

their former employee's and theirs is a huge establishment with several private rooms for facials and makeup. Here, too, one is struck by the youthquake, and one wonders what happens to coiffeurs when they reach their middle twenties. Where do they go? What is their fate? Among some of Carita's star performers are Marc, twenty-two, Lionel, twenty-one, François, twenty-four, Greta, twenty, Catherine, twenty-one, and Christophe, eighteen, who is known as "*Le Sorcier des Chignons*" (the sorcerer of the buns). The general impression of these coiffeurs is of youthful sprites, so thin, slim, elfin-looking, one wonders whether they ever get a square meal, live on pills, or what.

The competition between the two salons is played down, but it does not take long for even the uninitiated to sense it. Each one knows exactly who are the clients of the rival and who are those who alternate in their devotion to both. Carita numbers only one Rothschild but a very good one, the Baroness Guy (Marie Helene van Zuylen), and if she cannot claim the Countess de Paris or the Duchess of Windsor, she has in her care several of the sisters of the King of Morocco and the Shah of Iran, most of the Agnellis (Marella, Antonella, and Countess Brandolini), Princess Paola of Belgium, and Ira Fürstenberg. Carita's wigs—the prices go up to $500—have taken N.S. ladies by storm, and with several to choose from in their luggage are Brigitte Bardot, Soraya, Sophia Loren, Caroll Portago Hughes, Aline Romanones, and Maria Callas. Just who is the coiffeur of the last, on a steady basis, no one is quite sure. None of the big salons claim her.

Roger of Elizabeth Arden's is also the rage these days. Also very young and willowish, he is such a marvelous listener that women talk to him all day long. Princess Charles d'Arenberg, Mrs. Winston Guest, Beatriz de Rovazenda Patiño, Congresswoman Jacqueline Patenôtre, and Princess Amédée de Broglie are among his boosters. The last raises poodles for a hobby and often has one or two in tow so Roger can nip off some of their whiskers. Michele Morgan is another habituée. They share the same fortuneteller, which gives them an extra subject of conversation.

There are all sorts of currents in the air indicating that makeup experts are climbing fast on the C.C. ladder the way they did three thousand years ago at the courts of the Egyptian pharaohs. Pablo of the New York Elizabeth Arden salon, an Italian in this instance, is blazing new trails in this art. He is responsible for what Eugenia Sheppard has described as "the long, long eyes without end and a nude face." He is called for assignments outside Manhattan, which means that to the expense of a coiffeur, a chic woman is adding that of a makeup expert.

It is difficult to determine, except on a snobbish level, the reason why the barber, the equivalent of a hairdresser in the masculine field, is socially *persona non grata.* A husband would not dare invite his barber to a cocktail party, for his wife would take a dim view of it. For some unexplainable reason the consensus is that hairdressers are artists and barbers laborers. A few years ago when Sara Delano Roosevelt, daughter of Mrs. John Hay Whitney, married the talented pianist, Anthony di Bonaventura, son of an Italian immigrant barber, New York society approved of the intelligent way the Whitneys handled the situation and made no mystery of the perfectly honorable trade of the groom-to-be's father. At a dinner I attended the night of the day the nuptials had been announced, conversation centered on this event. "What a pity," I heard one woman say to another, "that the father could not have been a hairdresser. This could have made the announcement smoother." On a higher level the distinction that exists between coiffeurs and barbers repeats itself among couturiers and men's tailors or gymnastic instructors and masseurs. While the former are socially acceptable, the latter are never seen in society.

With the shift of interest to houses and objects, discussed in another chapter, decorators have become paramount in N.S.

and leaders in their own right. It is naturally far more original and amusing to import one who has news value and whose work has not been seen locally. Therefore, it is perfectly understandable that Mr. and Mrs. Matthew Mellon of the Pittsburgh dynasty should have imported Baron de Cabrol from Paris to lend a special aura to their chalet in Kitzbühel rather than employ the gifted Mrs. Jeffcott Pell, an American decorator who does much work in Austria; for Charles and Jayne Wrightsman to bring Paris' Stephan Boudin to New York to help them with their Fifth Avenue apartment; or for the Charles Engelhards to fly Mrs. Henry Parish to Johannesburg from Manhattan to decorate their mansion there instead of using a local Boer. One is sure, then, that all of one's neighbors will not have the same chintzes, savonneries, and bathroom tiles.

Then there is the client who would not dream of decorating a house, be it at the other corner of the globe, without the assistance of her favorite decorator. This is the case with Mrs. Gilbert Miller who admires "Billy" Baldwin greatly. Consequently, when she built her engaging whitewashed villa at Costa de los Pinos in Mallorca, there was no question but that he would get the job. It also provided a nice outing for this Baltimorean-by-birth New-Yorker-by-adoption, who needs to get away now and then since he is one of the busiest bestowers of happiness to a certain brand of American woman. He is worshiped by a group of them to such an extent that, in the name-dropping game, one knows instinctively when it is this "Billy" that they are speaking of for there is a tone of such cozy adoration that it is unmistakable.

When a close alliance between an employer and a decorator ends and another one is brought in, chic chat becomes absolutely frantic. After all, one knows that a love affair usually comes to an end, but a broken decorating relationship implies all sorts of exciting discords and quarrels over color schemes, materials, curtains, and furnishings. Usually there are fireworks and everyone hugely enjoys the echoes. But when Mrs. Jackie Kennedy quietly changed interior consultants, with Billy Baldwin replacing Mrs. Henry Parish, naturally no one spoke a single word and therefore curiosity knew no bounds. What transpired is still, at this time, a well-guarded secret.

All these houses, built either near or far from the main base, are in themselves a wonderful excuse for traveling weeks on end to find, with the help of the decorator, just the right fireplace or console.

Among the busiest decorating experts is Valerian Rybar, an American of Yugoslav origin. With offices in Manhattan and a representative in Paris, he flies across the Atlantic every few weeks, for he insists upon keeping in close touch with progress at hand. A true Balkan in countenance, with a narrow waistline and a gaunt, fiery expression, he has untold nervous energy and is, in fact, possessed by his work. He has expensive tastes and there are few internationalites with a more varied wardrobe than his. His marriage to Aileen Guinness, the Irish heiress, ended recently in divorce, after they had been leading separate lives for many years. This means that he is no longer the stepfather of the nephew of the Queen Mother, the Earl of Granville, whose wife is the former Mrs. Rybar's daughter by another husband, or the uncle of the Marquess of Dufferin and Ava, son of Mrs. Rybar's sister.

But if his connection with *Debrett's Peerage* is temporarily suspended, his relations with the top echelons of the jet set are excellent judging from the overwhelming number of assignments. Having completed the successful large Souvretta chalet in St. Moritz for the Ernest Kanzlers, he rushed back to the United States to plan the huge and spectacular coming-out party of Susan Engelhard in Bernardsville, New Jersey. In the process of finishing the large, brand-new mansion of the Konrad Henkels in Düsseldorf (he is the head of the third largest company of detergents in the world), he took on both the Ernest Boissevains' and the Graham Mattisons' apartments in

Paris' *Étoile* district, along with the Manueline-styled bowling alley pavilion for the Antenor Patiños in their palatial Quinta near Lisbon.

These European assignments have not interfered with his American ones, nor his Bahama one at Lyford Cay for New York's Mrs. Edmund Higgins. They are so many and varied, it is worth while listing them. Having finished the Palm Beach residence of Nicholas and "Bunny" du Pont, he was commissioned by them to do a new country club near Wilmington. On Long Island he is advising David and Joan Muss on their recently acquired house near Roslyn. In Grove Hill, Alabama, he is busy planning the décor for the Palladian villa Merlin McCullough, the eminent architect from New Orleans, has erected for lumber baron William Harrigan and his wife, rising right out of his own pine forest. This commission came to Rybar because of the work he had done previously at Las Vegas' Tropicana Hotel in which Harrigan has an interest. It is no wonder that when Rybar travels so many suitcases go with him. They not only provide the change in clothes for all the different climates he works in but they also contain all the maquettes and plans he must have on hand.

Henri Samuel, generally considered the No. 1 interior designer in France, is another gentleman in permanent orbit. Head of the celebrated house of Alavoine since 1946, with a long and distinguished background behind him at Jansen and Ramsey, he has acquired international fame for such masterpieces as the French Embassy in Lisbon, the Empire rooms he reorganized at the Palace of Versailles, the Castle of Belle Rive of Prince Sadri Khan and of Pregny of Baron Edmond de Rothschild, both in the vicinity of Geneva. He is busy, busy, rushing to Montreal for the redecoration of certain sections of the Ritz Carlton Hotel there, to St. Moritz for the huge chalet Herbert and Eliette von Karajan have just finished building, to Lausanne for the apartments of the Basil Goulandrises and George Embiricos, to Acapulco for two houses including one for himself, not to speak of all the glorious assignments in Paris. The last time I saw him, he was occupied making blueprints for a yacht some Greek clients were having executed in Japan. "It is not easy," he sighed, "at this distance but this is the way the world has become and we must learn to accept it."

The art gallery business has become another constant cause for travel and another reason for women not to spend their money at the dressmaker. There are many examples of clever people who have art galleries everywhere, constantly rushing from one to the other, to host a party here and to launch a certain artist or new art form there. In New York, Paris, London, or Rome the mails are flooded with invitations to attend openings, and only a tiny percentage of people turns up at them. It takes far more than just a beckoning card to attract the customers. There must be a significant build-up and a glamorous party which is useful for the double purpose of generating publicity and getting the clients there.

Alexander Iolas is a case in point. Born Cotsoudis, he changed his name many years ago when he was a handsome but not successful ballet dancer hailing from Egypt of Greek parents. Smart, he transferred his activities from *entrechats* to the more profitable world of the art merchant in the early forties in New York City. Some time ago he ran two galleries in Manhattan, but after his sister's marriage to wealthy Arthur Stiefel of Wheeling, West Virginia, who invested some money in his enterprise, he extended his range of activities on a cosmopolitan level. He now has galleries in Paris, Geneva, and Milan, and homes in these various cities, plus a magnificent marble mansion he has constructed in the Athenian hills where he has housed his stimulating collection. He never stays anywhere more than ten days and commutes across the Atlantic several times a year. He represents such big-name painters as Max Ernst and René Magritte and recently, for instance, in one swoop he sold twelve sculptures by Tinguely to the Houston Museum of Fine Arts' director, James Johnson Sweeney.

The diamond-studded watch and large diamond rings he wears he brushes off as part of his oriental heritage. But a friend of his explained it differently. "It is a sign of prosperity and also a common bond with so many of his female clients. They see those rings and decide to help him further. By acquiring a few more pictures from him, they know he will buy a few more rings."

5

Status Symbols

In every society there have always been status symbols. In the nomadic one there are so many it is impossible to enumerate them all, but some are worth examining for they are symptomatic of the current state of mind.

Social climbers of any intelligence realize that today, with local society dying everywhere, they must join the international one. But how to make a place for themselves? Undoubtedly, the two best possible entrées are collecting valuable antiques or paintings and buying unusual, glamorous houses.

It is axiomatic to assert that wealth and a certain flair are needed to join these particular ranks. Without a bank account, the problem becomes more difficult unless one is gifted with sufficient know-how and patience to become a member of several courts. Nothing is more helpful to a beginner in this world than an identification with the retinue of some V.I.P., patrician, business leader, or banker. It is undoubtedly the easiest solution for someone without the wherewithal to go into his own independent orbit.

Talk in N.S. centers on an endless jungle of sobriquets or Christian names. Last names are never, even by error, mentioned. This custom has spread to such an extent that even a British jet-setter who greatly respects the Royal Family will mention Marina, the dowager Duchess of Kent, by her first name when he never would permit himself to call her this to her face. This habit stems in part from the intense hurry of the nomads and in part from the knowledge that their colleagues suffer from the same disease. The mention of a surname impedes the swiftness of chic chat. But much of this custom originates from the wish to indicate a certain intimacy with a glamorous person, an intimacy which gives the name-dropper a certain reflected prominence. Bert, for instance, not only is a short cut for the Duke of Marlborough but also conveys a special coziness with the illustrious descendant of the great General. The same is true of Debo for the Duchess of Devonshire, Babe for Mrs. William Paley, Angy for Ambassador Angier Biddle Duke, and Stash for Prince Radziwill.

In this labyrinth of first names which belong to Americans, English, French, Spanish, Italians, Germans, and other nationalities, the uninitiated must exert and train his memory not only to avoid showing his ignorance but to prevent him from making an observation which can easily put him on the blacklist. Injured pride or feelings are often caused by an unflattering remark, in most cases made unknowingly, about a certain person who may be a future wife, mother or brother-in-law, forthcoming stepson, new mistress or lover, an employer or friend of someone present.

Any student of Roman history is right at home, for even the best informed would have a tough time recalling what the family names were of such illustrious personages as Ovid, Catullus or Virgil. The nomadic system of ignoring surnames has spread so and has reached such gigantic proportions that even in the most conservative milieus this is now a common occurrence. It is not at all unusual for children to call parents by their first names, and the only country where this habit is frowned upon by the upper crust is France. In many French families grown-up sons and daughters always address their parents as "Monsieur" and "Madame."

The French are the only race apt to make fun of those persons who advertise their intimacy with certain exalted figures by mentioning only the Christian names. Typical of their attitude is the story circulated about the Countess of Rosenborg, a French commoner who married into the Danish Royal Family. Seemingly, she mentioned with much affection "Cousin Nicky," but no one could recall, with the best of intentions, any relation by this name. After some investigation, it was discovered that "poor Nicky" was none other than the late Emperor of Russia, Nicholas II, whom the Countess had never met, since he was murdered during the Russian Revolution. Technically, the Countess was absolutely right, for the Czar's mother had been a Royal Danish Princess and therefore related. But the French thought it all terribly *drôle* and *amusant*.

I recall a minor magazine editor, making her climb onto the upper social spheres, arriving in Marbella from covering the Paris collections. "You poor thing," a chic nomad exclaimed, "how absolutely awful to be stuck in Paris in August!" "It was not dreadful at all," she replied, her vocal chords quivering with emotion. "It was sheer heaven! Diana, Eugenia, and Gloria are my closest friends, and to spend all day with them was positively divine." To count Diana Vreeland, Eugenia Sheppard, and Gloria Guinness as your closest friends, whether you are in the fashion field or not, and to call all three by their Christian names, is the best possible identification to think up for one sentence.

At a barbecue on Long Island, some people were discussing the pros and cons of flying to a certain ball in Palm Beach. "It must be worthwhile," a young matron explained knowingly, "or Charlotte would not be covering it." By indicating her familiarity with the comings and goings of Charlotte Curtis, the brilliant rising arch priestess of a new form of society writing, she established that she was on a first name basis with this important member of the *New York Times* staff and everyone was suitably impressed.

A very pretty young American girl—but there are so many pretty girls—was trying to make her stay on the French Riviera as memorable as she could. Competition was stiff, for there were more women than men and her social position was not, at that moment, impressive. At a cocktail party there was talk about the unfortunate wind which often blows along the Costa Smeralda of Sardinia and everyone had either just come off a yacht or was about to leave for the Italian island. This appeared a good chance for her to speak, so she took it. "I have just been there," she announced, "on Sam's yacht and we went to Karim's party."

"I don't have to ask you who Karim is," a very blonde dowager said, "but who might Sam be?" "Sam Spiegel, of course," the girl replied, unable to check her annoyance. "Is there any other Sam?" she asked. "Well, of Sams there are plenty," the interlocutor remarked, "Sam Newhouse, Sam Behrman, Sam Vallance, Sam Le Tulle to name a few, and all great friends of mine." "Do they all have yachts?" the girl asked, her temper mounting to a boiling point. "No, they haven't," the woman had to admit, disarmed. "In that case, I don't think your question really pertinent."

In many instances, name-dropping has become so intrinsic a part of nomadic life that there is not even the intention of impressing. It has become second nature to these people. But it is like a game to try to figure out who is being mentioned, for chic chat takes on such speed there is no time to interrupt or ask questions.

One is grateful when couples are mentioned, for in most cases the combination of two names provides a definite indication. When someone says "I am off to Arizona to play a couple of rubbers of bridge with Harry and Clare" the chances are the reference is to Mr. and Mrs. Henry Luce. If a C.C. member announces in Manhattan that he is driving on Sunday up to lunch in the country with Pamela and Leland and then take a turn or two on ice skates, one is proud to catch on right away that it can only be the Haywards. On the other hand, when a couple announces that their forthcoming weekend will be spent in Florida with Charlie and Jane, then the identification becomes more complicated. Should either this husband or wife, or both, be in the racing world or have definite fishing proclivities, it is sure to be the Englehards in Boca Grande, but if, instead, it is someone who drops "ormolu" and "lacquer" in the conversation, then it is undoubtedly the Wrightsmans in Palm Beach. But when Jane (Jayne) is mentioned in connection with *Radiant II,* the two-million-dollar yacht, one is on the high seas. This is the vessel the Wrightsman charter from the oil tanker baron Basil Mavroleon whose wife's name also happens to be Jane.

Let us take, among the countless examples, the mixup with the Joans confronting internationalites, particularly in New York. For instance, a friend will say he cannot come for dinner on a certain night. "I must go and hear Joan and then go to a party given for her. She is so divine, such a pal." One assumes that "to hear" indicates the Australian nightingale, Joan Sutherland, who is dazzling with her cadenzas either the Met Opera's or the American Opera Society's audiences. But not at all. One discovers later that it is Joan Fontaine, as socially inclined an actress as Miss Sutherland is a singer, who is reciting some poems by Marianne Moore at a Waldorf Astoria benefit. Actually the expression "to hear" was not incorrect. Of course, it is an enormous help if Joan is mentioned with either "Ricky," Richard Bonynge, the diva's mate, or Alfred Wright, the film star's fourth husband. But there is another adorable Joan, also social and an able actress, who pops up in chic chat. She is Joan Wetmore, in private life Mrs. W. Palmer Dixon. Another Joan, Miss Crawford, who has been in show business longer than in Pepsi-Cola, has her huge share of nomadic friends whom she meets on the five continents as she ably sells her wares.

If someone says "I am flying to California for the opening of the baseball season. It's so wonderful to go with Joan," this is no problem. It can only be Mrs. Charles Payson, Jock Whitney's sister, who has financial interests in this sport as well as an art gallery on Long Island and a racing stable. On the other hand, when one is told that Nonie (this can only be Mrs. Thomas Schippers) was lunching with Joan at Quo Vadis (a restaurant where most musical celebrities go), the chances are that it is not Joan Sutherland, despite the strong and obvious musical connection, but Joan Dillon, the daughter of the former Secretary of the Treasury, who lives in Paris and is one of Mrs. Schippers' intimates. But, again, when a chic person announces "I am going to spend a week with Joan in Salzburg where she has rented a chalet for the Festival," one might assume it is Miss Sutherland. This deduction could not be more incorrect. The redheaded diva does not sing in Salzburg, and Joan Dillon, musically minded, enjoys entertaining her friends there.

There is no greater confusion than in the Peggy department, but certain character reminders come in handy. Therefore, if some hostess is asking around where she can possibly find a band that can play waltzes because she must entertain Peggy, one feels relieved that it can only be Mrs. David Rockefeller, who is as enthusiastic a waltzer today as she was when she first met her banker husband, also a devotee of this dance. On the other hand, the fact that one hears Peggy has gone off to Spain for a shoot with her husband resolves absolutely nothing. There are two Peggys much involved in this pastime, Princess Charles d'Arenberg and Madame Claude Fossier, both with their base in Paris.

Name-dropping takes all sorts of directions. For instance, a snob, talking to someone who has been visiting a jet-set leader, will not ask news of the host but of a certain maid or butler. This implies his complete "at homeness."

On the other hand, servants everywhere are becoming more and more conscious of their own status in society and now often address each other as Mr., Miss, or Mrs. This system has been in use in England for a long time, especially in the case of housekeepers, but nowhere else. In Italy the change in the postwar years has been extraordinary, with the great intimacy which existed between the employer and the servant having practically ceased to exist. So afraid is the employer today of hurting the feelings of the recently acquired maid, butler or cook that he has become exceedingly ceremonial with them. In France those who do domestic work are most formal with each other, have their own get-togethers on Thursday and Sunday afternoons and evenings, and are provided, in many instances, with their own visiting cards.

In the wake of the new informality which characterizes the sophisticates, who all address each other by their first names, the non-sophisticates, who used to be on intimate terms with one another, are now aping the old-fashioned ways of the more rarefied classes and give the most enormous importance to their "Mister" and "Miss" status and their surnames. The elevator operator, who used to be known in the business building as Joe or Jane, now wears a tag on his uniform which reads Mr. Fork or Miss Spoon. In the various offices, banks, post offices, there is a sign on every desk or window indicating whether it is Mr. Milk or Miss Sugar. While the Chairman of the Board of a billion-dollar concern will say on the telephone, "This is Harry Sun," his secretary or unimportant assistant will say, "This is Mr. Joe Moon."

As the pendulum inevitably swings backward and forward, all these nice people who give such importance to their Mr. and Mrs. appellation will begin copying the higher circles. And what will the latter do then? After the confusion of first names has reached epic proportions, they will return to the good old times when both the Christian and surname were used.

With domestic help so rarely remaining on their jobs very

long these days, the familiarity in this department is, perforce, getting less frequent, and a new technique, the name dropping of dogs, is moving fast.

The Duke and Duchess of Windsor have several pugs, one of which is called Disraeli. Someone asked a friend of the couple, who had just returned from spending the weekend with them at Le Moulin de la Tuilerie near Paris, not how the Duke or the Duchess was but for news of Disraeli. The friend, less "hep," had to have this historical reference explained, and one could sense the immense satisfaction of the other person, who, I learned, scarcely knew the Windsors.

Since Princess Cora Caetani is frequently on the move in both Europe and Africa building up the stock of the Jansen Boutiques, she must sometimes leave behind her boxer, Fidelio. When she was in Turkey I heard an anxious Italian ask a French friend of the Princess, "Has Fidelio received any news from Cora?"

The soprano Renata Tebaldi has one of the most vocal and loyal group of fans imaginable, and all of them, naturally, want to show their awareness of the diva's activities. In standing room at the Metropolitan Opera, I heard one fan say to another, "I wonder if New is over his indigestion and whether he has come to the theater tonight." This, of course, shows what friendly terms she is on with the opera star's everyday companions, for New is her much-beloved poodle.

The Italians, along with the French, go in heavily for double Christian names, which is enormously helpful. When Maria Camilla is mentioned, one can assume that it is the charming daughter of the Princess Pallavicini. The same applies to Giannalisa who is one of the pioneering nomads, wears a monocle and has reverted to her first husband's surname, Feltrinelli (her second husband was Luigi Barzini, author of the best seller, *The Italians*). Maria Carmela surely means the estranged wife of Viscount Hambleden, mother of five sons and a member of Princess Margaret's set, and Maria Sole, the Countess Pio

Teodorani, sister of Gianni Agnelli, who has the wherewithal to indulge her passion: horses.

This double identity is absolute manna in the French labyrinth, and how gratifying it is that Marie Laure can only be the intellectual Vicomtesse de Noailles; Marie Louise, Madame Jacques Bousquet, whose Thursday afternoons in her home on the square of the Palais Bourbon are still a rallying point for persons of cosmopolitan quality; Marie Helene, the Baroness Guy de Rothschild, half-Egyptian, half-Belgian, adorer of clothes, horses, and cards; Jeanne Andrée, the third wife of the late Aga Khan and the handsome mother of Prince Sadri Khan; Paul-Louis and Paul-Annik, the very rich and hospitable Weiller father and son; Jean Noel, the handsome tennis player; Monsieur Grinda, married to the daughter of the famous attorney, Jean Michard-Péllissier; and Marie des Neiges, one of the delectable daughters of Prince Xavier of Bourbon-Parme. It also seems that to be a successful actor in France a double Christian name is a must. Such big time stars as Jean-Louis Barrault, Jean-Paul Belmondo, Jean-Claude Brialy, Jean-Pierre Cassel, and Jean-Louis Trintignant all answer to this formula. In the Nobel Prize winning game, it certainly does not seem to hurt a writer either. Jean-Paul Sartre did not accept it but he won it.

The French also go in for personalities who are known only by one name and introduced by that alone: Annabella and Capucine, the screen stars; Simone and Sylvie, the aging actresses; Poucette, the delightful painter who started her fabulous career selling her oils in the left bank coffee houses; Regine, who owns Chez Jimmy's and has recently become very social in a super-wayfaring group; Bettina, the former model who enjoyed the favor of Aly Khan's admiration; Fernandel and Bourvil, two of France's best male comedians. All are cases in point, along with Patachou, Dalida, and Barbara, the songstresses.

Since hairdressers are slowly but surely conquering society, their lack of a surname is considered amusing, elegant, and modern. No one knows what other connotation Kenneth, Alexandre, Claude, Roger, and all the others have on their passports and nobody cares. Approving this condition one day, a French duchess remarked, "When one is not born to a fine historical surname, it is much better not to have any."

Among the most easily recognized first names in international society are the Italians', for they have infinitely more imagination and creativeness in choosing unusual and musical ones.

One cannot go wrong, for instance, in assuming that, among the males:

Alberico is Prince Boncompagni Ludovisi;

Alvise is Count Robilant;

Annibale is the wealthy industrialist Scotti;

Antonello is Princess Paola of Liége's brother and a member of the Calabria branch of the princely Ruffo family;

Aspreno is the Prince Colonna, Assistant to the Pope's throne;

Bartolomeo is Count Attolico, in the diplomatic service;

Bettino is Baron Ricasoli;

Blasco is the Marquess Lanza d'Ajeta;

Cino is the Marquess di Laiatico;

Clemente is Prince Aldobrandini;

Flavio is Marquess Misciattelli;

Fosco is the explorer and author Maraini;

Fulco is the Duke di Verdura, the designer of jewelry;

Giacinto is the Marquess Guglielmi;

Gregorio is the Prince di Piombino;

Indro is the journalist and author Montanelli;

Leone is Prince Massimo;

Luchino is the stage and motion picture director Count Visconti;

Michelangelo is the film director Antonioni;

Tammaro is the outstanding authority on incunabula de Marinis.

It is just as gloriously easy in the ladies' name dropping department for one can rest assured that:

Afdera is the ex-Mrs. Henry Fonda, born Franchetti;

Alberica is Countess Lorenzo Attolico;

Andreola is Donna Andreola Corsini;

Andriana is the ex-Mrs. Timothy Hennessy, born Countess Marcello;

Degna is the wife of Ambassador Grabiele Paresce, born Marconi;

Delia is the Marchioness di Bagno;

Desideria is Countess Desideria Pasolini;

Domitilla is the wife of Don Sforza ("Lillio") Ruspoli;

Donina is the widow of Alberto Gnecchi;

Edda is Countess Galeazzo Ciano, daughter of Benito Mussolini;

Esmeralda is the wife of Giancarlo Sbragia, born Ruspoli;

Fiamma is the shoe designer Signorina Ferragamo;

Giulianella is Countess Filippo Senni;

Idarica is the Signora Ferdinando Gazzoni;

Ilaria is Countess Ginolo Ginori Conti;

Jacobea is the widow of Baron Giuseppe Sapuppo;

Lorian is Countess Loffredo Gaetani di Laurenzana dell'-Aquila d'Aragona Lovatelli;

Marozia is Countess Emanuele Borromeo;

Milagros is the Princess Colonna;

Minervina is the widow of Don Antonio Riario Sforza;

Mita is Countess Uberto Corti;

Moreschina is Madame Georges Piguet;

Olympia is Madame Paul-Annik Weiller;

Ornella is the musical comedy star Vanoni;

Selvaggia is the post debutante daughter of Count and Countess Emanuele Borromeo;

Stefanella is Donna Stefanella Barberini Colonna di Sciarra;

Valeria is the Marchioness Gianfranco Litta Modignani;

Verde is the daughter of Simonetta Fabiani and Gaio Visconti;

Virna is the film actress Lisi;

Wanda is Mrs. Vladimir Horowitz;

Xenia is the Duchess Visconti;

Yana is the wife of Don Fabrizio Alliata di Montereale;

Ylda, her sister, is the Marchioness Giacinto Guglielmi.

While Italian parents must be patted on the back for making the life of N.S. members much less complicated, there are a few from other countries who deserve an Oscar for assigning their children names that are rarely duplicated. Leather-bound volumes should also be filled with grateful signatures from the legion of name-droppers to the various nannies who, by assigning odd nicknames to their charges, have made the name game far less difficult to play. A prolific vote of thanks must be handed to the Aga Khan's thoughtful family for its exceptional choice of names such as Amin (the Aga's brother), Yasmin (the daughter of the late Aly Khan and Rita Hayworth), Karim (the Aga Khan) and Sadruddin (the Aga's step-uncle, who is usually known as Sadri).

Parents who must have had the gift of probing into the future were those of "Ari" Onassis who gave their daughters such high-sounding, mythological names that they can never be mistaken in the international society into which their brother's fortune has catapulted them. They are Artemis (Mrs. Theodore Garifalidis), Kalliroe (Mrs. Ierasimos Patrinicolas) and Meropi (Mrs. Nicholas Konialidis). Among the Italian couples to whom nomads should always be building monuments are Don Adolfo of the princely Caracciolos and his wife, the former Anna Visconti, for assigning their four daughters such unusual appellations as Meralda (Signora Emanuele Pantanella), Orsetta (wife of Don Marco Torlonia), Violante (married to a cousin, Count Gianmaria Visconti) and Allegra.

Among some very welcome first names which come to mind in N.S. are:

Ayesha, who is the Maharanee of Jaipur.

Aliki is Lady Russell and currently British Ambassadress in Ethiopia.

Barton is Mrs. Walter Gubelmann.

Berinthia is Miss Berenson, a granddaughter of Elsa Schiaparelli.

Borden is the late Adlai Stevenson's son.

Brooke is Mrs. Vincent Astor who has become a successful writer.

Carola is Mrs. Benjamin Kittredge.

Cobina is the columnist Wright.

Cordelia is Mrs. T. Markoe Robertson.

Cyprienne is the French-born wife of Don Marcellino del Drago.

Daria is Countess Mercati, ex-Mrs. André Firmenich and Mrs. Paul Palmer.

Dreda is Madame Ffoulke, Givenchy's assistant.

Drue is Mrs. H. J. Heinz.

Ermelino is Count Matarazzo, the Brazilian industrialist.

Erwein is Baron Gečmen-Waldek.

Felicia is Mrs. Leonard Bernstein.

Fern is Mrs. Charles Denney.

Fiona is the ex-Baroness "Heinie" Thyssen.

Gaea is the ex-Signora Sandro Pallavicini, born Fraulein Blozfedt.

Fleur is Mrs. Tom Meyer.

Galarina is Mrs. Salvador Dali.

Gertha is Countess Hans Czernin.

Gore is the author Vidal.

Ira is Princess Fürstenberg, ex-Hohenlohe, ex-Pignatari.

Jarmila is the ex-Met star Novotna, wife of Baron George Daubek.

Lais is the Senhora Hugo Gouthier, ex-Brazilian Ambassadress to Rome.

Lambros is the Greek M. P. Eutaxias.

Lauder is New York's most in demand bachelor Greenway.

Merle is the film actress Oberon, wife of Bruno Pagliai.

Militza is Madame Banac.

Mona is Countess Edward Bismarck.

Moura is the British pianist Lympany.

Mungo is the Earl of Mansfield.

Nedda is Mrs. Joshua Logan.

Neelia is Mrs. Stewart Reynolds.

Nela is Mrs. Arthur Rubinstein.

Niloufer is an Imperial Turkish Princess, now Mrs. Edward J. Pope.

Nuala is the wife of Senator Clairborne Pell.

Perla is Mrs. Graham Mattison.

Perle is Mrs. George Mesta.

Ragnhild is a Princess of Norway, wife of Erling Lorentzen.

Raine is the Countess of Dartmouth.

Roxana is Lady Vereker, formerly a Miss Bowen from New York City.

Scarlett is the widow of Vladimir Ivanovich.

Sharman is the daughter of Mr. and Mrs. Lewis Douglas.

Sita is the estranged wife of the former Maharajah of Baroda.

Soraya is the former Empress of Iran.

Speed is the novelist Lamkin.

Tania is Lady Bruntisfield.

Tassilo is Prince Fürstenberg.

Vala is Mrs. Ernest Byfield, Jr.

Valentina is Mrs. George Schlee.

Youka is Prince Troubetzkoi.

Some nicknames which stand out and are easily recognizable include:

Ala (Constantin Alajalov, the cartoonist)

Alfi (Prince Alfred Auersperg)

Ba (Mrs. Carter Burden, Jr.)
Barnesie (Lady Sassoon)
Bootsie (Mrs. William Randolph Hearst)
Boysie (Count Seherr-Thoss)
Britta (Mrs. Edward J. Behn)
Bubbles (Mrs. Carl Holmes)
Cappie (Mrs. André Badrutt)
Chico (Mrs. Hector de Ayala)
Chip (Charles Bohlen, American Ambassador to France)
Dado (Don Alessandro Ruspoli)
Daidú (Mrs. Edgar Church)
Deppie (Mrs. Despina Messinesi)
Doda (Mrs. George Embiricos)
Dulcie (Senora Edouard Martinez de Hoz)
Elizinha (Senhora Walter Moreira Sales)
Ella (Princess Maria Gabriella of Italy)
Etti (Mrs. Arpad Plesch)
Falello (Raffaele de Banfield)
Fifi (Mrs. John Fell)
Figuie (Madame Jean Ralli)
Foxey (The Countess of Sefton)
Ghighi (Igor Cassini)
Ghino (Count Guerino Roberti)
Gogo (Marisa Schiaparelli Berenson)
Grisha (George Gregory)
Happy (Mrs. Nelson Rockefeller)
Honey (Mrs. Richard Berlin)
Honeychile (Princess Alexander Hohenlohe)
Jay (The Maharajah of Jaipur)
Lillio (Don Sforza Ruspoli)
Lindy (Marchioness Dufferin and Ava)
Madina (Countess Arrivabene)
Maly (Signora Giovanni Falck)
Marita (Marchioness Antonio Sanfelice)
Missie (Mrs. Thomas Bancroft, Jr.)

Mitzi (Mrs. Samuel Newhouse)
Momo (Mrs. Warren Pershing)
Mucky (Prince Maximilian Windisch Graetz)
Pancho (Francisco Murature)
Piedita (Princess Maria de la Piedad Hohenlohe)
Pimpinella (the pimpleless Marquesa de Belvis and lovely daughter of the latter)
Porchy (The Earl of Carnarvon)
Poppie (Mrs. Joseph Thomas)
Prandino (Count Eriprando Visconti)
Princie (Sayah of Baroda)
Reynaldito (Reynaldo Herrera, Jr.)
Rockie (the widow of Gary Cooper, now Mrs. John Converse)
Roddie (Rodman de Heeren)
Rupy (Prince Ruprecht zu Löwenstein)
Sachie (Sacheverell Sitwell)
Sciusciú (The Duchess of Magenta)
Shipwreck (John S. Kelly)
Shrimpie (Jean Shrimpton)
Suni (Countess Urbano Ratazzi)
Sweetie (Carmen Larrañaga)
Tilde (Mrs. Alejo Vidal-Quadras)
Tillie (Ottilie Lady Carnarvon)
Tina (The Marchioness of Blandford)
Tinti (Prince Alessandro Borghese)
Tiny (Countess Carl Sailern)
Titina (Signora Emilia Sartori)
Toinon (Mrs. Lowell Weicker)
Tootie (Mrs. Cortwright Wetherill)
Tory (Mrs. Barend van Gerbig)
Tuckie (Mrs. French Guest)
Valodia (Vladimir Horowitz)
Vaughnie (Prince Max Emanuel Hohenlohe)
Viv (Vivien Leigh)
Vivi (Stokes, ex-wife of Count Marco Fabio Crespi)

Winkie (Winston Thomas)
Yayo (Princess Jean Charles de Ligne)
Zia (Lady Wernher)

Some of the Spanish feminine names are so very odd that they are not duplicated in the smart set.

Belen is the Duchess of Sueca;
Caritina is the Viscontesa de Villamiranda;
Casilde is the Marquesa de Santa Cruz;
Cayetana is the Duchess of Alba;
Lorenza is the Dowager Marchioness of Mohernando;
Pomposa is the Señora Escandon.

But with Spanish men one is knee-deep in trouble, for most of them, whatever class they may belong to, tend to be christened Luis, Antonio, and Manolo.

Initials are coming more and more into vogue, without mentioning the name. Until fairly recently, whenever BB came up, one knew automatically it was either the late art critic Bernard Berenson or the Marquess Amerigo Gondi. Today it's still the latter, but more frequently Brigitte Bardot. B is either Mrs. André Embiricos, Beatrice Lillie, or the pixy painter from Boston, Beatrice Dabney. Kay Key is Catherine Hannon, the ex-Mrs. John S. Kelly, who resigned from her important Tiffany assignment and is now at Bonwit Teller.

The late Lady Cunard, who was California's gift to London society, was in many instances ahead of her times. Aware of the importance of answering to a distinctive name, she changed hers from Maud to Emerald and it was not long before the original one was forgotten. It is indeed a pity that she did not have more imitators, as anyone who joins the ranks of N.S. soon learns.

Aristocratic name-dropping is in vogue, but there are many subtle distinctions in this phase. The appellation Rothschild is so evocative, for instance, of untold wealth, intellectual achievements, magnificent residences, and works of art that from one end of the world to the other, nomads drop the name into chic chat constantly. Whether the Baroness Marie Helene has resumed her vocal lessons, how many partridges the Baron Elie shot during his stay in Spain, what color pantaloons the Baroness Pauline wore at the dinner party she gave in the Chateau de Mouton, are all matters which are discussed with relish by those in the know and those who wish they knew more. On the other hand, on an international level, the name of the Duke and Duchess of Medinaceli draws rapturous expressions only from those who are well acquainted with the Spanish *Gotha.* There is no greater family in the Hispanic world, but to the average jet-setter they are just another ducal pair. The really introduced jet-setter, however, would rather dine at the Medinaceli Casa de Pilatos in Sevilla than touch heaven with ten fingers. The difference is that the Rothschilds are all in orbit and the object of tremendous publicity while the Medinacelis are not.

Name-dropping in the medical field is assuming gigantic proportions. Ailing or not, it is an essential status symbol in every nomad's place in society to be the client of certain doctors, chiropractors, dentists, or Yogis. The latter are, at the moment, overwhelmingly fashionable, and women discuss for hours whether such and such an instructor has, as the philosophy demands, renounced the pleasures of the flesh. To have one's check-up done in Switzerland or Munich once a year is an absolute must. Cures and watering places are mentioned frequently by certain internationalites and Montecatini, Ischia, Baden Baden, and Bad Gastein, at this particular time, top all the others. The chicer the jet-setter the more he claims that his restorative resort is not chic, and this is, of course, the ultimate form of snobbery, for it asserts the complete confidence in his power to rub off his own chic varnish on it.

There are other types of name-droppers in N.S., none more formidable than those of esoteric places. It appears, at times, to take on a sadistic ritual. This particular breed of globe-trotter, ever on the increase, is engrossed in discovering a locality of which his friends are ignorant. Ten years ago, to visit Petra and Palmyra was the *non plus ultra* in antiquity sightseeing, but now that these marvelous dead cities are within everyone's reach they no longer appeal to the offbeat traveler.

The latter will suddenly rave over the Early Bronze fortifications which recently came to light in Arad, neglecting to mention that all they consisted of were broken-down mounds. Or he goes into ecstasies over the mosaics representing a thrilling version of the Rape of Helen, unearthed a short time ago at Pella, the Macedonian birthplace of Alexander the Great. He does not reveal the fact that there are similar ones in various museums which do not necessitate a difficult journey.

The archeological dilettante makes the tourist, just returned from Egypt, very unhappy by asking him, for instance, whether he has seen the breathtakingly beautiful frescoes recently excavated from Alexandrian tombs. He has not, but the way his interlocutor carries on makes him feel that he has missed the most consequential sight in Egypt. And this is hardly the truth.

There are, naturally, commanding journeys undertaken by serious wanderers. No one is more in earnest, let us say, than Lady Alexandra Metcalfe, daughter of Lord Curzon, the late Viceroy to India, who has embarked on fascinating expeditions to remote valleys in China and the reed villages of Southern Iraq; and Roderick Cameron, the author son of the Countess of Kenmare, and Derek Hill, the gifted painter-writer-photographer, manage to reconcile peregrinations to distant outposts with their professions. But nowadays it is at times difficult to distinguish the traveler who is in earnest from the one who uses a journey as an aura of sophistication.

Another special form of name dropping is mentioning an invitation to a certain extremely U shooting party. This identification is particularly gratifying because everyone knows the group is limited by the sport itself.

The *non plus ultra* bid a nomad with gun can receive is to

partake in a tiger shoot organized by the King of Nepal in his mountain realm, usually lasting a week. This means sleeping in the most wonderful tents with velvet hangings, Persian carpets, and legions of servants in attendance. Fifty elephants take part in the trek, and members of the party sit in a howdah, placed on an elephant's back, with regular pillars and roof. An umbrella, symbol of royalty, indicates the King's.

All the hunts planned by the Maharajahs of Mysore, Udaipur, Hyderabad, Bundi, Kapurthala, and Gwalior are very desirable too. Those of the Maharajah of Jaipur are the last word in éclat, with such exalted guests as the Duke of Edinburgh, Winston and Cee Zee Guest, and Prince and Princess Charles d'Arenberg. These expeditions are likely to begin from Swai Mahdopour, set in a junglelike decor. In the city bearing their name, the Jaipurs reside in the splendid Raj Mahal Palace, having transformed another stunning residence, the Rambagh, into a hotel. The Maharanee is away from her husband's domains much of the time, discharging her heavy responsibilities in New Delhi as India's most glamorous Member of Parliament.

Her brother, the Maharajah of Cooch Behar, in Assam province, also plans brilliant tiger shoots, but these are less select for one must pay to join them. Needless to say, they are expensive and comfortable, with large tents, bathtubs, and orange-turbaned domestics.

Shooting parties keep many jet-setters on the move several months a year. In every capital and city, hostesses claim that entertaining in the fall has reached a formidable impasse because of the constant departures of such a large number of friends intent on partaking in the hecatombs of partridges, ducks, or doves—according to the season.

The success of these shoots is always in direct proportion to the number of birds bagged. To be asked to La Mandria, near Turin, the estate of the Marquess Luigi Medici del Vascello, is a cause for rejoicing for here not only does one run into the

Duke of Edinburgh (he manages to be everywhere), Baron Elie de Rothschild and the Marquess of Blandford but pheasant chat consists of a regular one thousand birds killed each day. At the end of the day these slaughters are artistically arranged in what is known as "Le Tableau" (the picture) and the proud gentlemen are photographed with the feathered deceased.

In Germany among the most sought-after invitations are those of the Margrave of Baden, Prince Albrecht of Bavaria, Prince Johannes Fürstenberg and Prince Karl zu Löwenstein; in Italy, those of the Duke Salviati at Migliarino, Count and Countess Uguccione della Gherardesca at Bolgheri, Marchesa Ludovica Niccolini at Camugliano and Marquess Giacinto Guglielmi at Cerveteri. At one of the latter's fabulous boar hunts, Consuelo Crespi made an unforgettable impression by coming as a sightseer in high heels.

Among the best Italian ladies with a gun is Princess Pallavicini, sister of the owner of La Mandria, and her shooting parties at the Chateau de Baillou, near Chartres, are magnificent. In France *la chasse* is an exalted national pastime, and U jet-setters rush, in an absolute frenzy, with their equipment to the magnificent estates, among others, of Barons Guy and Edmond de Rothschild, to the Alsatian property of Count Jean de Beaumont (Jacqueline de Ribes' father), the Chateau de le Potelet of Dany Roger Saint, and the Chateau de Craon of Prince de Beauveau-Craon.

In the Tyrol an invitation to a chamois or deer hunt by Belgium's Princess Liliane at her property, Hinterriss, or at Scharnitz, nearby, of Baron Elie de Rothschild is absolute bliss. Recent delicious gossip among these sturdy sportsmen was that, in a burst of enthusiasm, King Baudouin's stepmother killed stags which were too young, much to the distress of the neighbors.

At one of the Princess Liliane's house parties, the story goes that suddenly there were more guests than anticipated and that Prince Karl zu Löwenstein and Count "Pali" Palffy were asked to share a room. No greater contrast could exist between them. The Prince is so celebrated for all his good deeds that he is known as "Holy Karl," while the dashing Count has filled the drawing rooms with talk of his staggering number of celebrated wives, including two Americans, the late Dorothy Deacon and Eleanor Roelker. A wit supposedly congratulated the hostess on solving the accommodation problem so cleverly. "These two men have much to talk about," he said. "While the Prince can discuss his one and only marriage and the eight children resulting from it, the Count can list his eight wives and one progeny."

Much coveted in England are requests to participate in the pheasant shoots of the Duke of Roxburghe at Fleurs Castle, the Duke of Marlborough at Blenheim Palace, the Earls of Derby, Sefton, and Airlie, and those of the immensely rich, as yet unknighted Charles Clore, John Mills, and Kenneth Keith. Americans often lease some of the superb moors in Scotland of Lord Dalhousie for grouse. Partridge shooting is running into trouble because of the many insecticides killing off the beetles, bugs, and flies. The hedgerows, where the birds used to nest, are also fast disappearing. This explains why so many nomads now go partridge shooting in Spain. Here the Caceria Diana is a wonderfully organized syndicate with thousands of the best acres at its disposal, and it makes all the arrangements with great skill. Count Theo Rossi, for instance, rented a shoot for three days, with a grand total of close to 3,500 partridges slain. Among his guests were Stavros Niarchos, the Marquess of Blandford, the Duke Gaetani d'Aragona, and Prince Maximilian Windisch-Graetz. No American happened to be among them, but there are many who participate in these Spanish ventures. Joyce Blaffer, a Texas heiress, is always in the Iberian peninsula in the fall months with her ageless looking, pink-cheeked husband, the Marquis de la Begassiere, who runs a shooting syndicate in partnership with Prince José of Bavaria.

These syndicates are sprouting up all over Europe, for expenses are on the rise and even the very rich find that running a private shoot all the year around is a big drain on their resources. These associations usually consist of about ten members, who pay annual dues every year and have the right to take part in a certain number of shoots. There is a very U organization, known as the Mittersill, which does not operate near the castle-club of that name, but in the vicinity of Vienna. This is run by an American, Neil McConnell, together with Baron Hubert Pantz.

In the United States most of the big, important shoots are in the South on plantations which are, in most cases, owned by Northerners. In this region there is an abundance of quail, ducks, and doves. The best areas are South Carolina, Florida (in the Tallahassee district), and Georgia (in the Thomasville and Albany communities). These old plantations are beautifully run, and all the European nomads who get asked are struck by the efficiency of the old-fashioned Negro servants. Near Tallahassee it is very exciting to be asked by Mrs. George Baker, Sr. (the Duke and Duchess of Windsor and the Earl and Countess of Dudley are often guests here); Mrs. Robert McKay (she was an Emery from Cincinnati); Mrs. Sheldon Whitehouse (one of her sisters is Mrs. Winthrop Aldrich), who reigns over Newport in the summer; Lloyd and Audrey Griscom (their Luna plantatation is, un-nomadically speaking, "out of this world"), and John and Audrey Phipps.

In Georgia one of the most exclusive shoots is at Mackey Point of the George Wideners, and voices quiver with emotion when announcing invitations to Greenwood Plantation by Jock Whitney. In certain circles it is "heaven" to receive a bid to participate in the Georgian shooting parties of the former Secretary of the Treasury, George Humphrey, where ex-President Eisenhower is often present.

A torrent of name-dropping also occurs in connection with the great shots in whose company certain jet-setters have manned their guns. One soon learns that among the Europeans it is thrilling to have occupied a post near the Count of Teba, Claude Foussier, Jean de Beaumont, André Dubonnet, Prince "Alfi" Auersperg, or Luis Miguel Dominguin; and amidst Americans near James van Alen, Winston Guest, Michael and Ogden Phipps, oilman James Harrison, Houston's John Mecom Jr., the King's Ranch's Robert Kleberg, and his nephew Richard Kleberg, Orson Munn, "Sunny" Wainwright, and George Baker, Jr.

Kissing is gaining momentum all the time. Nomads adjudge it a direct, as well as a visual, assertion of their social status. It serves to contrive speedy connotations and assigns a frame to the rapidly etched portrait of a little-known person. We have actually reached the stage today where, if a well-known member of the C.C. does not kiss a person, it means that the unkissed one has not been accepted in the Club as yet. Nothing forges a membership card better than "pecking."

A kiss, however, is always in the form of a ritual, and a chic nomad never expresses pleasure at running into a colleague. He must greet him, even if the last meeting was six months ago, as if had seen him the day before. He must never say "How are you?" but "How long are you staying?" The kiss must be brief, on both cheeks, looking straight ahead. Any sign of warmth in this ceremony would indicate lack of sophistication, for chicness can never involve feelings. The two are anathema to one another. Social cosmonauts must be as tough and indifferent as the Gagarins and Glenns are in handling their problems in space.

It is essential to remember that these osculations have no sexual connotation whatsoever and are entirely on a social level. Sex actually rears its seductive head less and less in these migrants' existence. Love life demands leisure, and this new breed of people has none. Their calendar is one of such permanent agitation that those men and women who are enjoying a liaison together are confronted with the recurrent problem of working out their schedule for meeting somewhere, sometime. Continuous commuting to and from the country, weekend journeys, air flights, business entertaining, and automobile congestions contribute heavily to keeping them apart. A dashing Italian industrialist, ever so attractive to the fair sex, confessed to me the other day: "There is nothing I enjoy better and consider more relaxing than being occasionally unfaithful to my adorable wife, but to find the time becomes more and more difficult."

In reading the delightful, detailed biography André Castelot has written of *Josephine,* the wife of Napoleon, one is struck over and over again by how the enchanting Creole, despite all the duties her marriage entailed, was able to disappear every day and take off for her rendezvous with her various lovers. But there were no reporters in those days to follow her around and the carriage traffic in a smaller Paris was negligible. Had Josephine lived today, her love life would have been less active.

In the past decade the image of the playboy, an ideal status symbol for several generations of a certain type of man, has faded into oblivion. There are no young men to follow in the footsteps of Errol Flynn, Aly Khan, Alfonso Portago, and Porfirio Rubirosa, who all died suddenly without leaving successors to their crowns. To be a playboy takes not only considerable physical strength and independent means, but time. Granted that at this ever-increasing pace seductions are achieved more rapidly, certain attentions are still required to make a woman feel that she is wanted. These are hard to come by with one foot pressed on the Ferrari accelerator and the other in the doorway of a Convair. Gunther Sachs is so up to date that he has gracefully evolved from a Don Juan into a social cosmonaut.

A South American friend of mine, who has never made any mystery that bullfighters were her favorite pastime, is depressed at the turn of events. "The more successful ones," she told me, "now have their baby jets. Imagine that. El Cordobes fought thirty corridas within the space of thirty days all because of that cursed private plane he has acquired. Even the less successful ones, the moment a fight is finished, rush to the airport to fly on to another engagement. Ten years ago a bullfighter rarely averaged more than one combat a week; today he is booked constantly. A torero's sex life, naturally, has gone absolutely haywire as a result of all this rushing around and the increased dangers and responsibilities."

A kiss means so little nowadays that even on the screen those long love scenes of yesteryear have practically ceased to exist. The camera turns on the two seminaked bodies in bed. This vision is apparently necessary, for the sexual suggestion of a kiss in all classes is becoming less and less strong.

Globe-trotters who know their A's and Q's, are cognizant that a well-planted kiss in the lobby of Manhattan's Colony or The Caravelle on the cheek of the right person can only solidify their positions. Therefore, if they are connected with fashion, the receiver is probably Eugenia Sheppard of the *Herald-Tribune,* Constance Woodworth of the *Journal American,* or *Women's Wear*'s John Fairchild. If highbrow music is their hobby, the bussing is directed at the Metropolitan Opera's imperishable Madame Butterfly, Licia Albanese, or the prince of violinists, Nathan Milstein, and his pretty wife Therese. The entertainment-world snob, on the other hand, falls all over Merle Oberon, one of the most glamorous and nicest members of the film colony, or Joshua Logan, the ingenious director of so many hits, and his wonderfully warm mate, the former Nedda Harrigan.

A party-minded wayfarer expends his explosion of fondness on Mrs. William Woodward, Sr., the distinguished hostess with the mostest in New York City, or Serge Obolensky, the eternally handsome white Russian aristocrat who became an American parachuting Colonel.

The well-informed traveler is aware that a kiss bestowed at

Round Hill in Jamaica on Jane Pickens Langley, deeply loved there, or at Lausanne's Beau Rivage Hotel on the much in the swim "Vivi" Stokes Crespi; or in London's Annabel night club on Lady Pamela Hicks, daughter of Earl Mountbatten of Burma and wife of the noted decorator, can do no harm to his prestige. In Rome's Taverna Flavia someone who hugs Count and Countess "Manolo" Borromeo, one of the best pedigreed couples in the Italian capital, or Princess Carla Boncompagni in the lobby of the Hotel Excelsior rapidly establishes that he is no parvenu.

In Paris the nomad who spies the exquisite Madame Arturo Lopez Willshaw sitting in a corner of the Relais Plaza realizes that bussing her can only add cheese to his macaroni. Not only is she one of the top hostesses in Europe but she does not open the doors of her fabulous Neuilly palace to everyone. The same applies to a smack stolen at Maxim's from Mrs. Barry Sainsbury, the impish looking charmer in whose veins runs the historical d'Harcourt blood.

In Madrid the well-trained rover runs up to kiss Mrs. Albert Gelardin in the Ritz bar and in Rio de Janeiro he does likewise when he sees Mrs. Graham Mattison for he knows that identification with both these ladies is most desirable. The first, an Italian patrician married to the director of Pan American Airways in the Spanish capital, has the reputation of giving the most amusing dinners and the second, who was Perla Lucena before she left Guanabara Bay to become one of the chic-est ladies on the five continents, is "in" with all N.S. leaders, being one herself. All these people mentioned may be nonplussed at such an explosion of attachment on the part of a semi-stranger, but a well planted smack is hard to erase, particularly when stolen at rapid speed.

Not long ago I escorted Helen Hayes to a *première* of a play in New York. The lobby of the theater was jammed with the crowd that always assembles to watch the entrance of the various celebrities. A social climber was standing near one of the doors. When she saw us come in, she rushed through the mob and kissed Miss Hayes on both cheeks, barely nodding to me. As we proceeded further, the actress asked if I knew who she was. I told her and explained that this same woman had bussed me at cocktail parties, if and when she thought it would help her standing. But in theatrical circles a kiss on my face would have done no good at all, whereas embracing Helen Hayes meant that she was "in" with a famous stage figure.

When Mrs. Jackie Kennedy, at the time her late husband was President, attended the opening concert at Lincoln Center, the occasion was illustrious for this was the inauguration of a vast new project and Philharmonic Hall was the first of the theaters to be completed. The program was televised in its entirety, and at intermission, as the First Lady shook hands with Leonard Bernstein to congratulate him, the gifted conductor leaned over and bussed her. Some conservative Americans, sitting at home, were somewhat surprised, for they were not up on the new habits of the sophisticated class. It was never Bernstein's intention to indicate lack of respect toward Mrs. Kennedy, but this was the only means he knew to greet someone in his own society. The blurred image between distinguished people and celebrities was the basis for Bernstein's action. He is accustomed to buss Rosalind Russell, Betty Comden and Maria Callas, and subconsciously, because of the film magazines, the Fashion Institute voters, and public media, Mrs. Kennedy represented to him a vedette.

As democratic as Mrs. Franklin D. Roosevelt was—in fact, there were some persons who thought she went too far in some of her actions—Arturo Toscanini and Dimitri Mitroupolos, whose musical eminence two decades ago filled the concert hall the way Bernstein's does today, bowed and thanked her for coming to their concerts. They never would have dreamed of kissing her. But the habit is spreading so fast that even Heads of State have now adopted this form of greeting. Recently, all the newspapers carried photographs of President Johnson kissing Mrs. John Connally, the wife of the Texas Governor.

Along with name-dropping and kissing, the most important development for social advancement and standing in the international community is collecting and acquiring interesting houses. In an increasingly abstract way of life, where values on a human level are growing harder and harder to come by, those of objects, furniture, and paintings are easier to estimate and, therefore, to understand. In societies such as those of the eighteenth and nineteenth centuries, the best passport used to be the gift of conversation. Blind, old, and devoid of means, the Marquise du Deffand was lionized in Paris, as Hugh Walpole and all the writers of the time have attested so vividly, because of the enchantment of her repartee; and every ruler and prince was willing to undertake any form of acrobatics in order to have Voltaire as a guest in order to enjoy the bedazzlement of his wit. Today the acquisition of a Vermeer or an Ingres is far more indicative of social status than the presence of a literary figure in one's court.

Nothing causes greater emotion or anticipation to members of cosmopolitan society, including *Le Gratin*, than a visit to a new collection or to meet a new collector. All class distinctions vanish on the common level provided by Benvenuto Cellini bronzes and Nymphenburg salad plates.

What was taken absolutely for granted in preceding generations has today become the sign of unusual distinction. Collectors have, or course, always existed but it was all done quietly and discreetly for their own exclusive pleasure. Today, instead, it is a flag around which new friends and acquaintances rally. It never would have occurred to anyone previously to do more than say a casual word of admiration, when visiting a castle, a mansion or a house, upon noticing some unusual piece. "How very pretty," a person would say as if it were the most natural thing in the world for that particular object to be there. Today the most aristocratic, along with the hoi polloi, accept invitations from people they scarcely know purely because of the objects they own or the historical house they have acquired.

Because of the general insecurity of most people, art becomes increasingly more tangible and significant than the person who owns it. The quality of persons frequented today is unimportant provided their furnishings are of high caliber. The blue blood of a signed chair is far more important than the person sitting in it.

The patrician himself, who for centuries took for granted the fine furnishings collected by his ancestors, is suddenly enthusiastic about it all and conscious of the fortune it represents. Attics and basements are combed with an enlarging lens; each chair, desk, sofa, commode, stool, and bed turned upside down and scraped to see if it's signed. Decorators and antiquaries are, as a result, best friends with various princes, dukes, and billionaires all over the globe, for they can be most helpful in conferring a missing link of knowledge.

The Sicilian princess or English duchess who arrives in Paris or Vienna today is immediately entertained by the painting and furniture experts whose shop talk she considers of far greater impact than that of her friends. The merchant knows just where certain signed pieces by Boulle, Carlin, or Riseener are, whether a Capodimonte coffee pot at the auction sale of the Hotel Drouout in Paris was really a part of the Duke de la Fierte's collection, or who is most likely to buy a fabulous pendule, which carries the signature of both Lepaute and Vion. Will it be Mrs. Leon Barzin, Pierre David-Weill, or Stavros Niarchos? There is no more delicious gossip than this, far more titillating than learning who is sleeping with whom. "Sex chat is no longer amusing," the wife of a prominent American banker said to me, "since discrimination has gone out the window and people behave like dogs in a kennel."

Not to have seen the collections of Count Vittorio Cini in Venice, Fosca Crespi in Milan, Baron "Heinie" Thyssen in

Lugano, the Duchess of Alba in Madrid, Prince Colonna and Princess Pallavicini in Rome, Mrs. Albert Lasker, and Robert Lehman in New York City, Baroness Germaine de Rothschild or Jean Davray in Paris, to mention just a few, is far more embarrassing in N.S. than not to have been to the Poldi-Pezzoli Museum in Milan, the Frick in Manhattan, or the Jacquemard-André in Paris. Art sales are the rage, and people travel long distances in order to attend them.

The early fall exhibit of antiques, which began only a few years ago, at the Palazzo Strozzi in Florence is the scene of such mobs that, despite the vastness of the edifice, the sale of tickets must be stopped for several hours. This despite the fact that admittance continues until eleven o'clock in the evening, that the event is little publicized and the price of the objects very high. Two weeks after its opening, on the same visit, at short intervals, I ran into John Huston, Erich Maria Remarque and his wife Paulette Goddard, Gayelord Hauser, Princess Cora Caetani, Countess Sheila de Rochambeau and other well-known collectors.

When the René Fribourg collection came up for auction at Sotheby's in London, every hotel in the English capital was jammed to the rafters with anxious would-be buyers and spectators. If some rare painted paper by Reveillon is discovered in an attic of a Rhine Castle, its sale in Zurich brings the chicest persons. When a long-forgotten Gauguin representing a Tahitian woman and son, bought in 1923 for $3,390, was sold again at Sotheby's in 1964 for over $250,000, to the Hammer Galleries, the tension became unbearable. For whom was it bought? Horse racing was never this exciting.

But perhaps no sale ever created so much excitement in N.S. as the Venetian one of Palazzo Labia for, interestingly enough, its proprietor was the super example of a cluster of people who owe their cosmopolitan celebrity to the acquisition of important houses and antiques.

From 1948, when he acquired Palazzo Labia, until he disposed of it in 1964, Charles de Bestegui dominated the City of the Lagoons, which owes him two world-wide publicity stunts, a ball in 1951 and the sale. The two are connected since much of Bestegui's international glitter came from his housewarming ball. The auction, therefore, would not have made headlines had the ball not received such great coverage.

Collecting furniture and interior decor have been the main passions, all through his life, of this rich Mexican with excellent Spanish connections. Women have come a close second, but because of his high social standards he usually chose them from the aristocracy. When in 1938 he acquired the Chateau de Groussay, near Montfort l'Amaury, and started to restore it, shivers of delight went through those amateurs who would rather be asked to visit a renovated Chateau than eat caviar and drink champagne at Maxim's. Ten years later, when he became master of the magnificent Palazzo Labia, which boasts the sensational fresco of Cleopatra by Tiepolo, the excitement knew no bounds. Everyone was aware that the palace was gigantic, with innumerable guest rooms, and there were visions of the Mexican setting himself up as a Doge.

Plenty of castles were being renovated in France but a palazzo in Venice was a far more romantic prospect. Soon all sorts of gossip began circulating, including the accepted version that the reason he had been able to buy this masterpiece so reasonably, with treasure-filled salons, was that he had agreed to leave it, at his death, to the city. Bulletins never stopped flashing; at one point he had come across the table on which Lord Byron had penned some of his poems during his Venetian stay, at another the desk when Casanova composed some of his most burning, sexy letters. It was announced that he was importing entire ceilings from British country houses and later was in the process of creating a salon dedicated to the Venetian conquests, with exciting geographical charts and historical trophies.

All this talk kept interest alive in the doings of the Palazzo, but the discontent was whacking when it transpired that the new-styled Doge occupied these hallowed halls for barely a few weeks in each year. After the first flush of snobbism had worn off and the ball had taken place, spoiled members of the C.C. who went to stay with him complained that they had no freedom. There was no possibility of returning home independently at night, they said, for the host refused to part with any of the front door keys and no servant was on duty to let them in. Another source of irritation was the infrequency of cocktails or whisky. The palace, they all cried, was impractically located, much too far from the Piazza San Marco unless an expensive motorboat was at one's disposal.

His dinners were considered dull, since by ten-thirty the host began to yawn, a sign he wanted to retire. Those endless sightseeing tours of the palace were all very well, people said, the first three times, but then "*C'est toujours la même chose.*"

When the news broke that he was selling the palace with everything it contained, the stupefaction was immense, since it had been assumed the city of Venice would be his heir. Who would buy eighty-nine rooms? Being a national monument, it could not be transformed into a hotel, for any significant structural changes would never be permitted. Finally the R.A.I. (National Radio and Television of Italy) acquired it for a reported half million dollars.

The announcement that the Rheims brothers, Maurice and Philippe, two topnotch art experts, had been put in charge of the auction of the contents pleased everyone for these men guaranteed a degree of seriousness. Newspapers and magazines began writing up the sale daily. Despite the fact it was held out of season, in April, the city was filled with all the leading international names, including several Rothschilds. Countess Cristiana Brandolini was quoted by Dino Buzzati in *Il Corriere della Sera,* Italy's leading daily, as saying that "De Bestegui has ordered ten perambulators for paralytics and an equal number of servants to push them. He told me he would use them for his friends." "But have you so many paralytic friends?" I asked him. "No," he explained, "not yet, but I hope they will soon be in this condition." Just what this extraordinary statement indicated on his part was perplexing, except that he himself was coming out of a very long illness. Although *Paris Match* magazine quoted his age as sixty-eight, his old friends claim that seventy-eight, quoted by *Time* magazine, is nearer the truth.

Don Carlos, as he is often called, did not attend the sale, preferring to travel in southern Portugal and keep in touch by telephone. He had every reason to be pleased with the result, which netted close to two million dollars. This is a nice sum indeed, for apart from some fine tapestries—there were no valuable paintings—the bulk consisted of bergères, stools, benches, banquettes, sofas, mirrors, vases, tables, and damasks. He might have done better with the tapestries except for the fact that some of them were forbidden by the government to leave the country and this naturally limited the number of buyers. Apparently he had brought them in via the diplomatic pouch of some of his Embassy friends and had, accordingly, not declared them to the competent authorities. "Never did De Bestegui," Maurice Rheims was quoted as saying, "invite any member of the Superintendence for dinner and naturally their teeth were poisoned against him." The most recent news of Don Carlos' activity, reported by the press, is that he is planning a farmhouse at Groussay in neo-Gothic style, a gigantic mausoleum for the burial of a deceased dog and a towering rostrate column. Many write-ups concern his interest in adding more and more African animals to the park of his Chateau, including giraffes, ostriches, and some rare specimens.

On an infinitely smaller scale, but revealing what a person of energy, determination, and imagination can do, is the case of a French bachelor whose cosmopolitan celebrity is due entirely to a house. He has succeeded so well in his plan that the second biggest attraction in Tangiers today, after Barbara Hutton's palace in the Casbah, is Castle York. Despite its fancy

English appellation, it is an Arabic structure which, like most North African buildings, reveals absolutely nothing from the outside. Actually it is easy to miss, since it looks like an ancient wall. In the large square of the Casbah, dominated by the terrace with the glorious view over the Straits of Gibraltar, it is immediately to the right, marked by a solitary palm tree. Only a Moorish door, with neat nails forming geometric patterns, is visible.

The enormous amount of publicity the reconstruction of this ancient fortress has received, both in the United States and Europe, is due to the brilliant, calculated commercial sense of its restorer and owner, Yves Vidal, President of Knoll International, a top manufacturer of very modern furniture. He had the foresight to realize the possibilities this restoration would afford him, combining as it did the Moroccan setting with various articles his company sells.

A Marseillais by birth but Parisian by adoption, Vidal is a handsome, fortyish bachelor who says little but knows exactly what he wants. These ruins of York Castle cost him a relative pittance a few years ago. He acquired them at the time Tangiers was going through the difficult period of losing its international zone status and becoming one among many cities of the Moroccan nation. As Europeans moved out, real estate prices took a drastic tumble.

The ruins, with a magnificent position over the straits, offer a most compelling historical background. When, in 1662, Charles II of England married Catharine of Bragança, this Portuguese Princess brought Tangiers as part of her dowry. For a short period the brother of Charles II, the Duke of York, who was later to become James II, was governor of the city. It was in his honor that the fortress was named. Through the years that followed, the castle changed hands many times, eventually turning into a prison for those poor unfortunate European wretches captured by the pirates.

The heart of the building is an octagonal patio around which runs an arcaded gallery, and in the center a basin functions as both a fountain and a swimming pool, with tiles made in the ceramic factories of Fez. The various bedrooms upstairs are tiny, dominated by huge Moorish windows, all offering sensational views and always cool because of the breezes coming up from the Straits. The American interior designer Charles Sevigny, along with the Belgian architect Robert Gerofi, had a hand in doctoring up the castle with materials from Thailand bringing a Far Eastern note, and furniture of Eero Saarinen, Florence Knoll, Lewis Butler, and Harry Bertoia is emphatically displayed everywhere. Whether the effect is to one's liking is not the point. It is Monsieur Vidal's bread and butter, and his ingenuity in showing it off so advantageously must be admired.

The most spectacular example of a couple who has, in a comparatively short time, reached the pinnacles of distinguished social status through collecting is provided by Charles Wrightsman and his second wife, Jayne, many years his junior. When they first moved to Palm Beach some years ago from the West, they were not an immediate success. Since the old guard was somewhat indifferent to them, they joined what was then called café society. They went to Europe every year and started yachting, a habit they still follow but on an entirely different basis.

There is a story about one of those early trips which illustrates, better than any other, how far these two have come in the last two decades. As meticulous and careful planners, they presented their guests with an exact schedule of how the next day and evening would be spent. There was much hilarity on board when the list of forthcoming events for their stop in Barcelona mentioned a visit to a night club to watch the "flamingoes" dance. This sort of unnoticed slip on the part of a non-U secretary would not get beyond the Wrightsmans' watchful eyes nowadays. Not only would flamenco be spelled out correctly but it would probably be specified whether it would be Sevillanas, Bulerias, or which particular kind.

In these intervening years, with a discipline and will power which are truly astonishing and admirable, they have acquired culture with such a determination that only university professors and art professionals can keep up with their almost terrifying vocabulary and learning. It is no longer a question who receives the Wrightsmans but of who is received by them. Café society is but a dim memory and they rotate only in the most rarefied echelons. The Palm Beach old guard, whatever is left of it, could not interest them less for they are surrounded only by ambassadors, museum directors and curators, great collectors and really tip-top U hostesses, such as Mrs. Vincent Astor, Mrs. Sheldon Whitehouse, and Mrs. Albert Lasker. Everything about them is immensely discriminating, including Mrs. Wrightsman's way of speaking, a lesson in the art of elocution.

Their magnificent rise is due not only to their inspired decision of investing many of their oil millions in the finest furnishings, bibelots, objects, and furniture but to their capacity to absorb the knowledge which goes with them. Tax-wise, this was probably no mistake either. Although they utilized Monsieur Stephane Boudin's services in helping with the decoration of the magnificent mansion they acquired from the late Harrison Williams in Palm Beach and their superb Fifth Avenue apartment, Mrs. Wrightsman has become so enlightened about every masterpiece in her possession that she could earn an excellent living by expertising. Today she is also on the best-dressed list, which just goes to prove how one form of success brings another.

Now they no longer own their own yacht, since they deem it easier to rent one, thereby avoiding all the responsibilities and troubles that such an ownership entails. For the last few seasons they have chartered the magnificent snow-white British 680-ton *Radiant II* with a crew of twenty-three. Among those participating in these cruises have been Mrs. Jackie Kennedy with her sister Princess Lee Radziwill, the ex-French Ambassador to Washington, Hervé Alphand and his *Time* magazine cover girl wife Nicole, the former British Ambassador to the U.S.A. with Lady Harlech, the former Brazilian Finance Minister Walter Moreira Sales and his exquisite Elizinha, the President of the Metropolitan Museum of Art and Mrs. Roland Redmond, the Director of the National Gallery in Washington, John Walker, and his consort the former Lady Margaret Drummond and Versailles' Gérald van der Kemp with his wife, Florence Harris. These all-star casts have brought the hosts undeniable prestige all over the world. Wherever the *Radiant II* stops, the red carpet is rolled out by all the local collectors and museum staffs within a radius of hundreds of miles and they hurry to dance attendance on these unique patrons of the arts.

A case of poetic justice transpired in the relations between the Wrightsmans and Bestegui. When the latter gave his celebrated eighteenth-century ball in 1951, he did not know the Wrightsmans, or if he did it was on a very impersonal basis. At the time, since they were not the great international figures they are today, no invitation from the Mexican Amphitryon reached them. Matters would have stood there except that the Wrightsmans were starting their yacht cruise in Venice a few days before the ball was to take place. A well-known husband and wife who accepted an invitation to the ball had also consented to go on the cruise. What to do in order to partake in both these thrilling events? They talked the Wrightsmans into postponing the departure of the cruise until the day after the ball, absolutely convinced that they could get the Wrightsmans invited. Although the Wrightsmans had, so one hears, ordered costumes for the fete, their friends were unable to secure the invitation for them since Bestegui had found himself besieged with people begging for admittance on all sides. "May

I bring my brother?" "May I bring my best friend from Peru?" and that sort of thing. "The palace will sink in the canal," he is supposed to have replied to all the requests, making only a few last-minute exceptions. Somehow the story leaked out in the press, making it appear as if the Wrightsmans had tried to get invited, which was not at all the case. The point is that today their name would either have been on the original list or the host would not have dared to refuse to include them. In fact, as time marched on, the reputation of the Wrightsmans grew to such an extent that when Bestegui arrived in Manhattan, according to gossip, the one apartment he was anxious to visit was theirs.

A typical example of the reverence in which the Wrightsmans are held is illustrated in a recent, unsigned article in *Vogue* magazine. It is a glowing appreciation of their Fifth Avenue apartment in New York, and its title is "The Great Gesture; Masterpieces." Lest anyone think that collecting is facile, this piece will make him change his mind. In it you learn that "Mrs. Wrightsman, a scholar and a connoisseur, has undertaken the adventure of acquiring the special knowledge that these treasures exact to keep in condition. There is the vast scale of the minutiae of restoration—keeping up the parquet de Versailles floors, mending a Savonnerie carpet (made for the grand gallery of the Louvre to the order of Louis XIV), repairing, polishing, touching up ancient boiseries, the ormolu, the bronzes, maintaining the 72-degree temperature with the humidity at 55 percent, requiring the care just to dust the twenty pairs of Meissen birds. She has the eyes to see the swell in delicate marquetry, the bubble that may appear in the canvas. It takes work and love."

In the list that *Vogue* gives us of the extravagant marvels this flat contains, we read that in her bedroom there is "an invitation to a masked ball in honour of the marriage at Versailles of Monseigneur le Dauphin in 1745. It directs the recipient to enter at the left." What is an invitation to a contemporary Bestegui ball in comparison to anything as historically captivating as this? How many can claim possession of a bidding to a royal ball in the most glorious of all royal palaces over two centuries ago?

Vogue goes on to say that "Living with masterpieces in an eighteenth century atmosphere with the Fifth Avenue buses outside the windows, to live with masters whose works hang on sometimes the olive green walls of the entrance or on the gold and ivory colored boiseries, requires a triple ability far beyond money; erudition, time and a light heart, to make the great gesture." The journey from the wide open spaces of the West to those of taste has been so rapid and the results so meteoric that they have forged a new image for posterity of twentieth-century collectors.

Ever since the era of cavemen, influential people have always had retinues consisting of those less fortunate. In past centuries the most sought-after settings were the royal ones but today, with the exception of the British Queen, royal courts are modest in size and unobtrusive. Even the Pope, whose retinue appeared destined to remain unchanged, made some remarks recently indicating he would undertake radical innovations. The Count and Countess of Barcelona, who live in Estoril, Portugal, every month have a different aristocratic couple who comes from Spain to render "service." The service consists mainly of accompanying them to functions and acting as super-secretaries. The former King of Italy, who also resides in exile, a few minutes away from the Barcelonas, has a permanent gentleman-in-waiting but, unlike the Spanish, Italian royalists do not go for their period of "service." In Geneva, his independent wife, Marie José, having dispensed with all her Italian ladies-in-waiting, is usually accompanied by a Swiss, Madame Casaï.

Then there is the inverted phenomenon of Royal Princes whose families no longer reign adding sheen to the courts of the rich. Since influence is, more than ever, closely correlated to wealth, we find the affluent holding every possible shape and form of scepter. It is to their courts that the average person longs to belong since they can provide the finer amenities of life—the luxurious yachts, the private jets, the weekend country houses, the residences at the sea or in the mountains, a way of life which moves at an incredibly fast speed but, nevertheless, still exists.

No one has ever painted a more penetrating character study of a rich man's courtier than Diderot in his masterpiece *Rameau's Nephew*. When one reads this extraordinary dialogue, the two centuries that have intervened since it was penned fade away, so contemporary is its point of view. Rameau's nephew is angry because dozens of people he knows, without talent, merit or charm, are taken care of at the courts of the rich, while he has no patron. He asks himself what is the matter with him. "Don't you know how to flatter the way the others do? Aren't you able to live, swear, perjure, promise, maintain or fail as the others do?"

Loelia, Duchess of Westminster, in her absorbing autobiography *Of Grace and Favor*, describes with acuteness the inescapable presence of persons clustering around a rich, powerful man. By marrying the Duke, who was one of the wealthiest men in Great Britain, as well as one of the most eccentric, she describes how she found him "surrounded by a band of courtiers. All the classic types were represented, the advisers, the intriguers, the jesters, the toadies and the parasites."

With the increasingly hectic life they find themselves inexorably obliged to lead, the very rich have less and less time to make an effort and are consequently pleased that certain people keep them informed about what is happening or amusing to do. These hangers-on also bring into their lives jesters to provide entertainment, but are careful never to introduce those who might step in and take the unofficial position they occupy away from them. Although the courtiers of the wealthy never have official assignments, they guard their niches with enormous perspicacity, going to great lengths to defend them, for they are cognizant of how fragile they are.

In recent years, with nomadic life spreading like wildfire, the very rich are absent from their stately homes for long periods, leaving unemployed those courtiers who are unable to keep up with them at the same speed. The energetic ones—and it's amazing to discover how many there are—have taken to going right out and finding other retinues to which to attach themselves. Courtiers have realized that the old-fashioned system of belonging to one leader is today socially impractical and that it is inadvisable to place all one's eggs in the same court basket. Some of the wonderfully rich leaders give lifts in their private Caravelles or send air tickets to members of their suite to come and join them, wherever they are, but they are not in the majority.

It takes great ability to shift quickly from one court to the other, much like walking a tightrope, since some of the nomadic leaders are jealous of one another. The French have invented an expressive term for those who follow the rich around—*pique-assiette* (pick a plate). But great luxury is becoming more and more of an attraction for all, including those who are comfortably off. Even though the atmosphere of a certain household or yacht is suffused with boredom, guests are willing to forgive and forget provided all the comforts are there.

To visit is not only less expensive but far more convenient from every point of view, since no effort is required to organize anything. It automatically means to be part of a set-up group, following the tide of parties already planned. In an increasingly dehumanized society, it is a living proof of being wanted. The reason that many of the rich adore staying with their colleagues is not so much to save the money of a hotel bill, which they can well afford, but because it provides them with the cozy feeling that their company per se is desired. More and more the wealthy seek the company of their kind.

People are so conscious of this that many noticed at a recent private ball in Paris how Stavros and Eugenie Niarchos and Count and Countess Brando Brandolini never left each other's sides. "They are like the Cabots and the Lowells in Boston," remarked a well-bred young lady from New England. "You are behind the times," chirped a witty Frenchman, "they are far more like the oil-rich Gulbenkians and the Gettys in London." An exaggeration, no doubt, for the Countess, though very rich, being an Agnelli, is not in a class with the others.

The rich members of N.S. also have a marvelous way of setting trends for their own consumption. It was not long after the unique Mr. Niarchos became the Lord and Master of his private kingdom, the Island of Spezzapoula, that his ex-brother-in-law, George Livanos, acquired the one of Coronis, near Nauplion, and his ex-brother-in-law, Aristotle Onassis, bought Scorpio, a delightful part of the Ionian archipelago. Gianni Agnelli, in the meantime, has acquired the island of Dino off the Calabrian coast but, as yet, no decision has been taken as to what he will do with it.

But future island owners will have a hard time emulating or duplicating the high standards established by Niarchos at Spezzapoula, which is within swimming distance of the larger isle of Spetsai. His shooting parties here are the last word in polish and virtuosity. Over 20,000 wild birds have been imported, including partridges and pheasants, along with wild rabbits, hares, mouflons, stags, and roebucks. The feeding of all these animals is resolved brilliantly. Corn is specially grown for the birds, and grass is manufactured by scientific machines to take care of the appetite of the many stags. Water is constantly brought in by tankers. Two rapid motorboats, led by a walkie-talkie, rush around in the sea to pick up the birds as they fall dead.

On the beach every comfort is available, including Chris-craft for water skiing and pedaling contraptions. Each guest is assigned a little Fiat to drive around the island, seven kilometers long, and is housed in a cottage. The problem of reaching this luxurious private realm from Athens is facilitated either by a helicopter, which meets the new arrivals at the airport, or by *Beltram,* a tremendously fast boat.

This drift toward acquiring a private island is another aspect of the general pattern of the return of the fortress conception. These small domains, surrounded by sea on all sides, are today's answer to the impregnable castles of bygone centuries. Here the rich, who today have succeeded yesterday's aristocrats as the most influential class, find a refuge from the *hoi polloi,* the current enemy. The great change between the way of life of the Middle Ages and today's is that during their displacements from one castle to the other patricians took with them their favorite sticks of furniture. Not even with a fleet of private baby jets would this now be possible which is, of course, all to the advantage of the antique dealers.

6

The Royal Nomads

Royalty has become nomadic in the extreme. Those who are still ruling in Europe are frequently away from their thrones because of the number of official visits their duties subject them to abroad. In recent years the sovereigns of exotic countries such as Siam, Nepal, Laos, Ethiopia, Iran, Jordan, and Morocco seem constantly in orbit because of their many state engagements and because of these many contacts, which were nonexistent previously, they are now also asked to marriages, jubilees, and other events relating to their European colleagues.

Even the United States has contributed to the royal sweepstakes. Having already provided a Hollywood star as a consort for the Suzerain of the Principality of Monaco, they have now furnished the ruler of the mountainous Himalaya state of Sikkim with a charming wife in the person of Miss Hope Cooke. The only monarchs who appear to prefer staying close to home are the Emperor of Japan and the King of Libya. Until her recent death, the likable Majesty of Tonga also remained quietly in her Pacific island paradise after her sensational and triumphant appearance at Queen Elizabeth's coronation, where she stole the show from all the other crowned heads.

As a result of shrinking distances and the breathless search of reporters to uncover glamorous subjects for their writing assignments, royalty has become a twenty-four-hour target for the world press. The prominence assigned to their every small action or move is not in the least commensurate with the purely formal and representative functions they now fill. While their governing responsibilities have diminished steadily, their personal ones have increased immensely, and their everyday existences are under the permanent exposure of X-ray machines on all sides.

Royalty used to be well protected from the curiosity of the public at large and their private life much sheltered. Granted that they are all aware how important publicity is today in creating a certain impact on the world, the realization that they cannot even bathe quietly in a secluded swimming pool without every stroke being recorded by a distant lens is most disturbing. The Queen of England has vigorously protested about the invasion of her and her sister's moments of seclusion, but to no avail. Photographers continue to lurk everywhere. And this is not all. Former secretaries, maids, valets, cooks, write their memoirs and sell them advantageously after their period of employment.

Recently the Duke and Duchess of Windsor were spending, as usual, the weekend at their country residence near Paris. On a Sunday morning an attractive American house guest, whose silhouette is similar to the Duchess's, swam in the pool alone and talked to the Duke who sat on a chair nearby. The Duchess, instead, stayed indoors attending to some correspondence. Two weeks later the weeklies were full of photographs of the Duchess bathing while the Duke watched her. Of course, it was not the Duchess at all but the American friend. The cameraman, who had obviously recorded the scene from the very top of a nearby hill, had fulfilled his assignment and this is all that mattered.

It is not surprising, therefore, to discover that all European rulers have hideaways where they retire whenever the opportunity presents itself. Baudouin and Fabiola of Belgium, for instance, disappear in a villa at Zarauz, a village in the bay of Vizcaya; Juliana of Holland, with her husband and daughters, takes off to a charming home they have built in the Italian fishing village of Port' Ercole. Grace and Rainier of Monaco vanish into a chalet in Schoenried, Switzerland. The aging King of Sweden spends all his free time at his favorite occupation, archeology, digging away at the Etruscan tombs. And the reigning family of Luxembourg has an enchanting property by the sea between St. Tropez and Toulon.

The world press is equally interested in royalty which was dethroned as a result of the Second World War. These ex-sovereigns are all forced to live in exile because the various republics (Albania, Bulgaria, Egypt, Italy, Roumania, Yugoslavia) fear that their popularity might set off some revolution should they be allowed to return home as private citizens. As a result of their jobless status, they are all restless and one meets them far and near. None are subjected to more attention than the former King of Italy, Umberto, his wife, Marie-José of Belgium (aunt of King Baudouin), and their children. The Italian papers, weeklies, and monthlies do not leave them an instant's peace. They are haunted by the *paparazzi* (that extraordinary breed of Italian cameramen) every step they take. The fact that their headquarters are in different localities (Ex-King Umberto has a house near Lisbon, his wife resides in a Chateau near the Lake of Geneva, the Princesses use Paris as a base) allows photographers and reporters even ampler opportunity to obtain wider coverage by following the trail of each one individually. Italian editors are in agreement that they can never publish enough gossip on the members of this family, voted out by a very small margin during a national referendum, because the interest of their readers remains at a high pitch.

The eldest descendants of those who lost their thrones long ago and are allowed to live in their respective countries—they are known as the Pretenders—do not escape the vigilant eyes and ears of the press either. In the legion of pretenders, there is no doubt that the most efficient and best organized is a French one (but not the only French one by any means), the only member of royalty able to exercise a firm hold over the public chroniclers. He is so able and intelligent and has such know-how that even those royalists who disapprove violently of his ancestor, Philippe Égalité (who voted for the beheading of his cousin King Louis XVI), are now backing him. His name is Henri Bourbon-Orleans, Count of Paris. Many call him "King" and his wife, Isabelle Orleans-Bragança, "Queen." Wherever he goes in France he is accorded full honors, and General de Gaulle treats him with every mark of distinction. At the Te Deum Mass in Notre-Dame de Paris for the soul of Pope John XXIII, I watched the Count of Paris in his magnificent cutaway walk into the packed Cathedral, down the main aisle, through the two wings of the Republican guards in full regalia standing at attention, followed by his equerries. Having preceded by a few minutes President de Gaulle and all the high dignitaries of the Church, he sat near the main altar in the most reserved of reserved sections.

No one has mastered the art of publicity and public relations better than Henri Orleans, and the constant flow of articles that appear in all European publications about the accomplishments of the members of his large family are of the highest caliber. Often sent on missions for his country, he owns homes in Portugal and Morocco.

An old proverb claims that although a cassock does not consecrate a clergyman, it helps considerably. There is no doubt that a dignified appearance and a related way of dressing are prerequisites of the royal image. Everywhere people adore pomp and pageantry and although most of it is definitely on its way out, there is an incessant craving for it on the part of even the most democratic nations. Display and solemnity are the greatest weapons left in the hands of royalty. When they let go of it in a desperate attempt to be *à la page,* they lose their identity.

The Queen of England undoubtedly does not realize it, but every time there is a picture of her with a handkerchief tied around her head just like a nice matron from Liverpool or Birmingham watching one of her horses run, she does a slight disservice to the crown she wears with such dignity and to wretched milliners who are suffering such doldrums these days. Her grandmother, Queen Mary, who always appeared in the same styled dress and hat, was perhaps never in fashion but she established a unique royal image. The Beatle haircut worn by Prince Charles of Great Britain at one point did much to put the four entertainers on the map and harmed no one, but it did little to place the heir to the English throne on the pedestal which is the ABC of royalty. When the dashing and courageous King Hussein of Jordan, in order to prove to the photographers in Texas what a jolly fellow he is, subjected himself to posing in a cowboy hat, his royal solemnity inevitably suffered a slight set-back. The strength of monarchs and members of their clans (whatever is left of them) is to enhance the pride of their position, but never to detract from it.

An interesting incident, which proves this point so well, happened shortly before the death of King Paul of Greece in Athens. Princess Margaret and the Earl of Snowdon were spending a part of their summer holidays with Stavros and Eugenie Niarchos, alternately visiting the Niarchos' private island of Spezzapoula and cruising around the Greek islands on their hosts' yacht. Since the visit of the British Queen's sister was private, nothing was planned for her officially. It happened, however, that just at the time they were in Greece the Wiener Philharmonik Orchestra, conducted by Herbert von

Karajan, was scheduled for a concert in the classical open air theater of Herod Attikou at the foot of the Acropolis.

An invitation was extended by King Paul and Queen Frederica to the august English couple and their hosts to join them for dinner and then attend the musical event. Because the distance between Niarchos' island and the capital can be covered rapidly by those wonderfully fast motorboats the Grecian Croesus owns, the invitation was accepted.

When the news leaked out that Princess Margaret would be present at the event, the already S.R.O. concert became a must on the list of a multitude of persons who are not musically minded. Ticket prices went rocketing.

At these summer concerts the audience usually does not dress, since Athens is very warm at that time of the year. But for such a gala, with the Grecian sovereigns and the sister of England's Queen present, everyone made a big effort to look his chicest. The Maestro and all the men in his orchestra were wearing white tie and tails.

As the public sprang to attention, their Grecian Majesties, the Crown Prince (who is now King Constantine), his two sisters and brother-in-law, Don Juan Carlos of Spain, the Snowdons, the Niarchoses and all those who made up the royal party arrived in the kind of attire nice middle-class people wear at a summer picnic. The gentlemen were in sports shirts —some claim they had no ties—and the ladies wore simple hot-weather dresses which might have been sewn by the little seamstress around the corner.

The surprise was enormous, and the Greeks, who invented the word democracy, were shocked. The tremendous effort the Greek Royal Family had made to look as informal as their subjects do on so many occasions was not only unappreciated but criticized by all. What would the foreigners, including von Karajan, think, they kept saying, and above all what opinion would Princess Margaret hold about this appalling informality? The British newspapers, who enjoy taking potshots at their own Royal Family, criticized the Queen's sister, which could not have been more unfair in this case since she and her husband were guests and had to follow instructions.

The question of what to wear when royalty is present creates incidents all the way down the line. Another humorous episode in which Their Hellenic Majesties were involved, but which had no echo except in a restricted circle, happened in 1955 at the time of Elsa Maxwell's remarkable cruise around Greece and the islands. The S.S. *Achilleus* had been generously placed at her disposal by Stavros Niarchos and the famous party-giver had assembled a highly diversified international group of well over one hundred friends.

From the inception of the cruise there had been much talk on board that King Paul and Queen Frederica would in some way give a sign of their benevolence to Miss Maxwell and her galaxy of personalities, particularly since this sixteen-day trip was concocted to encourage tourism in their fair land. Their Majesties were not in residence at the Royal Palace in town—the time was September—but at their country home in Tatoi, and this appeared to create some difficulties. Then, suddenly, we were all informed that Their Majesties would honor a morning reception with their presence, which Miss Maxwell would herself host at the Yacht Club in Piraeus. This was to be a private affair, with no publicity, all photographers barred, and the journalists, who were on the cruise, to attend only as guests, not as members of the working press. These orders came directly from the court along with the instruction that all the ladies must wear hats.

This created quite a problem for most of these feminine cosmopolites had none with them, since it had already become unchic to wear bonnets. The time was short indeed, and our ship arrived in Piraeus only the day before the reception was to take place. Madame Louis Jacquinot, wife of a French Minister, was delightfully old-fashioned enough to own several hats which she kindly loaned around, but they were far from enough to satisfy the demand. So there was much rushing around to Athenian milliners, who were pleasantly besieged by frantic ladies in search of some pretty things with which to cover their heads.

Just before Their Majesties arrived at the Club at noon, last-minute instructions from the court were that, in order to facilitate the multiple presentation to the Sovereigns, the guests should form clusters according to their nationalities. This order threw some into an absolute panic since the passport on which they traveled did not correspond to the spiritual allegiance they felt for some other country. How should they be presented to Their Majesties? Some opined this should be decided by the nationality corresponding to their tax returns, others by what was written in their hearts. Then there were some persons such as Reynaldo and Mimi Herrera, Venezuelans, the Marquesa de Cadaval, a Portuguese, and Xavier de Satrustegui, a Spaniard (ten years ago the Spaniards were not in orbit as yet), with a few others who felt very lonely indeed for they were the only representatives of their nations. But they stood there, erect and alone, very much like soldiers on parade.

Finally, the great moment came, and the wonderful Miss Maxwell, who had gone up front to await the arrival of the rulers, appeared finally with the charming King and Queen in tow. The amazement was considerable when people began to realize that Her Majesty was not hatted. All the ladies felt terribly let down, but they plunged, hat and all, into their curtsies. Since the Queen is adept in the art of winning people over, this obvious slip on the part of some gentleman- or lady-in-waiting who had not coordinated the head question was soon forgotten.

There is another anecdote which is worth mentioning in connection with the prominence clothes have in the role played by royalty. This one concerns the beautiful Princess Alexandra of Yugoslavia (Maria Pia of Italy), the eldest daughter of former King Umberto. She and her husband were yachting with Stavros and Eugenie Niarchos on the *Creole* (at the time the Prince was employed by the Greek shipowner) which, after seeing off Miss Maxwell's cruise in Venice, caught up with it at various intervals.

In Venice, the night before the departure of the *Achilleus,* Countess Lily Volpi, who is one of the last great hostesses in Europe, gave a superb ball in honor of the cruise members in her palazzo on the Canal Grande. The evening could not have been more gala in feeling and looks with all the women dressed up as the occasion demanded. The Countess, following protocol, disappeared to await the Princess's arrival on the first floor. When, a few minutes later, the hostess made a grand entrance with Their Yugoslav Highnesses, the lovely Princess Maria Pia was wearing a vivid short day dress of Emilio Pucci. She had obviously not realized the significance of the party she was attending where many Italian royalists who had never met her before were eagerly awaiting her. The Princess had left Italy as a little girl when her father went into exile, and her presence meant a great deal to the faithful followers of the House of Savoy. In fact, outside in a square, hundreds of Venetians were crowded waiting for her to show herself at the window, which she did with the grace which distinguishes her. Had she not been a Royal Princess, the frock she wore would have passed unobserved by some, but in that assembly, where she was the center of attention, it assumed great importance because people felt she had let them down.

In reverse, I remember another occasion in Venice during the summer of 1938. It concerns the fabulous Countess Annina Morosini, a lady-in-waiting to Queen Helena of Italy (Maria Pia's grandmother) who, until her death a few years ago, was undisputed leader of society in the city of the Doges. She had been so wonderfully beautiful that on the day of her wedding, when she crossed the Piazza San Marco in her bridal gown, many knelt at her passage. An invitation to her palazzo was coveted by all, and on this particular occasion she was holding an afternoon reception for the King's cousin, the Duke of Genova and his Duchess.

The Countess Annina, who stood near the entrance to receive her guests, noticed to her utter dismay that the wife of a celebrated Italian Cabinet minister came in wearing neither hat nor stockings. Without wasting one instant, she first laughed, then, with that enormous authority which characterized her, said in her piercing voice, "You don't have to tell me, my dear, that you have come straight from the Lido and that terrible wind, which we are all subjected to in those nasty motorboats, has blown your hat into the Grand Canal, It happens to me all the time. I shall take you to my bedroom and provide you with another one so that later you can meet Their Royal Highnesses." Like a little lamb, the lady in question, considered by everyone an independent and somewhat rebellious person, followed the Countess and returned hatted. It was also noticed that the lady wore stockings, but the Countess would never reveal how she had managed that more difficult achievement.

Princess Liliane of Belgium, wife of former King Leopold, is a stunning-looking woman with enormous charm. But because of all sorts of circumstances, she has never succeeded in making herself popular and most of her compatriots cannot find one good word for her. For a long time, as the morganatic wife of the King, she was known as the Princess de Réthy, but later her stepson, King Baudouin, who succeeded his father, overcame much opposition and gave her the new appellation.

Because of this unfortunate lack of favor she suffers at home, stories abound about her in both Belgium and abroad. One of them concerns her first meeting with her future step-daughter-in-law, Donna Paola Ruffo di Calabria. This radiant Roman aristocrat had been asked in marriage by Prince Albert of Liége, but had not as yet met her future in-laws. Gossip has it that the first encounter was arranged in an Austrian ski resort in order to avoid publicity until the official announcement of the betrothal had been made by the palace in Brussels.

Upon her arrival with members of her family from Rome, Paola is said to have telephoned the Princess Liliane, who invited her to come alone for dinner that night. Having understood her to say to come just as she was, the forthcoming bride presented herself in sports clothes to find, to her acute embarrassment, that all the others were in full evening attire. The enemies of Princess Liliane claim this was a ruse to put the girl ill at ease, which does not appear likely, but we shall never know what really happened for no one is talking. However, this tale shows again the importance of the right garment in royal circles.

Until the Second World War, there was enough protocol left so that anyone who invited nonreigning members of royalty to his home always advised the other guests so that they would be on time and assemble before the royal entrance. In the casual atmosphere that prevails today, hosts often forget to do this. It also would have been unthinkable to leave a party until royalty had departed. Now it is done all the time.

Today, with the exception of those who are still sovereigns, much of the protocol has been thrown to the winds but not all of it—and this is where ambiguity arises. Royal and Imperial Highnesses attend receptions on an informal basis, but enough etiquette is observed so that you are introduced to them, never they to you. Therefore, in the middle of a terribly crowded cocktail party with everyone pushing on all sides, the hostess will say "Monseigneur (or Madame), allow me to introduce to you" and all you hear is your own name. She assumes that you must know who the royal personage is, but you don't. Suddenly you are left to your own resourcefulness to plunge into a working conversation.

The great democratization of royalty is often the cause of errors that are both ticklish and humorous. During Holy Week in Sevilla, the Countess de Fresno gave a large reception in her palace to coincide with the magnificent procession of her parish church. A rather plain-looking lady, dressed in black and wearing spectacles, came in and as all the women present curtsied to the ground, she became almost beautiful. She found a gracious word to say to each of them and carried herself with such dignity that it came as no surprise to discover that she was Princess Esperanza de Bourbon–Two Sicilies, married to one of the pretenders to the Brazilian throne, Pedro Orleans-Bragança, who comes from Persepolis every year to her Finca near Sevilla to spend several weeks.

When the Procession began, we all went onto the various balconies to watch it go by in the street below. In the penumbra, the British Consul General, Hamish Mackenzie, who had just arrived because of a delay at his office, mistook the Princess's back for that of his wife and, in a rare display of effusiveness for a Britisher, gave her a big pat on the shoulders. The Princess, quite startled, turned around and he apologized, smiling. When a few minutes later he learned the lady's identity, a moment of acute embarrassment followed and he rushed back to her side to apologize more profusely.

In the past this episode would not have happened, since the Royal Lady would have had the hostess at her elbow or a lady-in-waiting. As Princess Esperanza is a woman of the world and the Consul a delightful gentleman, no doubt this contretemps only helped them to become good friends.

A few years ago I escorted the titular Queen of Yugoslavia, Alexandra, to a Town Hall concert in New York, in the absence of ex-King Peter who had gone to Detroit to deliver a lecture. During intermission, as we were winding our way through the crowd to go out for a breath of fresh air, an acquaintance of mine stopped to speak to me. I immediately presented him to her. "Your Majesty," I said, "allow me to introduce to you Mr. Concert Goer." Since he was not sophisticated and I was unable to get across to him the nuance of the presentation, he said to the Queen, looking straight into her face, "I did not catch your name." She did not answer nor did I, evading the question and continuing to discuss the merits of the performer. But he did not give up so easily and asked a second time. As I was searching for a reply, she came to my rescue. "The name is Karageorgeovich," she said with great authority, and of course, this is the family name of the former ruling dynasty of Yugoslavia. This shut him up, and he did not ask her how to spell it.

Nowadays, on a beach or a yacht, we all witness the strange scene of a woman in a bikini making a profound curtsy to a gentleman or, on a golf course, a lady in tight pants dropping to her knees close to the green as a golfer in an open shirt, shorts, and a jockey cap goes by hitting the ball.

The etiquette that surrounded royalty was complicated and fascinating. There were definite marks of distinction for some of the patricians, such as having the right to stay hatted before the Monarch and being allowed to sit, some on chairs, others on stools, in the presence of the ruler. Now, with few exceptions, all that is left is curtsying, which is still a prerequisite of all the women who meet or know royalty.

I was present one day when an American wife was arguing the merits of curtsying with her aristocratic British husband. She was recalcitrant about going through the motion at a dinner they were to attend that evening where some non-British no-longer reigning royalty was to be present. This discussion is worth quoting for it expresses fairly vividly the two opposing viewpoints.

The husband was explaining to his wife that curtsying was nothing personal, but an homage paid to the institution the particular person represented. "I will go along with you," she retorted excitedly, "in the case of royalty which still rules. I can understand this. But it is the others one runs into all the time. It is such nonsense. Their families were dethroned some time ago so we are all equals."

"What are you talking about?" he replied, raising his voice. "Why do you insist on having a table at Annabel's in a certain given spot? Why do you refuse to go to Paris unless you can stay at the Ritz? Or go to the theater unless there are seats available in the first five rows? Is that equality for you? Why do you use my title? Call yourself Mrs. A curtsy is a gracious gesture to a symbol, that is all. So they have lost their thrones, I agree with you, but not the many centuries of glory behind them. Is it not then equally absurd in your estimation when the mayor of a city gives the keys to some distinguished guest? They are symbolic, too, since it has been a long time since cities had gates which were locked at night. Why do you seat an ex-Minister or an ex-Ambassador at your right for dinner? He is no longer in office, but you do it because of his past services rendered. If you are such an advocate of equality, then be true to your belief all the way." I heard later that his argument must have won the point for she curtsied that night to the Princess in question.

But the problem that comes up so often in chic nomadic chat is not so much whether women should curtsy to royalty, throned or dethroned—most of them do—but whether they should in certain very specific cases where the royal status is unclear. This anxiety—this is really the right word to describe this condition—manifests itself in all those increasing instances when men, born to the purple, marry those who are not.

In the case of royalty which still rules, there is always an immediate decision. Either the ladies, on the day of their marriage, are raised to the royal rank of their husbands or they are not. In Great Britain, the first is usually the case and, in fact, the Queen Mother, the Duchess of Gloucester and the young Duchess of Kent are all well-born ladies who have been raised to their husbands' level.

On the other hand, although Sweden is one of the most democratic countries on earth, the King has always decided against it. The many members of his family who married outside of royal circles not only were unable to raise their consorts to royal rank but lost theirs. All of them are simply known as Count and Countess Bernadotte.

It is when there is no longer an official sovereign that these rebuses find no really satisfactory solution. Some pretend that it is the nominal head of the royal clan who can make this decision, but others do not agree and the public at large is at a loss to know who is right and who is wrong.

This definition of the status of the feminine commoner who marries into royalty is important to her and to all those who have to deal with her. Her place at an official banquet or reception, or in a cortege depends entirely on this technicality. If she has been assigned this rank, then she is on an equal footing with her husband; otherwise hers is only a small supporting role. There is no question in anyone's mind that the former Queen of Albania, a very fine lady indeed, deserves a genuflection despite the fact her late husband, King Zog, lost his throne shortly after their marriage and that she was born nonroyal (her father was Count Apponyi, her mother Gladys Stewart from Boston). But there was consternation in Paris at the time of the state visit of King Hussein of Jordan about how to deal with his wife. He has not proclaimed her Queen but Princess Muna (Flower of the Desert), and her very middle-class British background does not help matters. So some ladies curtsied, some did not.

When, not long ago, former King Simeon of Bulgaria, an intelligent and worthwhile young man, married Margareta Acebo, a rich nonaristocratic Spanish orphan, the indecision about her case became most acute. Many of the ladies who had known the attractive Margareta in Spain and elsewhere opined that it would be ridiculous for them to pay the homage of curtsying to someone they had always treated as an equal and who had become the wife of a deposed ruler. On the other hand, the youthful former King felt strongly that they should. The Duchess of Alba, who is impulsive, made up the mind of all those who were uncertain. It seems that, after she curtsied, in a short time most of the others followed suit.

There has been much apprehension recently on the part of these nomadic members of the fair sex about what they should do upon meeting the brand new Princess Guy de Bourbon-Parme. Her young husband, handsome enough to be a movie actor, has the sort of pedigree a snob simply dies over, for he is the nephew of the retired Grand Duchess of Luxembourg, ex-Empress Zita of Austria, former Queen Giovanna of Bulgaria, and King Umberto of Italy. But his bride, formerly Brigitte Peu-Duvalion, is the pretty daughter of an ex (it is ex all the way you must agree) head of the police corps of Cannes. It was the tenderest of love matches according to the endless press communiques, for they fell deeply in love when they were children. But all of this, charming and touching as it is, does not make the decision about curtsying any easier.

Another source of current agitation is what to do in the case of Marina Karella. When the winsome and wealthy commoner became the wife of Prince Michael of Greece, it was announced that he had forsaken the rights of succession and that she would be known, henceforth, as Marina, wife of Prince Michael of Greece. Confusion reigned supreme when this couple came to Paris shortly after their marriage (the Prince is a nephew of the Count de Paris) for none of the Greeks who were asked by the French just what her status was could give a satisfactory answer. But no sooner does one think one has got the gist of the fascinating royal quest, an exception comes up to cloud one's horizon.

Alexandra of Yugoslavia was assigned royal rank at birth, although her mother, a Greek commoner, was never recognized as Queen to her husband, King Alexander of Greece, and never accorded royal status. So it is conceivable that, even if Marina will never receive official recognition, her children will.

In the opposite case, when a Royal Princess marries a commoner, the problem exists only in case she will reign. While there is no question that either the Earl of Snowdon or the tremendously popular Honourable Angus Ogilvy, husband of Princess Alexandra of Kent, merit a curtsy, what will happen to Claus von Amsberg, who is about to place the wedding band on Crown Princess Beatrix of the Netherlands? At this point there is no indication of what steps Queen Juliana will take to elevate her future son-in-law, but my Dutch friends predict that she will give the German diplomat royal rank in order not to make the protocol of his position untenable.

If etiqutte in dealing with European royalty may appear complex to some, it is child's play compared to African royalty, as the many royally minded nomads who travel on the dark continent perceive when they are received by the local sovereigns. Two monarchs with adjoining kingdoms who are delightful and hospitable gentlemen and who speak perfect English are Their Majesties the Kings of Buganda and Toro.

The first, the Kabaka, who is also President of Uganda, is Oxford educated, a short, slim man in his late thirties with intense, intelligent eyes and a cosmopolitan manner. King "Freddie" as he is known to his countless English friends—he spent some time in exile in London after running into trouble with the British authorities who ran his country before independence—received me in his capital, Kampala, at the palace erected on a hill and enclosed by tall papyrus reeds. I had to cross a very long room, filled to the brim with huge elephant tusks, and I advanced slowly looking where I was putting my feet. His equerries, who led me into the royal presence, walked on all fours, and so did the servants. Western visitors are fortunately excused from this bit of African protocol which appears most difficult to master. I never saw his Queen, the Nabageraka Damali, but Bugandian gossip was that they live more or less separately and that she appears only at official receptions. I heard that he would like to divorce her, having another Queen in mind, but he must be careful not to offend some of the sensibilities of his tribes. Since His Majesty was departing on a tour the following day, this was my only opportunity to see him.

In his capital, Fort Portal, the King of Toro, the Mukama, lives in a palace on a hill which overlooks the superb range of the Mountains of the Moon. His Majesty, George III, weighs well over two hundred pounds, has his head completely shaved, and is very loquacious. He asked me for lunch, and again the same protocol prevailed with people walking on their knees in his presence.

Since I had spent the morning on an excursion to see the pygmies, who are his loyal subjects, and had been unable to return to my hotel, His Majesty kindly asked me if I would welcome freshening up. When I accepted, he himself took me through several drawing rooms, all abounding with modern furniture of no distinction, to the bathroom, where, poised on a stool, polishing the tub with several rags, was a figure swathed from head to toe in pale blue veils. As she saw us come in, she dropped on her knees immediately. "Let me introduce to you Her Majesty," the Mukama said. Never having been presented before to a Queen squatting on the floor, I was completely at a loss about how to handle the situation. So small was the room that if I bowed the way one should before such a personage I would have hit my head against hers, and shaking hands was impossible. Her Majesty solved my difficulties by making a rapid exit on all fours, mumbling something in the local tongue in staccato style, punctuated by ever so many consonants.

When luncheon was finally served, to my surprise I discovered that although the large table had been set for twelve, Western style, the King and I were alone. Four butlers, who must have taken courses in circus acrobatics, brought the food in and out, always on their knees, covering the considerable distance from the center of the dining room to the door at fantastic speed. Later, when the time came for me to take my leave, the King accompanied me to the courtyard where the guards, standing at attention, also dropped to the ground.

"I suppose you think all this strange," the ruler said to me, pointing to them, "and perhaps it is. When I returned from my schooling in England, I made a few experiments to change some of this, since it did not seem quite in keeping with the times. But I soon realized that it would mean breaking an ancient tradition on which respect is based. And respect, however external it may be, is a much needed key in our society." As he said this, it all made so much sense that, although I did not drop on all fours, I did bow to the King of Toro far lower than I had two and a half hours earlier when I first met him. I was paying tribute to the intelligence of a wise man, who knows human nature.

The tremendous impact of the marriage of Grace Kelly to the ruling Prince of Monaco made it appear as if this were the first time that an actress had become a reigning Princess (the Grimaldis are Serene and not Royal, a step lower, but as rulers they go ahead of nonreigning royalty at official ceremonies). Actually Rainier's grandfather, Prince Louis, had also wedded an actress, Ghislaine Dommanget. Known in the theater as just Ghislaine, she made her reputation as an adequate interpreter of the leading role in Edmond Rostand's *L'Aiglon*. She now lives in a Parisian apartment and those who know her speak well of her. Since her step-grandson is reported not to long for her presence in his principality, she tactfully stays away. But if Princess Grace has shown her mettle, accomplishing her duties so well that even the most hard to please and conservative members of European society not only find nothing to disapprove of in her deportment but express praise, the decision of the former Empress of Iran, Soraya Esfendiari, to become a screen star has met with widespread objections. Although it is not her wish to pursue a career that has been frowned upon, her choice is one easily open to criticism and not in keeping with the lofty position she occupied for seven years. If she had proved to be exceedingly talented, she might have been forgiven, but her screen debut revealed only a vacant stare and no temperament. Many Iranians feel that the prestige of their country's crown, which she wore ineffectively, has received a severe blow.

As a former Empress, this very beautiful woman was invariably given precedence at all the parties she attended. What will happen now is hard to predict, but in many cases the problem will not present itself. Her social position, which was eminent when she first came to live in Europe after the divorce necessitated by her inability to give heirs to the Shah, has now lost much of its varnish, and her path rarely crosses that of U milieus.

Various examples exist of rulers who lost their thrones but maintained such nobility in their behavior that their situation remained unimpaired. When former Empress Eugenie of France, who like Soraya was also of nonroyal stock, retired in exile to England, she immediately stopped addressing Queen Victoria as "Beloved sister," the name which royal ladies called each other in those times, changing to "Your Majesty." The British Queen was so impressed with the great integrity and tact of this remarkable lady that she not only insisted she must continue to use the term "sister," but until her dying day, singled out the former Empress with many renewed signs of her friendship. When Eugenie's yacht, *Thistle,* by chance met several units of the German fleet in Norwegian waters, the Kaiser, who was traveling with the fleet, had the French flag hoisted on all of his ships to pay homage to this lady whose husband had been dethroned as a result of the terrible defeat his country had inflicted upon France.

Granted that those were different times, when a certain degree of chivalry survived and *beaux gestes* were still in fashion, it was Eugenie's great class that imposed itself, becoming a veritable legend and bringing immense luster to the Bonaparte dynasty. It cannot be said that in Soraya the recent Pahlevi dynasty has been as fortunate.

It would appear that Spain has the ability to produce aristocratic women who make superlative Queens. When Baudouin, the young King of the Belgians, singled out Fabiola Mora y Aragon to be his bride, his position was far from secure after the ravages the throne had suffered because of the intense criticism leveled at his father, King Leopold, and his stepmother, Princess Liliane.

There were many who felt that he was taking quite a risk, since Fabiola was neither royal nor well-known. What has followed in a very short time is one of the most extraordinary chapters in the history of kingdoms and thrones. For this gentle, dovelike Queen has created an impact of such intense devotion, not only among her husband's subjects but all over Europe, that it is difficult to evaluate the tremendous emotional force she has unleashed. Anyone who goes to Belgium immediately becomes conscious that most people speak of her not in human terms but in superhuman ones.

It is her enormous sweetness and dedication to duty that accomplished this miracle, along with the need of human beings to find a symbol of goodness in an increasingly selfish and dehumanized society. From morning to night she is on the job, never seemingly in a hurry, finding the time and the words to give comfort where and when it is needed. No one who saw them could ever forget the photographs of her tearstained, tired, tragic face when for days on end, twenty-four hours around the clock, she stayed with the King at the Brussels airport to give what consolation she could to the wretched survivors of the Congo massacres.

Throughout the Christmas festivities, when sovereigns and heads of state usually take a rest, she travels indefatigably to make the holidays happy for as many children as possible. In a tiny hallway of a concierge in Paris, I noticed a photograph of Fabiola hung on the wall. "Are you a Belgian?" I asked. "No," she replied, "I have placed the picture there because I think it is the kindest and most beautiful face in the entire world. It does me good to see it every day."

The fact that as yet there have been no children from this marriage and that the Queen has suffered some miscarriages has become a source of national distress among the Belgians. Every time a deceiving photograph appears of the Queen which might indicate some happy news, there is great rejoicing. But whether this blessing happens or not, Fabiola can always be comforted by the knowledge that, singlehandedly, she has given birth to a renewed, much needed aureole for royalty everywhere; the one of the heart.

The most special place royalty has in international society is that occupied by the Duke and Duchess of Windsor. With the swift passage of the years, their magic remains undimmed and the unique sense of elegance which the Duchess emanates will leave a definite mark in the history of taste in the twentieth century. Mostly time works against people, but occasionally it works in their favor. In the case of the Duchess, it is definitely the latter.

When the King of England gave up his throne close to thirty years ago, the unhealthy curiosity about her was such that rumors and stories were circulating so freely that it was impossible to put a real image into focus. The stage she moved on was so cluttered with envy, prejudice, and contradictions that, although everyone is always moved by a love story, this particular one placed on her shoulders a responsibility that was utterly staggering. She suddenly became the center of world attention, and every movement of hers was studied like the habits of a fish in a bowl.

In order to fulfill themselves, love stories, strangely enough, must have either very tragic endings or very happy ones. After three decades, one can safely state that the Windsor tale has been a blissful one and that, if Edward VIII disappointed his subjects as King by abdicating, he has not done so as a husband. Prince Felix Yussupoff, who played such an historical role in the First World War, has been living in Paris since the Russian Revolution. A wise man, he summed up the Duchess one day by stating that she reminded him of an iron lung through which the Duke breathed. Could a greater compliment be paid to a lady who shook an empire but who, with her continued strength, restored the balance of a sensitive man's life?

It is lucky for the former Wallis Warfield that, despite her small frame, she is vigorous in character and constitution. She has safely piloted her ship through highly stormy straits and very rough waves with an assurance that makes other captains admit that she has the firmest hand and knowledge. Now that so much passion has been spent, it is easier to evaluate her, not from an historical point of view—this is the task of historians—but for the remarkable impact she has had on our contemporary scene and society.

The supreme sophistication and grace of which she is today the exponent par excellence are actually the development and achievement of her American southern heritage. No one is more American than the Duchess, but this Americanism of hers is essentially the product of a southern aristocrat minus the accent. Her manners are such that the French, who criticize deportment for hours on end, admit that they are absolutely faultless. Being the center of attention, day in and out for a succession of years, would prove exhausting to anyone else but she carries this load apparently without effort and is always wonderfully well informed on all questions.

Anyone who has been to either the residence in the Bois de Boulogne in Paris or the Moulin de la Tuilerie at Gif sur Yvette, knows the absolute impeccability of the decor, the exquisiteness of every detail, the quality of every piece of furniture and every object. But these are not museums. They are cozy homes which are lived in and, although one could never find, not even with a lens, a speck of dust, there are innumerable newspapers, magazines, books, and flowers everywhere.

This taste is so personal, so essentially a part of her, that it becomes obvious that this is no work of decorators. They may have been called in to execute certain particulars, but that is all.

How was this super-discrimination achieved? A longtime friend of hers gave me a sensible explanation. "The Duchess," he said to me, "spent several years in China in her youth. There has never been an atmosphere quite like it in the world. It was one of such utter subtlety that today it appears as remote as Shangri-la. Just to give you an idea, imagine that customers never went to a shop. The merchants, followed by an army of assistants, brought the objects to the home. They left behind whatever was of interest for whatever time was necessary for the client to live with it and decide whether it was right or wrong for him. The Duchess, who is wonderfully susceptible, absorbed much from her stay in Peking."

Given the great casualness of servants today, one can only marvel at how the Duchess has imposed her will and meticulousness on such a mixed group. Name any nationality and she has a representative. One almost feels, when lunching at Le Moulin or dining in the Bois by candlelight, that these domestics are silent stagehands in some eighteenth century play obeying some invisible director.

The immaculate perfection of the Duchess in everything—ranging from her superb knowledge of clothes (she is never overdressed or underdressed for any occasion) to her singular sense of timing—is not in the least contemporary. Her discipline is such that never does she keep anyone waiting and those who invite the Windsors for dinner at eight-thirty can count on the clock to strike as they make their entrance.

Many royal princes never entertain, having been brought up on the formula that their acceptance to a party is a sufficient mark of distinction for any household. Nothing is less true of the Windsors, who return any invitation a hundredfold, and there are no better hosts than they. Never casual, they look after each and every guest with perspicacity, and the quality of the food, the china on which it is served, the wines, the crystals, the linen, all is a delight.

No intellectual—she is the first to admit it—the Duchess never takes on a pose. Full of energy and wit, born to be a leader, she has started, and will go on starting, all sorts of new trends. Her loyalty to the United States and her friends is admirable, and she is enough of an American to enjoy lunching with women alone. That she has a forgiving nature, too, she proved with Elsa Maxwell, who, after extolling her to the sky, decided one day it would make good copy to feud with her. To the repeated attacks in Elsa's columns, she never replied, ignoring the entire matter. But when Elsa decided she had been naughty long enough and asked to be readmitted to the ducal circle, the Duchess let bygones be bygones and was kind to her until she died. The Duchess, who knows human nature, undoubtedly must have been aware that Elsa's pronunciamentos were not, sometimes, in accord with her good heart.

Although the Windsors cannot be called jet-setters, since they never fly, they are frequently on the move. They go to New York and Palm Beach at least once a year and also travel frequently around Europe. There has been considerable talk of their building a house near Marbella where they have acquired property by the sea. At this moment, they are still undecided.

"I call our mode of getting around," the Duchess said to me, "a covered wagon. No one can conceive of the complications which crowd the path of those who do not fly. Since the Duke and I never travel alone, our journeys always are a big production. We have given up yachting, for I find women who are no longer young look absolutely terrible in trousers and, of course, they are the only sensible type of outfit for that kind of life. They are so easy to press: blouses and skirts are not. I am most intrigued by the way everyone and everything is on the move today. Older persons take on the most harrowing, uncomfortable treks and think nothing of sleeping under tents. Unfortunately a casual journey, which used to be such a joy, is no longer possible, since every hotel and motel is jammed and plans must be made long in advance. This has taken much pleasure out of trips as far as I am concerned."

When I asked her how she managed to run two such efficient households and was thinking about beginning a third one, she replied, "It is an all-day, all-lifetime job. While I still care terribly, the majority of people no longer do. Travel for them now comes first, and a house has become a station where they deposit their bags between flights. Good food used to be a leading item in entertaining, with the French never failing to take a second helping. But today they too are mesmerized by their doctors, who have advised them to eat sparely. No one takes fruit any more and it just rots away in the kitchen. Since guests now become restless if they stay in one place too long, I have given up serving coffee in the dining room."

Paris is still, in her opinion, the center of elegance, but parties have changed enormously in their recipe. Since everyone is away for such long periods, when friends entertain they do so on a large scale, which is easier since it takes less thought and time than assembling a few who are both homogeneous and stimulating. The Duchess also said that she was not knowledgeable about night clubs, since she rarely goes to them now. "One may not feel old but one looks it," she remarked. This is the only nonsense I have ever heard her utter. She truly does not appear a day older today than she did when I first met her over two decades ago.

The Bourbons are the greatest source of anxiety and distraction in N.S. There are so many of them that it is difficult to turn around without bumping into one. Since many of them are bright and attractive, they are considered a great addition to a dinner or house party and anyone in the jet set must seriously study his *Almanac de Gotha* (it is such good news that it is being published again) to try and unravel who is who.

The safest rule with the Bourbons is to find out first to which of the many branches they belong since few of the various groups really like one another. There are the Bourbons of Spain, the Bourbon-Orleans of France, the Bourbon–Two Sicilies, who should be Italian but at this point are likely to have other nationalities, the Bourbon-Parmes, who are several dozens—all bearers of different passports and residences, the Bourbon-Parme-Luxembourg, the Bourbon-Busset and the Bourbon-Chalus (these last two are no longer royal and therefore curtsies are not necessary). Then there are the Orleans-Braganças, who don't carry the Bourbon appellation but who are very much Bourbons.

Despite the confusing fact that some turn up their noses at the others, they have intermarried within the various sects. Often, therefore, a Bourbon princess goes to the altar and returns without changing her surname. Not only do these girls wed relatives, but sometimes, with special dispensations from the Pope, they wed their own uncles. There are a few fireflies to lead the way into the Bourbon Jungle, the most luminous being the custom followed by several of the Bourbon–Two Sicilies gentlemen who picked their brides from among highly aristocratic Polish families. If this slight Slavic accent makes them more easily recognizable amidst this huge royal herd, it is also the cause of many complications. The various successors to the last King of Naples and the two Sicilies, who have now joined the ranks of Pretenders, have invariably assigned royal rank to these Polish ladies on the day of their marriage, but the Spanish Bourbons have refused to recognize this elevation and, therefore, do not accept the children born from these unions as royal.

In Spain, in fact, they have never given in an inch on this point. Despite her eminently blue pedigree, Emanuela de Dampierre was never raised to royal status at the time she was married to the Duke of Segovia, the late King's son. Therefore, some experts claim that her two sons, Alfonso and Gonzalo, among the most attractive bachelors in Europe, are Princes of

Bourbon but not Royal Highnesses. They are so charming, however, all the ladies curtsy to them with joy.

Once one gets onto the Bourbon game—for that is what it is—one realizes how delightful it is. It reminds me of those vast puzzles that are sent, to while the time away when hospitalized. The mosaic is so gigantic it is impossible to finish piecing it together. Whether in Paris, Madrid, Lisbon, Rio de Janeiro, Vienna, Rome, Sevilla (where many of them make their headquarters), Brussels, or on the French Riviera, seating two Bourbons at the same dinner (one is easy) becomes an obsession, and each hostess finally concludes that this is a match from which she emerges defeated.

In the younger generation of the Bourbon–Two Sicilies there are nineteen members, but in the Bourbon-Parmes there are several dozens. There were twenty-three children alone from the two marriages of the late Duke Robert of Parma. Since many of these sons and daughters, all born at some distance from each other, followed their father's example and have begotten masses of children, to try to establish which generation they belong to becomes a fantastic riddle. Brothers and sisters are so spaced they look like fathers and daughters, aunts and nephews.

Let's be honest about it. Royalty still exerts a great fascination because of its authority to issue decorations. In principle, only the reigning ones should do this, but there are many exceptions to this rule, since most of those in exile or who were dethroned long ago continue to do so to everyone's great delight.

Much excitement can still arise over which prince has the right to bestow a certain order. In connection with one decoration, European aristocracy is completely divided into two fierce camps, just as in the times of the Guelphs and Ghibellines. If the reader should get lost in the story he can rest assured that much effort has gone into trying to simplify it as much as possible. Head of the Bourbon–Two Sicilies clan, up until his death in 1961, was a fine old gentleman by the Shakesperian appellation of Ferdinando, Duke of Calabria. Among his many brothers were Don Carlos and Don Rainier. As the Generalissimo of this vast clan, the Duke of Calabria was the direct-in-line heir to the nonexistent throne of Naples and the two Sicilies, the father of several daughters (no son), and most significant of all, the dispenser of the Holy and Military Constantinian Order of Saint George. The latter is a great favorite with decoration-loving persons because of its historical background, its enchantingly bejeweled design, and its lovely pale blue color.

Long ago the Duke had designated his younger brother, Don Rainier, as the heir of the pretenders to the throne and the order, skipping his other brother, Don Carlos. There was an excellent reason for this. An edict of Charles III, King of Spain, declared explicitly that no Bourbon Prince could aspire to two crowns, and at the time of his marriage to the heiress to the Spanish throne, Maria Mercedes, Don Carlos had to officially renounce his eventual rights to the Neapolitan succession. As bad luck would have it, his wife never became Queen of Spain, since her younger brother superseded her and eventually became King Alfonso XIII. After her death, Don Carlos took on a second wife, a Princess of the Bourbon-Orleans branch, begetting more children from this marriage. From the first there was a son, Don Alfonso, and from the second, Princess Esperanza, and the Countess of Barcelona. At the time Don Carlos died in 1949, nothing happened; but when the Duke of Calabria was called to the heavenly kingdom in 1961, all hell broke loose. The Duke's nephew, Don Alfonso, promptly declared that his father's renunciation was worthless, since his mother had never become Queen of Spain and therefore it was he, not his aging uncle Don Rainier, who inherited the pretensions to the Neapolitan throne and the authority to dispense the wonderful order.

Wasting no time, he took himself to Rome, called on the

Pope, and began assigning the decoration to many prominent persons. In their hurry to show off this lovely thing, they all accepted it without realizing the noisy storm which promptly burst over their heads.

Prince Rainier, the old uncle of Alfonso, who considers himself the only pretender and dispenser, immediately began his dramatic counterattack. He found in the Marchesa Matilda Serra di Capriola the most splendid of allies. She rallied all the Neapolitan aristocracy and middle class (the Bourbons are still adored in southern Italy, and whenever they go there, their reception is very touching) to his cause. Don Alfonso, who was en route to Naples, did not continue his journey and returned to his home in Madrid where Spaniards backed him enthusiastically.

In the meantime, since Alfonso died in 1964, the battle is currently being fought by his personable son, Don Carlos, who recently became the son-in-law of the Count of Paris by marrying the adorable Princesse Anne.

Nothing is more palpitating than royal gossip, and it is being whispered around that the Count of Barcelona, who is the accepted titular head of the Spanish Bourbons (although his brother, the Duke of Segovia, does not subscribe to this), is backing his step-nephew Don Carlos in this historical struggle. Apparently his attitude is prompted not only by the fact that it is nice to keep such a stunning decoration within the family, but also by the fact that Don Rainier is married to one of those patrician Poles whom the Spanish Bourbons refuse point blank to recognize as having been elevated to royal rank. Although both Don Rainier and Don Carlos continue to invest some lucky people with the order of Saint George, the wise Count de Paris is taking no sides. In order not to offend Don Rainier, gossip is that he insisted that, in the invitations to the wedding of his daughter to Don Carlos, the prefix "Two Sicilies" be dropped.

German royalty is the only one that presents few riddles in

N.S. since it rarely emerges from the Schlosses to mix with the globe-trotters. They are legion and perfectly happy to share each other's company. There are so many of them that they can marry within their own spheres and maintain certain standards that may appear out of date to some but are eminently satisfactory to them. Their marriages are splendid occasions to which many of the royal clans are invited.

The localities where the royally minded nomads are the most apt to run into their idols are Madrid, the Geneva-Lausanne region, and Lisbon. It is here that the greatest concentration of former rulers, hopeful future sovereigns, and Royal Highnesses can be found. Vera Espirito Santo, one of the most well liked hostesses in the Portuguese capital, was heard to say one day that the constant curtsying ladies were subjected to in the local society prevented arthritis from ever settling in the knees.

In the region surrounding Lisbon are Umberto of Italy, his sister ex-Queen Giovanna of Bulgaria, the Count and Countess of Barcelona, the Count and Countess of Paris (in the summer), the Countess's sister Maria Theresa Orleans-Bragança, and her commoner husband, Ernesto Martorell, and the widow of Carol of Roumania, currently known as Princess Helen of Hohenzollern. Also in evidence are members of the former Portuguese ruling family including Philippa of Bragança, a sister of the Portuguese pretender Don Duarte, who has been assigned an estate near Coimbra by the government, where he lives with his wife, another sister of the Countess de Paris and of Don Pedro, one of the pretenders to the Brazilian crown.

The Spanish capital is positively swarming with Royal Highnesses. The most prominent are the Infante Don Juan Carlos and his consort, Sophie of Greece, who have been recognized by the Iberian authorities as the future occupiers of the throne when the opportune moment arrives. But also very much on view are the Infante's first cousins Alfonso and Gonzalo (some Spaniards would rather see the former receive the coveted assignment); Don Carlos Bourbon–Two Sicilies with his wife

Anne of France; Hugues Bourbon-Parme and his handsome consort Irene of the Netherlands; ex-King Simeon of Bulgaria and his Margareta; the giantlike pretender to the Albanian throne, Leka, and his mother, former Queen Geraldine; the various Bavarian descendants of Alfonso XII's sister; and innumerable other relations of the former ruling family.

In the Geneva-Lausanne region we have ex-King Michael of Roumania with his wife Anne; Victoria Eugenia, widow of the last King of Spain, one of the last *grandes dames* of our era, and amusingly enough, listed in the Lausanne telephone directory as Reine d'Espagne; her daughter, the Infanta Maria Cristina, with her mate Count Marone-Cinzano; the intellectual and musically minded former Queen Marie José of Italy with her son Victor Emanuel; her husband's cousin, the Duchess of Genova, and countless others.

Two recent events struck me as indicative of the formidable buoyancy of royalty. Over a thousand Polish gypsies arrived a short time ago in Munich, some by air, others on foot, to ask hospitality of the German authorities. Their King, His Majesty Czorny, made a declaration that it was impossible for his subjects to go on living in a country that no longer had a semblance of freedom. When one of the Gypsy Queens recently died in northern Italy tens of thousands of her loyal tribesmen came from all over the continent to pay their last respects at her magnificent funeral.

The fact that gypsies, who are among the original nomads of Europe, are still so tremendously attached to their sovereigns is significant. Perhaps it is pure coincidence but it does show that nomadism and royalty are in harmony with each other. In this strange new world of caravans, gypsies not only can go on reading palms of royalty but can also advise them on the fortunes of the road.

7

American Social Leaders

Anyone with his binoculars focused on the nomadic scene cannot help being impressed by the showing the average American woman makes in it. Usually she is far more adaptable than her male counterpart and has better trained antennae. She is frequently an excellent observer, and her alert curiosity serves her in good stead. The greatest ability she displays is in coming to terms with every situation without losing her identity. Upon studying the upper echelons in the various capitals and resorts, one is struck by the solid position many U.S. members of the fair sex have achieved in each of them, either on an independent basis or through marriage with some local notable.

There is no greater chameleon than the American woman, and it is engrossing to watch this total and complete conversion to a new way of life achieved rapidly and successfully. On every side there are positive and convincing illustrations. In Florence the beautiful Marchesa di Laiatico was Aimée Russell from Islip, Long Island. Happily married to a member of the illustrious and historical Corsini family, she has not only become Italian in her point of view but so Tuscan in appearance that her noble profile today could be mistaken for one of the patrician Florentine ladies in Ghirlandaio's frescoes at Santa Maria Novella. This mesmerizing adaptability runs in the family, for the Marchesa's first cousin, Adelaide Johnson, the widow of the Count Alain d'Eudeville, is a bird of exactly the same plumage. Not only is she French in her ways and impeccable in her diction but she is a delightful exponent of that very special section of Parisian society, the old Faubourg.

In musical circles, most people assume that the gifted Metropolitan Opera coloratura soprano Gianna d'Angelo is Italian. So perfect is her knowledge of the Italian language and so identified is she with the many Latin heroines she has sung, it is hard to believe she was born in Hartford, Connecticut, has not a drop of Italian blood, and possesses a fabricated name.

In England everyone agrees that New York's Jane McMillan has become so British in the fifteen years since she married Colonel Tufton Beamish, who was knighted in 1961 and is currently M.P. for the Lews Division of East Sussex, that there is little trace of any Americanisms in Her Ladyship.

Because Americans are gregarious and enjoy having people around them, they are inveterate party givers. Wherever there is an American woman, a party cannot be too far behind. In most cases spontaneity and warmth are her greatest attributes. In the period between the World Wars some of the greatest hostesses in Europe were American. Recently two survivors from that happy era died, leaving behind a considerable void since, until their last breath, they kept the show going. The departure for the Elysian Fields of the Baroness Vincenzo Lo Monaco, who had been born Lilian Goldsol in Cleveland, Ohio, close to a century ago, and of Elsa Maxwell closed a chapter, and the new one is all the poorer for their absence. They were both unique characters whose main joy in life was to bring pleasure to their friends by entertaining them at all times.

No one ever thought the Baroness could die, for there was an aura of immortality around her. At ninety-six, she still went yachting with the Baron de Rede, danced with the enthusiasm of a schoolgirl, wore ball gowns with sweeping *décolletés,* swam like a seal, and traveled into the iron curtain countries without a maid. A convert to Christian Science, she read Mary Baker Eddy's book between parties. Despite her long, happy marriage to a Sicilian gentleman half her size who spoke no known language, she never undertook to learn Italian and her French was incomprehensible. Friends often wondered how the Baron and Baroness communicated with each other, but their Esperanto worked, for there was never a cloud on their horizon. She was a snob in the best sense of the word. She never settled for mediocrity. By closing her doors very firmly to the persons she did not deem worth knowing, she made it a privilege to be asked to the dinners which she gave wherever she might be in her incessant travels.

When, just before the Second World War, Mussolini passed some anti-Jewish laws in Italy, the Baroness, who was a Hebrew, moved to New York with the Baron, bought a house, had Salvador Dali paint a fresco, and settled there. In no time at all, she was a part of Manhattan's most exclusive drawing rooms. At a bridge table one day Doris Duke's mother is supposed to have asked her, with some condescension, her maiden name and where she came from. "I was Miss Nobody from nowhere," she replied with disarming facility.

At the war's end she returned to Rome in triumph and started again to entertain around the clock in the palace of Piazza Campitelli, as well as in her Parisian apartment in the fall and spring. At every costume ball she stood out for the originality of her conceptions and the humor with which she made herself look like the most unexpected characters, Stalin included. She always managed to keep out of quarrels, and it took much wisdom to avoid them.

When, at first, she appeared on the Roman scene, long ago, there was a formidable American to contend with. Jane Campbell, the wife of Prince San Faustino (she was Gianni Agnelli's grandmother), had galvanized the capital with her never-failing wit. When the Baroness began to show her mettle, the Princess was heard to say one day, "One American jockey can ride to victory in the Roman sweepstakes, but two will ruin the race."

Not even the Princess' family was safe from her bon mots. When her son Ranieri undertook the first of three marriages, to a nice girl from New York State, Katharine Sage, the Princess, upon leaving the wedding ceremony in Rome, sighed: "There go thirty years' snobbery out of the window." When her daughter Virginia became engaged to the enormously rich industrialist Edoardo Agnelli, she pretended she could not recall his name. Since Agnelli means lambs in Italian, she used to say "My daughter is marrying a man called Bah Bah Bah or something like that." To Count Marzotto, who was introduced to her one day on the beach of the Lido, she remarked, "I do hope that you are not richer than Edoardo. If this were so, I would be overcome with disappointment that she did not marry you instead."

It was at the Lido that the Princess, the Baroness, and Elsa Maxwell met every summer. Unlike her devoted friend the Baroness, Elsa adored a good feud, and if there was none in sight, she quickly manufactured one. Supremely conscious that nothing made better newspaper copy than a feud, she embarked upon them with an air of thrilling expectancy.

Elsa was born under the double sign of Gemini. Perhaps she was so full of intriguing contradictions because of this duality. For there were two sides to her: kindness, generosity, enormous appreciation for the arts and music, and respect for its performers, went hand in hand with a necessity to assert herself, the ability to keep the international set stirred up with her pronunciamentos, and the absolute conviction that everything she thought and said was right.

Like a child who could never accustom herself to some

wonderful new toy, Elsa never quite got over having become a world celebrity despite lack of looks, money, social position, and formal education. She could never let her intimates forget the importance in which she was held, a phenomenon which continued to intrigue her until the end. But with it all was ever present the blessed capacity of being able to laugh at herself.

The last time I saw her I escorted her to a concert in the courtyard of the palace of the Princes of Monaco. She walked with difficulty, dragging herself step by step, and several times I wondered whether she could make it. But her will was indomitable. As people clustered around us asking for her autograph, she turned to me and said, "It was all worth it just because of these nice, warm, human beings. They are my friends." That "it," she referred to, so difficult to translate into words, meant the great effort she had made for so many years to sustain the image of the celebrity. Later, after José Iturbi had finished a splendid rendition of a Beethoven Concerto, she remarked, "That was pure ambrosia. I feel so sorry for all the wretches in the world who don't love music."

The dualism was with her until the very end, the ego which had made her and the spirit which could transcend it. When, a few weeks later, the news flashed of her passing, I was not surprised. I had known that night that she was very tired and ready to depart. The cycle was closing, but it was one in which she had come out victorious because she had always been the giver. A pioneer, she established the new personage of the professional hostess and paved the way for many others. She also established that nothing was impossible and that a homely, penniless person could make of the world her splendid home.

This chapter would turn into several volumes if I were to list all the charming American ladies who have made a valid place for themselves abroad. In Rome we have legions of them; among them the Princess Chigi della Rovere (she was Miss Marian Berry, niece of the famous founder of Miss Berry's

School in Georgia); Countess Leonardo Vitetti (Nathalie Coe from Long Island); Countess Senni (Mary Gailey); Countess Alvise de Robilant (the former Elizabeth Stork from Lynchburg, Virginia); and the Marchesa Antonio Origo (Iris Cutting, a distinguished writer). In Florence there are the Countess Giangio Rucellai (Theresa Higginson from Boston) and Countess Lorenzo Emo di Capodilista (Barbara Steven), along with Mrs. Ernest Boissevain (Jean Tennyson) and Mrs. Frank Chapman (Gladys Swarthout). In Venice the Countess Carlo di Robilant was Caroline Kent of Biltmore, South Carolina.

In Paris everywhere one turns there are dozens of prominent Americans including Baroness Philippe de Rothschild (Pauline Fairfax); Countess Edouard Descazes (Caroline Scott from Richmond, Virginia); Madame Gaston de Bergery (Bettina Jones of New York City); the Vicomtesse de Bonchamps (Gale King of Hillsborough, California) and her niece the Marquise de Surian (Mildred Cowgill also from Hillsborough); Mesdames Georges Bernier (Peggy Rosenbaum of Philadelphia) and Leon Barzin (Eleanor Close, a half sister of Dina Merrill); Mrs. James Coleman, Mrs. Julian Allen, Mrs. Pinkney Tuck, Mrs. Ambrose Chambers; Mesdames André Magnus (Constance Coolidge of Boston) and De Croisset (Ethel Woodward of New York City).

In London again it's an embarrassment of choice and riches among the Countess of Bessborough (Mary Munn of Palm Beach); Mrs. Rudolph de Trafford (Kay Balkie Brooks Lo Savio); Lady Benson (Leslie Foster, formerly Mrs. Condé Nast); the Duchess of Argyll (Mathilde Mortimer); the Countess of Sefton (Josephine Armstrong of Glenns, Virginia); Mrs. Kenneth Keith (Nancy Gross who was first married to Howard Hawks and then Leland Hayward); the Duchess of Rutland (Frances Sweeny); and Lady Ogilvy (Virginia Ryan of New York).

With a vast choice among the many outstanding women the United States has sent into orbit, I found it awkward picking out a limited group. The decisions have been prompted by the particular contribution each one of these ladies has made to N.S., establishing an image or a trend that is underlined either by a marked adaptability or by the lack of it. If the leitmotiv running through all these scores is based on physical stamina and imperviousness to the difficulties of running several houses and to travel and party fatigue, it is also accompanied by the welcome strains of melodiously clinking bank accounts.

Some were born to an eminent social position, others were not but attained one. They all have their own brand of individuality, which nowadays is a far more valuable diadem to wear than a pedigree. Some are excellent linguists; others have managed to reach dazzling heights speaking only English. One of them, Lady Baillie, is only half American, but I have selected her, since she is one of countless Europeans whose American ancestry has contributed so much to her way of thinking and financial well-being.

The others represent many states, including Oregon, Kentucky, and Texas, and somewhere along the line in the huge nomadic tapestry their caravans have met or are bound to meet. Some of them are friends, others barely know one another, but they are all riding on the same carrousel. I must also include Mary Martin, for a very special reason. Because of their profession theater folks have always been extremely roving, but it's only because distances have ceased to exist that a star such as she can have a house in the Brazilian jungle and commute, backward and forward, from her tropical paradise to Broadway, London and television appearances.

When someone in Paris says, "I am dining at the Chateau of Versailles," it can only mean that Gérald van der Kemp, the Curator in Chief of this singular institution, and his American wife, Florence, are entertaining. They live, in fact, at the very end of the left wing of this most glamorous of all royal palaces, in the apartment occupied at one time by Louis XIV's outstanding Minister Colbert. A few other fortunate mortals, such as Assistant Curators, are housed in this august dwelling; but it is the Van der Kemps who are its magnets.

Despite the Dutch surname, the curator's family has been French for generations. A giant—he measures well over six feet—he dominates any assembly he is in, not only with his bulk and good looks but by his authority and responsiveness. His Jupiter-sized head is in perfect proportion to his statuesque features, consisting of a big nose, a strong chin, and pale blue eyes. It is the general consensus that he has done a fine job and that Versailles has never been better run, offered more worthwhile exhibits and spectacles, or been more alive. A man of energy and learning, he possesses a well-trained and gracious manner with all the rich benefactors of the Palace and the patience of a saint when listening with apparent interest to some of the nonsense expressed by opinionated amateurs. In his spare time he paints large, bold pictures that are a far cry from the eighteenth century with which he has been so closely identified, and he has had two exhibitions at Knoedler's in New York.

His second wife—they have been wed only a short time—is the most American woman imaginable. She has been wise enough to remain her own bright and humorous self, not assuming any airs of being an authority on art but admitting frankly where her knowledge begins and ends. I have heard it said that she is the freshest American breeze to enter Versailles since Benjamin Franklin turned up at the court of Louis XVI as envoy of the newly formed republic. Yet the captivating description Geoffrey Scott gives of Madame de Charrière in his masterpiece, *The Portrait of Zelide,* fits her like a glove. "A temperament impulsive, vital, alarming; an arrowy spirit, quick, amusing, amused."

Her father, the late Admiral Frederick B. Harris, became a very rich man through his knack for inventions, among them a clever system of sectional dry docks. Florence, who at one time wrote the Beth Blaine column for the *Washington Star* with

Phyllis Thompson (which was later taken on by Betty Beale and made her own), lived with her first husband, Donald Downs, on a farm in McLean, Virginia. Later, after her remarriage to a German, she moved to Mexico where her time was divided between a town house in the capital and a ranch near Taxco. These first two marriages brought three children. After her second divorce, she took back the surname of her first mate, and as Florence Downs appeared on the Parisian scene with her Mexican servants in tow. They are still with her and Versailles echoes again with the Spanish language, as it did at the time of Louis XIV whose Queen was a Spanish Princess. A practical hostess, at the time of her exchange of the gold bands with Van der Kemp, she sent her chef to take several accelerated Cordon Bleu courses so that he could cope with the exigencies of French cuisine.

For their large dinners—they usually give at least one a week—of thirty guests, divided into three tables to facilitate the nightmare of the protocol, she imports butlers in tails. The large midnight-blue drawing room, the smaller one, and the dining room are all candlelit. As the guests come in, they are shown the seating plan in the entrance so that when dinner is announced there is no confusion. The menu invariably consists of a fish dish, a meat entrée, salad, cheese and dessert, with quick service and little delay between the courses. As each wine is served, following the French custom, the name and vintage is announced to each guest by the steward.

Because the art of conversation is still alive in France, people talk to each other and no card playing is ever planned. Since there are always persons intrigued by furniture, objects, and pictures who are coming for the first time, there is much sightseeing in the delightfully decorated rooms. With the drive back to Paris to be considered, the evening usully breaks a little after midnight. "My main worry is not about the food," Mrs. van der Kemp told me in that incandescent, breezy manner of hers, "the French will put up with a bad dinner. But they never forgive you if they have wasted an evening being bored."

Whenever the President of the French Republic has official guests—be it the Sovereign of Morocco or Their Majesties of Denmark—there is often a large banquet organized in their honor in the Palace of Versailles, followed by a ballet performance in the exquisite theater. This sort of thing is done better in France than in any other country and it is invariably a feast for the palate, eyes, and soul. Van der Kemp is naturally much involved in these preparations, since the aesthetic responsibilities are his and his staff's.

From time to time the Van der Kemps escape to the simpler surroundings of a big house (it sleeps eighteen persons) at Grimaud, one of those attractive villages near St. Tropez. Here Florence and Gérald wear corduroy pants and entertain at informal dinners with spaghetti and red wine. Every summer they visit Mrs. Albert Lasker at La Fiorentina on Cap Ferrat, go on a yacht cruise with the Wrightsmans, and occasionally fly across the Atlantic to the apartment Florence keeps open in New York City.

Among those present at their stately Versailles dinners are likely to be two enchanting American women who have married Europeans: Her Serene Highness Princess Charles d'Arenberg and Countess Edward Bismarck, whose husband is the cultivated grandson of Germany's famous Iron Chancellor.

Baron de Cabrol said to me one day, "If Peggy d'Arenberg did not exist, she should be invented." Not a single nomad would contradict his statement. The Princess is a veritable pioneer in working out the most complicated flying timetables, which she accomplishes with infectious verve. In a society so often suffused with a touch of boredom, she simply does not know what the word means.

Scarcely thirty, the Princess already has behind her a reputation for having been, as Mrs. Thomas Bancroft, Jr., New York's youngest hostess with the mostest for several years, a position no one has filled since her divorce and remarriage in France. Born Margaret Bedford, but always known as Peggy, the only daughter of the late Frederick Bedford, who had strong Standard Oil connections, she showed from an early age her capacity to become an international figure. Today, be it Marbella, Biarritz, Formentor, Katmandu, Caracas, or Palermo, hers is a household name as one of the great caravan leaders and party givers.

What makes her unique is a combination of enormous sweetness and untold determined energy. While her good friends and co-international vedettes Jacqueline de Ribes and Ira Fürstenberg change their appearances daily, Peggy d'Arenberg is always the same, year in and year out, looking exactly as she did ten years ago. She never changes her style, and had she lived in the time of Gainsborough she would have become his favorite model. Blonde, with the most lovely skin imaginable, pale blue eyes, a ravishing smile, the countenance of someone who lives entirely on milk and honey, a youthful figure which she keeps erect, and clothed in light blues and pinks, she establishes the impression that she is the quintessence of naturalism. She takes no chances, however, and when in Paris she is at Elizabeth Arden's or at Guillaume's hair salon every afternoon. There she does much of her telephoning. Among all those Balmain and Balenciaga pink and Alice-blue dresses, she studies at length which is the most suited to her mood and face for a particular occasion.

When she reaches a party, usually late, she inundates it with rays of a northern crystalline sunshine which never fails to beguile. There is a childlike quality about her which is ever endearing, and never, in all the years I have known her, has she looked uninterested. She is a party girl par excellence and each one brings her a new pleasure. If it is humanly possible, she inevitably turns up and rises out of the ashes of yesterday's fête in London to give her all to today's in Colombo or tomorrow's in Papeete.

At the time of her divorce from handsome but non-party-minded Tommy Bancroft and her second matrimonial venture into one of Europe's oldest and most distinguished former ruling clans—there are various branches of the d'Arenbergs in Germany, Belgium, and France—there were predictions that in order to be the great success in Paris she had been in New York she would have to modify some of her habits. They all claimed that her lateness, considered amusing in Manhattan, would not be condoned in the French capital.

This prophecy did not come off, for these persons were unaware of the astonishingly disarming force that emanates from Peggy. It is impossible to get angry at her. A hostess will be having an absolute fit—really this is too much, she will be crying, the soufflé is hopelessly ruined, oh why did I let the chef talk me into one, never has she been this late—and the Princess finally enters with that adorable face of hers, mumbling some lavender-colored excuse, and all is promptly forgiven. The hostess is so pleased to see her that she embraces her and thanks her for having come at all.

Despite being one of those persons who is congenitally late, Peggy is a lady through and through, and the French cannot help but appreciate this quality. One of the reasons she is a topnotch hostess is that she knows who might be interested in talking to whom. The shooting parties she organizes with her husband at the family chateau of Menetou-Salon, rising out of a beautiful forest near Bourges, are exceedingly well thought out in every detail, down to what books or magazines a guest might enjoy reading in his room. So are her large dinners at Paris' Chez Maxim's, or Rasputin's, held there before her new mansion was ready. They invariably prove to be great fun because of the wonderful mixture of friends from all over the globe.

The Prince, who was born on time and is correctness personified, accepts his wife's special timetable with a wisdom dictated by his breeding and a philosophical acceptance of the inevitable. When on a journey, she surprises everyone by arising in the morning at the scheduled hour and underlining her sightseeing with much enthusiasm and an excellent photographic sense. If and when moon travel will be feasible, the Princess will be one of the first passengers, since there are not many corners of the world left for her to inspect.

Prince Charles is a fine shot, and in the fall is all over Europe, going from one expedition to another. He is also the head of the Rallye Vauzeron-Sologne's Chasse à Courre, and his riding prowess is much admired. His wife's immense energy is never channeled into sports, the reason undoubtedly being that the hours she keeps so seldom coincide with the outdoor calendar. However, after luncheon she does sometimes follow her husband's guests on shoots, wearing magnificent tweeds and fancy geometrical woolen stockings. In Spain she attends the corridas which conveniently start at six o'clock in the afternoon.

The Princess's lack of interest in sports is shared by Countess Edward Bismarck. Pulchritude experts agree that in the twentieth-century Venus would have guided Paris to the doorstep of the Countess, but nothing as dramatic as setting sail to a thousand ships or starting a war has happened in the life of the Kentucky-born lady. The reason can perhaps be attributed to the fact that, being a philosopher, the Countess has heeded Voltaire's advice and cultivated her garden.

As in the case of the mythological Queen of Sparta, the cruel passage of time has been unable to leave its traces on her extraordinary looks. Hers was and is forever the classical Grecian profile, taut bone frame, perfectly symmetrical nose, and poetic brow. But it is the eyes, pools of magic, which are spellbinding, and all the more arresting because of the very marked, but harmonious, distance that separates them. Their hue varies constantly from lapis lazuli and burnished emerald green to phosphorescent blue.

When she makes one of her rare public appearances, she

never fails to create a sensation. The few times during the summer season when she walks into the Piazza of Capri, the sudden stillness that descends upon the babel of voices is the signal that the island's Sovereign has arrived.

It is in Capri that she is at her happiest. Here she can indulge in her absorbing hobby and passion, gardening, the logical fulfillment of her early life in the Bluegrass country. Her botanical knowledge is staggering, and her green thumb all the more evident on this island, where, because of the rocky soil and lack of irrigation, there are usually no gardens. This challenge has proved an irresistible one, and at her estate, Il Fortino, on all the various terraces descending to the vibrant blue sea, she has succeeded in growing a variety of camelias and magnolias, wild crocus, cyclamen, iris, narcissus, and orchids, every possible variety of lilies, campanulas, and medinillas, all interspersed in groves of judas trees and oleanders and with the delicious perfume of jasmine impregnating the air.

Armed with baskets, scissors, and seeds, the Countess directs the work of several gardeners, who all admit that her eye is so discerning that nothing escapes her. In the nineteen-thirties her third husband, Harrison Williams (she had been married previously to Harry Schlesinger and James Bush), bought her this ravishing hill, the site of an ancient Roman villa, facing the bay of Naples, and she has transformed it with loving care into a corner of paradise. With foresight, way ahead of other jetsetters, she erected several low cottages independent from one another. Some have the sliding walls of Japanese homes, which can be opened in the summer so that, high on the promontory, there is always a breeze. The entrancing flower beds are all up and down paths and terraces on many different levels. Much of the earth had to be carried here, for the volcanic terrain was absolutely bare. Much of the water still has to be transported, at great expense, from Naples.

So complete is the privacy enjoyed by its owners that nothing can be seen from the road going up from Marina Grande to the town of Capri or from the sea. In recent years, after the death of Harrison Williams and her later remarriage, she has spent more time in Capri than before. In the summer the Bismarcks entertain on a breathtaking esplanade that looks over a forest of pine and olive trees, precipitously succeeded by honey-colored cliffs, and the shimmering Tyrrhenian Sea with, in the distance, the enchanting silhouette of Vesuvius appearing like an early Chinese etching.

Here late lunch and late dinner are served under umbrellas and awnings. Since she and her husband keep Spanish hours, they are fortunate in having Spanish servants who understand them. Exceedingly hospitable, they usually have house guests and never fail to entertain at dinner all the nomads they know who pause at Capri on board their yachts. It is easy to understand why the owners can so rarely be tempted to leave their serene domain even for a meal for it undoubtedly is one of the most hauntingly radiant private properties anywhere.

Although she has many times been on the best-dressed lists, it does not matter whether the Countess is wearing a Balenciaga ball gown or simple bucolic clothes. The intuitive Salvador Dali was so conscious of this lack of importance of clothes in her case that when he painted her portrait long ago he represented her barefoot in a dress which goes from an embroidered top to a tattered skirt. It is the eyes which command the picture and hold the viewer in a trance. The painting hangs over the fireplace of one of the superb drawing rooms in the Bismarck Hotel Particulier in the Quai de New York in Paris, facing the Eiffel Tower. In their collection are two fine Goyas and Tiepolos.

The Bismarcks never stay in Paris long. Apart from the trips to the United States, where the Countess still owns a town house in New York and a large estate on Long Island Sound, there are journeys to Rome, London, Dublin, to various flower shows held here and there, and to Germany where the Count has many relatives. There are also many marriages to attend in castles along the Rhine and of various members of European royal families.

The Countess's story is a tantalizing one, for in her various incarnations she was wise enough never to let go of her strong attachment for the earth and nature. Daughter of a well-known horse trainer, she stepped on the world stage with her third marriage to the utilities magnate, Harrison Williams. With magnificent houses everywhere, great wealth, unsurpassed jewels, and all a person can wish or desire, she remained basically simple. Pettiness and malice have never entered her makeup, but once someone is out of her life, the door is shut. There is no possible re-entry, as a couple who acquired a mansion of hers learned. Although she never discusses her experience with them, except to state that it was very unnerving, she is adamant about never attending a party that includes them.

Upon meeting her at a dinner in the dead of winter and learning she was off the next day to Capri, a far from ideal resort at that time of year, I asked her why. Her simple, direct answer gives a clue to her character. "I must go and see how my best friend is getting along," she replied. Someone, not very "hep," who was present at the conversation, asked me later who this friend was. But I did not even try to explain. In the jet age there are few Mona Bismarcks left who care to see their garden grow.

If Capri has only one Queen, Nassau has three. It is amazing to discover that the three, all of them very rich widows of the international set, are friendly and no boring sense of competition exists among them.

Lady Baillie, Mrs. Izaak Killam,* and Mrs. Charles Munroe remain in residence and in their respective mansions for several

* Since the book was written, Mrs. Killam has died. However, no coverage of Nassau in recent years would be complete without her.

weeks every winter and amidst the incessant coming and going, form a nucleus of steadiness around which much of the social life of the island revolves. Lady Baillie and Mrs. Killam, who live on a far more luxurious scale than Mrs. Munroe, are surrounded at all times by a veritable retinue of courtiers.

The prodigiously wealthy Lady Baillie not only never brags about her riches but underplays them. It has taken a very special genius on her part, through the years, to keep out of the public eye. As Olive Paget, no one could have been born to more prestige, position, or money than she. With her father, Lord Queensborough, providing a marvelous British background and her mother, Pauline Whitney, an equally glorious one in the United States, she had everything. It was her grandfather, William C. Whitney, who founded the illustrious dynasty and fortune.

The old adage "The rich get richer" applies to Lady Baillie. Her unmarried sister, Dorothy Paget, who grew to be enormously fat, was one of Europe's most discussed eccentrics. She loathed men to such an extent that she communicated with them mainly through the mail and lived at night, scheduling all her business appointments after sunset. When she died recently, she left no will. Therefore, despite the state of deep freeze which her relationship had reached with her sister—they had not said "How do you do" in years—Lady Baillie inherited everything.

She originally acquired Leeds Castle, a Tudor masterpiece encircled by water in the most romantic frame imaginable, with her sister but later bought her out. Being a meticulous perfectionist of impeccable standards, she spent fifteen years with Jansen's famous Stephane Boudin decorating it. Those who know what five minutes of this gentleman's time costs cannot help but be overwhelmed. The result achieved is pure magic. Apart from the unsurpassed aesthetic enjoyment, Lady Baillie's American heritage has come to the fore. Every possible modern gadget has been installed, and the staff is superb.

Several domestics precede their employer to Nassau every winter, thereby enriching the BOAC by a large number of fares. In their fore goes Mister Cooper, a master electrician and carpenter, to attend to the inevitable repairs every dwelling in in a tropical climate needs yearly.

Although Lady Baillie appears shy and reticent, she has been married three times and had a corresponding number of divorces. (The Honourable Charles Winn, who lasted six years, was followed by Arthur Wilson-Filmer for an equal period. Sir Adrian Baillie outlasted the two others by seven years.) Gray-haired and spectacled, she passes unobserved in a crowd, but this is hardly true in drawing rooms where people make the greatest fuss over her. The direct way to her heart is either a pack of cards—she craves bridge and canasta—or birds. An ornithology enthusiast, she devotes time and energy to elaborate aviaries in both Nassau and Leeds. Actually she owns so many birds that there always seems to be one which has just died. There are sad periods when there is often a burial every day.

Her son, Sir Gawain Baillie—he succeeded to the baronetcy upon his father's death in 1947—is a source of constant worry to his mother, since he is passionately fond of racing in his fast sports cars. He and his stepsisters, Mrs. Geoffrey Russell and Mrs. Boyd de Brossard, are apt to visit their mother in Nassau as well as at the villa "La Canzone del Mare" at St. Jean, Cap Ferrat. Her Ladyship's exquisite house in London is on Lowndes Square.

Frequent members of Lady Baillie's entourage—they appear for visits in all her various houses—are Viscount Margesson (Secretary of War in the early years of the Second World War), the Honourable Geoffrey Lord (who was Minister of Education in the last decade), the Marchioness of Huntly (Lord Kemsley's only daughter), Mrs. Charles Payson (a member of the Whitney clan and owner of "The Mets"), the Norman Armours, Bert Whitley who gave up the stage to become a favorite extra man all around the globe), George and Lydia Gregory, Mrs. Lyon Slater, John Galliher, and Chessie and Iva "Pat" Patcevitch, one of the most attractive couples on the international circuit. He is the Russian-born head of Condé Nast Publications and possessed with that indefinable Slavic charm which is characteristic of so many of the pre-Bolshevists.

Since Lady Baillie does not become intimate with people easily, Nassau residents were astonished to discover one day that she had become such a good friend of Mrs. Izaak Walton Killam, her neighbor on Paradise Island. There are infinite versions about how this surprising connection started. The most frequently told is that all activities in the large Baillie household came to a halt as a result of an electrical strike on the island. It was discovered that all the pumps worked to perfection in her neighbor's residence, since Mrs. Killam, being a provident person, has her own electric system. Since Mrs. Killam actually lives in another mansion in town and uses the one on Paradise Island only for swimming and picnics, she made its facilities available to Her Ladyship and her many house guests. But there were more lovely surprises in store: an olympic-sized heated swimming pool and the most magnificent gardens, also heated, all in the care of the famous Belgian landscape gardener, Van Bruggen, who had first been imported to the island by the late Axel Wenner-Gren.

Gossip is that, in order to show her gratitude for the courtesies received, Lady Baillie extended an invitation to her new friend to come and visit her in Leeds. It was accepted, and as is her custom, she arrived with a suite consisting of a maid, two nurses (she is always ailing), her butler, Mr. Perugia, a hairdresser, a masseur, a chauffeur, and a detective. She immediately asked her hostess to please advise her about which nearby country inn might accommodate her group. "Fiddledee," Lady Baillie is reported to have replied, "I have never heard any such nonsense. They will all stay right here at the Castle." Even the rich can be impressed with their fortunate colleagues, and one hears that Mrs. Killam was overcome with the ease with which the chatelaine met the sudden housing problem.

But the best was yet to happen. Mrs. Killam rented La Fiorentina, one of the beautiful villas on the Riviera owned by the Countess of Kenmare (she collects them), and Lady Baillie came to stay. Quite casually, one hears, Gianni Agnelli emerged from the sea one day and in his bathing trunks came to call on his old friend, Olive Baillie. This little visit led him to invite the Killam house party for dinner at his La Leopolda, the most splendid of all the mansions in the South of France, with a glorious view, a magnificent allée of cypresses, a delightful round swimming pool, a terrace to end all terraces, and a series of Empire-styled drawing rooms. Mrs Killam became so enthusiastic over it that she insisted on buying it. When the information leaked out that a deal had been made, Riviera residents could not believe their ears. At the time Agnelli had acquired La Leopolda, right after the war, the villa was going for a song. It is reported that he resold it for three million dollars.

It was the end of an era for, during the ownership of the Italian industrialist, which lasted almost two decades, it had become the mecca for all the chic-est people in the world. Mrs. Killam's regime is different, for she is apt to be somewhat dictatorial with her guests. A believer in olympic-sized swimming pools, she is busy adding one, and since she admires Lady Baillie's taste, she hired Monsieur Boudin to redo the villa's decor. On the Riviera, as everywhere else, a detective accompanies Mrs. Killam wherever she goes in the evenings to keep a vigilant eye on her necklaces and bracelets.

But who is Mrs. Killam? She was Dorothy Johnson from St. Louis, and is that rare specimen in the jet set, a woman who has been married only once. Only since the death of her Canadian husband has this lady stepped onto the international stage. He adored her so that his will is reported to have been one of the shortest on record. All it said was "I leave everything to my beloved wife Dorothy."

"Everything" supposedly consisted, among other gifts, of the Calgary waterworks, which supply water to the state of Saskatchewan, several banks, newspapers, and paper mills. In Wall Street it is figured that she is worth well over one hundred million dollars, and the chances are that her clever business sense is making her richer every hour. Among her other headquarters are a house in Montreal, a fishing camp in northern Canada, and a huge apartment on East End Avenue in New York acquired from Mrs. Vincent Astor.

Often dressed in long, flowing black robes, Dorothy Killam commands immense authority. Unlike Lady Baillie, who enters a room like a mouse, the Canadian millionairess enters with the assurance of a veteran general. In appearance, however, she suggests more an aging Florentine page, with her yellowish hair worn shoulder length in true Renaissance style.

Hairdressing is constantly on her mind. Gossip has it that when she charters a yacht she is much concerned about her coiffeur's comforts and is more likely to give him a single cabin than some of the guests. The story is told that when she went to visit Harry and Ruth du Pont at their celebrated house at Winterthur in Delaware she was unhappy because, despite their superb collection of Americana, they simply could not, at a few minutes' notice, supply her with a hair dryer.

Her stoicism is much admired by her friends. A few summers ago she hired a Swedish cadet ship, *The Flying Clipper,* for a Mediterranean cruise. Despite the delightful crew of handsome Scandinavian future officers, impeccably attired in their summer uniforms, all sorts of things went wrong. Something happened to the boiler so that there was scarcely any hot water during the trip, and just at the time of the worst heat wave, while the group was navigating around those barren Greek islands, the air-conditioning unit broke down. Her guests report that she took these adversities magnificently with the spirit of a true Missouri pioneer.

The third great hostess in Nassau, Mrs. Charles Munroe, lives on Cable Beach, amidst a verdant oasis of green, in a pink villa which is not at all splashy but comfortable and snug. In the drawing room, over the fireplace, hangs a superb version of Monet's "Lilies in a Pond." Liable to stay here four months of the year, since she has no other permanent home, she roams the rest of the time. She is a true wayfarer, taking her immense zest for life wherever she goes and making all her friends the richer for it.

Three times a widow and the mother of two sons, Rudolph Schirmer and Philip Benkard, she was born Ann Ditchburn in the state of Oregon. Gifted with a radiant voice, she studied singing in New York City and became, under the stage name of Ann Swinburne, such a first-rate musical comedy star that Victor Herbert wrote *The Madcap Duchess* for her. Her love for music has never faltered, and she renounced her skyrocketing career only to marry into the solid and well-established musical publishing family of the Schirmers. Today she is still an invaluable member of their Board of Directors. Her musical knowledge is genuine, and she is a familiar figure at the Spoleto, Bayreuth, and Salzburg (where she always rents a house) Festivals every year. An intimate friend of many of the musical great, she undertakes long journeys to hear anything new in which they are involved. An enthusiastic supporter of Samuel Barber and Gian Carlo Menotti from the very beginning of their careers, she has followed each step they have undertaken with something close to maternal pride.

She entertains often and easily, wherever she is. If it's Paris, it will be Maxim's; if London, Claridge's. Excellent at mixing people of all nationalities, she is enough of a linguist to cope with a professor of some German University or a French musicologist if it proves necessary. Restless in a gypsy-like manner, she moves incessantly with her small caravan, consisting of a maid and her English chauffeur, Sims, in a luxurious Mercedes, and rapidly puts up her tents, feeling at home everywhere. To be free to do what pleases her, upon the death of her husband she sold the huge Chateau of St. Jean on Cap Ferrat to Detroit's Ernest Kanzler.

In the thirty years I have known her, her spirit has not changed and her enthusiasm for everything she undertakes—the swim before breakfast in Nassau in the amethyst-tinted sea in front of her bedroom, the daily game of golf and cards, and the pause at the piano to go over a Mozart sonata ("It relaxes me so," I have heard her say often)—is part of the bubble of a charming human being unspoiled by riches or success. In Nassau she chooses her guests from all walks of life and they are apt to be Manhattan's dowager with the mostest, Mrs. William Woodward, Sr., Loelai, Duchess of Westminster, Conductor Thomas Schippers, lawyer Henry Hyde, or theatrical producer Gilbert Miller and his Kitty.

The latter couple have their own island home for the summer months in Mallorca, having recently built one in the new development of Costa de los Pinos, an enchanting cove about one hour's drive from both Palma and Formentor. There is no village but a series of emerald green pine forests descending to the Mediterranean Sea. Here, along with the Millers are, among others, the residences of the Spanish Foreign Minister Fernando Castiella, the Ambassador to England and the Marquesa de Santa Cruz, Countess Gaby Seefried and the Marquesa de Narros.

Although all these Spaniards naturally speak English, portly Gilbert Miller, who has just celebrated his eightieth birthday, is proficient in the Iberian language, having enjoyed part of his education in Spain. An excellent raconteur, he holds dinner partners spellbound with tales of all the great stage personalities and authors he has known. The Millers have only two guest rooms in their white villa, which is right on the sea and complete with a swimming pool excavated out of the rocks, and they are always filled with English and American friends. The interior is not at all Spanish in feeling.

An expert on comfort, Kitty Miller always runs her various households with precision and care. She trains her servants down to the last detail, and no one takes more trouble than she with menus, which she studies every evening with perspicacity, crossing out some suggestions, penciling in others.

Casualness is not one of her traits, and her background plays a part in this picture. She is the daughter of the late financial wizard, Jules Bache, and it is from her father that she inherited not only a delightful income but a clear, incisive, alert mind. Etruscan in looks, with a long, chiseled face, a high forehead and a full chin, she is no one to be forgotten easily. She immediately establishes an impression of impeccable neatness and fastidiousness. Despite her cool appearance, she is a warm friend, so much so that at times she gets carried away by her emotions and takes sides in some dispute in which a pal may find himself. Since fewer and fewer people bother to do this nowadays, not really caring any more who is right or wrong, her crusading friendships are apt to be a subject of conversation in jet-set circles.

Although the Millers spend the winters in Manhattan, the rest of the year finds them in Europe. In England they own two houses, a ravishing Georgian-styled dwelling in the center of London, five floors high, and one in the country. The latter dates from 1238 when it was erected to serve as a summer habitation for the Bishop of Chichester. There are several buildings on the 150-acre estate. One of them is called the Jaipur cottage since the Maharajah and Maharanee stay in it every year for Goodwood week when he is playing polo in nearby Cowdray.

Whether in Manhattan, Great Britain, or Mallorca, Kitty invariably lives up to her reputation as a great international hostess. When I asked for her recipe for a successful party, she answered, "The most important factor is for the hostess to want to have a good time and enjoy herself. Therefore I always start with a list of attractive people and as few obligations as possible. The wine and champagne must be the best, also the music. The decorations are the least important and do not make a good evening."

Two annual parties which the Millers give have become a tradition. In New York, ever since 1940, they entertain about fifty close friends at a big dinner on New Year's eve in their Park Avenue apartment. About one hundred more are asked in later for a dance which takes place in the lovely drawing room, cleared of some of the furniture, right under the inquisitive eyes of Don Juan Osorio, the enchanting little boy painted by Goya. In London, their annual dinner dance is one of the social events of the season. It is held during the first week of July at the Hotel Savoy since the house proves too small for so many guests.

In London's U drawing rooms one runs into the Baron and Baroness Leo d'Erlanger. So marked is the latter's southern accent that it hardly seems credible that, in the three decades that she has been married and lived abroad, she has lost none of her delicious Dixie inflections. Edwina Prue, daughter of a Virginian father and Texan mother, was brought up on a ranch in New Mexico and, after some schooling in California, worked as a model for Patou in Paris and for *Vanity Fair* and *Vogue* magazines in New York City. When she became the Baron's wife in 1934, she entered one of the most fascinating families on the continent. So mixed is her husband's heritage that it would take oceans of ink to describe it. Suffice it to say that in his veins runs the blood of a brilliant Jewish banker from Frankfurt, who started the family fortunes; of Miss Mathilde Slidell, whose father was the Commissioner to Paris of the Confederate States; and of Roman black papal aristocracy, who provided Pope Leo XIII with a Chamberlain—hence his name Leo. The D'Erlangers moved first from Germany to Paris and then, a century ago, to London.

Leo's father, Baron Rodolphe, was unusual in many fields of endeavor, but his lasting contribution consisted of his work in Arabic music. In the magnificent palace he built for himself in the bay of Carthage, near the most beautiful of all African towns, Sidi Bou Said, he pursued his studies of the difficult scales with an orchestra at his constant disposal. His talented wife wrote felicitous poems and sang German lieder, accompanying herself on the piano.

It was no easy task to become a member of such an erudite clan, but Edwina has been equal to it. Upon the death of her in-laws, her husband inherited the North African properties. Their olive and almond groves in Southern Tunisia, into which so much money and affection had been poured, have been nationalized, along with other farms belonging to Europeans, but Sidi Bou Said has remained and here the D'Erlangers spend several months of the year. The site of this Arabian fantasy is considered by archeologists to be where Hannibal's father, Hamilcar Barca, had the palace from which he used to search for Roman galleons coming into the bay. When the property was first acquired, there was little vegetation. Today the brilliant white dwelling emerges amidst groves of eucalyptus and cypress trees, the gardens a mass of oleanders, hibiscus, jasmine, and bougainvillea.

In North Africa, as well as in their two English residences, the Baron and Baroness keep open house. The servant problem in Tunisia is easy to cope with, for the domestics, who originally came from primitive settlements, have been in their employ for three generations. The chef, Salah, in his late thirties, knows French and Arab cuisine, alternating his menus with both types of cooking.

The D'Erlangers dislike giving large parties, but they always have people around them. Their available bedrooms are invariably occupied by friends, and diplomats from nearby Tunis often come with local acquaintances to be entertained at dinners. House guests find plenty to do. In the summer there is superb bathing off one of the nearby beaches and much sightseeing to be done in the zone. Conversation moves at a fast pace with the Baron, who is erudite and active. Apart from his banking interests, he has done much to develop civil aviation in Great Britain and currently is involved in the great undertaking of uniting, geographically speaking, England and France. He is, in fact, the Chairman of the Channel Tunnel Company. Their son, Rodolphe, a student at Harvard University, is already an ornithologist of merit.

In England the Baroness has her hands full. She runs a delightful Georgian house in London, in which is housed her collection of drawings ranging from Tiepolo to Augustus John and where she entertains at many small political or business dinners and luncheons, and a weekend cottage. This is situated near Banbury and its adjoining farm is of thirty-eight acres. Here her background comes to the fore and the atmosphere is very Southern indeed. The cook, who comes from the village, can even provide southern fried chicken at Sunday luncheon. The Baron is not apt to cross the ocean often, but his wife does in order to visit her sister, Mrs. Edward Warburg, in New York and to stay with Ronald Tree in his Barbados kingdom.

Douglas and Mary Lee Fairbanks are great friends of the D'Erlangers and often go to spend a few days with them in Sidi Bou Said. Since the actor-businessman and his Virginia-born consort are among the most popular American couples and their parties are usually considered among the best in the English capital, I asked Mary Lee, an immensely warm and natural creature, what her recipes for success were. In her spacious, sprawling, and yet cozy drawing room looking out on the Boltons Square in Kensington and surrounded by a private garden, she answered my questions in a straightforward manner.

"I am a regular hausfrau," she confessed. "While jewels and clothes play no role in my life, my house does. I adore every nook of it and my hand slides over the tables to catch the dust, my eye catches tarnished brass and I am fussy about the furniture being waxed and tended. I am lucky in having a fine staff, but I believe domestics are always pleased when someone takes as much concern in housekeeping as I do.

"Because of Douglas' varied business activities and also since we enjoy it," she continued, "we do a fair amount of entertaining. My dinners vary from six to eight to thirty-two guests. I am genuinely interested in food and wines, and I make a permanent effort in that direction. My opinion is that there must be one surprise in each party, a marvelous fish soup served in shells or yogurt soup made from cucumbers. My Hungarian chef often does exotic goulashes and if he serves a banal ice cream for dessert, then he adds an amusing sauce. Our small dinners often have more courses than the big ones, since I find that, despite all the planning behind it, it is hit or miss whether one is pleased by one's dinner partners and a long-drawn-out dinner may be too much of a good thing. At an intimate party, there is no such question for conversation tends to be general. For this reason I limit big dinners to three courses. I am very fussy about when the wine is served, for I know how helpful it is in loosening the tongue. The butler pours the first glass of white wine at the very beginning of dinner and then, as soon as the soup is taken away and before the meat is served, the red wine comes immediately.

"After the wine has been passed, the bottle is placed on the table so that the guest can serve himself again, and anyhow, it looks festive and sumptuous to have the decanters in evidence. I am a firm believer in decanting, and to everyone's surprise, I do it with champagne too. This I serve only at big dinners. We do not have a large cellar nor a checkbook that can afford a great one. It is essential, therefore, to buy wine wisely and if the hostess really cares, the wine merchant does his best to please her and gives her the best *vin ordinaire* in his stock.

Knowing, for instance, that 1961 would be a great year, I ordered several cases the moment the verdict was passed.

"It is essential," she went on, "not to overfeed the guests or they fall into a stupor and talk ebbs away into dull prattle. I never fail to consider the diet at least on one course, and I make it a point to remember whatever idiosyncrasy a certain friend has, whether he suffers from high cholesterol or allergies to fish. In certain cases, I have special dishes served and this proves flattering. China is immensely important. How can one enjoy eating food off a dark colored plate or drinking wine out of strongly colored glasses? Lace tablecloths are out. I believe in old-fashioned damask ones. I use pewter round mats, polished to look like silver since the real silver ones look too rich. Usually it's white candles all the way. I adore tables cluttered with nuts, mints, mustard pots, sea salt which looks like a series of snowflakes, Gayelord Hauser vegysalt, and also Lowry's seasoned salt. Along with peppermills, I insist on having white pepper available in shakers. If my silver does not look like water, clear and cool, I prefer to use Waterford candlesticks and bowls. On our tables we always have decanters with water, the hardest commodity to come across in Europe.

"Before dinner," Mrs. Fairbanks said, "I never serve hors d'oeuvres. They ruin a good meal. Nuts and popcorn are all right but that is all. We serve dinner after no longer than a half hour of cocktail drinking. As for cocktail parties, I loathe them so intensely that I never have them. Once a summer we give an afternoon party in the garden with a barbecue. Although it is apt to be on the cool side, there is no smoke, crowding, or noise. A form of entertainment I love is luncheons. People are never tired at that hour and enjoy a moment of relaxation during the busy day. It's also fun, since one can have actors, occupied with their professions in the evenings, and parliamentarians. Whenever I entertain for someone in particular, I always send him or her a guest list explaining who everyone is. I hate mediocre entertainers and never hire a so-so musician. If a talented friend feels like getting up and doing something, hurrah. But not otherwise. I am against shuffling guests after dinner unless there is a very beguiling one that everyone longs to talk to. But even then, I am very careful not to interrupt a discussion that appears to be of some consequence. I never forget to keep a seating plan for every party, nor the menu. I do not like repetitions. I invariably mix people. If a party is being planned for an author, I will not load the table with bankers. Nor with authors. There must always be a variety of persons who can discover several points in common."

Of all the countries in western Europe, Spain is undoubtedly by far the most singular, insular, and traditional. While it is easy to be enthusiastic about it, to become an integral part of it is no indifferent achievement. Two American women, each in her own manner, have successfully managed to identify themselves with many of the Spanish traits. Although their transformation has been necessarily incomplete, they succeed in suggesting otherwise. The Countess de Quintanilla-Romanones has become an international figure. Señora Rafaele Osborne, although also in orbit, has not. But they are both ladies to be reckoned with because of a marked individuality which Spain has helped immeasurably to bring out in them.

When I ran into Señora Rafaele Osborne at the Meurice Hotel in Paris, I could not believe this was the same person I had met some months previously at the Feria in Sevilla. The Parisian apparition was so eminently American and the previous one had been so very Spanish. As a matter of fact she had seemed so completely Andalusian that it had been a few days before I was informed in Sevilla that she had started her life as Claudia Heard in Dallas, Texas. Her jet-black hair, shiny and smooth, was classically combed and the marvelously tailored clothes had the pronounced Iberian touch of Balenciaga, who dresses her from head to toe. In Paris, she was a reddish blonde and, despite a superb red coat of the master, appeared as a healthy Westerner.

"It is easy to explain," she stated in her Texan accent. "I always revert to light hair when my husband and I go to Gstaad to spend the winter in our chalet. But the moment we return to Spain, I become a brunette again, since it is so much more becoming with the white and yellow colors I wear almost exclusively there."

Claudia has been married since 1948 to Rafaele Osborne, one of three brothers who own the famous brandy of the same name whose label dominates so much of the advertising space all over Spain. This family comes from Andalusia, the most romantic province in Europe, with its white villages, orange and lemon groves, and large clusters of gypsies. In a vast, old, magnificent country house of the early seventeenth century named Recredo, Claudia spends several months each year with her husband, who commutes to Puerto Santa Maria, a delectable town where the brandy bodegas have existed since 1772. Built in stone, with a flat roof and terraces, the house easily accommodates twenty house guests. The furniture is a combination of Spanish rustic and French Louis XVI, and the ceilings are all beamed in dark oak. There are three dining rooms in order to change the locale and atmosphere, but in the summer meals are often served in the orangerie, open on three sides.

"I like having tables of four," Señora Osborne explained, "since I find conversation is more stimulating, and it also facilitates the complicated Spanish protocol. It also fits in with my passion for china. While large sets are hard to come by, it is not difficult to find enough to serve four."

Since she dislikes the sun, which does not agree with her white skin, she does all her gardening in Balenciaga straw hats and gloves. She never joins her guests, who are apt to be business associates of her husband from all over the world or some of her Texas friends, when they go swimming at the nearby beach of Fuente Bravia. Those who want to picnic there do, but most of them return to lunch at the Recredo, since the Osbornes never sit down until four in the afternoon. Dinner, never served until eleven, is followed by flamenco every night and it lasts until at least three o'clock in the morning.

She always has a minimum of four gypsies staying in the house, sometimes more. They come from Sevilla in hired taxis and spend their days drinking coffee out of huge silver pitchers. "They are adorable," she told me, "but they are mercurial and inclined to quarrel among themselves. They loathe the country, refuse to go out, and stay indoors all day long. By the time midnight comes, they are wide awake and could go on dancing all night. At times they do." It is not difficult to entertain the house guests for there are many excellent bullfights to go to in the late afternoon in nearby towns, as well as parties given by hospitable neighbors.

The former Miss Heard's connections with Texas are far from severed. She owns a cattle ranch between Corpus Christi and Beeville to which she returns occasionally. She met her husband in Mexico and the reason Gstaad has become their winter headquarters is because their only daughter, Macarena, goes to the Marie José school there. They also have a large apartment in Madrid and their domestics, mainly from the city of Cordoba, follow them everywhere. Several times a year, because of Rafaele's business, she accompanies him to Paris and stays at the Ritz. Recently, however, on their way to and from Switzerland, they had to go to the Meurice because of the Siamese cat who traveled with them. There is a strict no-cat policy at the Ritz and it makes no exceptions for any feline subject.

Señora Osborne is, in keeping with all fashionable women, very hair conscious. I asked her how she solved her problem in the Andalusian countryside. "It used to be difficult," she replied, "so much so that I used to hire a small plane and fly to Tangiers where there was a very good coiffeur. But now Sevilla has come up with José Luis who is one of the wonders of the world. In fact, he is so great that he is deluged with offers to move to the big capitals. One of these days he will accept, but that emergency will be faced at its just time."

With marvelous lean looks and a vivid, retentive intelligence as her passport, Aline Griffith arrived in Spain during the Second World War from her home in Pearl River, New York, to work for the Office of Strategic Services. It is to her tremendous credit that from a pretty small town girl she has blossomed into one of the beauties of her generation, developed a fashion style of her own, and created an aura all her own. Everyone makes his own brand of luck but it is nice to start with at least one gold fish in the aquarium. Apart from her natural attributes, Aline had two. She married into a very prominent Spanish family and came on to the cosmopolitan stage when nomads were spreading their wings and anxious to discover Spain, still somewhat unknown.

I remember that in Madrid, when Aline was engaged to Luis de Figueroa y Perez de Guzman el Bueno Alonso Martinez y Salabert, Count of Quintanilla (it was only recently, upon his father's death that he moved on to the title of Count of Romanones), no one believed the marriage would come off. Luis, they all said, had been a great hero in the civil war and had no intention of really settling down. "Luisito has been engaged before," a member of his clan said to me, "but an engagement does not mean a wedding. In Spain people think twice before getting married, since it's for life." They were all wrong. In taking on Aline as his wife, Luis made his most brilliant decision. He picked out a winner and in so doing entered the international sweepstakes he so enormously enjoys.

Aline has learned a lot about Spain and has known how to glamorize it for her friends. She speaks the language well, dances the flamenco, rides horseback and shoots like a pro. She has advertised Pedro Rodriguez' embroidered outfits all over the world, acts as Madrid editor for the American *Vogue*, has written a charming book, *The Story of Pascualete,* which deals with her experiences in an ancient property belonging to her husband, and earns pocket money producing television commercials and dealing in real estate. She is also on the board of directors of two companies, one of which makes electric condensers for factory use and the other for those utilized in hospitals and laboratories. An excellent mother to her three good-looking sons, she does all that is required to keep in touch with Luis' innumerable cousins.

Some of the more conservative elements in Spanish society are stunned by Aline's vast web of interests and occupations. Why doesn't she relax? some of them ask. Since her husband is well to do, why not take life easy? Everyone enjoys going to her parties. She always has a mixture of people and has become the hostess for all the visiting firemen. There you will find, among others, the Duke and Duchess of Alba, the Marques and Marquesa de Villaverde, Deborah Kerr and Peter Viertel, Audrey Hepburn and Mel Ferrer, Ava Gardner, Luis Miguel Dominguin and his wife Lucia Bosé, Frank Ryan, Winston and Cee Zee Guest.

Her entertaining is provocative for it is done against three entirely different backgrounds. In Pascualete, her husband's ancestral country seat, a marvelously mellow old building, she and Luis give house parties, usually during the various shooting seasons; there are spectacular flocks of doves in September, partridges through the fall months and bustards in the spring. The last presents problems. One rides in a horse-drawn carriage until a flock is sighted. Then, quickly, while the carriage is still moving, participants throw themselves out and hide behind the nearest object they can find. The reason for this is that if the carriage stops to let them off, the wise birds notice and fly away rapidly before a gun can be pointed at them. Ava Gardner was on one of these expeditions and obeyed orders, jumping out at a given time and lying on a mound of dirt where she spent a long time waiting for the bustard to fly away. When, finally, she was able to rejoin the carriage with the others, she explained that the reason she smelled to high heaven was that she had been lying in the midst of manure but had not dared move, in accordance with Luis' instructions.

At Pascualete, the Quintanillas can easily put up thirty people who usually come for a period of four days. Luncheon is out in the woods, but dinners in the thirteenth-century dining room are formal. There may be flamenco at night with dancers imported from the nearby towns of Trujillo and Caceres where there is some wonderful sightseeing to be done by the guests who do not shoot.

In Marbella, their recently completed Arabic house—their property is next to the land bought by the Duke and Duchess of Windsor—is right on the beach. It was built around an enormous central patio and it is here that they give their dinners for about one hundred friends, the standard number for a party on the Costa del Sol.

In Madrid, they go on living in a relatively modern house, almost on the outskirts, although they own a magnificent one in the center of the capital. Their residence on the street Castellon de la Plana is bursting with modern paintings, some of which are the work of Luis, whose abstractions have met with success in New York and Palm Beach. They also have a small garden and a tiny swimming pool. In the warm months, the parties spill out al fresco and, as usual, the dinners are at many tables because of the complications of protocol. But Luis and Aline never stay consecutively anywhere very long. They go to the United States a minimum of twice a year and they are all over Europe rushing about visiting their glorious friends.

One of Aline and Luis' good friends is the mobile Mary McFadden Herrari. Everyone who knew this intelligent and energetic young woman during her incessant wanderings prompted by the House of Dior, which she represented in Manhattan, her skiing pleasures, and many other activities, was well aware that she would never wed a young man from the peerless but ever so slightly stuffy milieu she was raised in.

She took a long time to make up her mind, keeping the columnists in a state of permanent alert, but when she decided she did not let any of her friends down. She married a handsome, brilliant member of one of the top-ranking Jewish families of pre-Nasser Egypt and has gone to live with him in South Africa. In Johannesburg, she has rapidly become a social leader, which could easily be predicted since she has all the attributes for a fine hostess.

Mary's husband, Philip Herrari, a leading light in the De Beers diamond company, is constantly on the move looking after its interests which are now threatened on all sides in the slap-happy nationalization that is taking over Africa. Often Mary accompanies him to Rhodesia, Tanzania, Ivory Coast, Ghana and the Southwestern countries. Herrari is also a director of several diamond mine companies, as well as of other companies dealing with sea and industrial diamonds.

It did not take long for Mary to settle in her new surroundings for she is efficient, well organized and knows exactly what she wants. A large Dutch colonial house, surrounded by wonderful gardens, is the headquarters for the couple. Mary, who had never stayed put long enough anywhere to see the seasons come and go, has become a fanatical horticulturist, working to create an enchanting formal Italian garden as an amusing contrast to the rigid formality of the old Dutch gables. Women in South Africa are obsessed with gardening, and Mary has caught the disease. A young lady in a hurry, she has achieved the miraculous impression that the garden goes right through the house since there are plants and flowers everywhere.

She has combed the antique shops and discovered all sorts of curious objects, remnants of the Dutch East India Company, to use for flowers, ranging from snails with open backs to Chinese fish with big mouths. She has trained a maid to do imaginative floral arrangements and this takes her most of the day. Since there is no scarcity of servants in South Africa, Mary is taking advantage of this happy condition. Her theatrical flair has led her to dress up the male domestics in white pants, heavy gray jackets, and beaded hats. She has a chef, and hostessing two dinners a week presents no hurdles. Her parties tend to be a mixture of visiting business firemen, American and European friends who fly in for a few days' stay, and the members of the local society. The last are very bridge-minded and Mary has learned how to play. With her usual flair, she has become excellent. She has also imported baccarat sets, roulette and all sorts of games to keep her new circle of friends amused.

The interior of the house is a successful mélange of Venetian and red painted French provincial chests and rigid gilt Louis XV and XVI chairs, along with local colonial ones. The last are used with a thirteenth century refectory table in the Dutch dining room. Its fireplace, cupboards and beams are of dark wood. The paintings which she brought from New York are displayed on all the walls of the house. They include works by Dali, Tanguy, Kandinsky, Tamayo, Matta, Tapies, and others. There are also some Henry Moore sculptures. The classically ornate Spanish and Italian frames are far more admired by the South Africans than are the works, which are a little beyond the area of their appreciation.

How did Mary McFadden meet Philip Herrari? Nothing could have been simpler. Like countless other globe-trotters, Mary flew to Johannesburg to visit Charles and Jane Engelhard, whose hospitality is in the tradition of the Princes of the Renaissance. Love did the rest. Being so exceptionally prepossessing, Philip was not exactly lonely, but American girls have a way.

Charles Engelhard is constantly referred to as the King of Platinum but actually the network of the various branches of his colossal realm is so intricate and extensive that the labyrinth in the palace of Knossos was child's play in comparison. As Chairman of the Board of Engelhard Industries he has brilliantly aggrandized his father's legacy. He now has subsidiary and associated companies in sixteen foreign countries dealing in the processing and refining of precious metals. Then there are Engelhard Hanovia Inc., with subsidiaries in five countries, and the American–South African Investment Co., Ltd. A Port Authority Commissioner (New York–New Jersey), Engelhard has been a Democrat for a long time and a close friend of both President Johnson and the late President Kennedy. He served on several Presidential Advisory committees and was Presidential representative at the Independence Ceremonies in Algeria, Gabon and Zambia.

It would be difficult to create a woman who answers more fully to the description of an up-to-date, super-efficient, immensely capable wife of a cosmopolitan business leader than Jane Engelhard. Half Brazilian and half American, she spent much of her youth in Europe. A handsome woman, with a long, expressive face, she is marvelously turned out at all times, with fine clothes, hairdos and jewels. By contemporary standards she tends to be a shade overdressed, but she is right in wearing what she does for it suits her to perfection. She has such a good, youthful figure that she manages to look splendid even when she wears black leotards and does her Yogi exercises on the front lawn. Her most distinctive feature is her voice which combines a warm, velvety tone and a persistent *joie de vivre,* very much like a bubble that never bursts.

Endowed with overwhelming physical stamina, she takes on enough assignments in one day to exhaust the toughest astronaut. Her most onerous duty is to see that six households run like clockwork, for the Engelhard mode of life is a series of displacements and even the most efficient secretaries have a hard time keeping up with their schedules. Their permanent headquarters consist of large estates in New Jersey and Florida, an apartment in New York City, a fishing camp in Canada, and two residences in South Africa, one in Johannesburg and the other near Kruger National Park.

The procession of visiting celebrities and dignitaries from five continents who must be entertained is literally never-ending, and Jane is forever organizing house parties. She also has multiple public engagements to fit in, along with four daughters, Susan, Sophie, Sally, and Charlene, to look after. The fifth one, Mrs. Samuel P. Reed, is the offspring of Mrs. Engelhard and her now dead first husband, a German.

There are large families on both sides, and a cozy relationship is maintained by all. Mrs. Engelhard alone has four sisters, two of whom, Madame Jacques Bemberg and Countess Bernard de La Rochefoucauld, are in Paris. She is very close to them, and there is much coming and going.

Their racing interests also necessitate multiple journeys. They have stables in the United States, Great Britain, and South Africa. Since everything this couple undertakes is thought out and planned to the last detail, it is not surprising that in this undertaking too their efforts are crowned with laurels. Not long ago their horse Double Jump won the Prix Pekin in France, and Indiana conquered the St. Leger in England.

Despite the daily frenzy of activity into which she is catapulted, or maybe because of it, Mrs. Engelhard's tastes in people tend to be conservative. Representatives of the top echelons of the yé yé or beatnik milieus, which so many hostesses find increasingly amusing to have around, are unlikely to be asked to her parties. More probable guests at her husband's business dinners or house parties are the patrician and staid members of Bernardsville and Far Hills society, and in Paris, the dignified representatives of the old Faubourg.

If friends go along on the Engelhards' many journeys to distant countries, they are likely to be such stable people of the American Four Hundred dynasties as Mrs. Sumner Welles, the Alfred Vanderbilts, the C. Suydam Cuttings, and Mrs. French Guest. Traveling in their turbo-prop Convair, named *Platinum Plover,* is most comfortable. The center section is fitted out as a sitting room with a large table for business conferences.

The Engelhard residences are all large enough to accommodate many house guests. Cragwood in New Jersey, in the vicinity of Far Hills, is a Georgian house built on one of the many forest-covered slopes there, and it is surrounded by stately gardens and magnificent woodlands. Sundry peacocks furnish an exotic touch to the property, and the extensive kennels, populated by superb champion golden retrievers, are a dazzling investment.

Camp Chaleur in Canada is a big, rambling bungalow of pine with a long covered veranda. It is near the Grand Cascapedia in Quebec Province, one of the finest salmon rivers in the world. There is also a separate camp, which belonged to the first Governor of Canada, the Marquess of Home, for all the children and guests. A heated swimming pool is available, along with tennis courts and riding horses. Pamplemousse, on the island of Boca Grande in Florida, consists of several cottages around a tree-shaded Boquilla patio, each done in a different color scheme. Much in evidence is a large salt-water pool in a grove of palm trees.

While the mansion in Johannesburg is stately, with marvelous Queen Anne furniture emerging out of a formal garden, the one in Eastern Transvaal is sprawling and relaxed. It is called Mbulwa after a tree that rises in the middle of a large paved courtyard and that often affords a refuge for innumerable snakes. The thatched roof is reputed to be the largest in that part of Africa, and the roar of jungle animals is often heard. Not along ago a mother hippo got out of the nearby National Park with her baby, who fell into the pool. In trying to recover it, the mother followed suit. The Engelhards, awakened in the middle of the night by strange noises, managed to arrange for a derrick to come and lift the two out.

There are many tantalizing Marys in orbit but the most bewitching is Mary Martin. It is only fitting that in real life she, who has enchanted so many millions the world over with her warm, versatile talent, should suddenly discover a Bali-Hai of her own in the Brazilian jungle.

The chain of circumstances leading to the discovery of this paradise is engrossing. It all started with Janet Gaynor and her late husband, Gilbert Adrian, for many years the unforgettable fashion stylist for Metro-Goldwyn-Mayer. During a trip to Brazil, they were determined to see the interior of this virgin country. The natives did everything to discourage them but finally, after several unsuccessful efforts, they were taken to the primitive frontier town of Anapolis, in the state of Goias in the midst of a ravishing landscape where the monkeys swung by the hundreds from the trees. They promptly fell in love with the place and, despite the complete impracticality of it all, decided to buy some land. It proved enormously difficult, but they eventually managed to build themselves an attractive house.

After the long run of *Peter Pan,* Mary Martin and her husband Richard Halliday decided a complete rest was needed, and they took a freighter to South America. By chance, upon reaching Rio de Janeiro, they heard that the Adrians were on their farm and decided to surprise them. But the freighter's schedule was very tight and the time short. They booked a flight—a long one—to Anapolis one day with the return the next day. The trip, with many stops, proved uncomfortable and disappointing to such a degree that neither Mary nor Richard could understand what had possessed their good friends to settle for so many months of the year in such dreary country.

The disenchantment continued after reaching Anapolis and crossing the town. "But the moment we were up in the hills," Mary told me, her rich voice tingling with excitement, "both Dick and I were suddenly in a state of exhilaration and by the time we reached the *fazenda* we were raving. This was heaven with a capital H. Pink orchids were pinned to the trees, each and every leaf an unforgettable composition of Bruges lace, the sky and the earth an ecstatic symphony of blue and green."

The next morning, while breakfasting on the terrace, before

hurrying back to the airport, the Hallidays expressed the wish to buy some land too. "Right over there," Mary said, pointing to a nearby hill. Hurriedly, the feelers were sent out. Nothing was for sale, not one single acre.

Six months later Mary was in her suite in a hotel in Washington, D.C., during the run of Thornton Wilder's *The Skin of Our Teeth*, entertaining Noel Coward for tea. Suddenly she picked up the telephone and there were Janet and Adrian who, in order to make sure they could get a good connection, had flown all the way to Sao Paulo. Twelve hundred acres, the very ones she had pointed out had, through a chain of incredible events, come up for sale, but a decision had to be taken immediately. "All right," said Mary, without even talking it over with Dick, "go ahead, make all the arrangements and let us know." Noel Coward, who had been trying to talk the Hallidays into buying a small estate near his in Jamaica, expressed violent disapproval at such a plan. "It's too far," he said, "much the craziest thing I ever heard. You must cable the Adrians immediately that you have changed your mind." But Mary went ahead and every moment she can now snatch from the theater she flies there with her husband. Whenever some producer, composer, or director is interested in talking over a project, he must fly to the jungle to see her.

There are no telephones or electricity. Cables take anywhere from four days to three weeks to reach them and airmail anywhere between ten days and four weeks. The name of the fazenda is *Psalm 23* in accordance with the lines "He maketh me to lie down in green pastures." The sprawling house they erected is filled with Brazilian-made furniture. A swimming pool is not necessary, for there are beautiful waterfalls all over the place. They ride horseback every day, often taking a picnic luncheon with them which they eat in a bamboo forest. A mass of blue and yellow butterflies leads the way and hundreds of friendly parakeets fly over their heads making wonderful music.

Ernest, the faithful Negro cook-valet of the Hallidays who never leaves their side, directs the local servants. There is a native chef for the local dishes, but Ernest does the rest. Mary herself bakes the bread, rolls, pies, and cakes in the oven of the wood-burning stove. A permanent house guest is a nine-year-old monkey, Rebel, named after a beau of Heller, Mary and Dick's daughter, at the time the mischievous creature landed in the house from a tree and made it clear that she wished to remain. Since there are no bells because there is no electricity, a cow horn is assigned to each house guest so that when he wakes up in the morning and wishes to have breakfast served in bed he can let his wish be known.

Guests come all the time. One week it's Marge and Gower Champion, the next Oliver Smith or the Jack Paars. Jerry Herman, who composed the score for *Hello Dolly*, flew in from New York just to play six songs for a new show. Jimmy van Heusen and Sammy Cahn also arrived with the music for a new project.

Apart from Janet Gaynor, now remarried to Paul Gregory, all sorts of stimulating neighbors reside near Anapolis, and the Hallidays entertain them all the time. There are an English doctor, in charge of a medical mission, and his Mississippi-born wife; a Negro Brazilian lawyer with a very handsome wife who looks like a Wagnerian soprano; a delightful Chinese family from Formosa who run a textile factory; a huge Lebanese clan which deals with agricultural products; and several cattle ranchers.

There is hardly a jet-setter who goes to Hong Kong who does not look up Mrs. John Carey-Hughes, but the disappointment of not finding her often occurs, since she is pretty much of a cosmonaut herself. She emplanes with spell-binding ease, whether to occupy her Fifth Avenue New York apartment for a few days while she sees her daughter, Andrea Portago, who is at school in Manhattan; to visit her son, the eleven-year-old Marquess of Portago, Grandee of Spain, at Ludgrove, a boarding school in England; or to go big game hunting. She also breezes into Paris to have her clothes fitted at Dior.

She started her interesting life in Greenville, South Carolina, as Carroll McDaniel and through the years she has never lost the slow, somewhat haunting drawl of the natives of that state. After some years spent in New York modeling, she found her Prince Charming in the dashingly virile Marquess of Portago, a few years her junior and one of the last great playboys whose courage on the Cresta Run and in other sports became legendary. He was irresistibly attracted to the fair sex and vice versa. When he tragically lost his life in an automobile race, there were several ladies in the picture, including Linda Christian, who went into mourning. But despite his roving eye, he had not divorced and Carroll was his widow.

Restless and alluring, she eventually moved her headquarters to Hong Kong. Not long ago she relinquished the Spanish title to become the wife of John Carey-Hughes, a Welsh doctor, son of a Baptist minister, who has an excellent practice in Hong Kong where he has lived for eighteen years. He has dark hair, brown eyes, and a permanent suntan. He is a magnificent athlete, an excellent sailor, water skier, deep sea diver, and marksman. He too had been married previously and is the father of three children from his first marriage.

Carroll is a real Southern Belle, smooth, feminine, and good company. Hers is not an obvious type of glamor nor are her looks flashy but she grows on people, hour by hour. In the Far East she is the excellent hostess she has always been. She now resides in her husband's large two-story granite house, rising out of a garden, on the Kowloon side. The group she mingles with is cosmopolitan, and she has many friends among the Chinese.

Entertaining is no chore. There are several excellent servants who came originally from Shanghai, a wonderful maid who awaits her mistress's return every night whatever the hour, and a chef so well-trained that all he needs to know is how many for dinner. Sometimes there are about twenty. She usually receives her friends in her own modified version of the Cheongsam dress which the local tailors execute under her instructions (she likes a less pronounced split in the skirt). "This is all very well," Carroll says, "for the bamboolike, graceful Chinese leg, but for our Western one it is imperative to make some changes." The Carey-Hugheses collect Ming furniture and butterflies. The latter they go after on the hills near the city with special Oriental nets. Most of their weekends are spent on a forty-one-foot sailing boat. The coolies on the sampans are accustomed to seeing Carroll's svelte figure rush by on water skis, a sport she does very well along with many others. Currently she shares with her handsome mate a fiery enthusiasm for big game hunting, and they go on three safaris a year. The reason he can get away from his medical chores so often is that he has formed a partnership with four other physicians and they all take turns at their jobs.

So off they go to Alaska—Carroll shot an immense white bear there—Mongolia, and Africa, depending on circumstances, with a facility which stuns even the most seasoned travelers. In Kenya they are likely to encounter Mrs. Francis Kellogg, the former Fernanda Munn, who spends several months a year on a farm she acquired in full view of Mount Kenya.

Mrs. Kellogg's schedule in the United States is not exactly inactive. Happily married to a successful businessman, this truly blue-blooded patrician, related to ever so many distinguished Yankee clans, is the mother of a son, away in college, and a daughter who recently made her debut in society. The family has three other headquarters: a spacious Fifth Avenue apartment, a farm in Bedford, New York, and a Palm Beach mansion. Although her husband is not too keen on shooting, Mrs. Kellogg has always been a devotee of this sport and has hunted quail and turkey in Florida, pheasants in Hungary, roebuck and grouse in Scotland. Some years ago she went on her first safari to Kenya and it was love at first sight with Africa.

In her own down-to-earth and cool manner, she enthusiastically described to me her decision to spend some time every year on the dark continent. "The animals," she remarked, "the climate, the out of doors existence, the view of thorn trees or distant mountains. And there is always the chance of an unexpected rhino, elephant, buff. Almost as exciting is the varied bird life, and it keeps me alert and stimulated. When the opportunity came to acquire a farm, I couldn't resist it despite all the drawbacks.

"This estate, named Treffos," she continued, "is located at 8,000 feet above sea level, in the foothills of the Aberdares forest near Mwega. The farm has its own wheat and pyrethrum fields and pastures, water holes and thickets where wild game abounds. Here I feel a freedom from civilization and a rapport with nature which is simply glorious. The main house is roomy enough to accommodate several guests and while it is no architectural marvel, I find it attractive with its steeply pitched, thatched roof. Furnishings are typical of most homes in Kenya—a mixture of comfortable chairs and sofas of no particular period—and the over-all effect is pleasant. After safari tent life the rooms seem not only permanent but luxurious. Animals are far too fascinating alive and in their native habitat to intrigue anyone when they are dead. For this reason, most African domiciles, including Treffos, does not overflow with skins, mounted heads, or zebra rugs.

"With jet travel so easy and fast," she went on, "my friends descend on me in hordes. Last summer I even gave an East African coming-out party for my daughter Fernanda. Friends made the journey from Nairobi, the Mt. Kenya Safari Club and remote places. Among my American friends who came were Thomas and Durie Shevlin from Palm Beach. He is the loyal director of a wildlife charitable trust 'The Louwana Fund.' Tents were put up to take care of all the visitors, native musicians played, and the boys did wild dances and sleight-of-hand tricks.

"There is plenty of game in Treffos," she asserted with enthusiasm, "and I have even bagged a beautiful leopard who was preying on the herds. Bird shooting is also very active on the farm at times. The safaris I go on, however, usually start from Nairobi, one hundred miles away, which is the headquarters for the equipment and supply sources. The next safari is always a topic of prime interest, with much time spent studying maps and discussing every area in detail. It is based on game considerations. It is necessary to make applications in plenty of time in order to be able to hunt on certain tracts of land."

Then, looking me straight in the eye, she added, "Others may not think so, but I consider Nairobi the true crossroad of the world." Mrs. Kellogg is not only perfectly sincere in her point of view but absolutely correct. However, I cannot help but ask myself whether some years hence, when the nomadic fever will have reached its peak, the smart trend will not be to stay as long as possible in the same place and for a few weeks forget suitcases and airplanes. The chicest thing in Paris would be to make a luncheon date two weeks from Wednesday at the Berkeley instead of at the Focolar Restaurant in Mexico City, and in Manhattan to do the same at the Côte Basque in lieu of Alfredo's in Rome.

How restful it would be for these people not to overburden their memories trying to remember the dates of all the arrivals and departures of their different friends and not to be tormented by their anxiety or inability to entertain them on the run between international flights! To stay somewhere permanently and watch the unchic go by in orbit may become the sort of chic bliss of which dreams are made.

Appendix

A Guide to the Jungle of First Names and Nicknames

This Who's Who of first names that constantly crop up in nomadic conversation does not pretend to be either complete or definitive. I have only mentioned those that strike me as leading to confusion, even among the initiated.

Although each person mentioned may not have thousands of miles to his credit yearly, his name has been included since it rings a loud bell in N.S. Somewhere along the line, on one of the five continents, these men's and women's paths are apt to cross or meet.

The few paragraphs, written in telegraphic style, are not intended to be a profound character study of each individual but simply an identification tag to assist those readers who are interested in these wayfarers or plan to join them at some point or other. Although the information has been checked, rechecked and updated, it is inevitable that the vertiginous pace of life these cosmonauts are subjected to will bring some changes—occupational, residential, marital, or mortal—by publication time.

Adelaide and Adele

In both groups there are three outstanding ladies.

Countess Alain d'Eudeville is the former Adelaide Johnson of Islip, Long Island, and the widow of a very well-liked Frenchman. A superb apartment in Paris' Left Bank and a house in the country near the French capital form her base, but she undertakes many yearly journeys. She spends the winters in a cottage in the skiing resort of Mégève. A beautiful creature, she is very "in" with the old Faubourg set.

Mrs. Edgard Leonard is petite, gifted with a Dresden doll face and quick repartee. Twice a widow, she inherited from her first husband, a distinguished Dutchman, an estate in Holland which she visits yearly. A leading hostess in both Southampton and New York, where her residence in the East sixties is a small jewel, she travels far and wide, sometimes rents houses abroad.

Princess Kyril Scherbatow is a familiar figure in the resorts of Jamaica, Bermuda, and Nantucket, and is often called "The Island Princess." Born Sedgewick and first married into the Munroe family, she hails from conservative stock, but since her wedding to the white Russian patrician, she has been "in" with café society.

Mercurial and immensely entertaining is **Mrs. J. Kingman Douglas,** who, as Adele Astaire, danced her way to fame with brother Fred before she retired to become the wife of the late Lord Charles Cavendish. She now divides her time with her second Chicagoan husband between an apartment in Manhattan, a cottage in Round Hill, Jamaica, and a wing of Lismore Castle in Ireland.

Beautiful **Mrs. Stanley Donen,** the former Adele Dillingham, lives with her third mate, the successful motion-picture producer, in London and a weekend place nearby. Currently the Oklahoma-born belle is building a chalet in Klosters. She is a busy mother, since she has children from her first husband, Bill O'Connor, her second, Earl Beatty, as well as with her current one. She has a real knack for entertaining, and her parties in the British capital always provide a fascinating mixture of guests.

Another Adele, frequently mentioned in Spanish-loving milieus, is the wife of the Spanish Ambassador to Peru, **Señora Angel Sanz Briz**, sister-in-law of the Spanish Foreign Minister Fernando Maria Castiella. Chic, attractive, and intelligent, she does a fine job wherever her mate is sent.

ALAN, ALLEN, ALAIN

In U social and intellectual salons, one hears much about **Alan Pryce Jones.** With bases in New York City and Newport, he is one of the most popular British exports to the U.S.A. in the last twenty years. A contributor to various magazines and newspapers, he is alert, bright, and stimulating. A widower (his late wife, a member of the French-Austrian family Fould Springer, was a sister of the Baroness Elie de Rothschild), he is frequently in orbit visiting his mother-in-law, who lives in Florence, and his many friends in Great Britain.

In musical spheres all over the world, New York, and Anacapri (where he retires to a summer house), the name of **Allen Sven Oxenburg,** a first cousin of Howard Oxenberg (spelled differently) and Elizabeth of Yugoslavia, often comes up. He is the immensely clever *impresario extraordinaire* of the American Opera Society which has given, and continues to present, some first-rate, unique performances of forgotten masterpieces with great casts of singers.

In the entertainment world, it's **Alan Jay Lerner** whose list of hits is overwhelming. A refined, cultivated, introspective charmer with many adorable past wives, he made constant news with his last one, Micheline Pozzo di Borgo. Their matrimonial troubles were so vivacious it is to be hoped a musical script will emerge from them.

If the river Nile is mentioned, it is probably in connection with its great biographer **Alan Morehead,** who has also written so effectively about Africa's wild animals. An adornment of Port' Ercole society in the summer, this remarkable Australian is much on the move. Gardening is his hobby.

Particularly apt to get mixed up in *nouvelle vague* circles are **Alain Resnais** and **Alain Robbe-Grillet.** The first directed, among many other spectacularly successful films, *Last Year in Marienbad,* which the second wrote. Resnais is just about the most discussed film director in Europe, and since he is also handsome, the hostesses die over him. His favorite Egeria is currently Delphine Seyrig. Robbe-Grillet is wonderfully publicity conscious, knows how to promote himself very well, and never forgets to inject a sexy element in his novels which take place in an almost complete vacuum.

The richest of the Alains is the handsomest of the **Rothschild** Barons. A great yachtsman (his yacht's name is *Saita*), he is the most aloof of the celebrated family, happily married to Mary Chauvin de Treuil. Their house on the Avenue de Marigny in Paris, filled with treasures, is the scene of dignified luncheons and dinners.

The best looking of the Alains is the actor **Delon.** Discovered by Luchino Visconti and much in his company for a time, he made a bourgeois marriage after a long romance with Romy Schneider; plays gin rummy with the affluent set.

Alexander, Alex, Alec, Alexandre

In shooting, safari (he helps run the Mt. Kenya Safari Club in wintertime), Mittersill (an Austrian Club he directs with Baron Hubert Pantz in summer) chic-chat, the reference surely is to **H.R.H. Prince Alexander Hohenlohe,** a huge, Siegfried-like blond gentleman. His witty wife, the former Patricia

Wilder, is called "*Miel-bébé*" by the French and "Honeychile" by the English-speaking nomads. She is Macon, Georgia's, contribution to N.S.

Alexis may be Lichtenstein's **Baron de Rede,** one of the great hosts of the continent, a cool, sphynxlike bachelor with superb manners, taste, and great financial acumen. He gives marvelous parties in Paris at the Palais Lambert on the Ile Saint Louis. Some of the jetters call him Alec which proves confusing since a great friend of his, Count **"Alec"** (Alexandre) **de Casteja,** moves in the same circles. The latter is married to the late Mrs. Reginald Fellowes' daughter, a member of the very, very, very distinguished De Broglie family. He has four main bases (Paris, a house in Switzerland, a chateau in the Basses Pyrenees, and a residence in Monte Carlo), but spends the winters skiing and a good part of the year traveling.

In New York City and in art circles Alec is **Alexander Liberman,** the gifted Russian-born editorial director of the Condé Nast publications, a successful painter, a trend-setter and a good host. With his wife, Tatiana Duplessis (who designed hats at Saks Fifth Avenue), he entertains in Manhattan and in Beauvallon, near St. Tropez.

In royal international circles and in Paris, much uncertainty arises when a chic woman begins quoting Alexandre. It could be the coiffeur or **His Royal Highness Prince Alexandre of Yugoslavia.** Since the hairdresser reigns supreme in all these ladies' lives—they are willing to wait four and five hours in his establishment for a 30-second *coup de peigne* from the master —his pearls of gossip and wisdom are bandied about. But Prince Alexandre, who is also social and amusing, is often quoted too. His Royal Highness is the husband of Princess Maria Pia of Italy, the brother of Mrs. Howard Oxenberg, the nephew of Princess Marina, Duchess of Kent, and the father of two sets of twins. He lives in Versailles. Both Alexandres are always at all the royal weddings, the Prince as a relative (he is a cousin of everyone), and the hair stylist to make the bride, the mother, and the other princesses look as smart as he possibly can.

In and out of the British Isles, there is the **Marquess of Londonderry,** in his late twenties, personable and offbeat. An enthusiastic pianist—he plays both jazz and the classics—he is a vegetarian, has a marvelous pheasant shoot in Ireland, drives a fast Italian sports car (recently it was an Alfa Romeo), and spends much time at Annabel's in London, owned by his brother-in-law Mark Birley. His Marchioness is the Lorelei-like Nico Harrison whom he married in 1958 when she was a teenager.

In New York, Paris, Geneva, and Milan art gallery circles, the name cannot fail to be **Alexander Iolas,** a Greek born in Egypt who used to be a dancer and went on recital tours with Theodore Roosevelt's granddaughter Theodora. With homes everywhere, he entertains constantly. His niece is the current Marquesa de Cuevas.

In theatrical and film milieus, it is safe to assume that the reference is to **Sir Alec Guinness** whose many commitments keep him on the move most of the time. A quiet, unassuming, modest man with many interests, he is not a partygoer, but when he does appear he makes a considerable impact.

Sir Alec Douglas Home gave up his peerage for life in the fall of 1963. He would, otherwise, be known as the Earl of Home. A delightful person, he was one of the most individualistic Prime Ministers Great Britain had had for a long time and will, undoubtedly, be up in the front lines again.

In international racing circles, Deauville, the South of France, where he owns a delightful property, and in high financial echelons, there is oil-rich **Alec Weissweiller** whose wife Francine is a *salonniere.* She was a close friend of the late Jean Cocteau.

An Alesandro who lives in Manhattan and Southampton sometimes called Alec, other times Alex, is the **Marquess of Montezemolo** who first introduced the Vespa motor scooters in the U.S.A. and is now a Wall Street broker. He and his second wife, a *Vogue* fashion editor Cathy Murray (she is a sister of Jeanne Vanderbilt and Mrs. Frank Conniff), are in demand on many different circuits.

ALEXANDRA AND SANDRA

are names which cover much exalted ground. It fits the person of a former Queen, the cousin of a Queen, as well as her mother-in-law, a granddaughter of a King, a daughter of a Viceroy, a Cincinnati heiress, and the daughter of an owner of a baseball team.

Alexandra of Yugoslavia, who never was a reigning Queen, since she married King Peter when he was in exile in London during the Second World War, is the daughter of the late King Alexander of Greece. A likeable, curiously quixotic creature, she is enriched by great warmth and by the sort of impulsiveness that sweeps her into difficult situations. She and her husband are nomads without any kind of a permanent base. Peter is thirty-seventh in line to the succession of the British throne.

Princess Alexandra, sister of the Duke of Kent and the wife of handsome, ever-so-U Angus Ogilvy, is one of the most beloved members of British royalty. The fact that only the nicest things are said about her is a considerable help in the thick Alexandrian bushes. Her mother-in-law, the **Countess of Airlie,** sometimes called Bridget, is used to court circles, since her husband, who has continuously occupied positions of importance, is currently the Lord Chamberlain of the Queen Mother's household. A delightful hostess in the two family castles, Cortachy and Airlie, she comes in contact with Americans through her other daughter-in-law, Lady Ogilvy, the former Virginia Ryan of New York.

Alessandra Lequio, the striking-looking daughter of the Infanta Beatriz of Spain and the Prince of Civitella Cesi, became a world celebrity when she eloped and married Signor Clemente Lequio in a cloak-and-dagger sort of ceremony (her father was not in favor of it). Since she made a success of her marriage, the family is now blissful. She must not dislike publicity, for the Italian weeklies treat her as a *grande vedette* and are full of photographs of her various activities.

Lady Alexandra Metcalfe, sometimes known as "Baba," is a fabulous beauty, whose father was Lord Curzon and whose husband (she divorced him) was Equerry to the Duke of Windsor when he was Prince of Wales. She is one of the most interesting gadabouts, having accomplished all sorts of exotic, hard-to-take trips for a woman. She is very active on the "Save the Children Fund."

Mrs. Robert McKay, one of the celebrated Emery sisters of Cincinnati, is the owner of "Chelsea," one of the most beautiful estates on Long Island—it contains some of the finest work José Maria Sert ever did—and a widow for the second time (her first husband was Benjamin Moore by whom she had several children). She spends the winters on a plantation she owns near Tallahassee, Florida, but is a much-traveled lady, apt to rent houses for lengthy stays in England or Italy.

Since her estrangement from her husband, **Mrs. William Meyer,** the former Sandra Payson, spends more and more time in England rather than in New York where she was one of the reigning young matrons. She also visits her sister Mrs. Enrico Middleton in Florence and goes on shooting parties in Spain. Her mother, Mrs. Charles Payson, owns the New York Mets and her uncle, Jock Whitney, the *New York Herald-Tribune.*

In very chic Italian milieus there is the alluring **Countess Franco Spalletti,** who travels far less since she inherited the Castle of Bolgheri where she spends much time. A member of the illustrious Della Gherardesca clan, estranged from her monocled husband soon after her marriage, she decorated the salon of Elizabeth Arden in New York City.

Alfonso

The mix-up, particularly in Spain and Italy, over this name is considerable, for three of them are Princes and none of them the stay-at-home type.

Alfonso Falco is a source of bewilderment even to the most sophisticated because of his two heritages; in Italy he is Prince Pio and in Spain the sixteenth Marquess of Castel Rodrigo. A portly gentleman, he is exceedingly popular, as is his wife Sveva, sister of the Prince Colonna, assistant to the Pope's throne (her mother Princess Isabelle Colonna is the ruler of Roman society). The Falcos-Castel Rodrigos give famous house parties at their beautiful Villa Mombello on Lake Como, have an apartment in Rome and several houses in Spain (one of them was until recently the residence of the American Ambassador in Madrid).

Prince Alfonso Hohenlohe is another gentleman whose distinguished pedigree (German, Spanish, and Mexican) is so varied that he is at home everywhere. Married at one point to Ira Fürstenberg, he made continuous headlines in his lawsuits to retain the custody of the children. Among those most responsible for making the Costa del Sol elegant, with considerable real estate developments there to his credit, he also organizes automobile rallies to Morocco for celebrities.

Prince Alfonso of Bourbon, young, handsome enough to be a film star, and engaging enough to win all the ladies' hearts, is terrible eligible, one of the main adornments of Madrid society, willing to play the royal game and with definite pretensions to the Spanish throne. His father is the Duke of Segovia, his grandfather the late King of Spain, his mother the beautiful Emanuela de Dampierre, now Signora Sozzani.

The most affluent of all is **Alfonso Fierro,** who has one of the great industrial fortunes of Spain. The coming-out party held in Madrid in June 1964 for his daughter Carmen attracted all the big international names. He turns up in Marbella and Mallorca during the season with his wife, makes many trips to the United States.

Aline, Aileen, and Allene

can be spelled many different ways but, when it comes to the spoken word, they sound exactly the same. There are three Alines, three Aileens, and one Allene, all constantly on the merry-go-round and all valid exponents of the peripatetic philosophy. The first three are:

Countess Quintanilla (the old title by which she is better known)—**Romanones** (the recently inherited one at the death of her father-in-law) is the pride and joy of Pearl River, New York, where she started as Aline Griffith. She went on to a position of exceptional eminence in the turbine set and is on the well-dressed ledger. She is a point of reference for all the birds of passage in Madrid, Marbella, and Pascualete (a big *finca* her husband owns in Estremadura).

Mrs. Guido Branca, the former Aline Flannery of New York, a pet of many a set, including that of the Bismarcks, Pecci Blunts, and Dunns, is always taking off for many singular journeys from her home in Rome.

In aesthetic milieus Aline is the often-quoted widow of the internationally famous architect **Eero Saarinen.** She is a delightful authoress (her book *The Proud Possessors* is a masterpiece) on art subjects, was for many years an art critic for the *New York Times* (she was then called Aline Loucheim), and in her youth wrote poems.

The three Aileens are:

Aileen Mehle is known to the Hearst press readers as Suzy Knickerbocker. Her appearance is a delicious combination of a young Mae West and Debbie Reynolds, and her wit has already become legendary. She manages to be as good a friend as she is a reporter.

The **Hon. Mrs. Aileen Plunket,** a Guinness heiress, is a chatelaine out of a storybook—she owns the huge Lustrellstown Castle near Dublin—who commutes to an apartment in Paris. A party giver of tireless enthusiasm, she shares with her sisters a fabulous bank account, light eyes, blonde hair, a marvelous complexion, and the habit of calling herself by the name of a past husband. Having divorced the Hon. Brinsley Plunket in 1940, she later married Valerian Rybar, but upon untying this knot in 1965, again pulled out the old visiting cards, which had a more Anglo-Saxon sound. Her sister Maureen, currently the happy wife of Judge John Maude, her third mate, had wed and divorced a second consort after the death of the Marquess of Dufferin and Ava, her first husband. She, too, addresses herself now as the Dowager Marchioness. Sister Oonagh has been divorced from Philip Kindersley, Baron Oranmore and Browne and from Miguel Ferreras, but it is the coronet and name of the second marriage which she now uses.

Mrs. John Slocum (Eileen Gillespie) is the bright, cozy wife of an American diplomat, and nomads are always flying to stay with her wherever she is. She is a member of both Newport and Tuxedo societies and has two attractive daughters, Beryl and Marguerite.

Allene Talmey (Mrs. Richard L. Plaut) is the bright, inquisitive Associate Editor and writer for *Vogue* magazine, a frequent traveler because of her profession, a highly accomplished and skilled detector of trends.

Ann and Anne

is one of the feminine names which most contributes to the dismay of nomadic society name-droppers. There are dozens of them.

In royal circles there are so many of them that all sorts of good landing instruments are necessary to reach the correct coat of arms.

Apart from **Princess Anne of England,** daughter of the Queen, who is beginning to be more and more discussed, we have:

The titular Queen of Roumania, born **Anne of Bourbon-Parme,** the healthy, informal, attractive wife of former King Michael. She is the mother of four daughters and has a villa in Versoix, Switzerland, as a home base.

Duchess Anne of Aosta, a sister of the Count of Paris and widow of a dashing Italian Royal Prince, lives mainly in Florence and Sorrento, but despite failing health is an habitual traveler. Her niece, **Princess Carlos Bourbon–Two Sicilies,** is one of the most enchanting of the royal ladies. Beautifully brought up by her parents, the Count and Countess of Paris, she has a delicious snub nose which gives a will-o'-the-wisp look. Although she makes her home in Madrid, she is the guest of her many royal relatives all over Europe.

Her Majesty the Queen of Greece is the endearing, youthful Danish Princess who is learning, along with the arduous language, the difficult métier her marriage to King Constantine has imposed upon her. Although she was christened Anne-Marie, her subjects are tending more and more to drop the Marie from her name.

In the British Empire it can be Princess Margaret's mother-in-law, the vivacious **Countess of Rosse,** a sister of Oliver Messel, who commutes between two country seats in Ireland and a London home, or **Mrs. Ian Fleming,** the widow of the creator of James Bond, born Ann Charteris, who at one point was Lady O'Neill and later Lady Rothermere. A beguiling lady whom many consider irresistible company, she spends the winters on an estate in Jamaica or in the most U of U districts. **Lady Anne Tree,** a sister of the Duke of Devonshire, wife of Michael Tree, is a cool, dispassionately opinionated, swanlike peeress whose headquarters are the magnificent Mereworth Castle in Kent. She visits her father-in-law, Ronnie Tree, in Barbados and the Stavros Niarchoses in St. Moritz and Spezzapoula. Luckily the gregarious **Ann Lady Orr-Lewis,** who is recurrently mentioned in connection with Lyford Cay in the Bahamas, where she spends the winters as a successful decorator, is also referred to as Annie. Because of her many American friends, she is frequently in the United States.

Mrs. Charles Munroe is one of the three great hostesses of Nassau, a delightful, enthusiastic lady with many interests, who is a nomad for seven months of the year.

Along the many routes the entertainment people take, conversation is more likely to be about **Kirk Douglas**'s vivacious Belgian-born wife than about **Mrs. Jack Warner,** whose parties in Hollywood, New York, and on the French Riviera were memorable, but who leads a far quieter existence these days.

The thrice-widowed **Mrs. Ralph Robertson,** who inherited from her second husband, George Blumenthal, a collection of masterpieces, gives dinners in the great tradition and is a luminary in New York's more conservative echelons.

Mrs. Denniston Slater, whose trademarks are wearing dark glasses at all times, an ever-so-pleasing voice, and a remarkable capacity for adapting to the many different social scales her husband's various interests lead her up to, enjoys a merry life on the Long Island and Manhattan anything-can-happen circuit.

The **ex-Mrs. Henry Ford,** the former Anne McDonnell, is an expert on eighteenth-century furniture. That wonderfully hungry appearance on her beautiful, bony face, so craved for by magazines, has nothing to do with the hyperbolic settlement she received at the time of her recent divorce. Residing in New York and Southampton, she makes rapid excursions abroad, renting dwellings in Gstaad, and since she is now interested in horses, Ascot. Apt to be confused with her is her daughter **Anne** who has inherited her mother's looks and who, despite her youth, has joined the ranks of the best dressed and most sophisticated, appearing all over the world at the right time. Recently, following in the footsteps of her father and sister

Charlotte, she ignored the canons of the Catholic Church, in which she was born, to marry a divorced man. He is the personable **Giancarlo Uzielli,** the member of a well known Jewish Florentine family.

Anne Marie

Donna Anne Marie Aldobrandini, the estranged wife of Don Francesco Aldobrandini (a son of Prince Clemente Aldobrandini), is a daughter of Countess Lily Volpi's previous marriage to the French jeweler Lacloche. Recently turned theatrical producer, she uses Rome as her headquarters.

Princess Otto Bismarck is the Swedish-born consort of the head of the illustrious clan that provided Germany with the Iron Chancellor. A vivacious, friendly blonde, she divides her time between her husband's ancestral estates in northern Germany and a delightful estate in Marbella, sometimes visits her in-laws, Eddie and Mona Bismarck. In recent years she had to undergo several operations on her leg which was badly smashed in a skiing accident.

Madame Louis Malle is well-known in New York City, having lived there for several years while married to Giancarlo Uzielli. A stunning former model—she was French born, Anne Marie Deschodt—she is now the wife of the breezy film director who had nerve enough to costar Brigitte Bardot and Jeanne Moreau in *Viva Maria.*

Madame J. Louis François Poncet is a Swiss offering to Parisian society. Beautiful, young, and capable, she is not quite as much in orbit as her sister, Madame Paul Revay, with whom she is not on the closest of terms. No one ever makes a particular effort to invite them to the same small dinner party.

An **Anna Maria,** often called Anne Marie by her cosmopolitan friends, is the daughter of the late Count Volpi di Misurata, Italy's Minister of Finance and Governor of Libya, and the estranged wife of Count Cesare **Cicogna.** An intellectual, she presides in both Venice and Tripoli, where she dwells in magnificent residences, over a fascinating group of house guests ranging from Nancy Mitford to Jeanne Moreau. Her son Bino makes his headquarters in Milan, and her daughter Marina is a regular vedette of N.S.

ANTONIO

In Spain, Portugal, and Italy one swims in an ocean of men who answer to this appellation. The one whose surname never gets mentioned (it happens to be **Ruiz**) is the great dancer from Sevilla who has had his own company for many years. As a youngster, he burst on Broadway with a cousin of his, Rosario, making an instantaneous hit. The passing of the years has not interfered with his ability and growth as an artist. A bachelor who lives in both Madrid and Marbella, he is part of the Spanish party scene and a friend of the Albas.

Of late, another dancer by the same first name but who uses his last name, **Gades,** has made an enormous splash, and many consider him the best dancer to appear on the Iberian scene since his namesake. He is married to the Spanish musical comedy star Marujita Diaz, and they are in demand at all flamenco parties. In bullfighting circles, but on the social circuit too, it is **Antonio Ordonez** who, until the rise of El Cordobes, was everyone's (including Ernest Hemingway's) favorite torero. A striking looking hero, married to the sister of his long-time rival Luis Miguel Dominguin, he has just come out of retirement as all bullfighters inevitably do.

In sewing circles, it is **Canovas del Castillo,** who made his reputation as a designer with Elizabeth Arden and Lanvin. He is now in business for himself in Paris where he owns an apartment. He also has a country residence, much photographed by all the magazines, in Castilia not far from Madrid. He is unmarried and a member of the Loel and Gloria Guinness entourage.

The masculine **Antonio Muñoz,** of the Bank of Santander fortune, is still a bachelor and therefore a great catch in Spanish money-bag society. As he rides around every year with great authority at the Sevilla Fair, the women swoon.

In diplomatic Spanish shop talk and also among all the friends of the Lodges and the Braggiotti clans—they run into several thousands—it's the young diplomat **Antonio Oyarzabal,** who married Beatrice Lodge at the time her father was American Envoy to Madrid.

The **Marquess Origo,** a pleasant, easy-going gentleman farmer, married to Iris Cutting, the exceptionally gifted authoress of numerous interesting biographical studies, is well-known in Rome and among intellectuals.

Antonio Ghiringhelli, despite tremendous animosity on the part of many celebrated singers (he has had resounding differences with Renata Tebaldi, Renata Scotto, Giulietta Simionato, Giuseppe Di Stefano, Mario del Monaco, Cesare Siepi, to name a few), manages to remain at the helm of La Scala Opera. He made his fortune in the shoe business.

Another Antonio is the industrialist **Sozzani,** married to Emanuela de Dempierre, first wife of the Duke of Segovia and mother of those two Prince Charmings, Alfonso and Gonzalo de Bourbon. He turns up in Milan and on the French Riviera.

The half Portuguese–half American (his mother is New York City's prominent Mrs. Paul Warburg) **Antonio Almeida** is a talented and good-looking conductor, who has made the most of his career in Germany directing symphony orchestras. Married to an American, he keeps Paris as his headquarters.

Audrey

is limited to four prominent ladies.

Mrs. Stephen Currier is young and one of the richest women in the world. Shy by nature, she is nevertheless continuously catapulted into prominence. A granddaughter of the late Andrew Mellon, she has David Bruce, American Ambassador to Great Britain, as her father, Mrs. Ailsa Mellon Bruce as her mother, and Mrs. Edward Warburg as her mother-in-law.

Audrey Emery, one of the most glamorous and witty ladies of our times, has three headquarters: a farm in Virginia near Charlottesville, a house in Cincinnati, and an apartment at the Ritz in Paris. With two Russian husbands in her past, Grand Duke Dimitri of Russia (as his morganatic wife she was then known as Princess Ilynaska) and Prince Djordjadze, she was reportedly engaged to the late Prince Pierre of Monaco (Rainier's father), but he died before the marriage took place.

Audrey Pleydell Bouverie is much talked about in jet society. Born Audrey James, half English and half American, she is well-known on both sides of the Atlantic. Her second husband was Marshall Field, and her third the Hon. Peter Pleydell-Bouverie, from whom she also divorced, is so fond of the name Audrey that he has taken on, as his second mate, Audrey Kidston. There ensues much confusion in England because of two Audrey Bouveries. The divorced one, who was long ago the light in the eyes of Lord Louis Mountbatten (but he married, instead, Edwina Ashley), has her abodes in England, the Bahamas, and on Elba.

Audrey Hepburn is among the few of the current crop of stars who is in the social whirl, gliding with grace through the sets of the Loel Guinnesses (how these two love movie people) and Count and Countess Romanones-Quintanilla. With houses in Switzerland and Marbella, she and her husband, the bearded Mel Ferrer, are constantly moving but never convey the impression of haste.

BEATRICE, BEATRIZ, BEATRIX, BEE

H.R.H. Infanta Beatriz of Spain, the wife of the Prince di Civitella Cesi, is sometimes referred to by her intimates as

"Baby." She lives in Rome and rides to the hounds. Being a daughter of the last King of Spain, she is treated accordingly, and visits her mother, Queen Victoria Eugenia, in Lausanne. Her two daughters married commoners (Clemente Lequio and Paul-Annik Weiller). Her two sons, Marco and Marino, are passionately interested in horses. Because her husband is half American, she comes in contact with many Yankees.

H.R.H. Princess Beatrix, Crown Princess of the Netherlands, although constantly traveling as the good-will Ambassadress of her nation, spends part of each summer in Port' Ercole. A member of a very conservative clan, she, like her sister Irene, caused storms of protest with the choice of her future husband, the German diplomat Klaus von Amsberg. She often visits the United States and has been the house guest of Jack and Drue Heinz.

Lady Ormerod is one of the most prominent figures in the Caribbean. The widow of the aviation-rich Frederick Sigrist, she remarried a former member of Great Britain's diplomatic corps, Sir Berkeley Ormerod, lives in Nassau in the winter, in England in the spring and fall, in the South of France in the summer.

The Dowager Countess of Granard is the American-born widow (she was Beatrice Mills of New York and Staatsberg on the Hudson) of the Eighth Earl. She has a magnificent residence in Paris' Rue de Varenne, but also spends time in the British Isles and in Florida, where she visits her sister, Mrs. Henry Phipps, every winter. Her way of talking causes comment, since, much like Gertrude Stein's prose, it has little punctuation.

Madame Antenor Patiño was Beatriz de Rivera before becoming Countess of Rovazenda. Since her marriage to the Bolivian tin king, she has been plagued by lawsuits on the part of his first wife, the Duchess of Durcal, who does not recognize, sometimes successfully, the validity of their marriage. Exceedingly well liked by her many friends, she shares, with Patiño, residences in France and Portugal and roams part of the year on a yacht named *Beatriz.*

Mrs. André Embiricos divides her year among Petali, the island her husband's family owns in the Aegean Sea, a magnificent Parisian residence, and skiing quarters in Klosters. American-born, often called Bee, she was a successful model before her marriage to the English-educated Greek shipping tycoon.

Beatrice Dabney, who counts the great Whistler among her ancestors, is also referred to as Bee. With a strong Bostonian background, she uses New York as her headquarters and moves quietly in many sets. She is now married to *Vogue* photographer, Penati. A delightful elfin-like creature, she paints with flair and talent.

Beatrice Monti is never called Bee but she is a busy one nevertheless, competently running an art gallery in Milan and roaming the capitals in search of new artists. In the summers she takes a breather and occupies a delightful house in the town of Lindos on the island of Rhodes.

Bettina

Mrs. Elsbridge Bruce is rarely seen, but constantly discussed because of her courage to say good-by to the lavish Long Island set, marry a Negro, and make a success of it. The daughter of the late Marshall Field and the opinionated Mrs. Diego Suarez, she divorced her first husband, left behind her a formidable social position, and went to live in England with her new mate and later in France where mixed marriages are accepted with ease.

In Parisian gilded salons and couture circles—she is currently a promoter of Madame Gres's work—it's **Madame Jacques de Bergery** whom New Yorkers will recall long ago as the graceful Bettina Jones. At one time French Ambassadress to Turkey, she stuck loyally to her husband when he ran into temporary political trouble at the end of the Second World War following the liberation.

Another Bettina is the late Aly Khan's companion, the divorced wife of *Paris Match's* **Gilbert Graziani.** She recently published her memoirs of her life with the Prince, to the reported annoyance of his son, the Aga, who deemed them unnecessary. A firm believer in bangs, she always wears them during her incessant wanderings in the company of her current beau, baby-faced Maurice Jacquin, Jr., reputed to be as young as he is wealthy. She was among the first to build a house in Sardinia's Costa Smeralda.

In Great Britain's ultra-U establishments and the United States, it's **Elizabeth Countess of Lindsey and Abingdon,** one of the great beauties of the post–First World War era and the possessor of a mellifluous voice. Herself a member of the Montagu-Worthley-Stuart-Mackenzie tribe, she never bore children, and therefore, following her mate's recent demise, the Earldom has passed to a cousin.

Bill and Billy (William)

Both **William Randolph Hearst** and **William Nichols** are publishing luminaries. The first is exceedingly likable, an easy conversationalist, and a fine observer of the political scene on an international scale. He takes trips to interview world leaders with his own staff of experts. His third wife, Austine, usually called "Bootsie," is a delectable Southerner, who is an accomplished hostess in both Manhattan and at San Simeon. Nichols is the guiding light of *This Week* magazine. An erudite, sensitive man, with a variety of hobbies, he is often emplaning for business conferences, but home is a fine apartment on Park Avenue. His mate is one of the most attractive canceled Czechs to come out of middle Europe as a result of the upheaval in that part of the world.

William A. Burden holds the gigantic position of Chairman of New York City's Museum of Modern Art. Slightly pompous, able and opulent, he collects art himself. Some years back he was United States Ambassador to Belgium.

In New York City, Long Island, Nassau, Jamaica, and New Hampshire (he owns houses in all of them), in high finance and entertainment circles it's bound to be **Bill Paley.** Immensely rich, married to one of the most elegant women in the world, "Babe" Cushing, he is one of those lucky men who, having received many opportunities from life, took each and every one.

A Bill with marvelous connections on both sides of the ocean is **Viscount Astor,** whose mother was the unique Nancy Langhorne from Virginia, and whose manorial seat, Cliveden, is always in the news. He enjoys fathering children, having produced a son and two daughters from his three marriages. His current wife is the lovely Bronwen Alun Pugh, who has the good luck of being blessed with a name which never gets confused with that of anyone else.

Bill McKnight, a lawyer prominent in Southampton society and U echelons of the Eastern Seaboard, is fairly easy to spot for he is usually mentioned with his wife "Brunie." They are devoted to each other and neither has ever been divorced.

In the quiet Swiss valleys (he has a house there), at the Mt. Kenya Safari Club (in which he has an interest), and in many phases of the entertainment spheres (he is an astute businessman) it is **Bill Holden,** who started life with the less prepossessing name of William Beedle. A complex character, he keeps the attention of his public and friends at high pitch.

There is considerable confusion on the West Coast and in Beverly Hills society, for there are several Bills who move in the same set.

Bill Goetz, whose wife is Louis Mayer's daughter Edith, is one of the big hosts out by the Pacific waves. His mansion is large and so is his art collection so amusingly written up in Hedda Hopper's *The Whole Truth and Nothing But.*

Bill Haines, former leading man of silent Metro Goldwyn Mayer films, is now the most successful interior decorator amidst the California palm trees. Therefore when one hears "I love what Bill did with the Tibetan wallpaper in the bathroom," one knows just who it is.

Bill Dozier, one of Joan Fontaine's former husbands and currently wed to Ann Rutherford, is a producer of television films who travels for this reason. So, when Merle Oberon tells one in Mexico City, "Bill has just arrived from Hollywood on business and I'm giving him a tiny dinner tomorrow night," there is little question whom she is talking about.

If, instead, there is mention of oil wells and deals, it's bound to be **Bill Dugger,** a Texan who also lives in Los Angeles. He was recently divorced from the lovely British movie actress Mara Lane, who not so long ago provided the light in Prince "Dado" Ruspoli's eyes.

All along the West Coast, but in San Francisco particularly, if there is talk of his legal cleverness, it is **Bill Wallace,** an able lawyer. In love with the enchanting, mercurial Ina Claire for a long time, he patiently waited until she accepted his proposal. The waiting period was worthwhile, for their marriage has been a smash. In his role as the President of San Francisco's Legion of Honor Museum he comes in contact with many artists.

Not to be confused with Bill Wallace is **Billy Wallace,** who was for a long time one of Princess Margaret's favorite escorts. In his late thirties, exceedingly prosperous, he owns a fine manor house in Berkshire and is welcome everywhere. He recently married a wealthy heiress, Elizabeth Millar, whose father is the first Baron Inchyra.

But along the British U trail there are others to create a mix-up. **Prince William of Gloucester** is one of them. A first cousin of the Queen, he is generally considered the most attractive male specimen of the Royal Family after Prince Philip. Educated at Cambridge and Leland Stanford University in California after Eton, he is a great traveler and very social. Independent and sophisticated, he makes friends easily. Recently there was quite a to-do about his twice flunking the entrance exams into the British diplomatic service, but he took a non-career job in West Africa.

Then there is **Viscount Ednam,** eldest son and heir of the Earl of Dudley. A good-looking and easy-going gentleman, this Billy is currently married to Maureen Swanson. His first wife, Stella Carcano, daughter of the former Argentinian Ambassador to the Court of St. James, is in orbit too, and much confusion arises between the two Lady Ednams. Billy and Maureen often have Jamaica as their stamping ground, and Stella (but known as "Baby") has Mallorca. The first Lady Ednam is a sister to the English Mrs. John Jacob Astor (there is an American one also).

Bill Ballard, an architect whom the chic set of the Caribbean often uses, was first married to Lucinda Ballard, the theatrical costume designer, and then to the late fashion expert Bettina Wilson.

There is only one **Billy** in the decorating field according to some wonderful ladies, including Mrs. John F. Kennedy and Mrs. Paul Mellon. A spectacularly successful interior designer, **William Baldwin** is small in size but a shining glory in Baltimore's (that is where he was born) bosom.

Among the affluent, as well as among the not so rich, **Billy Graham** is not only their favorite evangelist but also part of their society. At Round Hill, Jamaica, for instance, he is lionized. His name often comes up with that of Eleanor Whitney, the ex-wife of "Sonny" Whitney, who has followed him to darkest Africa and on other expeditions to sing at his religious meetings.

BIRGITTE

provides a trap I have seen many persons fall into when a member of that inner, inner C.C. mentions this name. The final

TE is so well-pronounced it soon becomes obvious that it cannot be Birgit Nilsson, the eminent Wagnerian soprano, they are talking about, for, with all due respect to her formidable voice, the Swedish soprano is not a darling of the smart set. So who is Birgitte that entrancing people like Leonard and Felicia Bernstein, John and Jane Gunther, and the Bill Paleys speak of in such rapturous tones? It turns out to be **Vera Zorina,** for this is her Christian appellation and this is what her husband, Goddard Lieberson, and her intimate friends call her.

Bunny

is shared as a nickname by both men and women of prominence. With the ladies it could be either **Mrs. Nicholas Du Pont** or **Mrs. Paul Mellon.**

The first is an enthusiastic gardener and an expert on botany. She divides her time among a large estate in Delaware, a pastel-shaded mansion in Palm Beach, and traveling. A stunning blonde, she is warm, friendly and easy-going.

The second seldom circulates in society, although she has spectacular residences in Upperville, Virginia, Washington, New York, Cape Cod, and Antigua. But she is always mentioned in chic chat, for she is fantastically rich and buys wonderful jewels, pictures, and furniture. Recently she made the best-dressed list. She is a famous gardener.

It could also be the sweet-looking **Honorable Mrs. Dominic Elliott,** daughter-in-law of the Earl of Minto, who travels in Princess Margaret's set. Her mother, Mrs. Arpad Plesch (one of the most-often-married ladies of our times), lives on the French Riviera, and her stepfather keeps his fine studs in Ireland. Her father was Count Thomas Esterhazy of the historical Hungarian clan.

Among the gentlemen, Bunny could be either **Prince Boncompagno Boncompagni** or **Ernest Boissevain.** The first is a member of the old Roman nobility, lives in New York with his second wife, the former Selma Borger, and is successful in the textile business. The second is the serene, pleasant, Dutch-born husband of Jean Tennyson, who divides his 365 days among a villa in Florence, flats in New York and Paris, a house in Vermont, and visits to the music festivals and to his native Holland.

Carla

The mix-up in Rome is intense, for three of them are apt to turn up in chic chat. They are:

Princess Alvaro of Bourbon-Orleans, who is the rich daughter of the late Senator Leopoldo Parodi-Delfino and the wife of the eldest son of the Infante Alfonso of Spain. Well-liked, she has been busy educating four children and does not travel as much as her other namesakes except in summer on a yacht she owns.

Princess Carla Boncompagni, a handsome lady in whose veins runs the bluest blood imaginable. Born a Borromeo, that glorious family which boasts not only a Saint but a private island on Lake Maggiore, she is excellent company and lives entirely in hotels, turning up often in Paris, St. Moritz, and other centers of amenities.

The **Marchioness Lanza d'Ajeta,** an immensely vivacious, sympathetic, efficient ex-Ambassadress—her husband the Marquess filled the jobs of Italian Envoy to Brazil and Argentina for several years—she is born a Visconti, which means she is related to everyone who counts in Italy. Currently she lives in São Paulo where her husband is in business.

To simplify the confusion, it is fortunate that the fourth Carla, **Mrs. Peter Thorneycroft,** left Italy a long time ago to become a brilliant light in London society. At the time when she was Countess Giorgio Roberti, many considered her the most beautiful woman in Europe. Her current husband has been a member of the British cabinet on many occasions and is a popular member of the Conservative Party.

Cesare

No singer is a greater contribution to a successful evening than the Metropolitan Opera bass **Cesare Siepi.** Handsome, gifted with a glorious voice and remarkable stage presence, he is as at home on the concert platform as he is donning costumes and beards. Since his marriage to an American ballerina, his excursions into society have diminished.

In St. Moritz, where he and his wife can be found at the Palace Hotel, Milan where he lives, and Montecatini, a spa he helps run, the portly and good-natured **Count Bonacossa** is very much in evidence.

Count d'Acquarone turns up everywhere with his beautiful wife, the former Claire de Dierex. His late father played a dominant role at the Italian royal court, his mother, the Dowager Duchess d'Acquarone, is a familiar figure on the French Riviera where she owns a splendid house, and his brother the Duke is a famous rose-grower in San Remo.

Casare Balsa is a self-made Catalonian who went to Mexico and made his fortune in the hostelry and restaurant business. A gentle man, with laughing eyes, he is quiet, unassuming, and never misses a trick.

Count Cicogna, often referred to as "Coco," is the husband of Anna Maria Volpi, but they have led independent lives for many years. He shuttles from the French Riviera, where he has a charming house, to Milan where he has his stock brokerage office, to the Caribbean, which he visits every winter.

Charles and Charlie

Charlie is a tantalizing name in the talking game, for behind this simple appellation are some very important men. Easy to mix are Messieurs **Wrightsman** and **de Bestegui,** since they live and breathe antiques, although in reality no two more different men could exist in the same antique-loving species. Another Charlie, fabulously rich, who comes up in conversation all the time is **Charles Engelhard.** He might prove confusing to the uninitiated since his wife's name, like Mr. Wrightsman's, is Jane. All one can do is listen attentively to the inflection of the voice for Mrs. Engelhard is Jane, just simple Jane, while Mrs. Wrightsman is more likely to be referred to as Jaynie. There are, however, some greater aids for distinguishing between them. The Engelhards have no home in Palm Beach but one in Boca Grande, and their score on homes absolutely annihilates the Wrightsmans'. While the latter have two fabulous ones, Palm Beach and New York, the Engelhards have an apartment in New York, a farm in New Jersey, a camp in Canada, an apartment in Rome, and two residences in South Africa. They also travel in a private jet and, along with diamonds, platinum is their main business interest.

Among the American Charlies, there is a large choice. The painter **Baskerville,** not rich like those mentioned above, has talent and is a favorite extra man. Since he has been to the Orient many times, his name comes up with all the Maharajahs and tigers he has put on canvas. Then there is the sometime real estate broker, sometime columnist for the *Journal American,* **Van Rensselaer,** also a bachelor—he was married at one point to the daughter of an Italian diplomat but later divorced—who is an amiable fellow and thinks positively about his jet-set friends.

In Palm Beach, where he is the reigning sovereign, in Paris—he owns a house there too and races some of his horses—and along U circuits one can bet it's **Charles Munn,** father of those two charmers Mrs. Frances Baker and the Countess of Dessborough. His current wife is Dorothy Spreckels ex-Dupuy, ex-McCarthy.

Charles Wacker III, single and a gift to the fair sex, travels in turf circles, in the backgammon set and in Chicago's millionaires' corner. Recently, his heart throb was Patricia Rawlings, who has the gift of being in the news all the time.

Because of his great gifts as a cartoonist and conversationalist, **Charles Addams** plays a very definite role. Also a bachelor, he is often reported to be involved in torrid love affairs.

Charles Blackwell is one of the lights of wealthy New York, Long Island, and Palm Beach society. An urbane, smooth gentleman, he takes off with his wife Katie (they have never been divorced) on long journeys, rents houses in far-off places such as Hong Kong, and enjoys taking cures.

In England the alternative is among:

The **Duke of Rutland,** who is the host at two famous country houses, Haddon Hall and Belvoir Castle, and is married, on his second round, to Frances Sweeny. One of the handsomest of the British aristocrats, he is enthusiastic about journeys and goes with his Duchess to exotic places. In the summer, however, he prefers to stay closer to home and rents a house in Biarritz.

His father-in-law, **Charles Sweeny,** one of many Americans settled in Great Britain, is an enthusiastic golfer and currently a single man again.

Charles Clore is a big draw on the marriage market since he divorced his French consort. One of the wealthiest men in the British Empire, he travels far and wide, gives one annual dinner dance during the season in some London hotel, and entertains often at large shooting parties on his estate near Newbury in Berkshire.

Lord Charles Churchill, the younger son of the Duke of Marlborough, was educated partially in the United States and was a great favorite of his grandmother, Madame Jacques Balsan (Consuelo Vanderbilt), who remembered him nicely in her will. He is married to a Texas heiress, Gillian Fuller.

Elsewhere, we discover **Charles Feldman,** who gave up his career as an agent to become a film producer. He has remained on excellent terms with his former wife, Jean Howard, and for a while showed great interest in the career of Madame Capucine.

Terribly eligible is **H.R.H. Prince Charles of Luxembourg,** the brother of the reigning Prince and related to every family in the Gothas. Attractive and easy-going, he is involved in the Pris Unic activities in the Grand Duchy, has been to the United Nations several times as a member of a delegation from the principality, and has many American friends.

Charles Collingwood is much quoted in television milieus in both the U.S.A. and in Europe. He now lives in London, planning many important CBS shows. He entertains a lot with his wife, the actress Louise Albritton, and roams the world constantly.

Charles de Guigné, a marvelous mixture of French know-how and California sunshine and money, was picked by *Town and Country* as one of the most eligible young men in the cosmos. He has started, with Susan Stein and other friends, a travel agency called "Ports of Call." He is the ex-nephew of the Vicomtesse de Bonchamps.

In Queen Victoria Eugenia of Spain's society and many other top Swiss drawing rooms, **Charles Chaplin** is mentioned constantly. A devoted husband to Oona O'Neill, ever so many years his junior, he is opinionated and yet a far greater conformist than people expect him to be.

In France, Charlesses are rarely referred to as Charlies, which is a blessing. Among the most frequently mentioned are:

H.S.H. Prince Charles d'Arenberg, undoubtedly the greatest cosmonaut of all the French Charlesses, seldom gets the opportunity to enjoy the quietness of the Chateau de Menetou-Salon, surrounded by a beautiful forest, or his Parisian mansion, recently completed. He is always catching a plane with his wife Peggy or in the process of joining her somewhere.

The **Vicomte de Noailles** owns a series of enchanting houses, among them the celebrated Pavillon Pompadour at Fontainebleau where the mistress of Louis XV lived when the court occupied the royal palace there. He is an immensely cultivated gentleman with a rare knowledge of gardens. Married to the unique Marie Laure Bischoffsheim but not exactly in the same *avant-garde* artistic league, he arranges for the yearly visits of the Queen Mother of England to France. His name also comes up on the Riviera where he owns an estate near Grasse not far from that of his widowed sister, the Princess de Ligne, an enthusiastic gardener too.

Coming up fast indeed is the **Count de Cosse-Brissac,** a member of the younger set. He is a little easier to recognize among the French, for he is sometimes referred to as Charlie. Married to Anita Lobkowicz, who is half American, he owns the beautiful Chateau de Blanville near Chartres, and when in Paris enjoys night club excursions.

In hotel snobbish chat it is usually Monsieur **Charles Ritz,** who is in his early seventies and does a fine job upholding the high standards set by his father, the famous Cesar, and mother, Mimi.

Although he became an American citizen well over two decades ago and his home is in California, the French frequently refer to **Charles Boyer,** for they consider that he has never let his country down, has never been involved in any form of cheap publicity. He has been married to the same woman for thirty years and has kept high the prestige of French charm and acting.

The most sought-after **Charles** in Europe is **Aznavour,** who has triumphed over his small frame of body with his immense skill as a song writer, performer, and actor. Although his white overcoats and sports cars are very yé-yé, members of the C.C. court him incessantly.

Not a Greek Charles, but a British one holds sway over international shipping. He is the third **Baron Aberconway** whose family is alphabetically listed first in Debrett's **Peerage.**

Chairman of John Brown & Co. whose shipyards are building the gigantic new Cunard liner which will replace the **Queen Mary** in three years' time, he is married to New York City's Ann Lindsay.

Christina

presents infinite pitfalls in the nomadic society jungle. Even the most U of nomads are overcome by the number of glamorous ladies who answer to this name and constantly cross each other's paths. In royal circles there are three born to the purple, and a fourth who married into it.

One can be deeply grateful that the **Infanta Maria Christina of Spain** is referred to as "Crista." Daughter of the last King of Spain, she is a handsome, intelligent, well-adjusted lady who is an asset to royalty anywhere. With residences in Geneva and Rapallo, she accompanies her husband, Vermouth industrialist Count Marone Cinzano, on long goodwill tours of South, Central, and North America, and visits her sister the Princess of Civitella Cesi in Rome.

Christina of Aosta is unmarried, tall, a little shy in manner, passionately interested in riding. She is always on the move visiting her royal relations all over Europe, but makes her headquarters in Florence and Sorrento with her mother. Her father, the Duke of Aosta, died in Kenya after being taken a prisoner in Ethiopia during the last war, where his cousin, King Victor Emanuel of Italy, had sent him as Viceroy.

Christina of Bourbon-Parme, unmarried sister of the head of the immense Parma royal family, is short, blonde, nearsighted, marvelously gay, trains dogs like a pro and sings Viennese songs with real schmaltz. Although her base is Vienna, one runs into her everywhere. She sometimes wears some of the inherited jewels of Queen Marie Antoinette.

Countess Carl Johann Bernadotte, the commoner daughter-in-law of the King of Sweden, is in constant search of plays and musicals to produce in Stockholm. A close friend of Garbo, she goes to New York frequently, and in the summer, cruises with her husband on one of the yachts Jacques Sarlie charters.

In the legion of nonroyal Christinas, the most prominent are:

Marchesa Emilio Pucci, the ravishing, Botticelli-life wife of the member of the Italian Parliament who is the top sports designer in the world. She makes her home in Florence (in both a palace and a villa), but accompanies her nomadic husband around the world at the drop of a hairpin.

Countess Bernardo Rucellai, whose domain is also Florence (she is quite a hostess there) and the Tuscan countryside (several villas and a beach house), goes to the United States because of her husband's many American connections (his mother was American). She is friendly and enthusiastic.

Mrs. Henry Ford, the former Christina Vettore, arrived in the nomadic sweepstakes when the car Czar started taking an interest in her. Once married to a Canadian officer, William Austin, she is described as an Italian Melina Mercouri. A bohemian at heart.

France has numerous Christines also. The most discussed there at the moment is (every hostess is trying to latch on to her) **Christine de Rivoyre,** a tiny woman in her forties, who drives around in a small red car and whose novels are riveting because of the deep understanding she shows for the anguished society of our times. Her latest, *The Sultans,* became an immediate best seller.

The enchanting **Christine de Caraman** is a sloe-eyed creature whose engagement to Taki Theodoracoupolos, the sexy Greek tennis player and skier (once the escort of Linda Christian), was one of the longest in recent social history until it culminated in wedding bells in 1965.

Christina de Heeren, the bright, active daughter of Rodman and Aimee de Heeren, commutes in the summer between Biarritz and anywhere an important bullfight is held, and in the winter between New York and Palm Beach, where her parents have homes.

In Spain it's easier to distinguish them. If a lawsuit is mentioned, one can assume it is the still breathtakingly beautiful **Duchess of Durcal** (in her own right) who has been suing Antenor Patiño ever since anyone can recall. She claims (and some courts agree) that she is still his legitimate wife, but he insists she is not (and other courts, it seems, agree with him).

If skiing is mentioned, it is sure to be their daughter **Frau Ernest Schneider,** whose husband was a skiing instructor. The independent, adorable Christina who divorced Prince Marc de Beauvau-Craon in order to marry a man after her own heart, will some day inherit the title of Duchess of Durcal and, in case her first marriage is annulled, Herr Schneider will be the Duke.

Christina Mattossion, married to an Egyptian and the splendid sister of the Duke of Albuquerque, shoots down quail and partridges like a pro. She is Countess de la Torre in her own right.

On the West Coast it's **Christina Kaufman,** who has made husband Tony Curtis very happy; and elsewhere it may be **Christina Paolozzi,** the eccentric Italian-American Countess who threw her clothes to the winds and posed, for the sake of art, in the nude for *Harper's Bazaar* readers. She is married to Dr. Howard Bellin.

The Christina on everyone's lips in London and the British Empire is Italian-born **Lady Cholmondeley,** internationally known for her fun parties. Her husband is the son of the Marquess of Cholmondeley and the brother of the Earl of Rocksavage.

Two Cristianas, who are always referred to as Cristinas, are:

Cristiana Torlonia, who has reverted to her maiden princely Italian surname after two American marriages and divorces. Half American herself—her mother was Elsie Moore from New York City—she now lives in Rome, leads a sporting life, playing much golf.

Countess Brando Brandolini d'Adda, who has a palazzo in Venice and a house in Paris, often crosses the ocean and is a visitor to St. Moritz every winter. Because of her Agnelli background, she is very rich, and since she occasionally does not recognize people who have been introduced to her several times, she has the reputation of being exclusive. She is always exquisitely turned out.

One *Christina,* whose name recurs, is not a person but a yacht belonging to Aristotle Onassis. Not to have gone up that gangplank at least once is liable to give any "in earnest" nomad the kind of inferiority complex that will eventually enrich a psychiatrist.

Cristóbal and Christobel

are fraught with peril. The three men who answer to the first name are considered very chic and their exploits crop up all the time among name droppers.

Although **Balenciaga** leads a retired existence in both Paris and Spain, where he has various houses, there are plenty of women who know him slightly but mention him in affectionate terms by his first name. When the tone of the voice is reverent and hushed, it is surely this master of the hems and simple classical lines.

The Cristóbal of the historical snobs is the **Duke of Veragua,** a direct descendant of Christopher Columbus and named after his glorious ancestor. An officer in the Spanish Navy, he is often the Iberian representative at Hispano-American celebrations. A most agreeable and attractive gentleman, he is one of the best Spanish Ambassadors of good will.

Constantly in orbit is the son-in-law of Generalissimo Franco, the **Marquess of Villaverde,** consort of his one and only daughter Carmen. A dashing fellow who is a surgeon, he has enormous vitality and goes on shooting expeditions. He is sent with his charming wife to represent his country on official missions.

Not Cristóbal, but Christobel is the **Hon. Mrs. Neville Berry,** a daughter-in-law of Viscount Kemsley. English by birth, she was at one point married to Lanfear Norrie, a wealthy American who has his European headquarters in Biarritz. Despite houses in England and on the French Riviera, she crosses the ocean often with her husband. Her blonde curly locks recall those of German actress Lilian Harvey.

David

David is a fascinating name, for it grows like grass in England but not much elsewhere. Since all of the most attractive men in the British peerage and outside of it appear to answer to this appellation, a regular course must be taken to follow the many intricacies and nuances. King George V and Queen Mary were responsible, for they named their eldest son, the Prince of Wales, now Duke of Windsor, after the young hero who slew Goliath, and everyone followed suit.

Although the **Duke of Windsor**'s first name is Edward, members of his family, including his wife, call him David. If this name is mentioned in royal circles in England today and in very exclusive Mayfair drawing rooms, it may refer to the **Earl of Westmorland,** fifteenth in line, who has been the Queen's Lord-in-Waiting since 1955. Not in the least a nomad, he keeps very close to Buckingham Palace, lives at Ormeley Lodge in Surrey, and is just the last word in top-drawer British society.

The **Hon. David Somerset** has many attributes: his wonderful looks, his talent at selling paintings (he is a Director of the Marlborough Galleries), and a future Dukedom (he is the heir to the Duke of Beaufort). A close friend of Stavros Niarchos, he is apt to be his guest at Spezzapoula's shoots or in St. Moritz.

If the names of Fulke (The Earl of Warwick) or Rosie (his

mother) come up, then it's bound to be the handsome **Lord Brooke.** Since his marriage to Sarah Beatty has collapsed he is much sought after as an extra man at dinner parties.

If the subject is houses, antiques, and that sort of thing, connected with much travel, one is sure it's **David Hicks,** the decorator, who married the daughter of the Earl Mountbatten of Burma.

If there is mention of the Duke of Edinburgh (he is his first cousin) or the King of Sweden and Lord Mountbatten (his own uncles) or Yvor Bryce (his wife's uncle), then it cannot fail to be the very personable **Marquess of Milford Haven** who, since his second marriage, is less in the news.

On the other hand, if Tangiers is discussed (he makes his home there), a private zoo (he has a small one), Wilton (a famous country house in England which belongs to his brother, the Earl of Pembroke), one is sure it's the **Hon. David Herbert.**

David Metcalfe may be mentioned in connection with the Duke of Windsor (his father used to be the Duke's Equerry and close friend), Lord Curzon (he was his grandfather), the insurance business (he is in it) or the late Sir Alexander Korda (he married his widow, from whom he has had three children, and is now divorced), or some marvelous girl he is involved with.

In California society (he has a farm in the Valley of the Moon within driving distance from San Francisco), in the Astor clan (he was the late Alice Astor's fourth husband) and in the Radnor one (he is a relation of the seventh Earl of that name), it's **David Pleydell Bouverie,** a gentle, quiet but energetic gentleman in his early fifties who travels far and wide six months out of the year.

Among the jettiest of the jet set, with houses on the French Riviera and in Gstaad, are actor **David Niven** and his wife Hjordis.

The U.S. Ambassador to London is the tremendously popular **David Bruce,** who made a flop of his marriage to the heiress

Ailsa Mellon but a great success of his current one to his former assistant, Evangeline Bell.

Owner of the enchanting yacht *Sea Huntress* and popular in shooting circles is **Earl Beatty,** the half-brother of Ronald Tree. His American heritage (his mother was from the former colonies) has come to the fore in his choice of wives. Three of them were American and only the current one is a Britisher.

Then there is **Baron David de Rothschild** of the youthful jet set. In honor of his twenty-second birthday his father, Baron Guy, gave an unforgettable ball in 1965 for 1,600 guests at the Chateau de Ferrieres which was transformed for the occasion into a replica of the castle described in *Sleeping Beauty*. The young Baron's friends came from all over the world for it.

For several years one of the hosts at the sought-after New York ball of "The Bachelors" was the personable **David Bartlett.** He was first the husband of the current Mrs. Lewis Preston, and recently he took on Paris' Stephane Abeille de May as a bride.

David Bailey is the prodigiously successful, highly paid British photographer. Sporting a Beatle haircut and wearing a turtleneck sweater, he was on all the front pages when he slipped the ring on the finger of Catherine Deneuve, the adorable French actress who made Roger Vadim a father some time ago without the benefit of a wedding.

Deedee, Didi and Tetee, Titi

The first three are Deedees:

Mme. Jean-Claude Abreu, born Mary Ladd in New York City; daughter of Mrs. Russell Davenport, wife of a Cuban exile, owner of *L'Oeil* magazine, with homes in Paris and Zermatt, a frequent visitor to the United States. In demand in the top echelons of the French young, she is blonde, adorable-looking, and marvelously organized.

Mrs. John Barry Ryan III, whose headquarters are in New

York City, spins around a little less. She has excellent taste in clothes, sophisticated interests in the theater, and connections with intellectual circles. She is often referred to as the young Diane Vreeland although she has no current connection with any magazine (but used to be on *Harper's Bazaar*).

Count John Kesselstadt is a German bachelor with wine interests, whose mother, Gabrielle of Lichtenstein, is a member of the family ruling the principality. A good shot and just back in circulation after a job in Africa, he has an apartment in Geneva.

The others are:

H.R.H. Princess Maria-Beatrice of Italy, the youngest of the children of the last King of Italy and his Belgian Queen. With a turned-up nose, dimples, and a spontaneous manner, she is full of fun, restless, and permanently on the go, but knows, when circumstances demand it, how to make an effort with her elders.

Mrs. John Schiff is one of the most genial ladies on the Long Island–Jamaica circuit. A daughter of the immortal looking Mrs. George Baker, apart from her mate's considerable fortune she is deliciously rich in her own right.

Titi Blaffer, the divorced wife of Texas oil heir Edward Hudson, roams between New York and Newport in a Rolls-Royce, collects modern pictures and at one point was in the art business just for the fun of it. She is currently inseparable from French and Company's Spencer Samuels, but where business ends and social life begins is hard to say.

Denise

might be either the elfin-like widow of the late, immensely talented painter **René Bouché**, formerly Denise Lawson Johnston, a member of the court of Princess Charles d'Arenberg and popular with many sets; or **Mrs. Vincente Minnelli,** the attractive Yugoslav who fled to freedom across the Adriatic in a rowboat and appears at lunch with a long tress down her back, like an old-fashioned schoolgirl, and at night with it piled on top of her head, creating an 1890 picture. As the wife of one of the busiest screen directors, she is ever in orbit.

There is also the enchanting soprano of the Paris Opera, **Denise Duval,** a great Mélisande and the touching interpreter of the Poulenc operas *Les Mamelles de Tiresias* and *La Voix Humaine.* In Parisian drawing drooms Denise is bound to be the witty, cultivated **Madame Edouard Bourdet.**

Diane and Diana

Mrs. T. Reed Vreeland makes and destroys fashions with the bat of an eyelash as the supreme priestess of *Vogue* magazine.

Lady Diana Cooper is the ex-British Ambassadress to France, ex-star of Max Reinhardt's *The Miracle,* authoress of several autobiographical volumes, and related through her father, the late Duke of Rutland, to much of the blue blood streaming in the English aristocracy.

In London we have the widowed **Mrs. Harry Phipps,** daughter-in-law of Mrs. Marshall Field and Ogden Phipps, and a cousin of the Bismarcks, who has made herself popular, as she had done previously in New York, with the young, intellectual, slightly offbeat cliques; the youthful **Mrs. James Archibald Wolfe Murray,** the daughter of the former British Prime Minister, Sir Alec Douglas Home, wife of an executive of a large whisky manufacturing concern, whose lucky sister is a Lady of the Queen's bedchamber; and **Lady Beatty,** pretty and young, who manages to hold her ground as hostess at the grand Chichely Hall in Buckinghamshire and on board the *Sea Huntress.*

Mrs. John Traina, Jr. (her father, Wiley Buchanan, was the American Ambassador to Luxembourg and then Chief of Protocol during the Eisenhower Administration) is the attractive Diane who defied her father's wrath and married the man of her dreams, an executive of the American President shipping line.

Mrs. Huntington Hartford, exactly thirty years younger than her A.-and-P.-rich husband, was formerly Diane Brown, a model. Born in Massachusetts, the daughter of an accountant, she worked as a guide in a steel plant before joining the Plaza Five agency. She follows her mate in his constant travels, and her hobby is riding. A different type from his two previous wives, she is socially quiet. Recently there have been divorce rumors.

Diane Cilento has entered N.S. since the star of her consort Sean Connery has risen in such a meteoric manner. Always a busy actress—she recently completed a run in London in the play *Four Seasons,* by Arnold Wesker, and is appearing on all the giant screens in *The Agony and the Ecstasy*—she follows the protagonist of James Bond on his journeys when it is necessary to disprove that their marriage is on the rocks.

The beautifully groomed and dressed **Countess of Wilton** turns up in Nassau for the winter and in Great Britain. An excellent card player and a good hostess at her husband's shoots, she used to be married to David Naylor-Leyland, who now makes the Palm Beach scene with his American wife, Dita Douglas.

Dolores

applies to three exquisite beauties in different age groups, whose international fame has rested mainly on their looks.

Dolores del Rio, who was a great motion-picture star in the twenties, is still dazzling, and manages to overshadow many of the younger crowd. With a busy career, she is ever fulfilling assignments in different locations. One of the few actresses who always was in society, she is an addition anywhere.

Dolores Fürstenberg, widow of Patrick Guinness, is one of the most sensational of the young beauties. Like her mother,

Gloria Guinness (the wife of her late husband's father), she poses incessantly for the fashion magazines, and her name is bandied about by many who don't know her personally. With headquarters in Lausanne and Paris, she is ever a rolling stone, visiting her mother and father-in-law in their many residences, her mother-in-law Princess Joan Aly Khan, and her stepbrother-in-law the Aga Khan.

Another **Dolores,** with spectacular jewels and furs, is the Brooklyn belle **Miss Sherwood,** whose marriages and divorces to those wealthy gentlemen George Guinle and the late Georges Litman have filled the chronicles for years. Currently she is married to Don Mario Ruspoli. If the discussion centers on how late Dolores was arriving at some party, it's bound to be this brand-new wife of the Italian nobleman, for she belongs to that flock of ladies who are never, not even by some error, on time for anything.

Doris

is hard to figure for there are several such ladies who are much in the entertainment world. Apart from Doris Day, who does not partake in N.S., we have:

Mrs. Yul Brynner, a Chilean by the non-Spanish appellation of Doris Klein. Her best friends are such rich and glorious ladies as Gloria Guinness and Marie Hélène de Rothschild. With a house in Switzerland, she is much in Paris, wearing very simple, marvelously cut clothes and stirringly simple, arresting coiffures. Since Klein rhymes with Stein and Yul is not far in sound from Jules, there is understandable confusion with **Mrs. Jules Stein,** who was a member of N.S. long before Mrs. Brynner. An indefatigable hostess in Beverly Hills, New York, and Paris, this white-haired wife of the inventor of Music Corporation of America loves her friends and parties.

There is also a Doris on the West Coast, who has had three

husbands, all well-known—Mervin Le Roy, Charles Vidor, and Billy Rose. A daughter of Harry Warner, very rich and intelligent, she recently reverted to calling herself **Doris Vidor.**

Doris Duke has never played the social game and is only referred to occasionally by old friends who see her. With many homes—an estate in New Jersey, an apartment in New York, residences in Hawaii, California, and Newport—she is always on the move but manages to follow her own interests without fanfare.

An independent **Doris** is **Miss Lilly,** who at one time was a columnist and now fills a job with a large cosmetic concern. The authoress of several humorous books, she never followed the advice she gave in *How to Marry a Millionaire* and never married one.

Dorothy

Metropolitan Opera Star **Dorothy Kirsten** commutes to her assignments from her house in the Hawaiian Islands. Married to Dr. John French, Brain Research Doctor at UCLA, she was a protégée of the late Grace Moore and has made the Puccini repertoire her own.

Green-eyed **Mrs. Oscar Hammerstein,** the attractive and eloquent Australian-born widow of the musical comedy lyricist and librettist, occupies a very special place on Broadway and in international theatrical circles.

In Canada, New York, the Caribbean, and the French Riviera it's **Mrs. Izaak Walton Killam,** wonderfully rich and living accordingly, with retinues of courtiers and servants.

Mrs. George Mahana summers in Monte Carlo and is well-known in certain sections of New York City society. She is fond of visiting her daughter, wife of a diplomat, often in some far-off place on some assignment.

In New York, Washington (her late husband occupied some

important posts in the government), her native Philadelphia, in Paris (where she visits her sister-in-law the Dowager Countess of Granard), and ultraconservative society Dorothy is **Mrs. Ogden Mills,** recently in bad health. A stunning beauty in her day, she is the grandmother of one of today's most glamorous young matrons, Mrs. Frederick Cushing.

In England it can be either:

Lady Brownlow, the American-born wife of the Gentleman-in-Waiting to the Duke of Windsor at the time he was King, an excellent hostess in stately Belton House (one of Sir Christopher Wren's masterpieces) and in Jamaica where they spend the winters; or:

Lady Dorothy Macmillan, a sister of the late Duke of Devonshire and wife of the former Prime Minister of Great Britain, a pleasant lady, who has been a great asset to her husband's career.

The original **Mrs. Randolph Kidder,** wife of the American diplomat, is renowned for her extraordinary clothes, hairdos, and jewels. She speaks French to perfection and made quite a place for herself in the French capital when her mate was Counsellor at the U.S. Embassy in Paris. Her mother is the musically minded Mrs. E. Gerry Chadwick of New York City.

Dorothy Gish, with her sister Lillian, frequently takes off incognito for strange, interesting places. These two imperishable stars who have afforded so much pleasure to the public and their countless friends over the years are also on the move for professional engagements.

The United Nations party circuit is the most exhausting in the world, but **Mrs. Arthur Goldberg,** whose husband, a former Supreme Court Justice, succeeded the late Adlai Stevenson as head of the American Delegation, is up to it. An energetic woman who paints abstract oils in her spare time, she decorated the Waldorf Astoria Tower apartment which is their official residence with paintings loaned by different museums.

Earl

In these democratic times, when an Earl is called by his first name and not by his title, this denomination in N.S. comes down to:

Earl E. T. Smith, a tall, handsome gent who makes his headquarters in New York and Palm Beach, is sometimes a Republican, sometimes a Democrat. A great friend of all the Kennedys, he wrote an excellent book on the Cuban crisis (he was Ambassador there during the Eisenhower administration), is the father of one of the prettiest young matrons in American society, Mrs. William Hutton, and the widower of one of the most attractive, Flo Pritchett.

Earl Blackwell invented Celebrity Service and the *Celebrity Register*. He manages to know terribly bitchy people without ever having a bitchy thought. He travels constantly, with offices in New York, Hollywood, London, Paris, and Rome, organizes celebrity junkets and cruises, never loses his patience when many others would.

Earl McGrath keeps changing jobs, so it's difficult to know just what he is doing at the moment, but he is surely in some phase of the entertainment world. Married to Camilla Pecci Blunt, and therefore related to many of the top nomads, he is an excellent host.

Earl Wilson and his B.W. (that is the way he always refers to his cozy consort Rosemary), the popular columnist of the *New York Post*, is a guest on a great many junkets, gads around constantly, writing with a fine homespun humor about the personalities he meets.

Edouard, Edward, Ed and Eddie

boils down to:

Count Bismarck, the grandson of the German Iron Chancellor, husband of Mona Strader (for several decades a reigning glamour Queen as Mrs. Harrison Williams), divides his time among a magnificent Hotel Particulier in Paris, a beautiful estate in Capri, and traveling. An excellent linguist, he speaks Italian and English like a native, is cultivated, and has great taste in pictures and furnishings.

Vicomte de Ribes, a successful banker (Rivaud and Co.) and administrator of many societies, has his home in Paris, but his many interests take him to Asia and Africa. He is married to one of the most publicized women of our times, Jacqueline de Beaumont, and is a topnotch skier.

H.S.H. Prince Lobkowicz is Czech through his late father and American via his mother, Anita Lihme. He has his base in Paris, where he runs a prosperous brokerage firm, a country house in Normandy, and a permanent air ticket to all the world capitals. He is a firm believer in royalty, being married to an attractive representative of this rarefied class, Princess Françoise de Bourbon-Parme.

Edward Condon, one of the United States' best-looking men, discussed for his mercurial temper, has been in various business enterprises in Europe, with Rome as a point of reference. Married first to Paynie Payson, currently Mrs. Enrico Middleton, he later became the husband of pretty Elizabeth Guest, a daughter from the first marriage of the current American Ambassador to Ireland, but this union too shipwrecked.

In egghead society no one is more desirable than **Edward Albee,** a quiet introvert who watches the contemporary scene and writes scathingly about it in his plays. A bachelor, he is considered a great catch by any hostess, but he plays the dinner and cocktail party circuit very carefully indeed.

Now back in the fashion field after a long hiatus is **Edward Molyneux.** English by birth but French by adoption, he divides his life among a property on the Côte d'Azur, an apartment in New York, and long stays in Paris to prepare his new shows. A talented painter in his own right, he is also a collector and some years ago sold most of the masterpieces he had acquired to Mrs. Mellon Bruce.

Ed frequently means **Sullivan** who travels fast and furiously to be in the know about who is successful where. His enormous prestige has not changed his point of view, which has remained sharp, realistic, and human.

Ed Russell, the estranged husband of Lady Sarah Churchill and therefore the son-in-law of the Duke of Marlborough, was the publisher of *Vogue* for a while, but he has now reverted to his previous job in another part of Newhouse's publishing empire.

Edward Stone started life in Fayetteville, Arkansas, but made the world his home. Among his spectacular architectural achievements are the U.S. Embassy in New Delhi, the American Pavilion at Brussels' World's Fair, and the National Geographic Society's Office Building in Washington, D.C. More recently, he has been making news on the divorce front.

The conservative **Edward Bemberg** of the famous Argentinian dynasty makes Manhattan his base. His American wife is the former Georgia Hatch whose sister also made an international merger, living with her Sicilian mate, a member of the Villarosa clan, in Milan.

Elie, Helie, and Heli

present very specific problems in and out of French U milieus.

The most in orbit of the group is **Baron de Rothschild.** A magnificent looking man, he is a great polo player (as is his son Nathaniel), a wonderful shot (his property in Austria is the scene of superb parties), a great collector of art with his wife, Liliane Fould-Springer, and has financial interests in every nook and corner. His name spells magic everywhere, but in Paris particularly he is treated like royalty.

The delightful **Duke of Talleyrand-Perigord,** whose knowledge of antiques and pictures is legendary, has been a widower since the death of his enchanting American wife Loelia Emery of Cincinnati. An indefatigable traveler, the Duke takes off all the time for different destinations. He resides in the treasure-filled Pavillon Colombe at St. Brice, near Paris, and in Rome's Palazzo Pecci Blunt.

The Count de Pourtales, whose grandmother was Anna Gould, lives with his wife mainly in Geneva, where he pursues his banking career. Taking an active part in the social life on Lake Leman, he is a marvelous skier, with Gstaad as his winter base.

Elie de Brignac's name is familiar to anyone interested in racing. Unmarried, in his middle thirties, he lives in Normandy where he breeds horses for such turfmen as Raymond Guest; rides superbly to the hounds; looks swarthy; is definitely a man's man.

The **Count de Ganay,** also a bachelor, went to Harvard Business School, is an agricultural authority, runs the family estates, is a topnotch shot and fishing expert.

ELISE

presents problems, especially in Paris and the United States, for there are three ladies who have homes in Paris but cross the ocean several times a year. The two most nomadic are:

Mrs. Basil Goulandris, one of the most beautiful of the wives of the Greek shipping tycoons, spends all her winters with her husband skiing (wherever the snow is good), the summers divided between Greece and Southampton (where they have a house), and on and off periods in a magnificent apartment on the Avenue Foch in the French capital.

Elise Hunt is a warm-hearted, pretty, highly talkative Californian who makes her stays, but never for long, in a magnificent house in Neuilly where she entertains on a large scale. She spends every fall running from one big shooting party to another.

Mrs. Halsey Malone, a gentle, conservative lady, is an important hostess in Paris where she moves in Embassy circles. This is a big help for whenever one hears "I saw Elise at the Embassy last night" or "I was talking to Ambassador X last night at Elise's" one knows just which Elise it is.

Elizabeth, Liz, and Betty

The first is the name of the British Sovereign and her mother, known in England as the Queen Mom, who are never referred to in nomadic society except by their rank.

Elizabeth Arden (in society Mrs. Elizabeth N. Graham) is a queen in her own right. Endowed with an energy which leaves her thousands of employees out of breath, she is always visiting the various outposts of the brilliant empire she has created with her genius and over which the sun never sets. Her name is likely to pop up anywhere, at any time, for everything that concerns women affects her. She is, however, at her happiest when off to the races to watch one of her many yearlings run.

Mrs. Howard Oxenberg, a beautiful creature, would be a great adornment to society even if she were not Her Royal Highness Princess Elizabeth of Yugoslavia. Married to a manufacturer of pregnant ladies' outfits, she is much in transit. Should one hear of some Elizabeth having given a party it surely is not this charmer, for she is somewhat allergic to entertaining.

Countess Ferdinand von Bismark is acknowledged as the smartest member of youthful Brussels society. A Belgian by birth—her father is the famous ornithologist, Count Leon Lippens—and married to Prince Bismark's son (an official of the European Economic Commission in the Belgian capital) she is an accomplished rider, skier, and tennis player.

Mrs. Richard Burton spells such magic in the screen world that she receives a cool million dollars per picture. Hard to nail down socially, when she does make an appearance she often creates a riot. A very young woman, with four marriages behind her, she had the ability, with her fifth wedding, to shake the uncertain morals of our time.

Four charming ladies who have been subjected to the nickname Liz:

The stunning **Lady Elizabeth Von Hofmannsthal,** who shuttles between London and her husband's Austrian schloss in the Salzkammergut. She is connected through her parents with the foremost English patrician clans and through her late father-in-law (one of Austria's most illustrious authors) with Mittel Europa intellectuals.

A star of Long Island and Virginia society and the nomadic skiing trails, **Elizabeth Guest** is the daughter of Raymond Guest and the ex-wife of Edward Condon. She took on as her second mate George Stevens, Jr., son of the screen director.

In horseracing circles it's a hopless mess. Liz could be either **Mrs. Cloyce Tippett** or **Mrs. Theodore Weicker.** The first used to provide much fodder for the columnists and the press in general, but everything is much quieter on her front now. Born Mary Elizabeth Altemus of Philadelphia, she was once married to Jock Whitney and currently lives on a farm near Ocala, Florida, from where she takes off to follow her wonderful horses. She breeds them in Ireland and owns a helicopter. The second is an energetic, well-liked lady who shuttles among her various houses on the Eastern Seaboard and an apartment in Paris' Ile St. Louis. She also follows all the important races wherever they are taking place, having a good stable of her own in France.

Three of them answer, instead, to Liza. They are:

Lady Glendevon, the daughter of the late W. Somerset Maugham, who was the protagonist of a well-publicized lawsuit against her father which kept the entire continent in a state of uproar with much of the British nobility taking her side. Her husband, the brother of the Marquess of Linlithgow, has held several political appointments of note.

Liza Minnelli, the daughter of Judy Garland's marriage to Vincente Minnelli, is a talented singer in her own right who appears headed for a notable career.

Wherever rarefied society gathers in Virginia, Washington, or the Cape, **Liza Lloyd,** the daughter from a previous marriage of Rachel Lambert, currently Mrs. Paul Mellon (known as "Bunny"), is sure to be present. Her coming-out dance, given at the famous Mellon estate in Upperville, Virginia, received little publicity (the Mellons hate it), but all those who attended said it was one of the fanciest balls to be given in the United States in the last two decades. She is very eligible.

In the cream of the cream's youthful Roman set Elisabetta often means **Countess Alvise Robilant,** who started life as Elizabeth Stork in Lynchburg, Virginia. Beautiful and serene, she is an adornment to any party.

Elsa

With the recent death of Elsa Maxwell this name, so evocative of the Princess of Brabant, Lohengrin's unhappy bride, narrows down to:

A toss-up in Paris between **Elsa Schiaparelli** and **Elsa Martinelli,** the former model turned actress, who has settled there. Here are some pointers about how to distinguish one from the other:

Schiaparelli's name is apt to come up with shocking pink (she created it), turbans (her personal trademark), her daughter Gogo (the very well liked widow of Berry Berenson), two attractive granddaughters, all the glamorous society ladies who used to be in her employ, or some cool remark she has made.

Martinelli's, with her estranged, handsome husband Count Franco Mancinelli Scotti, her current beau, flowing-haired photographer Willy Rizzo, yé-yé parties she gives, bangs which she wears all the time.

Among those nomads who manage to find time to read reviews or books (rarely the latter), there is much name dropping of the two writers **Elsa Morante** and **Elsa Triollet.** The first, wife of Alberto Moravia, the top-selling Italian author, is a wonderfully sensitive novelist in her own right with two masterpieces to her credit (*The Island of Arthur* and *Falsehood and Sorcery*). The second, wife of Louis Aragon, one of France's leading leftist literary lights, is also a fine author and a brilliant translator of foreign works into French.

In exclusive billionaire milieus it's **Ailsa** (but it sounds like Elsa) **Mellon,** the divorced wife of David Bruce, sister of Paul Mellon, one of the richest women in the world, who sticks to the United States (she has four apartments in New York and houses on Long Island and in Connecticut and Florida), beloved for her great generosity, discussed for her inability to make decisions.

Emanuela

suits to perfection the two Italian ladies, who answer to it, both being as unusual as the name they bear. Since each has a romantic background and is gifted with a sort of Renaissance beauty, they are constantly discussed.

Signora Sozzani, the elder of the two, resides in Milan. Half French (her father was Viscount Dampierre, Duke of San Lorenzo, related to all the French nobility) and half Italian (her mother, Donna Vittoria Ruspoli, is connected with the best of the Italian aristocracy), she married in 1935 the Duke of Segovia, the deaf and dumb son of Alfonso, King of Spain. Despite her superb genealogy, she was never given royal rank, and therefore, never rated a curtsy. For this reason her two handsome, ever-so-popular sons, Don Alfonso and Don Gonzalo, are not Infantes of Spain. In 1947 she had her marriage dissolved in Roumania, of all places, and then married an Italian industrialist with whom she has not found happiness. But she makes everyone happy when she appears at any sort of gathering, for she is one of the most distinguished, wonderful-looking ladies in international society.

The **Duchess of Acquarone,** who lives in Rome, is the daughter of the love merger of Count Emanuele Castelbarco and Wally Toscanini. (They had to become Hungarians in order to get married because it was impossible for him to obtain an Italian annulment from his first wife.) Her husband was heir to the late gentleman-in-waiting of King Victor Emanuel of Italy. Their interests have separated them (he hates society and is all wrapped up in growing flowers on the Italian Riviera), and nomadic society has been the gainer, for she is now able to be everywhere, and like the other Emanuelas, bring her enchanting gazelle-like appearance to all sorts of fetes.

Eric, Erich

The Earl of Bessborough is known as Eric although his first names are Frederick Edward. Half French through his mother, a Baroness de Neuflize, he is married to an American, Mary Munn, daughter of the acknowledged Czar of Palm Beach society, and is a busy gentleman with a labyrinth of interests.

The Earl of Dudley is the most quoted among the Erics for he has the habit of saying exactly what he thinks. With two wives behind him (the first was the daughter of the Duke of Sutherland, the second is presently Mrs. Michael Canfield), he is happy with his third, Grace Kolin, has many weekend guests at his Great Westwood estate, spends the winters in Nassau and a considerable amount of time in the United States and the continent.

Eric Loder is another thrice-married English gentleman who made many feminine hearts flutter in his day. His first wife was the dancer Gabrielle Ray, the second Iris Fitzgerald, and the third the handsome, bejeweled Eleanor Curran from New Orleans. She, again, had been married twice before; the first husband was Count Moroni, a member of the Italian diplomatic corps, and the second, the colossally rich Canadian whiskey industrialist, Sir Mortimer Davis. The French Riviera (where they own a villa), Deauville, Paris, London, Switzerland, New York, New Orleans, and Canada see them every year.

In literary and entertainment environments **Erich** can only mean the German writer **von Remarque,** who has written so many bestsellers and has been such a penetrating reporter of our times. Happily married to Paulette Goddard, because of poor health he now leads a somewhat secluded existence in Porto Ronco near Lugano and Rome but maintains a New York apartment.

Denmark has provided N.S. with two Erics:

Bruhn is one of the best ballet dancers in the world today, a quiet, sympathetic man who enjoys parties and has been, ever since his first appearance in Europe, a close friend of Nureyev.

Nielsen has as his mission in life to amuse people. His name is recurrent in chic chat concerning Gianni and Marella Agnelli, Gloria Guinness, Jimmy Douglas, and Countess Lily Volpi.

Baron Goldschmidt-Rothschild is impeccably dressed, wears a red carnation in his buttonhole, and walks with a stick. Although his name spells riches, this is not the case. But it does not matter. He has lots of charm and this is what counts. The women worship him and in every capital—he turns up in all of them—they make a great fuss over him. His tents shift from Los Angeles, where his late wife lived (she played, for a lark, the role of the Queen of Ruritania in the film version of *My Fair Lady*) to Rome. His name pops up in the columns because of the long walks he takes in New York's Central Park with Greta Garbo.

Eugenia, Eugenie, Gina

The last Empress of France, who died in 1920, would be surprised to learn how relatively few of her namesakes grace the current scene. There was a long period during the last century when there was a veritable epidemic of the name because it was reputedly the most elegant possible.

Constantly mentioned and quoted today is **Eugenia Sheppard,** the brilliant fashion columnist whose eyes see absolutely everything and whose clever pen so humorously twists what has become a huge industry with not much fun left.

Mrs. John Willim has her base in New York, but she roams the world for several months of the year, often staying at the Ritz in Paris. The sensational burglary of her jewels in Baden Baden and their equally brilliant recovery by clever German detectives made of this well-dressed, very articulate lady one of the top heroines of the 1964 summer. Formerly Mrs. William F. R. Hitt, she is now married to a much younger man in the real estate business.

If N.S. members refer to "poor **Eugenie,**" it's bound to be the ex, third wife of Stavros Niarchos who agreed to the most silent divorce in recent jet-set history so that he could marry Charlotte Ford. Very rich in her own right—she is a Livanos—her record as a wife and mother was always above reproach. Everyone is now filled with curiosity to see how and where she will reshape her life.

Mrs. Hussein Rahim, the beautiful former Eugenie Thayer, is one of the rare blossoms in the social register garden whose marriage to an Arab, an Egyptian to be more specific, dark, suave, and handsome, is the kind more often seen on the screen than in real life.

The Eugenias are often called Gina or Gena, and prominent among them is **Mrs. William G. Breed,** Roumania's rare gift to New York society. First married to a baritone and later to a prominent attorney (Breed, Abbott and Morgan), she is today a widow who regularly crosses the ocean and is a familiar figure at Paris' Ritz and on the French Riviera. Her main interest is music—she is one of the guiding lights of the New York Philharmonic—and she often travels with her good friend Mrs. Joseph Kennedy.

A Gina, who is not a Eugenie but a Giorgina, is Her Serene Highness the **Reigning Princess of Liechtenstein.** With her headquarters in the ancient ancestral castle of Vaduz, she spends part of the winter skiing with her husband, often in St. Moritz, and takes off on goodwill official visits. At home she entertains a string of glorious guests including the Duke of Edinburgh, Prince Charles and Princess Anne of England. A charmingly democratic ruler with simple tastes, she permits her old friends to call her by her first name.

In recent years, **Gina Lollobrigida** has emerged out of all those spangled dresses she used to wear to become increasingly sophisticated and social. In her villa in Rome and in her Parisian apartment she entertains more and more, and with an uncanny sense for publicity, is now as much in the social gazettes as in the film columns. Not officially separated from her husband Milko Skofic, but rarely seen with him, she appears to enjoy members of the Middle European aristocracy.

Florence

can be boiled down to four ladies, all immensely vital and very different.

Mrs. Schuyler Smith (Florence Kimball), teaches voice at Juilliard Institute, is responsible for the careers of many excellent singers including Leontyne Price, and gives delightful musicals in her New York flat.

Mrs. Gérald Van der Kemp is fairly easy to spot, for she is the most exotic American-born flower ever to grace the Palace of Versailles. With two marriages behind her, she is currently the wife of the formidable Curator of Louis XIV's extravaganza and she is mentioned either in connection with some refreshingly un-French remark she has made or with the wonderfully rich people (she is rich herself) she must entertain to express gratification at the fabulous gifts they present to the Palace. She owns a house near St. Tropez.

Mrs. Frank Jay Gould, widow of the American Croesus, keeps open house on her estate near Cannes and in the French capital and is always surrounded by artists of note. She has founded three French literary prizes: the Prix des Critiques, the Prix Max Jacob, and the Prix Roger Nimier. When someone asked Mrs. Gould if the sound of the trains rushing by her property on the French Riviera annoyed her, she supposedly answered, "Why should it? All my money comes from the railroads."

Mrs. Jean Noel Grinda is a delightful looking, tiny creature with enormous personality in her way of dressing. She is absolutely dwarfed by her huge, blond, handsome husband, a tennis champion. She is the daughter of one of France's most powerful attorneys, Jean Michard-Péllissier, who has a large villa on the Riviera.

Frances, Francis, and Françoise

are a source of agony, for many Franceses amuse themselves by giving their name the French twist. They are legion. In France:

Françoise Sagan never gives the impression of enjoying herself, but she is immensely social and is present at parties not only in Paris and St. Tropez but all over the nomadic trail. It's immensely chic to know her, to quote her, to be seen with her.

Two members of top social echelons are the **Viscountess Amaury d'Harcourt,** a classical beauty who is also enormously gifted (she writes novels, paints excellent portraits, rides superbly to the hounds), and **Her Royal Highness Princess Edward Lobkowicz,** a member of the Bourbon Parme dynasty, a leading Parisian hostess, a gentle, dovelike, well-organized tiny creature, who moves in the American society of her husband's mother, Anita Lihme.

Françoise de Langlade, the energetic *Vogue* magazine fashion editor, manages to be a member of many courts, much to the envy of those who are left trailing behind. With a fantastic vitality, she is in and out of planes and cars, constantly going somewhere.

A Françoise who is really **Frances** is the daughter of Charles Munn, the stepdaughter of Jacques Allez, the sister of the Countess of Bessborough, and the divorced wife of George **Baker.** Equally at home anywhere, she belongs to the vanishing race of great ladies. Although New York is her base, she is seen in Paris, Capri, and England.

Mrs. Alexander McLanahan was painted by Augustus John, is a good pianist, and entertains many musicians in New York. Her husband owns a chateau in France.

An indefatigable hostess in both New York and Newport, an inveterate traveler, known from Hong Kong to Lisbon, a party giver and goer twenty-four hours a day, seven days a week, is **Mrs. Harold Brooks.** Despite failing health, she is in the thick of the social season everywhere.

Francis (it's a woman but she prefers to spell it this original way) **Carpenter,** who used to be the wife of du Pont heir Bill Carpenter, gives parties that really swing in whatever part of the world she happens to be.

If someone in California says, "I am going to a small party at Frances's," he is talking about the popular and easy-going **Mrs. Samuel Goldwyn.** Her dinners are always intimate and discriminating.

The pretty and linguistically accomplished **Duchess of Rutland** was born Frances Sweeny, and her celebrated mother is

Margaret Duchess of Argyll. Her house parties at Belvoir Castle (pronounced Beaver) are coveted.

Franco

is really confining, mainly in the entertainment sphere.

Franco Corelli is, at the moment, the top tenor in the world. Gifted with not only a spectacularly sized voice but one of beautiful quality, he is tall and good-looking, and lends verisimilitude to the romantic roles he must undertake.

Franco Rossellini, the former nephew of Ingrid Bergman and son of one of Italy's most contemporary composers, Renzo Rossellini, is a personable, smooth bachelor who moves in all sorts of different sets. Recently having proved his mettle as a film producer, he is a member of the entourage of Ernest and Rosemary Kanzler, who invest money in his film ventures.

Franco Zeffirelli is, undoubtedly, the busiest of all directors and stage designers. With prodigious pep, he indefatigably rushes across the ocean and around Europe on a wide range of assignments which include opera, Shakespeare, and offbeat revivals of such plays as Giovanni Verga's *La Lupa,* in which Anna Magnani made a disappointing theatrical comeback. Conceited, elflike, and very opinionated, he moves with a court of his own.

Dynamic, bright **Franco Palma** is always making money, what with Squibb and many other companies in Italy. He has digs in Rome, Port' Ercole, and St. Moritz, and his wife is politically minded.

Franco sometimes is **Frank Pogson,** the Englishman who made one of the great postwar marriages. His wife is the Princess Orietta Doria Pamphili, last of the celebrated family, proprietor of one of the great private collections of paintings in Europe and fine palaces. Since she is the last of her line, he has added Doria to his Anglo-Saxon name.

Now that his wife, Virna Lisi, is hitting the jackpot on the screen, **Franco Pesci,** the architect, is constantly thrown into the jet set. A big, handsome man, who has a villa near Rome, he made news when, in a night club on Sardinia's Costa Smeralda, he socked a young man, who he thought had made impertinent remarks about his consort, in the jaw. A classic brawl followed.

Forty years ago, **Count Franco Spalletti** and his brother Antonio were the prototypes of the most swinging and elegant men in Europe. In Florence, where he lives, this exponent of the old-fashioned monocle is still impeccably turned out and is the most sought-after bachelor in the city. He has been separated for decades from his wife.

Frederick, Fred, and Freddie

Wherever the name actress Rosalind Russell is mentioned, her affable, efficient husband of Danish origin, producer **Frederick Brisson,** is quoted. With many hits to his credit, he has managed to keep his own personal identity, no easy task when confronted with such an effervescent, strong-willed, and attractive wife.

Frederick Guest, a son of Winston Guest's first marriage, is a son-in-law of Joan Bennett and Walter Wanger, having married their daughter Stephanie. A good polo player, following in the family tradition, he is a Wall Street broker and has the same wonderful manners as his father.

Frederick Eberstadt did not follow into his father's banking world, but has become an excellent professional photographer. He is always clicking away for the best papers and magazines. Being rich on his own, he can give wonderfully original parties with his wife Isabel in their large New York Park Avenue flat and in summer rent houses in offbeat places around the world.

With his wife, Nathalie Fell, **Frederick Cushing** forms one of the most engaging of the young U couples in American society. Although thus far their fame has centered mainly in the United

States, the tremendous barrage of publicity his lovely mate has been receiving lately is spreading their reputation on a more cosmopolitan level. Because Mrs. Cushing's mother, Mrs. John Fell, is a close friend of all the Kennedys, they are part of that particular picture.

In the same set is another attractive fellow, **Frederick Melhado,** the estranged husband of the pretty and rich Lydia Melhado. He has a ready smile and has fallen in love with the English way of life.

In high Beverly Hills society and wherever his mercurial sister, Mrs. J. Kingman Douglas is, Fred is the nimble-footed and popular **Fred Astaire,** who was born charming and will remain so until the end of his days. He is one of the few stars about whom there has never been one nasty word in print.

Frederick Rheinhardt is one of the most prominent career men in the American diplomatic service. A specialist on Russian problems, he has recently been the United States Ambassador to Italy but has not mingled often, much to their chagrin, with Roman society. Affable, good-looking and tough, he is the son of a distinguished mother who efficiently ran Mills College in California.

Well-known for his tasteful work as a decorator, **The Baron de Cabrol** is, with his wife Daisy d'Harcourt, prominent on the U party circuit all over Europe. He and his Baroness are also excellent, faithful riders in the Duchess of Magenta's celebrated Chasse à Courre in Normandy.

George and Georges

George Baker is the ever-smiling, pleasant heir to a large Wall Street fortune. First married to Frances Munn, he is the husband of the sister of the late Kay Kendall, turns up every winter to ski in the Alps, attends many shooting parties, looks as well in sports clothes as he does in tails, for he has a youthful, taut body.

George Braga, the result of a beguiling mixture of Cuban and New England ancestors, is still rich despite the confiscation of all his sugar plantations on Castro's island. An urbane, cultivated gentleman, with a fine home in New Jersey, he travels many months of the year because of his business interests. He is accompanied by his popular wife, the former Gioia Marconi, whose father was the celebrated Italian inventor and who, through her mother, an O'Brien, is related to countless Irish aristocrats.

Georges Cravenne is the most influential promoter and press agent in France. He continuously arranges for big junkets and *premières,* has the best list in Paris of personalities willing to lend their names to some project in exchange for free journeys to Russia, the Cannes Film Festival, or other fields of pleasure. He is married to film star Françoise Arnoul.

George Cukor is the director in Hollywood whose sun never sets. A confirmed bachelor, he is the reason for parties being hosted in his honor whenever he takes off on holidays. His latest effort, the film version of *My Fair Lady,* will run forever.

An original writer of plays and screen treatments dealing with the perturbations of marriages, **George Axelrod** is charming, attractive, and easy to talk to.

George Embiricos is a wealthy Greek shipping tycoon, currently estranged from his wife "Doda" Goulandris, sister of all those rich brothers. Serious in his business and tastes, he collects paintings, uses Switzerland as his base.

George Guinle, a Brazilian, won the affection of the Brooklyn belle Dolores Sherwood, only to lose it to the late George Litman. The stunning model was married to, and divorced from, both. Guinle, whose family owns the famous Copacabana Hotel in Rio de Janeiro, has since made the jet set richer with his attentions to such big-name ladies as Kim Novak, Jayne Mansfield, and Zsa Zsa Gabor.

George Hamilton is a rare exception in the recent crop of film actors, for he enjoys going to parties and arrives on time.

Linked romantically with Susan Kohner, Charlotte Ford, Marina Cicogna, and Lynda Bird Johnson—and briefly with Jeanne Moreau whom he played opposite in *Viva Maria*—he remains a cool bachelor with a handsome face somewhat devoid of expression. He has shown good sense in the way he has handled his career and he is a devoted son to his much-married mother, Anne Stephens Potter Hamilton Hunt Spaulding.

George Hoyningen-Huene, a Baltic Baron, has enriched the field of photography in the last four decades. A tall, athletic, impulsive artist with immense talent and discipline (a rare combination), he was the star photographer for *Harper's Bazaar* for many years until he chose to dedicate his time to art books and motion pictures. He has acted as photographic consultant on films directed by George Cukor.

George Livanos is staggeringly rich, single, and finds time both to work hard at his shipping business (his sisters are Mrs. Eugenie Niarchos and the Marchioness of Blandford) and to play. Although London is his station, he is everywhere and has acquired an island, in the tradition of his wealthy compatriots, near Nauplion. It is difficult to keep track of his conquests, for the members of the fair sex find him irresistible.

George London and **George Szell** have nothing in common except that both are big musical personages, but somehow, it is easy to get them confused, since they are in the same world. London is a towering Canadian baritone who does as well as Scarpia in *Tosca* at the Metropolitan as in his Wagnerian impersonations at the Bayreuth Festival. Szell is an elderly Czech who has put the Cleveland Symphony Orchestra in the forefront among the world's most distinguished musical organizations.

In a minor key for the great public but in a major one for Maria Callas is the young and talented **Georges Pretre,** who is currently making his way up the musical Olympus. With the Greek diva so solidly behind him, his name comes up among her fanatical fans all the time.

Georges Pompidou, the French Premier, is a delightful gentleman who gets all the hostesses excited because he accepts social engagements not in line with his job, a rarity nowadays. He is often a guest of the Rothschild family.

George Revay is a Hungarian hunk of man who is married to the very pretty Swiss heiress "Bichette" Givaudan. One finds him on the Parisian party circuit, in St. Moritz—where he and his wife ski all winter long—and in Marbella in the summer where they rent a bungalow.

George Sebastian is a Roumanian native and a favorite of the Windsors and Countess Volpi. He is a man of great taste, and the house he built and occupied for over thirty years at Hammamet, Tunisia, has won the enthusiastic praise of all the cognoscenti. In fact, the Duchess of Windsor so fell in love with it that she may ask him to create a smaller version for her on the Costa del Sol. There is an American connection here, too, for he was married to the late Flora Stifel of West Virginia.

If one hears of **George** having commissioned someone to write a book, it's certainly **Weidenfeld** whose publishing house in England is a colossal beehive. His parties in his Eaton Place apartment are famous, and so are those (always very crowded) he gives during his long, annual stays in New York. Frequently in Italy and France, he is madly social and devoted to an author he has published for many years, the British socialist leader Harold Wilson.

George Widener is one of the most respected gentlemen, with residences in New York and Philadelphia and a beautiful plantation down South, where exciting shooting parties are organized. He travels to Europe with his wife, the former Jessie Sloane, whose sister, the Baroness de la Grange, lives in Paris.

When it comes to the muse Terpsichore, **George Balanchine**'s name evokes many admiring comments. The tours of the New York City Center Ballet have made his work known to the entire world and hundreds of thousands of people refer to him as if they knew him personally. His friends speak of him very highly, especially for his kindness to his fourth wife, Tanaquil Leclerq, so cruelly attacked by infantile paralysis.

Heavily mustached, ruddy-faced George Ansley is an elderly Britisher who lives in Paris. He is the devoted admirer of the Countess Mercedes de Bendern, who used to grace the late Aly Khan's parties. His daughter "Penny" is married to Lloyd Franklin, Barbara Hutton's guitar-strumming ex-beau.

In the very large Antenor Patiño cosmos one hears mention of **George Ortiz-Linares,** small in size as all that Bolivian clan, but bright and able. Deeply interested in archeology and a collector of ancient bronzes, he takes off with his second wife from Paris or Geneva to the Isle of Crete where he owns a house in an archeological zone.

The third **Earl of Cromer** holds the glorious post of Governor of the Bank of England. A godson of the late King George V, he is married to the daughter of the press czar Viscount Rothermere. Known to his intimates as Rowlie, he has many friends in Manhattan, where he worked for Morgan and Co., and in Washington, D.C., where he has been on economic missions.

George Plimpton, despite his Social Register status, is *avant-garde*. Lanky and with Harvard mannerisms, he is an editor of *Paris Review,* writes articles, drives a Mercedes, and although close to forty, is still an extra man.

George Gaynes (an adaptation of a long Finnish surname) is a handsome sandy-haired six-foot singer who is nimble enough to go from Mozart (*The Marriage of Figaro* and *Don Giovanni*) and Menotti (*The Consul*) to musical comedy (*Wonderful Town*) and the legitimate stage (*Luv*). Socially inclined and good company, he is an excellent husband, father, and son. His mother, a famous beauty of the nineteen-twenties, is "Ya," Lady Abdy, a Russian-born sculptress.

The **Earl of Harewood** is the only member of the British Royal Family deeply interested and active in musical organizations. He recently resigned from the Presidency of the Edinburgh Festival. When some years ago he married Marion Stein (an Austrian) a relative who did not take too kindly to this alliance dryly observed, "The main advantage I can see is that we shall have a Steinway in the family." His mother was the late Princess Royal, an aunt of the Queen.

Gloria

is tricky. Three of them are great vedettes, one of them is a vedette's twin, and the fifth and last is a member of an entrancingly flashy family.

The most imperishable is **Gloria Swanson,** who, like the phoenix, comes out of the ashes of her own past from time to time, making sensational comebacks. Five times married, intensely glamorous from head to toe, a crusader along many avenues, she never stays put for long. She adds a welcome spice and strong opinions to any assembly she graces.

Gloria Guinness, several times a bride but better known by the surname of her last mate, is one of the supreme Nomadic Queens. In her husband's yacht or baby jet, she moves like a robot among her five houses (distributed among Switzerland, Mexico, France, and Florida), but also hops in and out of her native Mexico, New York, and London at the drop of the hat she rarely wears.

Gloria Vanderbilt, unlike Mrs. Guinness, whose consorts have all been of different nationalities, has picked out four American husbands, albeit they have all belonged to different ethnical groups (the first, Pat de Cicco, was of Italian extraction, Leopold Stokowski English-Polish, Sidney Lumet Jewish, the current Wyatt Cooper of mixed backgrounds). Her interests, like Mrs. Guinness's, are on the intellectual side and both of them write plays (unproduced so far). While Mrs. Guinness sells articles to *Harper's Bazaar,* Mrs. Cooper sells her oils at exhibitions, proving that old adage "The Rich Get Richer" is appropriate. Gloria Vanderbilt has also written poetry and tried acting, but Mrs. Guinness has not.

Gloria O'Connor Schiff has been married only twice and is the twin of the great café society star, Consuelo Crespi. Since she works for *Vogue* magazine and Mrs. Guinness for its rival *Harper's Bazaar,* there is an endless muddle when it comes to their professional lives.

Anyone who has read **Gloria Braggiotti Etting**'s autobiography knows what entrancing parents, brothers, and sisters she was fortunate enough to have. Of mixed Italian, Turkish, and New England ancestry, she is a citizen of the world which she roams with her eyes, and what is more essential, her heart wide open. She and her painter husband Emlen Etting (her first and only one) have their tents planted in Philadelphia and the Jersey shore.

Harry

Harry is, by all standards, one of the simplest names in the International sweepstakes, but it can present nightmares to a nomadic newcomer.

When it's reported in connection with *Cristina* (the Yacht, not a person), Tina (the ex-wife), Maria (Callas, the prima donna), Scorpio (an island he owns), the Radziwills (great ex-friends), oil tankers (he owns many), Monte Carlo (he controls 53 percent of the Societé des Bains de Mer), it's **Aristotle Onassis.**

Five boys (his sons), Maria Carmela (his wife), marital difficulties, book and magazine distributing (his family owns Smith's), and Henley on Thames (his attractive country seat) are attributes of **Viscount Hambleden.**

Hit plays (he writes them), screen plays (he concocts them), Gloria Guinness and Frank Sinatra (he belongs to both their courts) spell **Harry Kurnitz.**

In case there is talk about the attractive girls he dates,

Tiffany (he is the Vice-President), skiing (he is excellent at it), it's bright-eyed, cheerful **Harry Platt.**

If there is indication of after-dinner speeches (he always makes them) or superlative feats on the dance floor, one can draw a sigh of relief and know **Harry Evans** is being talked about.

Sex appeal, reference to Ghislaine (his wife), Sonia (his mother), and Violet (his aunt)—both daughters of the late Mrs. George Keppel, the great friend of Edward VIII—construction (that's the family business), and the principality of Monaco (he is the Honorary Consul General in London) are signposts for **Baron Ashcombe.**

Talk about China (he was born there), *Time, Life, Sports Illustrated,* and *Fortune* (he owns a great majority of the stock), and of the times his wife was Ambassador and Congresswoman, means **Henry Luce.**

In the New Frontier society and certain sections of the musical world **Harry** is "Mr. Calypso" **Bellafonte,** the renderer of the Caribbean folk songs of which he has become the supreme interpreter.

Harry O. King, a bulky Chicagoan in his middle seventies, has for many years lived in a Manhattan town house. A widower with two daughters, he is rich, amiable, a great traveler, and a friend of the Duke and Duchess of Windsor, Mrs. George Baker, and Mrs. Lyon Slater.

An expert on "Americana," **Harry du Pont** gave marvelous advice for the restoration of the White House to its pristine splendor. His world-renowned collection is housed in his mansion "Winterthur" in Delaware. He also owns an attractive village of eight bungalows in Boca Grande, Florida, and a magnificent cottage on the Southampton Dunes. He and his wife Ruth go on world cruises at the drop of a hat.

The richest of all the **Harrys** is reputed to be **Oppenheimer** whose fortune staggers even the very wealthy. With tremendous holdings in both Anglo and De Beers, of which he inherited the Chairmanship from his late father, he makes his home in Johannesburg, but is ever in motion in his private jet to satisfy his worldwide interests. He is noted for a stupendous collection of diamonds and paintings.

One of the most popular Italian diplomats is **Ambassador Carlo Enrico Giglioli,** universally known as Harry. Currently doing his bit in one of the African countries—all envoys get such a post sooner or later—he leaves friends galore behind him whenever the time comes to move again. A Florentine, he has enjoyed bachelor status since his marriage to Gabriella de Montemayor collapsed long ago.

Henry and Henri

Henry Fonda, who was married in 1965 for the fifth time, is blessed with two very talented children, Jane and Peter, who are making heavy inroads in the acting medium which made him famous. Often called "Hank," he is a sincere, well-mannered, considerate person with no visible axes to grind. His last ex-wife, Afdera Franchetti, brought him into the social orbit.

Henry Hyde is an international lawyer always taking off for some new destination. Divorced from Mimi de la Grange, from whom he had two beautiful daughters, Lorna and Isabel, he remarried a professional model, Elizabeth Prokoff Piper. Because of his late French mother, he speaks French like a native.

Henry Sell, whose conversation is as stimulating as champagne and whose appearance is similar to that of the magician Klingsor in *Parsifal,* combines being an authority on Buffalo Bill with manufacturing paté. For a long time the editor in chief of *Town and Country* magazine, he is at home all over the globe.

Henry Ford of the automobile kingdom is as well known in St. Moritz and yachting circles as he is in Detroit. His recent wedding to Christina Vettore made the Catholic clergy angry to the complete indifference of N.S. members who sympathized fully with the plight of the groom and bride.

H.R.H. Prince Henry of Hesse, one of the most respected members of European royalty and an immensely talented painter and stage designer, divides his time among a villa in Rome, a house in Forio d'Ischia, and castles in Germany where his father, Philip, and his brother, Maurice, make their headquarters. Because of his close relationship with the Italian Royal family (his late mother was Princess Mafalda of Savoy) and much time spent in Italy, he is also known as Enrico d'Assia.

Prince Henri de la Tour d'Auvergne, who used to be in the news when he escorted Barbara Hutton, is in the horsy set after his marriage to lovely Patricia Galvin, the American-Irish heiress who rode in the American team at the Tokyo Olympics. With bases at Chateau Lafitte and on the French Riviera, he works for a Swiss Financial Corporation.

The Marquis de la Falaise de la Coudraye, who knew Hollywood in its glorious days, having been the mate of both Gloria Swanson and Constance Bennett, is happily married to a South American. He commutes among Paris, a Chateau in the Vendée region, a house in Biarritz and St. Moritz, where he is one of the top officers of the Corviglia Club.

Count de Beaumont, married to Graziella Pecci Blunt, is a handsome charmer (his late uncle was one of the greatest hosts Paris has ever known), who shuttles among an apartment in Rome, a house he built on the Costa Smeralda in Sardinia, and the family chateau in Normandy.

The **Vicomte d'Origny** is a Prince Charming who has thus far escaped the bonds of marriage. A brother of the beautiful, artistically inclined Vicomtesse Françoise d'Harcourt, he is also a superb exponent of the *chasse à courre,* managing a horse like someone born in the saddle, an excellent shot (he runs a syndicate) and a much in demand designer, by profession, of textiles and scarves.

Count du Chastel de la Howarderie is married to Ina del

Merito, a niece of Antenor Patiño. Because of his wife's Spanish heritage, they own one of the most beautiful houses in Spain, the former Monastery of San Jeronimo near Cordoba. He visits Andalusia, is a familiar figure at the Sevilla Fair, and participates in many shoots. In Spain, he is Marquess del Merito, courtesy of his wife.

Henri Samuel, a bachelor in his early sixties, is among the successful decorators of our time. He finds time to be social, aside from his various assignments, in Canada, Switzerland, Greece, England, the United States, Luxembourg, and of course, France, and entertains in his houses in Paris, Montfort, and l'Amaury.

Henry Clifford is a highly witty, cultivated patron of the arts. Much involved with the Philadelphia Art Museum, he is a good client of the travel bureaus. Apart from their mansion in Pennsylvania, he and his wife Esther have a villa in Florence which belonged to the illustrious Capponis, an estate in Vevey, and one near Cuernavaca.

Henry McIlhenny is a bachelor with a superb art collection housed in a great house on Philadelphia's Rittenhouse Square where members of the *Who's Who* from every nation are entertained. In an unusual castle, Glenveagh, in Donegal, he gives large, interesting house parties. A world traveler, he charters a yacht every summer in the Mediterranean and is civic-minded. (He is on the Board of Directors of the Metropolitan Opera.)

A wonderfully eccentric English Henry is the **Marquess of Bath,** whose stately house of Longleat is graced by live lions. His reactionary declarations are cannon fodder for the British press, and his appearance, which reminds some of a prizefighter, is commented upon.

Henry Tiarks, a successful businessman, is in and out of the United States where he has many friends. As the proprietors of a cottage at Round Hill in Jamaica, he and his wife are familiar figures in the Caribbean. His daughter Henrietta is married to the Duke of Bedford's eldest son, the Marquess of Tavistock.

Part of the spreading-like-wildfire movement of young men marrying older women is good-looking and rich **Henry Jurgens,** who married Baroness Monique de Nervo, once the official Ambassadress of French Couture to the U.S.A. They appear in St. Moritz every winter and seem happy.

Nothing puts a young man more on the international map than a romance with a movie star. **Lord Herbert,** who is the son and heir of the sixteenth Earl of Pembroke, holder of one of the finest titles in Great Britain and proprietor of the celebrated stately home of Wilton, has entered N.S. by dating Jill St. John, the ex-wife of Barbara Hutton's son, Lance Haugwitz-Reventlow. He is now engaged to Claire Pelly.

Around Athens, the most probable gentleman mentioned by this name is **Henry Labouisse,** ex-American Ambassador to Greece and now Executive Director of UNICEF, who hails from New Orleans, but lived in Virginia before taking on his international assignments. He came on to the jet stage some years ago when he married the cool, impersonal, beautiful Eve Curie, daughter of two great scientists, Pierre and Marie Curie. For a long time she lectured successfully around the U.S.A.

IRENE

is an aristocratic name almost all the way. Here we have three Royal Princesses and a Lady in their own right, a dress designer-patrician, and a famous journalist-editor.

The Dowager Duchess of Aosta, the good-looking mother of the Duke of Aosta, owns a villa at San Domenico near Florence within walking distance of her sister, the former Queen Mother Helen of Roumania. A Grecian Princess by birth, she is an aunt of the present King, and since Italy became a republic, has led a quiet, dignified existence.

Irene of Greece is the pretty niece of the Duchess Irene, for whom she was named, and until her brother King Constantine had an heir, was next in line for the Greek throne. She lives in Athens with her mother Queen Frederica and is active in civic works when she is not sent on various official assignments.

Irene of Bourbon-Parme, the strong-willed daughter of the Queen of Holland, lives in Madrid with her husband. Handsome and responsive, she created a furor when she gave up her Protestant faith to become a Catholic and make a love match. She thus did not live up to the famous motto of the Royal House of Orange: "I will maintain."

Lady Irene Astor, born Lady Irene Haig, is the daughter of the famous British Field Marshal, Earl Haig. She is married to the Hon. Gavin Astor, the eldest son of Baron Astor of Hever, and because of her husband's many activities (among others he is Chairman of the Board of the Times Publishing Company) travels extensively.

Irene Selznick is the handsome and aristocratic-looking daughter of Hollywood's great rajah, Louis B. Mayer, and the divorced wife of the late David Selznick. Operating out of Manhattan, she is now and then in England, for she produces English plays in the United States with rare discernment.

Countess Irene Cittadini is the Polish-born beauty who, after the death of her first husband, Philadelphia's John Worden, became the spouse of an Italian diplomat. A rover by choice, she usually lives in hotels. In Lausanne, Geneva, Gstaad, New York, and Hot Springs she is an accomplished hostess and patroness of the arts.

Mrs. John Emery is the daughter of the famous artist Charles Dana Gibson and his wife, one of the celebrated Langhorne sisters of Virginia. Tall, slender, and graceful, she is at home everywhere. With four Emery children, she is also the mother of George Post, a son from a previous marriage, who married her current husband's niece, Linda Moore, whose mother is Mrs. Robert McKay.

Irene Brin, the wife of Obelisco Gallery's Gasparo del Corso, is an adroit and ingenious journalist and writer, as well as *Harper's Bazaar's* Italian representative. Her looks are the sort Boldini would have enjoyed painting, but her wit is sharp and up-to-date.

Irene Galitzine, in whose veins flows the blood of the Russian elite, is the sparkling and glossy-looking fashion designer whose at-home ensembles have swept the world market. Full of vitality, she travels globally with her consort Silvio Medici, combining business trips with pleasure.

Irene Dalis is the Metropolitan Opera and Bayreuth Festival's gifted mezzo-soprano of Greek-Italian parents from California. Her name comes up among top Cuban exiles, for her husband is George Loinaz, a Cuban in the publishing business in London and New York.

Jack and Jacques

actually sound exactly alike, and there are so many Jacks who have strong connections with France and Jacques with England and the U.S.A. that one never knows which is which. Among the most frequently mentioned American Jacks are:

John Emery is often referred to as Mr. Cincinnati, with an education which includes Groton, Harvard, and Oxford. A brilliant, gray-haired charmer, he is busy in Ohio's art and musical world, apart from his manifold business occupations there. Married to Irene Gibson, and therefore a nephew by marriage to all the famous Langhorne sisters, he counts among his own sisters Mrs. Robert McKay of Long Island, Audrey, who used to be married to the Grand Duke Dimitri of Russia, and the late Duchess of Talleyrand.

H. J. Heinz, Mr. Fifty-seven Varieties, roams the world constantly to check the various items of his ever-growing empire. With many houses and interests, he gives the impression of being able to stretch his twenty-four hours a day into a hundred. Youthful looking, he is an enthusiastic photographer, snapping everyone at his own parties, and then, what is even more remarkable never failing to send a copy to each and every one. His third wife, Drue English Maher, is a sputnik who keeps up with him.

Senator Javits is a man of tremendous energy, managing to squeeze in a social schedule with his various senatorial responsibilities. A traveler on various missions, he has the capacity to remember faces and names, helped all along by his intense and warm-hearted wife Marion.

Jack Warner remains one of Hollywood's biggest wigs, but in recent years has been less prominent on an international social scale, spending comparatively little time in his house in Antibes, and therefore being less of an adornment for the casinos along the Riviera.

Jack Heminway, who has been a widower for a short time, is identified with the Charles Engelhard and Anne Ford sets. He is a son of the late Dolly O'Brien, whose beauty and allure kept her in the news for several decades.

Jacques Allez, a gentleman of the old school, has been prominent in the development of aviation in France. In his Paris house he entertains many Americans, for he is the widower of one, a member of the Paul family, and has as his house guests his stepdaughter Frances Baker and Mary (Countess of) Bessborough.

Jacques Bergerac, one of the most attractive-looking French lawyers roaming the world, never did reach the top when he turned to movie acting. At first he made his bride, Ginger Rogers, so blissful she insisted on having him sit next to her at dinner. After a divorce and another marriage with Dorothy "Peyton Place" Malone, whom he provided with two children, he is a free man again and perhaps will marry Debbie Minardos, widow of Tyrone Power.

Jacques Sarlie is a Dutch-born financier who pitched his tent in Manhattan and is at some times very rich, at others less so. His many business interests keep him air-borne, but when he comes down, he stays at the best hotels or charters a yacht to which he invites Count and Countess K. J. Bernadotte, Jean Howard, Marina Cicogna, Baron Geçmen-Waldek, and John Galliher.

The books by **Jacques Barzun,** Columbia University's Provost, are quoted everywhere. In demand socially, he manages to put in appearances from time to time.

Janet

In Washington, Newport, and Long Island, Janet can mean only **Mrs. Hugh Auchincloss,** an affluent matron, whose chief claim to fame is that she is the mother of those two great international stars, Mrs. John F. Kennedy and Princess Stanislas Radziwill, the result of her previous Bouvier marriage.

The widow of Gilbert Adrian, now **Mrs. Paul Gregory,** the former Janet Gaynor, is one of the most adorable of the screen actresses. Petite, warm, cozy, and chic, she is never bitchy or egocentric. She owns a delicious farm in Brazil.

Janet Newbold Stewart, still a great classical beauty, is among the few Manhattanites who entertain at tea time, and in recent years has become passionately interested in theatrical ventures and people. Among her husbands: Allan Ryan, William R. Stewart, and James Bush.

The Marchioness of Milford Haven is the second wife of the nephew of the Queen of Sweden and the Earl Mountbatten of Burma. Quiet, humorous, and charming, she is seen in London, the Caribbean, and Saratoga (where she often visits her uncle Ivor Bryce and his wife, the A. and P.'s Josephine Hartford).

The **Hon. Mrs. Thomas Kidd** spends the winters in Barbados. She is the late Baron Beaverbrook's daughter. At one point she was the Duchess of Argyll and later the Hon. Mrs. William Montagu. With children from her various husbands, she has a vivid intelligence and a zest for living.

Along the intellectual paths and in Paris, the most quoted is

Janet Flanner, who has written those brilliant articles on France for the *New Yorker* for many years.

JEAN AND JEANNE

in the English language sound the same, but in French the final NE is heard distinctly.

Alfred Vanderbilt must like both versions, for his second wife was Jeanne and his third is Jean. The current **Mrs. Alfred Vanderbilt,** the former Jean Harvey of the Chicago restaurant dynasty, is rapidly becoming a devotee of fine clothes and has climbed the best-dressed ladder. A gentle, horse-loving (like her husband) young lady (many years his junior), she is equally at home at a gala opening of the New York Philharmonic or on a safari in Africa.

Jeanne Vanderbilt, the ultra-sophisticated second ex-wife of Alfred Vanderbilt, has intellectual and political friends, wears her hair in an old-fashioned bob, and belongs to the offbeat rich set.

Baroness Eugene de Rothschild, an English beauty, **Jeanne Stewart,** with a milk and honey complexion, dabbled on the stage before marrying Bernard Docker (at the time he had not as yet been knighted), and later wed into the Austrian branch of the famous banking family. She now divides her time between New York City (where her husband found refuge during the last war) and Europe.

Mrs. William van den Heuvel was born into the Music Corporation of America (her father is Jules Stein). Always an independent, original thinker, she cleverly manages her own career (television and magazine writing) along with her husband's (he is a lawyer), and mixes interesting people at her soirées in New York City.

Lady Jeanne Cram is one of the most interesting characters in nomadic society. The only child from the Duke of Argyll's marriage to the late Lord Beaverbrook's daughter, she is brilliant, unconventional, and writes cleverly for British publications on every sort of subject. First married to the controversial author Norman Mailer, she has now adopted a more conservative allegiance by marrying John Sargeant Cram, a gentleman farmer from South Carolina. She spends much time in Jamaica.

Mrs. Ernest Boissevain, with homes in Florence (the splendid Villa delle Rose), Paris, New York City, and Vermont, is the former opera and radio star Jean Tennyson. Widow of the late scientist-industrialist Camille Dreyfus (Celanese Corporation), she is now the wife of a member of an old Dutch family, entertains beautifully (mainly in Florence), is passionately interested in musical projects, and most generous in the upkeep of several of them.

Jean Howard, an ex-Follies girl, who was married to the Hollywood agent turned producer, Charles Feldman (with whom she has remained on excellent terms), inherited all the lovely jewels of Mrs. Cole Porter, is ever on the move, sometimes on fascinating film assignments, sometimes just for fun.

Mrs. Stephen Smith, the attractive sister of the late President Kennedy, rarely stays in residence very long in her duplex in New York City and, like all the other members of the large clan, is always on the move.

The sensationally successful writer-playwright **Jean Kerr** is the bright wife of the New York *Herald-Tribune's* theater critic. Her God-given ability to make people laugh has, thus far, helped her play *Mary, Mary* to gross over ten million dollars.

Mrs. T. Suffern Tailer started life as Jean Sinclair and was the victim of two unhappy marriages before the current happy one. She is excellent company and easy to talk to on the Long Island and Florida circuit.

With San Francisco as her home, but constantly on the move, **Mrs. Grover A. Magnin** is one of the chicest ladies on the Pacific coast and the wife of a prominent member of the famous store. One of the best hostesses to visiting jet-setters in the Golden Gate City, she has a fine collection of paintings.

In the Jamaica–Round Hill area, in the Hamptons, in New York City, and on the New England skiing slopes, the wealthy **Mrs. Harcourt Amory Jr.**, is an excellent hostess and is always giving some kind of party. Her name appears in all the columns, and Eugenia Sheppard picked her out among the best housekeepers who can run four residences efficiently.

The gifted **Jeanne Moreau** from time to time makes excursions into the best society, holding on to that very special individuality of hers and never sacrificing it to run-of-the-mill dialogue. In Paris she dines at Baron Rede's and in Venice visits Marina Cicogna. She has recently taken on a very youthful Greek beau, actor Theo Rubanis.

Jeanne-Marie presents no problem, since the two ladies who answer to this name are very different. The ex-**Princess Guy de Broglie** born De Maillé de la Tour Landry, has shown such spartan discipline on distant, exceedingly uncomfortable journeys and such an interest in abstract art that she has made a top place for herself in high international beatnik society. **Princess Martin Lubormiski**, the half French, half American wife of one of the most illustrious names of the Polish nobility, is one of the busiest partygoers in Paris, rarely returns home with her husband without some night club excursion.

Jerry and Gerry

is one of the most confusing of all, for it applies to women and men alike. Among the ladies:

Mrs. Andrew Fuller, the blonde and intense former Geraldine Spreckels of California, also married at one time to a Spreckels, has a New York apartment filled with up-to-date art and a house in Fort Worth, Texas, where her husband has oil interests, and travels in Europe. She is the mother-in-law of Lord Charles Churchill, son of the Duke of Marlborough.

Geraldine Stutz is dazzling because of her air-tight energy and the way she has been able to put Bendel on the map again. She gave up her bachelor status to become Mrs. Arthur David Gibbs.

The melancholic and pretty former **Queen Geraldine of Albania,** who lost her throne shortly after her marriage to King Zog, lives in Madrid. A beautiful creature who has great dignity, she is half American and half Hungarian.

The American-born **Mrs. Dick de Lisser** at one point divorced her rich husband, a member of one of the ruling families of Jamaica, to marry a British member of the police force, but later remarried No. 1.

Geraldine Chaplin is a personality in her own right. The eldest daughter of Charles Chaplin and Oona O'Neill came to the fore as an untalented ballerina, but her marvelous face was so photogenic that all sorts of motion-picture contracts followed. Her reported romances with a diversified group of men, including El Cordobes and *Paris Match* editor Gilbert Graziani, keep the columnists in a state of agitation.

Harper's Bazaar's **Geri Trotta** goes off quietly on all sorts of fascinating assignments. She belongs to the group of girls who always wear bangs.

Among the gentlemen:

Jerome Zerbe is the inimitable gift of Cleveland, Ohio, to the international set. Witty, bright, and a good friend, he covers hundreds of miles every year for some beautiful art books and for *Town and Country* magazine, for which he functions in the double capacity of Society Editor and Photographer *Extraordinaire.*

Jerome Zipkin is a rich bachelor equally known in Manhattan, Beverly Hills, and the Barbados where he turns up to stay with his great friend, Claudette Colbert. A good card player, he is a favorite in the gambling set and efficiently administers his real estate holdings.

Gerald Gordon is a handsome, well-liked broker who has been for many years Anita Colby's favorite cavalier, although they have never married because of religious complications.

The Duke of Wellington is one of England's favorite dukes. With fine Spanish, Portuguese, and Dutch titles in his family tree and a superb property in southern Spain, given to his celebrated ancestor for services rendered, he is an excellent architect. Everyone longs to be asked to his beautiful country estate in England, Stratfield Saye.

Jimmy and James

James Dunn is among the most attractive, popular ambassadors the United States ever had. Now retired, with his wife Mary, he centers his activities in Rome and New York City.

The Duke of Cadaval has one of the most distinguished names of Portugal, where he owns several properties. He also can be found in Paris, San Moritz, and Capri, where he rents a house. A long-time friend of Geneviève (widow of Jacques) Fath, his romance with her ended long before his walk to the altar with Claudine Pritz.

James Caffery, a nephew of the former American Ambassador to Egypt and Sweden, has established his base of operations in Marbella, and is the landscape architect par excellence of all those new gardens there.

James Donohue, Barbara Hutton's first cousin and a favorite of hers (she usually spends Christmas with him at his Long Island estate) is a great opera-goer whose wit sometimes has left people breathless.

Jimmy Douglas is a rich young American aristocrat who dwells in a Paris flat where he plays the harpsichord. Often a member of some court (at one time Barbara Hutton's) or other, he is considered "very sweet" by women.

Count of Pourtales, son-in-law of the late Anna Gould, Duchess of Talleyrand, is the erudite and civilized owner of the beautiful castle of Bandeville near Paris and a polo enthusiast.

James King, rising young tenor on the operatic stages of Vienna, Berlin and Bayreuth, is one of many American singers who had first to prove himself abroad. Unmarried, pleasant, and not conceited, he is as at home in German and Italian opera as on the party circuit.

Since his divorce from Pamela Kellino and his friendship with Countess Vivi Crespi, **James Mason** is seen more and more in fashionable drawing rooms. Everyone finds this British actor delightful, and women are particularly struck by the enchantment of his flutelike voice and his choice of words.

In Mrs. Jackie Kennedy's society as well as in Jock Whitney and Bill Paley's—he is their brother-in-law—**James Fosburgh** appears often with his wife, Minnie Cushing. He likes eggheads, paints oils with much skill, and has American anchorages in New York City, near Mt. Kisco, and in the Adirondacks.

With his wife, the former Candy Alig, **James van Alen** participates in big international shooting expeditions. His mother, Mrs. Louis Brugiere, is one of Newport's most imposing grandes dames and he has the distinction of having been the brother-in-law of two Mdivanis, since his sister Louise was wed to Alexis and then to Serge.

The Metropolitan Museum's fine director, **James J. Rorimer,** is widely traveled because of his job. With his wife, the former Katherine Serrell, he is at home in the society of such distinguished members of the Board of Trustees as Mrs. Vincent Astor, Roland Redmond, and Arthur K. Watson.

There will soon be more cowboy pictures made by the Tiber than in California, and scores of Italian actors are taking on American appellations. None of them has made the impact of **Jim Mitchum,** the strapping son of Robert Mitchum, on Rome's Via Veneto. This young man is "hot" property both in screen and girlie talk.

Jo and Joe

can apply to either sex.

Among the ladies:

Princess Ruprecht zu Löwenstein is a cool British-born beauty whose German husband is a banker in London. She arrives regularly in all capitals for the big parties and has a variety of friends of all ages.

Mrs. Yvor Bryce is torn among all the various residences she owns, going from England to the United States to the Bahamas. A sister of Huntington Hartford, she shares with him a cozy income from the A. and P., has changed her surname several times in various matrimonial ventures.

Josephine Hughes successfully runs De Pinna's fashion department and corrals all the internationalites into seeing the various collections at her fashion shows. She tears around Europe during her frequent trips, leaving everyone agog at her Texan zest and vitality.

Among the gents:

Joseph X. Dever is the civilized and exceedingly well-liked society columnist of the New York *World-Telegram.* He manages to be everywhere, never forgetting his good manners and never becoming irritable.

Joseph Meehan swings much of the time in the world of Henry Ford, for whom he works. He is a familiar figure in Southampton with his very pretty wife Kay, and turns up in the winter with his boss in St. Moritz.

Joseph Pulitzer III is St. Louis's gift to the international set. Fine-looking, a fabulous skier (all the snow resorts are acquainted with his prowess), and the able publisher of the *St. Louis Post Dispatch,* he flies around in a private company plane with his consort, the former Louise Vauclain of the Baldwin Locomotive clan.

Joseph Thomas is another familiar figure on the snows of the Alps, although he owns a house in Jamaica's Tryall settlement. An esteemed member of the Lehman Brothers Investment Brokerage firm, he and his popular wife Poppie entertain well wherever they go.

J. Kingsbury Smith is the popular, smooth publisher of the New York *Journal American.* Social inside and outside of the confines of the Hearst Empire, he has many European friends because of his long stay in Paris where he directed a news service. His cozy and charming wife is the former Eileen King.

JOHN, JOHNNY, GIANNI, JEAN

In N.S. John, Jean, and Gianni have a way of getting all confused, especially since it is chic to Italianize, Anglicize, or Gallicize a name, according to the country one is *not* in.

The most glamorous Johnny is **Gianni Agnelli,** probably because he is the richest, the smartest in business (he is the head of Fiat Motor Company, which he inherited, and innumerable other corporations), the handsomest (he looks like a Greek marble faun), and the most blasé. Kind to his kin and generous to his friends, he can never keep still except at the heart of his empire (Turin). All the various people who are dying to entertain him have the most terrible time, since after turning up anywhere, he usually leaves within thirty-six or forty-eight hours.

A favorite extra man is **John** (often called Johnny) **Galliher** whose Irish dimples some hostesses find irresistible. He has apartments in London and New York City.

Johnny Halliday, a tall, lanky, sexy singer, is in the process of graduating from European ye-ye society (which is growing all the time) into more staid company.

The distinguished and urbane **Prince Faucigny Lucinge,** who used to play a leading role in the affairs of the principality of Monaco, centers his activities in Paris. Now the President of the Union Interalliée (an important cultural organization in France), he is constantly off on business to London and Brazil.

Also a Parisian luminary is the **Count Jean de Beaumont,** known for his novels, his influence in banking spheres, and his shooting (he is one of the great shots of the world). His name comes up with that of his famous daughter, Jacqueline de Ribes. His other two children are not in the news.

As celebrated along the California coast as in Paris is the aristocratic, impersonal **Marquis de Surian,** whose wife is wealthy Mildred Cowgill from Hillsborough. Since she happens to be the niece of another American who married a Frenchman, the Vicomtesse de Bonchamps, their names pop up together in the cauldron of nomadic talk.

Another French Jean whose wife is an American—she was Frances Kier—is the **Baron de Pellenc,** a portly gentleman who has a Parisian home, a chateau in Seine et Oise, and a famous Hotel, La Gazelle d'Or, which he created in Taroudant in the Atlas Mountains of Morocco, a favorite retreat of Barbara Hutton.

Barbara's favorite Jean, however, is the **Count de Baglion** who is almost a permanent fixture in her court and known for his interest in antiques.

Among Shakesperians, John is always **Sir John Gielgud,** the fabulous actor-director who finds time for everything, including a busy social life on both sides of the ocean.

Hong Kong has its contribution in **Doctor Carey-Hughes,** the handsome Welsh physician who, after a long courtship, persuaded Carroll McDaniel, widow of the Marquess of Portago, to allow him to slip the gold band on her finger. A passionate sailor, he also loves big game hunting.

Renowned for some new romance or other is **John Ringling North** of circus fame, who never loses his calmness amidst elephant and lion crises.

John Barry Ryan III, of New York's theatrical and egghead drawing rooms is a bright investment broker-banker, a grandson of Otto Kahn, happily married to Dorinda-Deedee-Dixon, a junior edition of Diana Vreeland.

Count Palffy is in the news of Wall Street, Geneva (where his wife, the former Lila Kerr, owns a house), and central Europe as a whole. Son of the famous eight-times-married charmer, Count "Pali" Palffy and the late Dorothy Deacon, whose sisters were Mrs. Henry Gray and Gladys Dowager Duchess of Marlborough, he gives dinners in a Manhattan town house which has been photographed by *Time* magazine as a representative of a certain elegance.

The most humorously quoted of all the Johns is the columnist **Crosby,** who in recent years moved to London. An original thinker, he always has a fresh point of view, observing the scene at large with perspicacity and humor.

Although, unlike his father who was wonderfully eccentric and well-known for his artistic enterprises, he keeps quiet, the **Marquis de Cuevas** is an N.S. topic because of his marvelous Rockefeller heritage and his matrimonial venture with the niece of Art Gallery tycoon Alexander Iolas after a long marriage to Antonia Cobos (many, many years his senior).

John Drexel, marvelously polite, well-educated, and well-read, has traveled high and wide, but feels most at home in conservative Newport, Hobe Sound (where he is the President of that very exclusive club), Philadelphia, New York, and among the British nobility (his wife is the daughter of Lord Camoys).

John Gunther, the reporter *extraordinaire* makes New York his base, but he is constantly taking off to obtain material for a new book. Socially minded, he is a jewel in many lucky hostesses' salons with his wife Jane (Greta Garbo and Mary Lasker adore them).

John Fairchild has achieved miracles in promoting American fashions globally and has made *Women's Wear* one of the leading publications in the apparel industry. He is constantly quoted and his recent book, *The Fashionable Savages*, was a big success.

Sir John Russell, a member of the Duke of Bedford's clan, has lived in Teheran, Warsaw, Rome, New York City (where he held important diplomatic posts), and now resides in Addis Ababa (where he is the British Ambassador). Bright and sympathetic, he has the good luck of having a winner for a wife, an extraordinarily interesting Grecian beauty, Aliki Diplarakes, ex-Miss Greece, ex-Miss Europe, ex-Madame Paul-Louis Weiller, at one time one of the Queens of Parisian Society and recently the mama-in-law of Olympia Torlonia.

The polo playing **Marquess of Waterford** has as his family motto *Nil Nisi Cruce* (No Dependence but in the Cross), which is surely among the most eloquent in the British Isles. This young man, who has fine mansions in Ireland; is provided with several American aunts, for the mother of his wife, the Countess of Dunraven, is a sister of Mrs. Carroll Carstairs, Mrs. Henry Payne Bingham, and Mrs. Wolcott Blair.

In Ireland **John** could easily be **Huston**, the genial, brilliant film director. A compelling personality, he lives between film assignments in an Irish castle, and renounced his American citizenship to become a full-fledged Irishman. His latest assignment is the biggest of his career; it's *The Bible*.

The Johnny who is involved in the marriage sweepstakes is the fourth **Earl of Kimberley.** He started marrying only in 1945 and recently obtained his fifth divorce which gives a brief average to each matrimonial tie. According to *Debrett's Peerage*, he has four addresses in England.

The Jean whose name is uttered constantly in revered tones in the United Nations is the redheaded **Count de Noue,** who, after many years in New York, has now moved to Geneva where he continues to be a brilliant Protocol Chief. He is married to a daughter of the Duke Decazes.

Just when one thinks the career of **Jean Marais** is waning, it picks right up. This former romantic actor, who graced many of the Jean Cocteau productions, has now become a reincarnation of Douglas Fairbanks in French adventure films, and he is again in the news. The Comédie Française, of which he was a member, was never like this.

Wherever women with taste show off marvelously set jewels, **Jean** "Johnny" **Schlumberger** has been at work. A talented middle-aged bachelor and a charmer, he retires to do some of his designing on an estate he owns on the island of Guadeloupe and at a cottage in the nearby Island des Saints. He goes around the world once a year to acquire inspiration, and spends part of each year in New York City and Paris.

Many ladies who have undergone his plastic operations are grateful to **Dr. John Converse.** He is currently married to the former Mrs. Gary Cooper.

Every waterfall and cove in Jamaica echoes with the name of **John Pringle,** a member of the clan who has brought so much sheen to this island. Handsome and able, he has been married for a decade and a half to a beautiful Canadian model, Liz Benn. He runs the Tourist Board of this new independent republic and was responsible for the creation of Round Hill, the special compound-club which now has been copied by so many others.

In exalted museum echelons and on those fabulous cruises Mr. and Mrs. Charles Wrightsman organize every summer, Johnny means the brilliant director of the National Gallery in Washington, **John Walker,** an erudite and delightful scholar who had much of his training with the late Bernard Berenson. His wife is Lady Margaret Drummond, whose father, the late Earl of Perth, was British Ambassador to Rome.

Johnny de Braganca, whose father belonged to the Portuguese Royal Family, frequents the Long Island set, Gstaad (where he house guests with Anne Ford), and exclusive clubs around the world. His mother was an American Stewart. He is considered a catch not only as a husband—at the moment he is single—but also at a dinner party.

In the Caribbean (where he often visits with his wife), in Florida (where he moves in the Winston Guest set), and in shooting circles (he gives marvelous parties at his estate, Knowsley), the handsome eighteenth *Earl of Derby,* with the Eton and Oxford background one would expect him to have, is very much at home.

Traveling here, there, and everywhere on a large number of assignments is actor **Jean Sorel**, often referred to as John. Married to the Italian film actress Anna Maria Ferrero, he lives in France and Italy and is bilingual. He is always making news. His love scenes in *Le Bambole* with Gina Lollobrigida filled the papers for weeks and almost provoked the fall of the Italian government. His most recent motion picture, Luchino Visconti's **Vaghe Stelle dell' Orsa,** has raised countless eyebrows for he plays a brother in love with his sister (Claudia Cardinale).

Kitty and Kiddy

From Florida and the Caribbean (where she visits) to England and Mallorca (where she owns three homes) the chic and witty **Mrs. Gilbert Miller,** daughter of the late financier Jules Bache and wife of the theatrical producer Gilbert Miller, reigns supreme.

But in New York, where Mrs. Miller is one of the hostesses most in view and in conservative British company, Kitty might also be **Kitty van Heukelom,** another American, the divorced wife of the Honorable Charles Winn, whose first mate was none other than Lady Baillie. Many English visitors arriving in New York call on this green-eyed Kitty.

The widow of Moss Hart, **Kitty Carlisle,** makes professional appearances from time to time and is a cozy friend and a gifted entertainer. In her New York apartment she throws fun parties at which all the top names of the milky way are present.

Mrs. James Coleman divides her time as best she can among

Paris, Boston, and California. Formerly Margaret Gardner of the famous New England clan which included the great patroness Isabella Gardner, she first married Parmely Herrick, son of Myron Herrick, one of the most popular ambassadors the U.S. ever sent to France. Upon his death she married this Californian whose list of previous wives totaled three. Gay, vivacious, and good company, she owns the apartment in Paris which at one time was the scene of the late Princess George Chavchavadze's famous parties and later the Baroness Lo Monaco's.

Confusion invariably arises in Paris and California between Mrs. Coleman and the **Vicomte de Bonchamps,** whose nickname is Kiddy. In N.S. language Kitty and Kiddy often sound exactly the same, particularly over the cocktail party babel of voices. The Vicomte, who is very French, is married to Burlingame's Gale King Christiansen and visits California every year. Naturally, like Mrs. Coleman, she entertains all the visiting firemen from the West Coast in Paris.

Lee

Princess Stanislas Radziwill is the third wife of the handsome Pole and one of the most resplendent social vedettes of our times. An arresting-looking young woman, she is indefatigable, crossing the Atlantic as if it were a lake, maintaining homes in New York and London, renting houses for the summer in Italy, Portugal, or Greece. At times a fashion editor—her row with couturier Givenchy made headlines some years ago—she was reported recently to be considering a theatrical career. When her sister Mrs. Jackie Kennedy was First Lady, she accompanied her on some of her official trips. Her first husband was Michael Canfield, who has since married the Earl of Dudley's former wife.

Mrs. Robert Lehman, an Italo-American from California, is almost an exact copy of Gina Lollobrigida, even in her choice of clothes. A warm, enthusiastic person, she often escapes from the magnificent homes and collections of her banker husband to a simpler life in Puerto Rico or wherever she can find it.

Mrs. Lawrence Copley Thaw is terribly social not only in New York, where she entertains well in her maisonette off Park Avenue, but also in the capitals she is forever visiting. She started her way in the international jungle as Elizabeth Francis in Boston, later was a researcher at *Vogue* magazine (has anyone escaped this publication?), resigned her job to marry the Marquess Lottaringhi della Stufa whom she later divorced to wed again. Recently widowed, she always appears undernourished, but this appearance is from choice for she attends many important dinners.

Mrs. Carman Messmore, the former Leonora Highet, is a quiet, blonde Britisher who is married to one of the directors of Knoedler Galleries. In the swim of all the millionaires who buy paintings from her husband, she designs sweaters which she manufactures successfully.

Lelia, Loelia, and Leyla

are names which raise havoc, since three of the ladies who answer to them are in the same sets.

The **Hon. Mrs. Hubert Howard** lives in England and Italy (on the two superb estates of Sermoneta and Ninfa); is the only daughter of the late Duke of Sermoneta, who devoted his untiring energies to composing classical music, and the American-born Duchess, Miss Margaret Chapin, who contributed so much to culture for many years by publishing the magazine *Botteghe Oscure*, which discovered many talented writers. An enthusiastic painter who has held exhibitions, she is religious and related to half of Rome's aristocracy.

Loelia, Duchess of Westminster, the most traveled of the British Duchesses, is always paying a visit to her friends around the world. The divorced wife of the late eccentric

Duke, she has written her own autobiography and has been a long time contributor to the English *House and Garden*. She is tall and regal.

Madame Jean Ralli is a tiny Grecian lady who lives in Paris, works for Dior, wears large round glasses and blows kisses to her friends. A firm believer in royalty, she is surrounded by them and is ever entertaining them in her spacious Left Bank apartment. Like her English namesake, she is a frequent guest at large house parties.

Often heard, but rarely seen at social occasions because of the traveling demanded by her professional engagements, is **Leyla Gencer,** Turkey's contribution to opera. Comely and intelligent, she is such a good musician that she can sing almost any opera. In 1965 she scored as "Norma" at La Scala in Milan and at Verona's Arena and as "Anna Bolena," in the rarely performed work by Donizetti, at the Glyndebourne Festival.

Lily and Lil

The **Countess Volpi di Misurata** has residences in Venice, Rome, Monte Circeo, Paris, Geneva, and Misurata in Libya. A striking-looking woman who wears huge black bows in her high coiffure, she is a generous hostess in all her encampments, has a genuine love for music (she used to be a charming amateur soprano). Her first husband was the jeweler Lacloche.

The **Marchesa Gerini** travels between Port' Ercole and Connecticut where she was born into the Italo-American clan of the Polis. A big, good-natured creature, she owns the famous property of Santa Liberata on the Argentario.

Actress **Lilli Palmer** is sure to turn in a good performance. At one point the wife of Rex Harrison and a regular in Italy when they lived in Portofino, she is now here, there, and everywhere with her current husband Carlos Thompson.

Mrs. Herbert Pulitzer, a glamour girl in her own right, has made a big success with her fashion designs called "Lillys."

Fond of going barefooted in her Palm Beach palazzo, she helps her rich, successful husband with the Pulitzer Groves Fruit Shop and visits her mother, Mrs. Ogden Phipps, in Long Island. When in Europe, she is in the Peggy d'Arenberg set.

Lily Cushing is a wonderfully slim, chic, bony-faced post-deb who, through her mother, Justine Cutting, is related to many delightful American aristocrats. She appears in the pages of *Vogue* magazine.

Whether in post-deb chat or in *Paris Match* circles (her husband is the New York representative), on the H. J. Heinzes' yacht excursions, or on St. Moritz's snowy slopes, **Mrs. Stephane Groueff** looks just as young as her daughters, Jill and Tina Isles, who recently made their bow to society.

The first Mrs. Raymond Guest (she preceded Ellen "Tucky" French and the current one, formerly Princess Caroline Murat) is now styled **Mrs. Polk Guest** and is associated with Washington and Virginia's horsy set. Divorced long ago, she is the mother of Mrs. George Stevens, Jr., and post-deb Virginia Guest whose photographs are beginning to appear in all the sophisticated magazines.

Lily Pons, the former reigning Queen of the coloratura sopranos, has, since her divorce from André Kostelanitz, made Texas and Palm Springs, where she spends her winters, her homes. Always pert, *soignée,* and every inch the prima donna, she looks youthful and well.

Louis, Luis, Lewis

In Spain or wherever there is talk of Spaniards, it's quite a job to unravel which one is being referred to. They include:

The Duke of Alba, the consort of the Duchess and not a Duke by birth, although on his own he is a member of the Ducal family of the Sotomayor. An excellent shot, he pursues this sport, and he also skis well. A gracious man, he is overshadowed by his colorful wife.

The Count of Quintanilla-Romanones paints abstractions and shoots well, has three dwellings in Spain (Madrid, Marbella, and Pascualete), visits the United States at least twice a year with his American wife.

The Marquess de las Marismas del Guadalquivir is a bachelor who, despite looking like a Saint in an El Greco picture, has a vivid humor. He is considered the best director in the world today of the plays of his great friend, the late poet Garcia Lorca, and is invited to put them on in different countries.

Luis Miguel Dominguin is the most social of all the bullfighters. He had retired for a while, but recently was preparing for a comeback. Married to the Italian actress Lucia Bosé, he is popular in Grandee and jet-set cliques.

Before their separation, the Cuban-born designer **Luis Estevez** and his wife Betty were indefatigable hosts in New York, Acapulco, and Paris. He is a man of enormous vitality who recently settled in California.

Louis Jacquinot has occupied a variety of outstanding positions in General de Gaulle's Fifth Republic, and has been sent on numerous international missions. With his ash-blonde wife Simone, a member of the enormously rich Lazard clan, he finds time to be social.

The Pretender to the imperial French throne, **H.I.H. Prince Louis Napoleon Bonaparte,** is far less in the spotlight than his competitor, the Count of Paris. He divides his time between France and Switzerland, leads an exemplary family life with his wife, Princess Alix, and makes the French proud when he does grace a social occasion.

When he is not working, **Louis Jourdan** appears at parties, contributing his usual, smooth performance. He is one of those actors who, upon accepting a dinner invitation, turn up.

Louis A. Benoist is a regular sputnik, who manages to crowd in his schedule an astounding number of engagements. He and his mate Kay have several residences in California, one in Mexico, and one in Virginia, traveling from one to the other by yacht or private plane. He is the bigwig of the Almaden Vineyards and of the Lawrence warehouses.

The Bankers Trust's lean, ascetic looking, bright **Lewis Lapham,** whose father used to be San Francisco's mayor, roams the world on business, sometimes leaving his delightful spouse, the former Jane Foster, to keep the fires burning in a Manhattan apartment and a Connecticut country home, sometimes taking her with him.

A Louis referred to as "Dickie," is the **Earl Mountbatten of Burma,** the most resplendent figure in the British Royal Family. His list of past posts make one dizzy, and among the most celebrated were those of last Viceroy of India, before independence was proclaimed, and Chief of Defense Staff. He has two residences in England and one in Ireland. On his many missions abroad he is sometimes accompanied by one of his two daughters. His popular wife, Edwina, died a few years ago.

Margaret, Maggie, and Marguerite

The most often photographed and mentioned is the **Countess of Snowdon,** sister of the Queen of England, who has taken to traveling more and more, and turns up in such nomadic nests as Venice, the Greek Islands, and Sardinia. She is the most controversial of the members of the British Royal Family.

Ever since her earth-shaking divorce from the Duke of Argyll, **Margaret Whigham** has been seen less and less in the exclusive Mayfair drawing rooms and therefore is talked about less frequently.

The Marquesa de Cuevas, widow of the Ballet Maecenas, was born Margaret Strong, a granddaughter of the founder of the Rockefeller fortunes. An intelligent and cultivated lady, with so many homes at her disposal all over the Unied States and Europe it must be difficult for her to remember them all, she is more discussed than seen.

Margaret Leighton is one of Britain's most talented actresses. She commutes across the Atlantic for theatrical and film jobs, but she prefers British husbands. She is married to Michael Wilding after divorcing Laurence Harvey, and is a part of international society.

Margaret Chase Smith, the Senator from Maine, is definitely not in the jet set, but is quoted by its members, for she makes all sorts of epoch-making statements on such pertinent subjects as the disappearance of the "square" state of mind.

Her Royal Highness Princess René de Bourbon-Parme, who was born Margaret of Denmark, is the mother of Queen Anne of Roumania and Prince Michael (one of the most gadabout of the royal princes), a dignified, popular lady in France, where she resides at Saint Cloud, and in the Caribbean where she visits in the cold months.

Mrs. John Ambler, one of the three charming, easy-going sisters of the Crown Prince of Sweden, now the wife of a British businessman, divides her life between London and Stockholm.

In three cases, two in the United States and one in Paris, Margaret becomes Maggie:

Margaret Case has been an institution at *Vogue* magazine since time immemorial. Eternally young in mind, spirit, and body, she has an energy that is one of the wonders of our times, and like the Navajos and Cherokees, she keeps her ear close to the ground so that there isn't anything she does not know about the nomads who check in with her the moment they arrive in Manhattan to find out who is there.

Mrs. Clyde Newhouse has had a successful career as a torch singer, television and radio interviewer, and more recently as a fashion commentator under the name of Maggi McNellis. A jet-setter, she is endowed with a definite brand of American humor.

Baroness Egmont Van Zuylen, a handsome Egyptian, widow of a rich Belgian patrician, with homes in Paris and Holland—

she is quite a chatelaine there in the Chateau of Haa–adores to gamble, goes off cruising on Aristotle Onassis' yacht, rarely misses a Maria Callas performance, is often a weekend visitor at Ferrières, the fabulous castle of her son-in-law Baron Guy de Rothschild.

The unmarried **Countess de Limburg Stirum** is an amateur painter with a certain flair and an excellent horsewoman. A member of one of Belgium's oldest families, she has one of the many daughters of the Count of Paris, Hélène, as a sister-in-law, and is therefore constantly in royal circles. She usually winters in New York.

The **Archduchess Robert of Hapsburg,** tall and thin, the former Princess Margherita of Aosta, is a *grande dame* in appearance and manner. She is a familiar of royal society everywhere, particularly in Paris, where her husband is prominent in banking.

Wherever the House of Orange has interests, from Holland to Port' Ercole, there is talk of the democratic, fun-loving **Princess Margaret of the Netherlands,** who recently announced her engagement to a Dutch commoner. She will not have to give up her rights to the throne, since the Parliament has sanctioned her decision.

Marguerite Lamkin has a Southern drawl which becomes more pronounced with the passing of time. A sister of Speed Lamkin, the novelist, divorced from a motion-picture director and an actor, she put her Louisiana accent to good use earning big money teaching all the big stars in Hollywood, when they needed to sound Southern. She lives in London with her third husband, the brilliant British barrister, Mark Littman.

Margot

Because the three ladies who answer to this name have their respective domains in London, Rome, and Paris, they should be easy to distinguish, but alas, they are frequently in the same place at the same time, attracted like magnets to one another.

The reigning **Margot** is **Fonteyn,** the compelling ballerina who found a new dimension in her profession the moment Nureyev became her partner. As the wife of a Panamanian political figure, Rodolfo Arias, an international lawyer who has been an ambassador at various times, she is sometimes torn from artistic milieus and thrown into political and business ones.

In Rome, Margot means the estranged wife of **Prince Gianfranco Alliata di Montereale,** the only contribution of the Republic of El Salvador to world society. Born Margarita Guirola della Cotera, she made her dent in Mexico City as Bruno Pagliai's mate after a first marriage to a Frenchman. Wonderful-looking, her white hair framing a youthful face, she is an excellent skier and rider to hounds.

Mme. Edmond Bory, the former Madame Champin, is an exquisite Parisian hostess whose husband's many holdings keep her on the move between two continents.

Marina

The most prominent of those who answer to this name, so evocative of the beauties of the sea, is **Princess Marina, Duchess of Kent.** Most people don't call her by her first name to her face, but they do so behind her back. Although she has retired from the party circuit and is reputed to stay at home in Kensington Palace watching television, her rare appearances are magic, for she is still every inch a regal beauty. She travels on good-will missions for her niece, the Queen, visits her sister, Princess Paul of Yugoslavia, in Paris or Florence, and members of the Greek Royal Family, into which she was born, in Greece.

The discussed and nomadic **Marina Cicogna** has blossomed from an ugly duckling into a beauty. Her progressive theories of living contribute enormously to the amenities of general conversation from Manila to Timbuktu.

A marvelous contrast to her is her aunt, **Countess Enrico Luling Bruschetti,** who was Marina Volpi, the owner of one of the most beautiful houses in Europe, the Villa of Maser, near Venice. A tireless traveler, she knows café society, but is not part of it. Her guests range from Princess Margaret and Lord Snowdon to Barbara Hutton, an old friend.

Marina Doria is the tall, good-looking Swiss cheese heiress who has been the off and on fiancée of Prince Victor Emanuel of Italy, son and heir of former King Umberto.

Marina Sulzberger, the intelligent and personable wife of the *New York Times* correspondent, is at home in her native Greece, in Spetsai (where she has a summer house), in Paris (where they have an apartment), and all over the world when she follows her husband Cy on his different assignments.

Marina, wife of Prince Michael of Greece. This is the official way she must be addressed in Athens, creating much embarrassment because she has not been given royal rank. Very rich—she is a member of the banking family of Karella—she is not beautiful, but bright and attractive. In order to marry her, the Prince had to renounce his rights of succession. He is a cousin of the King and the son of the late Prince Christopher and Françoise of Orleans, sister of the Count of Paris.

Mary

with all due respect to the Virgin Mother, is a fountain of anxiety in airborne enclaves. There are dozens of them, all wonderfully energetic, popular, and unable to remain long in any one place. Among the Americans are:

Mrs. Howard Cushing, one of Newport's reigning queens, related on all sides to distinguished families, mother of the adorable Mary Cushing and mother-in-law of one of American society's most frequently photographed young matrons, Mrs. Frederick Cushing (Nathalie Fell).

Mrs. C. Suydam Cutting, born Mary Pyne and widow of

Oliver Filley, recently married the well-known explorer and Tibetan specialist. She is one of the truly great *grandes dames* of the United States. A gentle and whimsical human being, she commutes from New York to an estate in New Jersey to an eighteenth-century fort in Nassau.

Mrs. James Dunn, with *pieds à terre* in Rome and New York, is a beguiling, universally esteemed, wonderfully cultivated former Ambassadress (her husband was envoy to many countries) and a leader of worthwhile nomadic expeditions.

Mrs. James Fosburgh, usually called Minnie, one of the epoch-making Cushing sisters, married an excellent painter after her divorce from the late Vincent Astor. With three houses in the United States, she has moved farther and farther away from society to dedicate her time to the intelligentsia, seeing very little of anyone who is not an actor, director, writer, or artist.

Mrs. Albert Lasker, the widow of the philanthropist and collector of great impressionist paintings, despite bases in New York City and State, is constantly traveling because of the activities of the Foundation to which she is dedicated and her strong Democratic political affiliations. In the summer she rents the Villa La Fiorentina at St. Jean, Cap Ferrat, but entertains wherever she may be.

Mrs. Philip Herrari, the dynamic daughter of Mrs. Watson Blair, the former Mary McFadden, renounced her de luxe gypsy life in order to marry a handsome Egyptian who is in the diamond business in South Africa. A born leader, she will surely become a magnet in Johannesburg's smart set.

Mary Martin, in private life Mrs. Richard Halliday, is a unique blithe spirit from Texas, the greatest possible addition to her theatrical profession, society anywhere, and the Brazilian jungle, which she loves best of all and where she spends every available free minute on a heavenly farm in the State of Goyas amidst flying parrots and swinging monkeys.

Mrs. Ricard Ohrstrom, another Texan gift, was Mary Murchison, and to start life with such a name in the Lone Star State means being born with a platinum spoon in your mouth. A delectable, delightful lady, an excellent wife and mother of a large brood, she alternates among four houses (New York, Virginia, Jamaica, and Deauville).

Mrs. Laurance Rockefeller is all wrapped up in worthwhile projects. Because of the numerous responsibilities she fulfills, she is always coming in contact with people in the highest places.

Mrs. Mary Roebling, the most discussed woman banker in the United States, spends most of the evenings of her crowded life on some dais, delivering a speech; is an indefatigable hostess in Trenton (New Jersey), New York, Washington, and Philadelphia; often a delegate to economic and commercial missions to various capitals.

Mrs. Edward Warburg, Southern accent and all, is another welcome present from the Mary-minded State of Texas to international society and to New York in particular. Her sister is London's Baroness Leo d'Erlanger, whom she visits. Despite her girlish appearance, she is a grandmother, courtesy of her son (from another marriage), Stephen Currier, and his arch-millionairess wife, Audrey Bruce (a granddaughter of Andrew Mellon).

Mrs. Sheldon Whitehouse, a real patrician, shuttles among her houses in New York, Newport, and a Southern plantation, is always off to visit her son, who is a diplomat, and her daughter, who is married to one.

An American Mary married to an Englishman is the **Countess of Bessborough,** formerly Mary Munn. Her husband's many businesses take her on long trips to the Orient. She is a good amateur painter, and one hears the remark "how pretty Mary's latest oil is."

Mary Duchess of Roxburghe, the buxom, good-natured daughter of the late Marquess of Crewe, is divorced from the Duke whose title she still carries. She bore the Queen's canopy at the Coronation of King George VI, and takes a lively interest in Mayfair political circles.

In Athens, after the death of **Madame Vassili Dendramis,** who was for many years the brilliant Greek Ambassadress to Washington, Mary now means **Madame Mary Dracoupolos,** Stavros Niarchos' sister, who is part of all those splendid house parties her brother and sister-in-law give on Spezzapoula.

Senhora Ricardo Espirito Santo divides her time between a great town house in Lisbon and another marvelous one in Cascais, is the owner of rare art collections left by her banker husband, and entertains with style the many royal personages who have chose the Portuguese capital as their favorite haunt.

The Parisian Mary is definitely the **Baroness Alain de Rothschild,** who lives in a splendid town house full of treasures, is an accomplished *connoisseuse* of art, and shares her husband's enthusiasm for yachting.

Mrs. Efrem Zimbalist (Mary Curtis) plays a leading role on Philadelphia's Main Line, at the Curtis Music Institute, and in Curtis Publishing circles. A splendid lady, who has single-handedly done more for music in the U.S. than any other living person, she discovered, among others, the talents of Gian-Carlo Menotti and Samuel Barber, and made it possible for their careers to soar.

MICHAEL, MICHEL, MIKE

includes three Royal gentlemen who appear everywhere:

Former **King Michael of Roumania** is huge in size, shy, attractive; lives in Geneva with his wife, Anne of Bourbon-Parme, and four daughters; works for an aviation concern. Since his mother, Helen of Greece, is the aunt of King Constantine, he visits in Athens where he is apt to be confused with his cousins by the same name.

Prince Michael of Greece, son of the late Prince Christopher of Greece and Françoise of France, was left an orphan at an early age and educated partly by his uncle and aunt, the Count and Countess of Paris. He renounced his rights to the throne in order to marry a rich commoner, Marina Karella.

H.R.H. Prince Michel of Bourbon-Parme, brother-in-law of ex-King Michael, is always in the news, in Paris on the automobile racing circuit and in Copenhagen (his mother is Princess Margarethe of Denmark). He is estranged from his wife, Princess Yolande de Broglie, who has provided him with five children.

Prince Michael of Kent is in his early twenties, an enthusiastic pilot, automobile racer, and bobsled rider. He is a cousin of the first two Michaels mentioned.

Michael Tree, whose wife is Lady Anne Cavendish, sister of the Duke of Devonshire, is quoted for his witty remarks. With Mereworth Castle as a base in Great Britain, he is a frequent guest of Stavros and Charlotte Niarchos, both on Spezzapoula and in St. Moritz, and visits his father, Ronald Tree, in the Barbados.

Because of his great taste and imagination, **Sir Michael Duff's** estate in Wales, Vaynol Park, is one of the most appreciated in England. He married Lady Caroline Paget, sister of the Marquess of Anglesey.

Michael Phipps (his wife is British, Muriel "Molly" Lane), an eminent sportsman, an outdoor gentleman with vast real estate holdings, and father of the glamorous Mrs. Thomas Schippers, is well known in American-British circles, Long Island, and Palm Beach.

Michael Paul inherited millions at the death of his wife and a magnificent Palm Beach mansion which he used to lend to the late President Kennedy. He plays the violin quite well.

Michael Canfield looks after the publishing interests of *Harper's* in London. An American, he is handsome in a British way, has much charm in his quiet manner. First married to Lee Bouvier and therefore a brother-in-law of Mrs. Jackie Kennedy, he is now the husband of Laura Charteris, ex-Countess of Dudley, and consequently a brother-in-law of the widow of Ian Fleming.

Dark, personable, polo playing **Michael Carcano,** whose father was the Argentinian Ambassador to London, is settled in Paris with his wife, Rosina Bemberg of the rich Argentinian aristocracy. He has an estate in the Algarve, southern Portugal, at his disposal, and is a topnotch skier.

Just how French society would function without the five De Ganay brothers is a matter of conjecture. **Count Michel de Ganay** is, along with Jean Louis, André, Charles, and Paul, an adornment to the jet set, as is his exquisite wife, the former Victoire de Montesquiou. Because of his mother's many interests in Argentina—she too is a member of that fabulous Bemberg family—he spends several months a year in the country where the tango was born.

Michel David Weill, the dynamic, short-in-size-but-not-in-brains member of the French banking dynasty Lazard Frères, has houses in New York and Paris. His wife, Hélène Lehideux, is small, gothic-looking, and a personality in her own right.

In Deauville, where he is Mayor, in cosmetics (his family owns the cosmetic firm Orlane), and in many of the European drawing rooms, **Count d'Ornano** holds sway. With a good stable of horses, he is much in the swim with his wife Anne de Contades.

White-haired, well-read **Michel Valery Olivier,** has a splendid house in Biarritz where he entertains with his wife, born a d'Harcourt (one of the most illustrious clans in France), at one point the Duchess of Vivonne. Sometimes he is referred to as "Kim."

Michael Cacoyannis is the island of Cyprus' gift to the theater and cinema. Dark, intense, and originally a lawyer, he sprang onto the world scene with his films *Elektra* and *Zorba the Greek,* and tore the roofs off the Palais de Chaillot with his direction of Euripides' *The Trojan Women* in the Jean-Paul Sartre adaptation in 1965.

There are two Miguels, sometimes referred to as Michael, who are always in the news:

Miguel Ferreras, the tempestuous Cuban dress designer who divorced his first wife to marry the Irish heiress Oonagh Guinness and move his dress designing business from Manhattan to Paris. He later divorced again, closed down, and took off for a third wedding ceremony, this time with the daughter of the late Dominican dictator Trujillo, much-married Flor de Oro, who figured long ago as Porfirio Rubirosa's first mate.

Miguel Aleman, the urbane, terribly rich, former Mexican President and king of Acapulco's various developments, loans his house in the Pacific resort to all sorts of celebrities. It is here that Merle Oberon and Bruno Pagliai gave their epoch-making party for the Duke of Edinburgh.

A Mike who is not a Michael is **Gardner Cowles,** the brilliant, affable leader of the destinies of *Look* magazine. With his current enchanting wife Jan, he has three houses (New York, Connecticut, and Florida), but is a world traveler of note.

A brand-new **Michael** whose star is soaring in the jet set is the British cockney actor **Caine.** Thirty-two years of age, he created such a sensation in *The Ipcress File* that assignments all over the globe are piling up on his calendar. To *Glamour* magazine, this sexy newcomer asserted "My main interest in life is women."

The **Mike** whom every "hep" egghead party-giver tries to latch onto is the actor, director, and gag writer **Nichols.** His bon mots are constantly quoted, and there was much to-do about what his relations would be with Burton and Taylor on the film set of *Who's Afraid of Virginia Woolf?*, which he directed. Born in Russia with the less easy surname of Peschlowsky, he has two divorces behind him and a tendency to be chubby.

Mimi

is an utterly international nickname.

In Spain it's the **Duchess of Medinaceli** in her own right. She carries some of the finest titles in the peninsula on her small shoulders and her real name is Victoria Eugenia, after the Queen, who was her godmother. With many houses, she owns the Casa de Pilates in Seville, the crowning glory of her family, one of the most beautiful residences in the world. Well-liked, she is civic-minded and a cozy hostess.

In Italy it can be either the **Duke of Brindisi,** a member of the famous Aldobrandini clan, a gentleman of the old school who never married, or/

Countess Cecil Pecci Blunt, a niece of Pope Leo XIII, a muse of all the arts, particularly of music. She is identified with famous house parties at the Villa Reale de Marlia, near Lucca, the residence of Elisa Baciocchi, Napoleon's sister, when she ruled Tuscany.

Mimi di Niscemi, whose father is a Sicilian Prince and whose mother is a Philadelphian, is the successful designer of costume jewelry, Mimi di N. Her business headquarters are in New York City.

In Manhattan there is always mention of:

Mrs. de la Grange Hyde, French on her father's side and American on her mother's, who is divorced from Henry Hyde and mother of the glamour girl of 1965, Lorna Hyde. An enthusiastic skier, she spends time in the Caribbean area and every summer visits her brother, who has a big property in Corsica.

Mimi Russell, the attractive young daughter of Lady Sarah Churchill and Ed Russell, is a regular guest at her grandfather's historical Blenheim Palace in England.

Mrs. Edward Alexander, the former Gloria Baker, leads a quiet life since she married the Brigadier General, and is no longer in N.S. A half-sister of Alfred Vanderbilt, she was one of the several wives of Henry J. Topping.

Mrs. Reynaldo Herrera keeps an apartment in Manhattan and goes from there to Caracas, where her husband's family is prominent. A perfectly beautiful woman, she is warm, intelligent, and wise.

An offbeat Mimi is **Mrs. Browne-Cohaine,** who has started a successful business entitled "Ruins Incorporated." She buys old houses in wretched condition, fixes them, and resells them at Cadaques, the Island of Minorca, and other places. She used to be married to Ogden Goelet.

The rising **Mrs. Joseph Verner Reed, Jr.,** was born Marie Byers. Educated at Foxcroft, she married the attractive Chase Manhattan executive who is active in Republican politics. New York City, Newport, and Hobe Sound, where her husband's family occupies the No. 1 place, are her main encampments.

In South America and Italy, Mimi may be **Countess Vettore** Marcello, who, with her two sisters, the late Princess Francesco Ruspoli and the Princess Alliata di Montereale, was born into the prominent industrial family of Matarazzo. At one time an Italian congresswoman, she is the mother of Piero Mele (from a previous marriage), the former playboy who explored Tibet and squired Brenda Frazier onto the front pages, and the aunt of the never-out-of-the-newspaper-columns Dado Ruspoli.

Molly

Two matrons conspicuous in Florida and Long Island U beach and golf clubs answer to this nickname:

Mrs. Edward B. McLain, Alfred Vanderbilt's first choice in the marital go-round, the former Manuela Hudson, a regular commuter between Manhattan and Palm Beach, and often a bird in passage abroad; and **Mrs. Michael Phipps,** the former Muriel Lane from England, wife of the real estate squire. They are both well-liked, so it is difficult to tell them apart, since there are never any bitchy remarks made about them.

Mrs. Sigourney Thayer is a great expert on the Middle East. She is one of the few social registerites who has made a success of a writing career on several different fronts (including a column), and she is a tremendously articulate personage on all subjects.

The **Duchess of Buccleuch** is related on every side to the British Royal Family. She was born a Lascelles, into which clan the Queen's aunt, the Princess Royal, married, and her sister-in-law is the consort of the Duke of Gloucester. With an overwhelming background of marvelous historical houses filled with paintings of the finest old masters, she is modern, up and coming, a doer and a traveler. She appears in the United States at least once a year.

The unique and jolly **Countess of Berkeley,** the former Mary Lowell of Boston, is the widow of the last Earl. (The title will die out since there are no direct descendants.) She has masses of houses in Italy (a beautifully restored old convent in Assisi, two towers in San Gimignano, a house in Rome, and a villa in Ischia), and an adopted war orphan Vittorio Manunta, who made an everlasting impression as the protagonist of the film *Never Take No For An Answer.*

The strongminded, very positive **Hon. Mrs. Molly Burns** is the only daughter of the great merchant of old masters, Lord Duveen. Now with her second husband, Bryan Burns, she spends the winters in a comfortable house near Montego Bay where she entertains a lot.

Nancy

The darling of British U society, Paris, Venice, and highly *outré* circles, **Nancy Mitford** is currently at work on a book about Versailles at the time of Louis XIV. One of the most original personalities of our era, she is wit personified, sometimes at the expense of Americans who are not truly U in her opinion.

Nancy Perkins, whose three husbands have been Henry Field (brother of Marshall Field), Ronald Tree, and "Juby" Lancaster, is a niece of Nancy Astor, for whom she was named. Upon Lady Colefax's death, she bought her decorating business and has been at it ever since. A woman of impeccable taste, whatever she does in interior decoration is news in England, where she lives, and in the United States.

The youthful new **Princess "Dado" Ruspoli,** the former Nancy La Charbonnière, whose Joan of Arc styled bangs clash with the unsaintly décolletés she wears, has houses in Italy and France and is one of the leaders of yé-yé society.

Mrs. Horace Tritton, the former Nancy Oakes, ex-wife of Count de Marigny and Baron Lyssard Hoyningen Huene, whose father Sir Harry Oakes was mysteriously murdered in Nassau over two decades ago, is a warmhearted globe-trotter with residences in Mexico City, London, and Nassau, and what counts more, friends in every port.

Nancy Hartung, the ex-wife of Chris Holmes, who is now the ex of Arlene Dahl, makes her home in Gstaad, but is a roamer with frequent magazine assignments. She is striking in appearance and typically American.

Mrs. Kenneth Keith, the former Nancy Gross, mercifully is called Slim by some of her close friends. Her first mate was Howard Hawkes, and her second Leland Hayward, the theatrical producer. Although her home is in England (a flat in London's Eaton Square and a Norfolk estate), because of her British banker husband she is ever crossing the Atlantic. Handsome and intense, she gave up wearing dark glasses, her trademark, on her husband's request.

Wherever fashion and the magazine business are discussed the name of neat and trim **Nancy White,** who succeeded her aunt, Carmel Snow, as editor-in-chief of *Harper's Bazaar,* comes up.

The **Nancy Randolph** column of the *New York Daily News* is written by Julia McCarthy, who has been doing a bang-up job for a long, long time. "In" with the British, she always has some exciting news to tell about the British aristocracy.

A collector of modern oils, **Mrs. Henry Ittleson** has remained perfectly natural despite her husband's wealth. They surprised everyone by building a terribly modern house in the old, mellow village of Roquebrune on the French Riviera.

The **Countess of Perth**, whose Scottish husband has held many important positions including that of Minister of State for Colonial Affairs, is the daughter of Manhattan's Reginald Fincke.

Another American-born **Countess** is the widow of the Earl **of Dunraven,** who has a fine estate in Ireland's Limerick County. This Nancy, who is a sister of Mrs. Carroll Carstairs, Mrs. Robert P. Bingham, and Mrs. Wolcott Blair, constantly nips over the ocean to visit them in their various encampments.

Mrs. Nicholas Biddle is the auburn-haired, genial daughter of Colony Restaurant regular Mrs. George Harris. Her first husband was Lewis Preston, who is now the husband of a member of the Pulitzer family.

NICO, NICHOLAS, NICOLETTA, NICKI, NICKY

are a source of endless mix-ups because the slightest change in linguistic inflection modifies the sound. **Madame Hervé Alphand** usually escapes a sobriquet and is called Nicole. The beautiful and able wife of the former Ambassador to Washington, where she made a smashing success and landed on the cover of *Time* magazine, is a joy to the eyes and good company. No Ambassador had ever changed wives in midstream before but Alphand did when he divorced No. 1 to marry Nicole while he was in the American capital. He now has moved on to the post of Secretary General of the French State

Department, and his wife decorates the Parisian scene, working for Pierre Cardin.

The Duchess of Bedford is the most unusual and on-the-go of the British Duchesses. French by birth and with four smashing Milinaire children from her first husband, she became a television producer of note and only gave up this lucrative profession when she entered the portals of Woburn Abbey as the Duke's third consort. A ball of fire, immensely active and capable, she has helped her mate enormously in making his estate the most visited and highest paying stately house in Great Britain. The Bedfords also have residences in London, Paris' Ile St. Louis, Collares (in Portugal), and the French Alps, and cross the Atlantic and Pacific oceans in order to drum up clients for their tourist trade and make television appearances.

In England there is another Nicole, mostly referred to as Nico, the current **Marchioness of Londonderry** whose hair is as long as her interests. An exquisite beauty, she is a definite leader of a certain young set.

Among the male Nicos, there are two constantly referred to:

Nicholas Goulandris and **Prince Boncompagni Ludovisi.** The first is a leading figure in Greek shipping, who spends the winters in a cottage at Nassau's Lyford Cay and the summers fishing off his yacht among the Grecian Islands. In between he can be seen in New York, London, Paris, and all the capitals on behalf of his large business interests. He has an apartment in Athens and is planning a house on the island of Skiathos. He is always accompanied by his engaging wife, Dolly. The second, who will eventually succeed his father as Prince of Piombino, belongs to one of Rome's leading families and has married a girl whose pedigree is most impressive. She is Benedetta Barberini Colonna di Sciarra. Currently studying in Zurich to complete his courses in engineering, he is serious, and with his wife is considered among the most attractive young couples in the *beau monde*.

Closely associated with Florence, the villa I Tatti, and the world of the late Bernard Berenson is **Signorina Mariano,** who for several decades was the guardian angel of, and unique assistant to, the venerable and unsurpassed art critic.

Countess Edoardo Visconti has residences on both Capri and Lake Como and winters in Milan or Rome. With her sister, Countess Madina Arrivabene, she established many new trends and was one of the most breath-takingly beautiful women of her generation.

In and out of all the dressmaking establishments in New York and Paris is the **Baron de Gunzburg,** who has the looks of the Egyptian pharaohs of the eighteenth dynasty and is as cool and self-collected as they were. French by birth, he has lived in the United States for a long time, beginning his training as a fashion editor with *Harper's Bazaar* and now in the employ of *Vogue*.

Prince Aragona Pignatelli Cortes is the head of Gulf Oil in Italy, a bright, dynamic, and prepossessing man. His marriage to Luciana Malgeri, Rudi Crespi's stepsister, ended in one of those rapid, mysterious shipwrecks that plague N.S.

Nicky Hilton is heir to his father Conrad Hilton's hotel empire. The first to head the long list of Elizabeth Taylor's husbands, he is now married to "Trish," the pretty daughter of Mrs. Horace Schmidlapp.

Nina, Nin and Nini

The **Duchess of Cesarò** is the swan-necked and patrician mother of fashion designer Simonetta Fabiani and the Countess Umberto Corti. She is on affectionate terms with both daughters, although they don't speak to one another.

Mrs. Anthony Harwood, the witty and wise sister of the much-married Mdivanis (most of them dead), at one time or the other counted among her in-laws Barbara Hutton (to whom she has remained a loyal friend), Louise van Alen, Virginia Sinclair, Pola Negri, Mae Murray, and José Maria Sert. Upon the death of her mate, Denis Conan Doyle (son of the creator of Sherlock Holmes), she remarried a cultivated American several years her junior, has houses in Paris and India, and stays with Miss Hutton in Morocco.

The **Countess of Seafield,** a peeress in her own right, and therefore a member of the House of Lords, is the bearer of many proud titles. Colossally rich (she is reputed to be the second wealthiest lady in Great Britain), with much of the money inherited from her stepgrandmother, a New Zealand heiress, she owns two famous castles and a shooting lodge, besides a house on Paris' Left Bank; is the head of the Grant Clan, divorced from Grenadier Guardsman Derek Studley-Herbert, the mother of Viscount Reidhaven and the Master of Deskord.

The adorable-looking German heiress **Nina von Opel** is an adept sportswoman and lovely enough to have been elected Miss Corviglia 1964, a much sought-after distinction in the most exclusive of all skiing clubs.

Intensely intelligent and petite, the indomitable **Princess Pallavicini** is called Nini and is one of the last great hostesses of Europe. Her stupendous Roman palazzo, overflowing with superb works of art, is the melting pot for society and intelligentsia in the Italian capital, and the Chateau de Bellieu in France is the scene of wondrous shooting parties.

Also known as Nini is redhaired **Mrs. Francis Martin,** a daughter of the Joseph Tobins, leaders of San Francisco society. She is a cordial and compelling wife, mother, and friend.

Nin, when said aloud, is either:

Mrs. John Barry Ryan or **Nine Fenaille,** who recently divorced the Duke de Montesquiou-Fezensac. The first, the former Margaret Kahn (her father was the celebrated financier

Otto Kahn), is all over the place in New York, Newport, and London (she has houses in all three), and her great interests are politics, the United Nations, and the Metropolitan Opera (of which she is a director). The second is a serene, blonde beauty who has combined personal elegance with hard work in hospitals and much skiing. Her daughter, the Countess Michel de Ganay, is reputed by many to be the most ravishing young matron of French society.

OLGA

In Portugal, where she reigns as the supreme and indefatigable hostess to all artists; in Venice, where she has a residence in her own ancestral Robilant palace; in Germany, where she often visits her daughter, Countess Karl Schoenborn, at the treasure-laden Castle of Pommersfelden in upper Franconia, and at all the music festivals, the **Marquesa de Cadaval** can be found. A lady in the grand tradition, with a variety of absorbing hobbies, she is an authority on the prehistoric settlements found in the Mouge.

Señora Ysidro Martin y Montis owns and runs fine encampments in Gstaad, Biarritz, Paris, and Lausanne, and is an enthusiastic cardplayer and dispenser of amusing stories. Born Olga Leighton in England, she inherited a considerable fortune from her first matrimonial venture with Frank Mackay, an American sportsman. From her second husband, the Marquess of Portago, also a great figure in the sports world, she had a son, Alfonso, who succeeded to his father's title and died tragically in an automobile race, and a daughter, the Marquesa de Moratalla. Her third mate, a brother of the Marquess of Linares, is a cultivated gentleman with a sense of humor proved by his unforgettable appearance at the De Cuevas Biarritz Ball when he came as Don Quixote in full armor, followed by Elsa Maxwell as Sancho Panza on a donkey.

Olga Deterding, the daughter from the marriage of the celebrated oil tycoon and a Russian lady, is an eminently resplendent figure in Paris and London, where she now resides. A much talked about person because of her impulsive nature, she showed her mettle when she assisted the late Dr. Schweitzer at his hospital in Lambarene.

Another **Olga** well-known in Africa is the former Countess Olsoufieff, of a distinguished Muscovite family and the consort of Don Vanni **Corsini** of the princely Tuscan tribe. Commuting twice a year between Mozambique, where her husband conducts his business, and Mezzomonte, his country seat near Florence, she is intelligent, capable, and translates Russian classics into Italian.

Pamela and Pam

Pamela Drexel, daughter of John and Noreen Drexel, is a student, linguist, and music lover. She can gracefully switch from the gilded drawing rooms of Newport or breathing the millionaires' air at Hobe Sound to follow courses at the University of Florence, inspect the Arab countries, and do social work in Harlem.

Mrs. Leland Hayward is one of the brighter lights of the postwar glamorous ladies. A daughter of Lord Digby and at one time wedded to Winston Churchill's son Randolph, she belongs to many different sets, including her husband's eminently theatrical one (he is a producer of many hits). She capably runs Jansen's boutique in New York.

Lady Pamela Hicks, daughter of the Earl Mountbatten of Burma, spent the war years in the United States as a guest of the late Mrs. Cornelius Vanderbilt. She is a cousin of the Queen of England and is married to a gifted decorator.

The Marchioness of Huntly, who was Lady Pamela Berry, is the daughter of one of Britain's most powerful men, Viscount Kemsley (owner of the *Sunday Times*), and wife of the premier

Marquess of Scotland. She is an important hostess and loved by the highbrows.

Lady Pamela Berry, easily confused with the Marchioness of Huntly, is the daughter of Lord Birkenhead and the wife of the strong man of the *Daily Telegraph* and *Sunday Telegraph.* A petite brunette with a very birdlike face, she is among Britain's most influential women, has an important salon for the intelligentsia and the political groups, is much involved in promoting British fashions.

Pamela Kellino, no longer Mrs. James Mason after a marriage of twenty-three years, is often quoted as a sharp observer of the Hollywood scene. While the settlement for her services rendered as mother and wife (two children) came to about a million and a half dollars, her income as a columnist and as a radio and television commentator must not be insignificant.

Pamela Turnure got in the swing when she became Mrs. Jackie Kennedy's social secretary at the White House, and her pretty looks have kept her there. Her courtship by Canadian mine scion Bob Timmins has been well-publicized.

The attractive **Viscountess Egremont,** formerly Lady Wyndham, whose husband was Private Secretary to Prime Minister Macmillan, loves traveling to offbeat places. She has crossed the Sahara, and one of her most interesting accomplishments was to accompany the Bakhtiari tribes in southern Iran during their annual migrations.

Pamela Hansford Johnson not only writes delightful novels but also happens to be the wife of the great dispenser of words and thoughts, Lord Snow, at present Parliamentary Secretary of the Ministry of Technology in Britain's Labor Government.

PAOLA

Many call the widely discussed **H.R.H. Princess Paola of Liége** the most beautiful woman in Europe. After her wedding to the brother of the King of the Belgians, she was so crucified by the press that a strong public reaction ensued in her favor. Her seeming indifference to the vicious attacks helped to create around her lovely head the halo of a stoic martyr. There is no doubt that at first this fun-loving Italian-born Princess did not adapt herself too well to her new and exalted position, but she has learned the royal métier so well that she has become a goodwill ambassadress for Belgium on a staggering number of official and semiofficial visits the world over.

Amidst the greatest excitement the former Paola St. Just, now **Countess de Rohan Chabot,** broke her engagement to an Italian nobleman, and eventually married into an ancient French family. A leader of the younger egghead set, she used to be the inseparable friend of Françoise Sagan. She has now had her own first book published to rumors that Mlle. Sagan disapproved of her new vocation. Judgment of this first literary effort would indicate that the reason for the cooling of their friendship was not caused by any sense of rivalry.

Another intellectual Paola of Paris is **Countess Jean de Beaumont** of the rich De Rivaud de la Raffinerie banking clan. The mother of three children, including the Vicomtesse de Ribes, she leads a stupendously active existence.

Mrs. Orson Welles, the former Paola Mori, is both handsome and charming, playing to perfection the difficult role of wife to a genius. Able, stable, and affable, she makes new friends for her husband wherever his varied screen assignments take him. In recent years they have lived mainly in Madrid.

Signora Enrico Piaggio, whose expensive tents are pitched in Genoa, Portofino, and on the ravishing estate of Varamistá in Tuscany where so many ultra-chic shoots take place every autumn, is a strenuous participant in horse shows. The widow of an immensely wealthy industrialist husband (Vespa scooters), she is the mother of Signora Umberto Agnelli, a daughter born from her first marriage whom Piaggio later adopted.

Patrick and Pat

A traveler in strange places who writes about them with knowledge and a somewhat heavy hand is **Lord Kinross.** Since the motto of his house is "Nothing Rashly," one assumes that his divorce after four years of marriage was not impulsive. His books on Turkey, *Europa Minor* and *Within the Taurus,* are currently fashionable, since Turkey is coming into the nomadic sphere and very few people have written about it.

Lord Plunket, Equerry to the Queen of England and Deputy Master of The Household, is so eligible and engaging that women drool when his name comes up. He is a grandson of America's music hall star Fanny Ward.

No longer a bachelor—he married recently—is the polo playing **Lord Beresford,** brother of the Marquess of Waterford, Captain of the Royal Horse Guards, with headquarters in Ireland.

Patrick Broome, who sometimes acts as the Aide de Camp Extraordinaire to Yvor and Jo(sephine) Bryce, is in the antique business. He opened a shop at Ramsbury in England in partnership with Lady Ashcombe and called it "The Bleeding Horse." A bachelor, he is a favorite extra man.

Patrick O'Higgins for many years was inseparable from the late Helena Rubinstein. And lucky she was to have such an extraordinarily able, well-liked, righthand man, bursting with the charm that men from the Emerald Isle are inclined to possess.

Iva Patcevitch, always called Pat, is the handsome, white-haired White Russian who has headed the Condé Nast organization since its founder's death. Kind and gentle, he operates on an impersonal basis which saves him from physical collapse, for his is a tough, never-ending schedule of business and people. He is lucky to have as second wife Chessie Lewis Tull Hall Amory (he is her fourth husband), one of the most engaging and sunny ladies around.

All nomads who wander through the Greek Islands soon become aware of **Patrick Fermor** whose home is on the island of Eubea and who writes with such fervor and knowledge of Hellas.

Mrs. Sheldon Cooper is a shining light in Burlingame and San Francisco. Married to a capable, smooth lawyer, she is a member of the most important clan in northern California. Her mother, Mrs. Joseph Tobin, was born De Young, and with her three sisters, ran the entire social scene in the Golden Gate district. Educated in France, where she often returns, she speaks faultless French.

Bright, capable **Patricia Coffin** is a fixture at *Look* magazine and wears dark glasses at all times.

Mrs. Peter Lawford is the handsome sister of President Kennedy. Recently divorced from her actor husband, she is an indefatigable traveler who has not changed her hair style over the years. A loyal friend, she flew to Paris from the United States to be present at the burial of Porfirio Rubirosa.

Two London Patricias are so different that they are not difficult to tell apart. **Baroness Brabourne** will eventually succeed her father to the Earldom of Burma, a rare privilege in British aristocracy. The eldest daughter of Earl Mountbatten, she partakes in many royal events, being the first cousin of the Duke of Edinburgh, and therefore of the Queen. From her husband, a film producer, she has had five children. **Baroness Selsdon** is much younger and in another set. A well-known model, Patricia Donald-Smith, who at one time worked for Pierre Balmain, she continued with her work after her marriage in 1965, claiming she was bored "doing nothing." Her husband is employed by a firm of industrial consultants.

Paul and Paolo

Prince Paul of Yugoslavia, Regent of that Kingdom during the childhood of King Peter, husband of Princess Olga of

Greece, hence brother-in-law of Marina of Kent, father-in-law of Princess Maria Pia of Italy and of Howard Oxenberg, lives in Paris and Florence. He inherited the Villa Demidoff from an aunt. He visits his wife's relatives in Greece; is a very erudite gentleman more often quoted than seen.

The **Vicomte de Rosiere,** having resided in the United States half of his life and being married to the American beauty Harriette Moeller, is as well-known in American N.S. as in Paris, where he now lives. He works for jeweler Harry Winston and manufactures swimming pools.

The young **Count de Ganay** is eligible, rich, an inveterate wayfarer, and an indefatigable dancer.

Both **Paul Getty** and **Paul Mellon** are synonymous with money. The first now lives in the British Isles in magnificent, historical Sutton Hall, once the seat of the Dukes of Sutherland, and in a castle near Rome. There, this American oil billionaire entertains, but his hospitality is not in the least flashy and house guests are mesmerized by the pay telephones they must use to make their long-distance calls. The latter is a sensitive man of great taste—his collection of pictures by English masters (from circa 1700 to 1850) is in the fine tradition established by his father—and civic-minded. He moves in his private jet among his many houses. His wife is "Bunny" Lambert. At his estate in Antigua he entertains the Kennedy and Radziwill clans.

The mercurial actor **Paul Newman** makes excursions into society, sometimes with a beard, sometimes without.

Prince Ilynski, a handsome young six-footer and dead ringer for Emperor Alexander III of Russia, makes quite a splash in Cincinnati, where he is in the real estate business, and in Palm Beach. Married to Angelica Kauffmann, of the *Washington Star* dynasty, he is the father of four children. He is the son of the late Grand Duke Dimitri of Russia and Cincinnati's Audrey Emery.

Paul Bowles is idolized in Tangiers and is as talented as he is nice. A music critic, composer, and author, he achieved fame through a series of excellent novels. Youthful looking, he understands and loves the Arabic world. He recently gave up an island he owned off Ceylon.

Anyone of importance who goes to Naples lands at the delightful island of La Gaiola, a stone's throw from Posillipo, to be entertained by **Baron Paolo Langheim,** a *bon viveur* who goes to bed early in order to watch those incredible sunrises in the Bay of Naples from his terraces. He is a nephew of the shipping queen, Madame Militza Banac.

Another Neapolitan Paolo is **Count Gaetani,** whose lovely villa near Castellamare has one of the most enthralling views of Vesuvius in existence. With his second wife, the former Edda Guggenheim, he is a polished host to his many N.S. friends, and he in turn visits them at various times during the year.

A Roman Paolo who is much invited for his impeccable manners, dry wit, and excellent card sense is **Count Quintieri,** a middle-aged bachelor who is quite a catch on the marriage market. He makes frequent trips to his estates in Calabria and is a globe-trotter.

In England, **Paul Channon,** Member of Parliament, is the youthful son of Lady Dorothy Svejdar (a daughter of the Earl of Iveagh) and the late Henry "Chips" Channon, a Chicagoan who became a Britisher and was for many years a Member of Parliament and one of London's most celebrated hosts. Through his mother, Channon is related to all the Guinness clan and is the nephew of Prince and Princess George of Prussia. To complicate the picture for the outsider, his wife Ingrid Wyndham was briefly married to the Hon. Jonathan Guinness, a relative of his mother.

Peggy

sometimes is a Christian name in itself and in other instances it is a derivative of Margaret.

Mrs. Lewis Douglas is equally well-liked in New York City,

Arizona (she spends the winters there), and England, where for several years her husband was the American Ambassador. Born Peggy Zinsser, she is active on the Metropolitan Opera Board.

Mrs. Cecil Singer, the former Margaret Stout, also has musical connections. Her son from her first husband, David Thaw, is a member of the Munich Staat Oper in supporting tenor roles, and her daughter-in-law, Clair Watson, is one of the best Mozart and Strauss sopranos in Europe. She follows with great interest the careers of her singing family.

Her Serene Highness Princess Charles d'Arenberg, the former Margaret Bedford and Mrs. Thomas Bancroft Junior, seems to live in airplanes. However, when on the ground she packs and unpacks her suitcases in a mansion in Paris and a delightful chateau near Bourges.

Her good friend **Peggy** (Margaret) **Hitchcock,** daughter of the celebrated polo player Thomas Hitchcock, finally, after many courtships, married **Dr. Luis Scarrone.** She travels high and wide, sometimes with her charming, rich mother, born **Peggy** (Margaret) **Mellon,** and her sister, **Mrs. Peter Stephaich,** who lives with her Hungarian husband in Paris and Kitzbühel.

With her husband, **Madame Georges Bernier** is one of the editors of the art magazine *L'Oeil,* and also runs the art gallery of the same name, in Paris. Born Peggy Rosenbaum in Philadelphia, she pinched the harp in her youth, then lived in Mexico as the wife of **Lewis Riley** (now the husband of Dolores del Rio), and later worked for *Vogue* magazine.

The unique **Peggy Guggenheim** has built one of the most outstanding private modern picture collections of our era. She is settled in Venice's Palazzo Nonfinito.

Senhora Aloysio Salles of Brazil's smart Copacabaña set made a big splash in American fashion history when she modeled under the name of Peggy Haley.

Baroness George Grippenberg, the English-born wife of a distinguished former Finnish diplomat who turned successfully to the insurance business some years ago, is so kindhearted to society newcomers that her name is bandied about like a flag in all sorts of lately gilded houses.

The wife of the President of the Chase National Bank, **Mrs. David Rockefeller,** was born Margaret McGrath. She loves to waltz, is nearsighted, and like all the members of that wonderful family, is civic minded and impersonal.

With her banker husband, **Countess Paul Munster** has England, Austria, and Venice as her stamping grounds. Tall, thin, elegant, English-born, she is an enthusiastic gardener.

Madame Claude Foussier is an American by birth (Margaret Feist) and her current husband is one of the great shots. Formerly married to Philip Uzielli, she wed the ex of his current wife, Ann Dubonnet.

Peggy Glanville-Hicks, a bright English composer, has had several esoteric operas performed and is in the process of writing one based on a libretto by Lawrence Durrell. She owns a house on Mykonos and another in the vicinity of the Athenian Acropolis.

Whether in Palm Beach, where she visits Michael and Molly Phipps, Caracas, where she stays with Reynaldo and Mimi Herrera, or all over the Mediterranean, including Mallorca where her sister lives, **Peggy Scott-Duff** is forever roaming. An English blonde, she never seems, despite many beaus, to reach the altar and change her surname.

Peter

Peter Glenville is an articulate, attractive Englishman and among the most brilliant stage and cinema directors of our generation. A great social asset to any gathering, he has a fine wit and an amusing mind.

Peter Lawford played a prominent role in New Frontier and Frank Sinatra society. Recently divorced from Patricia Kennedy, this British-born charmer always knew what he wanted and became one of Hollywood's most colorful figures.

Peter O'Toole is a superb actor who has hit the jackpot with a few films and many great stage performances. He is a constant source of curiosity and chic talk with his nonconformist ways.

Pieter van Vollenhoven, the bespectacled, marvelously rich Dutch commoner, is the pride and joy of Rotterdam now that Her Royal Highness Princess Margaret of the Netherlands has decided to make him her consort. He spends much time in Port' Ercole visiting his future in-laws and to please them was baptized in the Reformed Dutch Church.

British *House and Garden* editor **Peter Coats,** a pink-cheeked bachelor in his early fifties, is a favorite extra man in London and at many of those glamorous house parties in the stately homes of England.

Peter Wilson functions as Chairman of the Board of both Parke-Bernet Galleries in New York and Sotheby's in London. Quoting Peter, on the part of the ever-increasing multitude of object lovers, is Bliss with a capital B. He has a house in the south of France.

Eligibility, skiing, shooting, Southampton (where he owns a famous estate, 'The Port of Missing Men'), New York City and Madrid, (he has apartments in both) and frequent business trips to Germany are trademarks of Count **Peter Salm,** the handsome, quiet, hard to catch (every girl is trying) believer in long, romantic hair styles for men. His mother was the fabulous Millicent Rogers, a rare rich creature of quality. He is often mentioned in connection with two half brothers, Arturo and Paul Ramos.

The trademarks of **Peter Duchin** are popular music, the St. Regis (his orchestra plays there and packs them in every night), the Averell Harrimans (who brought him up), charm, and his wife, Cheray.

A lost bank account in Switzerland, exile, the French Riviera (where he lives with his wife Alexandra), or Venice (where he visits his mother-in-law) spell the former **King of Yugoslavia.**

Deborah Kerr (his wife), Klosters and Marbella (where they have houses), Biarritz (where they go in the summer and he surf rides), writing (his profession), mean **Peter Viertel.**

Peter Fonda is known for his talent as an actor, his father Hank, his sister Jane, his ex-stepmother Afdera, and his wife, Susan Brewer.

Another eligible young man and a member of one of Greece's richest shipping families, **Peter Nomikos** is gentle, quiet, and unassuming, and spends part of every year in London.

Peter Ustinov, because of his triple profession (actor, writer, director), never stays put anywhere but is welcome everywhere.

He is easy to confuse with **Peter Sellers,** also very funny and social, who is usually mentioned along with his young, pretty, adoring wife Brigitt Eklund or his great friends Princess Margaret and Lord Snowdon.

In and out of the Burlingame Peninsula; Southern California, where he runs a spectacular ranch; Newport, where his wife, the former Leta Morris, widow of Byrnes MacDonald, opens her house every summer and reigns as a Queen, one can find **Peter McBein.** Since both McBeins adore shooting, sailing, and every sport known to man, they are as likely to take off for a fishing trip to the Chilean lakes as to ride dolphins in the Aegean Sea.

Peter Widener III is a familiar racing figure, particularly in Florida where, at Ocala, he has his celebrated stud farm.

Peter Townsend stayed on the front pages of the international press all through his romance with Princess Margaret. Although he leads a more prosaic life now, with his Belgian wife and children, representing an important champagne company in New York, he is still a romantic figure.

Philip, Philippe

Philip van Rensselaer is the soft-spoken exponent of La Dolce Vita, American style; made headlines for his friendship with Barbara Hutton; has written two highly publicized novels supposedly based on personal memoirs. His name comes up in N.S., particularly in the Marina Cicogna, Cristiana Brandolini, and Norma Clark sets.

Philippe Jullian, Bordeaux's gift to writing (his grandfather, a member of the French Academy, Camille Jullian wrote an important book trying to prove that the Gauls were more civilized than the Romans), has penned delightfully about snobbism and other subjects including the dead Queen of Portugal; is a clever illustrator who spends much time in England where he knows the historical houses inside out.

Baron Philippe de Rothschild is accepted as the least rich but the most intellectual of that glorious family; translates Christopher Fry into French; built the Pigalle Theatre; owns the fantastic Chateau de Mouton; has a daughter Philippine (who acts under the name of Philippine Pascal) married to a gifted actor Jacques Serreys; lives in separate flats in Paris from his American wife Pauline Fairfax-Potter (but he adores her). His first wife died in a Nazi concentration camp.

H.R.H. Prince Philip of Hesse is related to every princely family in the *Gotha.* His has been a tragic life—his wife, Princess Mafalda of Italy, died in a concentration camp during the war and he himself spent much time in one—but he finds comfort in his children and his many friends.

Philip Johnson has given new dimensions to contemporary architecture. A lean, gray-haired bachelor, he calls a glass house in Connecticut home.

In the British Empire, the Caribbean, Biarritz, and sophisticated conservative areas the handsome, middle-aged, jolly **Earl**

of Hardwicke whose eldest son Viscount Royston missed becoming son-in-law of the Count of Paris, is right at home.

Philip Pool, a cool-looking, polite, and considerate businessman, entertains well at "Casa Rosa" in Nassau with his attractive wife Virginia, a sister of Tucky French (the ex-Mrs. John Jacob Astor and ex-Mrs. Raymond Guest).

The Duke of Mouchy, a member of the Noailles clan, and through his mother, of the La Rochefoucaulds, belongs to the bluest of blue French aristocracy. To add to all this glory, his wife is Diane de Castellane. Exceedingly hospitable, he gives large buffet luncheons at his chateau of Mouchy, surrounded by a stupendous forest, on Sunday for all the top nomads. Some of them also go swimming in the pool or play tennis.

Last but not least is the **Duke of Edinburgh** whom his old friends call by his first name. Born a Prince of Greece, he gave up his succession to the Greek throne, somewhat distant but nevertheless real, to go into the British Navy and then become the Queen's husband. Handsome, articulate, and an irresistible Ambassador of goodwill, he pilots his own plane. He is an excellent polo player and skier.

Pierre

is a name which gives many anxious moments whenever French people are present and to all those who have French friends.

Two of the most important figures in the world of Haute Couture, **Cardin** and **Balmain,** answer to the name. The former is usually mentioned in connection with the splendid actress Jeanne Moreau (they were inseparable), his way-out styles or his own manner of dressing (very youthful, collegiate), and the latter with the Island of Elba (where he entertains house parties), the Queen of Siam (whom he dresses), or his fabulous energy.

Pierre Millet, the bright and able French Ambassador to

Laos, spent much time at the French Embassy in Washington and at the French delegation of the United Nations. He is married to the chic Julia Mosquera Graux, a Colombian.

In the French Riviera, night club, and movie-making sets Pierre is dark-haired film actor **Pierre Brice** (some of the ladies think his torso is marvelous), and in more conservative film groups and along the *Paris Match* circuit it's **Pierre Galante,** the likable and at times estranged husband of Olivia de Havilland.

Every attractive girl who arrives in Paris meets the dashing **Count de Segur** whose pertinent remarks are appreciated more by some and less by others. He is separated from his wife, a Brazilian, Emita Sanchez de Larragoiti, much a part of Parisian salons.

Pierre Daninos, a columnist for *Le Figaro* depicts with civilized humor the contemporary scene in his latest book, *Snobissimo.*

The **Duc de Brissac,** a fine-looking man with two chateaux and an *hotel particulier* in the French capital, a wife and four children, has a stupendous position among the list of European aristocracy.

Lazard Frères' **Pierre David Weill,** well-known all over the world, has a sophisticated marriage arrangement with his beautifully dressed wife Berthe Haard—she lives in New York City, Connecticut, and La Costa Brava, and he in Paris, the Valley de la Chevreuse, and on the French Riviera. They visit each other from time to time in their respective abodes.

Pierre Lazareff runs, among other important newspapers and magazines, *France Soir.* With his wife, Hélène, who has made a huge success with *Elle,* he entertains all the visiting firemen who come to Paris at his country estate "*La Grille Royale*" near Louveciennes.

No member of the New Frontier received more publicity than the late President Kennedy's press secretary, **Pierre Salinger,** who has remained in the news ever since. For a brief period a California Senator, after a divorce he succumbed to the charms of French magazine writer Nicole Gillman, whom he married.

Count Cheremetev, a curly-headed, youthful, and blond descendant of an ancient Russian family, lives in Paris and is married to a daughter of the marriage Princess Marie Clotilde Bonaparte contracted with Serge de Witt. The Countess, his consort, is so proud of her Napoleonic ancestry that she rarely lets people forget it. She likes to wear saris.

When a hostess in Manhattan has a problem seating some important guests at luncheon or dinner, she tries to get through to "dear Pierre." He is the bespectacled Chief of Protocol at the United Nations, **Count de Meulemeester,** a Belgian bachelor, whose job lasts twenty-four hours a day seven days a week. His resistance to party fatigue is a wonder. During the Pope's recent visit to the glass palace, this Pierre never left his side.

Raymond, Raymund, Raimundo, Raimondo

Raymond Guest is the current Ambassador of the United States to Ireland. A member of a wealthy family, with strong Phipps connections, he has an important stable of race horses, turns up in Paris, where he has an apartment, and in Deauville with his third wife, Princess Caroline Murat; goes off on shooting expeditions in the wilds of Ethiopia.

Raymond Loewy, whose name has become synonymous with industrial design and the extraordinary clothes he wears, has five headquarters: Paris, a country house in Seine et Oise, the French Riviera, New York City, and Palm Springs.

Raymund von Hoffmanstahl, the son of the late Austrian playwright and librettist for the Richard Strauss operas, married first Alice Astor, a sister of Vincent Astor, and then Lady Elizabeth Paget, thereby becoming heavily connected with the British nobility. On the European staff of *Time* magazine, he lives mainly in London but also occupies a castle he inherited in the Salzburg region.

Raymundo de Larrain is a Chilean with a flat in Paris who is a pioneer in the long hair style now worn by so many young men. Discovered as an imaginative designer of sets and costumes by the late Marquis de Cuevas, he was catapulted into prominence with the assistance of the Vicomtesse de Ribes who helped him co-produce the ballet *Cinderella* in which Geraldine Chaplin played a modest but much publicized role.

Prince Raimondo Orsini, one of the handsomest of the Roman aristocracy, had former Empress Soraya swinging for a while. Still a bachelor, he is accused, as is the custom these days, of being the father of illegitimate children, which makes his reputation as a Don Juan all the more tantalizing. He attends the Fair at Sevilla splendidly riding a horse in the necessary Andalusian trappings.

Raymond Olivier, a great chef who has even given lessons in the culinary arts for television, is the author of several cookbooks which have grace and spirit.

A newcomer to the nomadic sweepstakes is **Raymond Doan,** a mining engineer of Indochinese-French parentage who paints as a hobby and is currently Barbara Hutton's lithe and graceful seventh husband. Educated in Saigon but settled in Morocco, he has one divorce behind him. Shortly before his colorful wedding to the glamorous heiress in her Japanese house near Cuernavaca, he became known as Prince de Champossak, a reported courtesy of a leading Laotian aristocratic clan.

Robert and Bob

Robert de Balkany is a wealthy Transylvanian whose father pitched his tent in France. Married but estranged from his wife, the adorable Genevieve François-Poncet, he is devastatingly attractive to the fair sex. His company having acquired the *Gaviota* from Baron de Rede, he takes royalty cruising on it.

Robert Coe, the rich American bachelor who was the United States' Envoy to Copenhagen, owns a magnificent residence in the south of France and a ranch in Wyoming. He is a dedicated gardener.

Because of his exalted position with American Express, **Robert Clarkson** has done much wayfaring in his life. With his wife, the former Cora Shields, he constantly entertains in his Park Avenue apartment.

Robert Sweeney is a curly-haired American whom the ladies find irresistible. The uncle of the Duchess of Rutland, he has many friends in Great Britain and was at one time one of Barbara Hutton's beaus. His two wives were the late Joanne Connelly and Pamela Curran.

Robert Brady, an American painter and designer of fascinating taspestries, is a bachelor with a ready smile and much taste who entertains beautifully in Cuernavaca where he owns a resplendent Bishop's palace filled with interesting objects.

Author **Robert Graves** lives in Mallorca but appears in his native England and for lecture tours in the United States. He is a mellow raconteur, and his knowledge and imagination are a delight to all those who are fortunate enough to know him.

Cat-food heir **Robert Hornstein** originally hailed from California but can now be found in Capri, where he is the lord and master of "Capricorn"; in Rome where he has an apartment; or in Paris, where he is a frequent house guest of Elsa Martinelli. An excellent amateur painter, he is famous in Capri for his large parties.

Françoise Sagan's ex-husband, **Robert Westhoff,** a pottery designer, sits more or less silently with his former wife at parties. Since his ex-mate is so friendly with Juliette Greco, he is often referred to in connection with her.

Brenda Frazier's good-natured, kind husband **Robert Chatfield-Taylor** moved to New England to be with her in the new surroundings when she chose to refashion her life.

Robert Zaguri is the curly-headed Brazilian of Moroccan origin who knows how to handle Brigitte Bardot's moods and needs. Having lasted as her permanent escort longer than any other, he has become one of the most publicized males in the world.

A serious banker, the **Archduke Robert of Hapsburg,** brother of Otto, Pretender to the Austrian throne, has the long Hapsburg face and prominent chin. Married to Margherita of Aosta, he lives in Paris and in the summer takes his family to a secluded property in Calabria at the tip end of the Italian peninsula.

Robert Lehman of the banking and investment clan has a superb collection of paintings and objects which was started by his father and continued by him. A gentle man, hospitable and generous, he is a fine ambassador of American good will wherever he goes.

Actor, producer, director, and Jack of all trades, **Robert Hossein** has a much discussed private life. Now in his late thirties, he has always demonstrated a marked preference for youthful mates. His first, Marina Vlady, was reported by the press to be seventeen when she married him; the second, Caroline Eliacheff, fifteen. Currently it looks as if the next Mrs. Hossein would be Marie-Pierre Pisier, not quite eighteen.

Robert Leibus is renowned for his great knowledge of Ming objects and his splendid hospitality. At one time he was an important host in London's Eaton Square, but taxes being what they are, life in Morocco presents advantages and he has moved to Tangiers.

Sir Robert Throckmorton, whose family was already famous in Elizabethan days, often travels to India. Amusing and warmhearted, he is married to Lady Isabel Manners, who was Loel Guinness' second wife.

Robin

Mrs. Angier Biddle Duke, the fourth wife of the American envoy to Spain, is willowy, gaunt, and enormously resistant to the exhausting life she must lead. With radio, television, and promotion (she worked for Pepsi-Cola) experience behind her, she has the knack of never being caught unaware. An exception to this rule occurred when she turned up at Madrid's PX in pants, which is tabu.

Robin Boyer, the divorced wife of Michael Butler, is one of the adornments to New York's younger set interested in the theater and jazz. She works for Dior in the U.S.

Robin Douglas Home, a nephew of the former Prime Minister, writes a column for the *Daily Express* and nowadays rarely plays the piano, which gave him notoriety some years ago.

Robin Fedden, an officer of the National Trust, is the author of some delightful books and is the great authority on Crusaders' Castles in Lebanon and Syria.

Robin Beare is considered one of the top plastic surgeons in the world. The ladies die over him and cannot wait to subject their sagging faces to his *bistouri.* Being a superb mimic, he is in demand socially on both sides of the Atlantic. His holidays are usually spent salmon fishing with or without his wife Iris, but his professional assignments keep him on the move.

The Marquess of Tavistock, the eldest son and heir to the Duke of Bedford, is a serious young man in investment banking. Educated at Harvard University and with many American friends, he married the pretty and reputedly slightly spoiled heiress Henrietta Tiarks.

Rose, Rosemary, and Roz

Gertrude Stein wrote that a rose is a rose is a rose and Shakespeare, many centuries before her, that a rose by a rose by another name would smell as sweet.

Rose, plain Rose (never Rosie), is the splendid mother of the late President, **Mrs. Joseph Kennedy,** an exceedingly strong and calm dowager who has managed to rise heroically above the many sorrows which have come her way (along with the many satisfactions). A real wayfarer, commuting among her Palm Beach, New York, and Hyannis Port houses and on trips to Europe, she is often accompanied by Mrs. William C. (Gina) Breed.

Rosie usually means **Mrs. Hugh Chisholm,** the exquisite, Greuze-like former Rosemary Warburton, who has the uncanny ability of making news wherever she is, be it California (she owns a splendid house on the Burlingame peninsula), New York, Long Island, Paris, or Biarritz (where she is the possessor of a fine manor).

Another prominent **Rosie** in Biarritz—and in England as well—is the sparkling one who was born **Bingham,** twice married and divorced from the Earl of Warwick and Ted Bassett.

Three prominent Rosemarys are (a) **Mrs. Ernest Kanzler,** (b) **Lady Rosemary Muir,** (c) **Rosemary Clooney.** The first is one of the rare Swiss gifts to nomadic society. With five homes to look after (two in Europe and three in the U.S.A.), she is a definite leader in her own right, with her special court and her own brand of buoyant style. Her fourth, current mate is a prominent Detroiter whose late first wife was Mrs. Edsel Ford's sister. The second is a daughter of the Duke of Marlborough and has many American connections (her grandmother was the famous Consuelo Vanderbilt Balsan). She is very U in and out of the great English houses. The third is always making news with her many best-selling recordings and her off-and-on marriage to José Ferrer, to whom she has borne several children.

Roz can only be **Rosalind Russell,** a remarkable woman who has made a huge success of her career (still going strong), her marriage (to Frederick Brisson, the producer), and her social position to which she was born and which she has maintained. With a definite mind and viewpoint of her own, she is one of the few stars whose ego is kept well in check.

Rudi, Rudy

Rudolph Nureyev is not only the greatest attraction of any ballet performer but also the most lionized star on the party circuit. With his long, flowing hair and incredible clothes, he is a compelling guest who can make a transition from dazzling entrechats to the most recent dance craze. He owns a house in the south of France where he spends short holidays.

For fifteen years **Rudolph Bing** has been the Lord and Master of the Metropolitan Opera, over which he rules with an iron hand. Popular with some members of the Opera Board and all the United Nations Ambassadors whom he invites to his box, he is not so well-liked by many of the singers. Gothic looking, he is a whiz at publicizing himself. He travels all over the United States in the spring when the opera goes on tour, and in the summer goes abroad to hear new voices.

Rudolph Firkusny is a talented pianist born in Czechoslovakia and now a resident of the Hudson River Valley. For many months of the year on tour, he is popular socially with the most conservative sets in the United States and abroad.

Count Schonburg, a dashing cousin of Prince Alfonso Hohenlohe, is in his middle thirties. He helps run the Marbella Club, on the Costa del Sol, and all its dependences and interests. Since sooner or later everyone stays there, his name is constantly referred to, particularly when there is a difficulty in obtaining a reservation. "Don't worry, I shall wire Rudy," one hears. "He will find you a bed."

Count Crespi is an Italo-Brazilian who has spent most of the postwar years in Italy but who will, in the future, spend more time in Brazil because of an inheritance he received from his grandmother. The exponent par excellence of café society, he launches people and products on the international scene. He recently made news by entering into a fashion controversy with

Emilio Pucci. His wife, Consuelo O'Connor, is a *Vogue* editor and one of the most photogenic of the social *vedettes.*

Rudolph Schirmer, the lanky, handsome, and articulate Vice-President of the famous music publishing firm, uses Santa Barbara as his base, but is all over the place with his second wife, the petite and feminine Iris Flores, whose grandfather was President of Costa Rica. Schirmer's mother is Mrs. Charles Munroe, a leading American hostess.

Sheila

The **Viscountess Bridport** is also **Duchess of Bronte** (there is the apocryphal story that she and her husband change coronets on their luggage when they cross the Channel, going from the Italian title to the English). She is dainty, blonde, Dutch-born, and maintains three houses in Italy.

Princess Dimitri of Russia came into the world in Sidney, Australia, as Sheila Chisholm. She first married Lord Loughbrough (her son from this marriage is now the Earl of Rosslyn), divorced him, and then became the wife of Sir John Millbank, who died ten years ago. Now for the third time a bride, she owns a successful travel business in London.

Countess Jean de Rochambeau (her mother was the late Loelia Emery from Cincinnati, her father a Britisher, Alistair Mackintosh) is hearty, good-natured, has a passion for monkeys (it's the decorative motif of her homes) and a marked gift for entertaining. (Her masked ball in June 1964 at the Pavillon Colombe in Saint Brice, near Paris, was fabulous.) She contributes her verve to the American *Vogue* from the French capital.

Sheila Graham writes an excellent Hollywood column and is an F. Scott Fitzgerald specialist.

Ever since *A Taste of Honey* first appeared on the stage, **Shelagh Delaney** has become the darling of Chelsea and the entertainment world. The novelist was last heard of working on a film script for Albert Finney entitled *Charles Bubbles,* which deals with some of her own experiences.

SOPHIE AND SOPHIA

H.R.H. Princess Sophie of Bourbon is the sister of the young King of Greece and the popular wife of Don Juan Carlos, who is the acknowledged pretender to the Spanish throne. She lives in Madrid with him and the children, is called on constantly on semi-official assignments, goes to her native country, royal weddings, and the U.S.A.

The **Princess di Leonforte,** widow of a member of the Borghese family and mother of all those children who are always making news and have so brilliantly developed the resort of Port' Ercole, is a Sicilian by birth and related to all the prominent clans on that island. Her headquarters are in Rome.

Mexico City's **Señora Ignacio Bernal,** green-eyed and stupendous looking, is cultivated, cozy, and a marvelous asset to her husband, a distinguished archeologist-author responsible for much of the success and look of the great new museum which has risen in Chapultepec Park. Her sister is married to the Count of Teba, a nephew of the late Duke of Alba.

Sophie Sturges, the widow of **Thomas Sturges,** born of the princely Neapolitan family of the Pignatellis and a Russian mother, lives in Geneva, but because she is gay, well informed, and amusing, she is welcome in many orbits.

On the New York fashion trail, it's bound to be the handsome **Mrs. Adam Gimbel.** Her husband successfully runs Saks Fifth Avenue, for which she designs wardrobes every season.

The well-dressed **Mrs. Anatole Litvak,** wife of the film director, turns up regularly in Klosters, St. Tropez, and all the places one expects to see her.

Sophia Loren, whose marriage to her Pygmalion, Carlo Ponti, many years her senior, is continuously coming up in the Roman courts because of the antiquated Italian divorce laws, is popular with all those whom she deals with professionally. She is much too busy earning several million dollars a year to be social. Her official residence is in Switzerland.

Sophie may be **H.R.H. Princess George of Hanover.** One of the three sisters of Prince Philip—they all married into German royal families—she was first the wife of the Prince of Hesse, who died during the last war. Her current husband, a brother of Queen Frederica of Greece, is the head of the School of Schloss Salem in Baden. They have three children. While neither she nor her sisters went to their brother's wedding to the future Queen of England—it was rumored at the time that it would prove embarrassing to have so many German relations—they were all much in evidence when Her Majesty and the Prince went on their first official visit to Germany in 1965.

A Sophie who has many friends in Spain (her mother was of the powerful family de la Gandara), Switzerland (which she visits), and Florence (where she makes her home in the huge Palazzo Serristori she inherited from her father) is **Countess Uberto** Bossi Pucci. A former lady in waiting to Marie José, the last Queen of Italy, she sometimes accompanies her to royal weddings. Her intimates call her "Chiffon."

Susan, Suzanne, Suzy

In Paris there is often a mix-up among the first three ladies mentioned.

Madame Gerard Mante was born Proust and is the niece of the celebrated author. This is only the beginning of her extraordinary connections with the intelligentsia. She married a nephew of the creator of *Cyrano de Bergerac,* Edmond Rostand, and their daughter Marie Claude is the wife of Claude Mauriac, nephew of François Mauriac. A real *salonnière* in the old tradition, the name-dropping of great literary names in her apartment on the Quai de Béthune in Paris is absolutely legitimate. It is said that if her uncle had seen her function as a hostess he would have used her as the model for his immortal Madame de Verdurin.

Tall and blonde, **Madame Leon Dazenas,** the former Suzanne Champin, independently from her husband (whose hobby is hunting) organizes the famous concerts of "Concrete Music" in Paris which are followed by large receptions in her home.

Suzanne Luling, for many years a director of Dior, is now with Revillon furs, and is often a jet passenger on visits to Japan and the United States. Very gregarious, she adores to talk and dance.

In Washington, Palm Beach and Long Island, there is much mention of **Mrs. Arthur Gardner,** whose husband was American Ambassador to Cuba. She is husky voiced, blond, and a dynamic hostess, prominent in the Windsors' set.

A frequent visitor to the U.S.A. is the beautiful **Mrs. John Ward,** who with her husband has houses in London, Barbados, and Monte Carlo. Her mate's late mother, Lady Ward, was a member of the Reid family, former owners of the New York *Herald Tribune.*

Mrs. Peter Ustinov, the former Suzanne Cloutier, gave up a promising acting career to marry the actor-director-author. She is a perfect foil to her immensely witty mate's repartee wherever his varied and distant assignments take him.

Suzy Parker, the sometime mannequin, sometime actress, is the darling of the clothes-horse set and Bradford Dillman, her husband.

Susan Stein, the daughter of Jules and Rosi Stein, a young lady of diversified interests, has acted on Broadway and is in the travel business ("Ports of Call"). A student of the Mandarin language, she wears Chinese robes and is a vivacious party-giver in her Manhattan flat.

Mrs. André Hakim, Darryl Zanuck's daughter, is a frequent visitor to the United States, but her address is in Paris. Despite having provided her dashing husband with three children, she is now separated from him.

Paris' **Madame Leon Volterra** is ever earning sought-after racing prizes, and her photograph with winners is a commonplace in all European newspapers. Dressed exclusively by Pierre Balmain, she has marvelous jewels and turns up at Hialeah during the season.

Madame Jacques Delbac is entrancingly rich, since her previous husband was the banker Robert Lazard. It was her castle in Provence which provided hospitality to England's Queen Mother for several days in the spring of 1965.

Sylvia

Mrs. Leonard Lyons, the wife of the columnist, is a small blonde with enormous zest and energy, always in motion, covering the world scene for her husband with pep and ability.

Sylvia Fine, the wife of Danny Kaye, is a bright, wisecracking counterpart to her illustrious husband and writes much of the material he uses in his sketches and songs.

Princess Jean Louis Faucigny-Lucinge is a Brazilian who was brought up in London, where her father was the Brazilian Ambassador for several decades. When she is not in the south of France, where she and her husband own a house, or in Brazil where she must go from time to time to look after her interests, she lives in Paris.

Mrs. Killian Hennessy is the recent bride of the Cognac scion. Of Spanish parents, she was married first to a Castellane, then a Talleyrand. She worked for several years for the dress house of Lanvin and was part of the court of Barbara Hutton.

Sylvia Hawkes, the former Lady Ashley, Mrs. Douglas Fairbanks, Sr., Lady Stanley, Mrs. Clark Gable, and now the estranged wife of Prince Dimitri Djordjadze, moves from England to Florida to California. An exquisite blonde who spends much of her time combing her beautiful hair, she has always been the quintessence of British femininity and has always personified the chorus girl who made good.

Mrs. Azamat Guirey, whose mother was the late Alice Astor, sister of Vincent Astor, and whose father is the most splendid gift Imperial Russia ever gave the United States, Colonel Serge Obolensky, is settled in a cozy house in the British capital where she is an easy, effortless hostess. She is currently estranged from her second husband.

Lady Harlech has returned to London after a successful stay in Washington where her husband was the popular British Ambassador and an intimate of the late President Kennedy. Her friends call her Cissie and her children always make news for their beatnik habits.

Mrs. Cesare Spadacini, who was Sylvia Casablanca, filled the gazettes with her comings and goings until she wed a Milanese. She is a Mexican beauty and heiress who was in the Aga Khan's court for a while.

Sylvie Vartan is the French yé-yé diva whose zest and charm are more significant than her small voice. A clothes horse, she has established her own brand of style which is admired by all the leading fashion magazines. Her wedding to another yé-yé star, Johnny Halliday, caused much buzz in Europe.

TED, TEDDY, THEODORE

Ted Bassett is God's gift to the ladies, who all adore him. The battle is always raging about who will have the pleasure of the company of this sophisticated American who remains on excellent terms with all his past wives. Currently the favorite escort of Mrs. Anne Ford, he is a marvelous cardplayer, appears in Biarritz where an ex-mate lives, in Gstaad, and all the places where such a fascinating man is at a premium.

Ted Weicker is currently married to the popular turf lady Elizabeth "Liz" Robertson. A brother of Lowell Weicker, he is heir to the large Squibb pharmaceutical fortune and has lived all over the world developing branches of this company. He divides his time among New York, Long Island, Florida, and an apartment in Paris. Often a guest on his brother's yacht in the Mediterranean, he also is a good golfer and currently a senior partner of Reynolds and Co.

Ted Rousseau is an important adornment of the Metropolitan Museum of Art's staff. An excellent curator, a wonderful linguist who is as at home in French as he is in Spanish, he is a most elusive bachelor.

Baron van Zuylen, half Belgian, half Egyptian, with houses in Paris and Holland (the famous Castle of Haa is the family seat), brother of Baroness Guy de Rothschild, travels constantly with his wife Gaby, and has publishing interests in Brussels. He is young, handsome, and immensely rich, with a large racing stable.

Senator Edward Kennedy is, like all the members of his family, much on the go, and despite the serious accident which he suffered, has kept bravely on discharging his duties. In Europe he turns up with his wife in Marbella, for the Sevilla Holy Week, and in Paris where many people entertain him.

TERRY

There could not be four more different Terrys in looks, personalities, interests, and backgrounds; yet they all know the same five thousand people and their names echo in and out of the same conversations.

The greatest nomad of the four is the many times married **Baroness Hubert Pantz,** the American-born Therese Genepive, who has houses in New York, Vermont, Paris, and Austria. She is a dynamic and enthusiastic follower of her husband's real estate projects and shooting.

The **Duchess Canevaro di Zoagli,** who lives in Rome and Florence and summers in Port' Ercole, is the widow of a diplomat; is half American (her mother was Eleanor Terry from Annapolis); has staunch, devoted friends all over the globe, being such a formidably loyal friend herself; and has seven irresistibly attractive children.

The Marquess Lottieri Lottaringhi della Stufa, from an old aristocratic Tuscan family, is the busiest decorator in Brazil, rushing from Sao Paulo to Rio de Janeiro biweekly. Formerly a world traveler with no set home, ex-husband of Mrs. Lawrence Copley Thaw, he is a portly, amusing fellow with gigantic moustaches that bring to mind those worn by the great explorers of the last century.

Madame Guy de la Valdene, a daughter of Palm Beach banker Loy Anderson, is a pretty and wonderful water skier. She is the wife of a nephew of Winston and Raymond Guest, whose sister Diane married Jean de la Valdene and settled in Paris long ago.

TINO

is the diminutive of Constantino and Constantine.

His Majesty the King of Greece is called this not only by members of his family but my many internationalites as well. Young, attractive, sporting, he is fast learning the métier of king and the labyrinth of pitfalls that face him and his attractive bride, Anne Marie of Denmark.

Constantine Karamanlis is the sadly missed former Greek Prime Minister who was a close friend of all the U Athenians and big businessmen and who did so much to bring back prosperity to Hellas. He now lives in exile, mostly in Switzerland.

H.S.H. Prince Constantine of Lichtenstein, a first cousin of the reigning Prince, spends the winter in St. Moritz, where he helps run the Corviglia Club. His daughter, Monica, married to André Spitz Jordan, lives in South America.

Ambassador Soldati has made the Swiss Embassy in Paris

the most sought-after and elegant of all with the help of his very intelligent, capable wife, the former Countess Daisy de Contades. Her sister is the ex-Senator, current Deputy, Jacqueline Patenotre, who is also Mayoress of Rambouillet. The Soldatis own a weekend country home near Paris and spend their holidays in an old mansion between Lausanne and Geneva.

Count Vitetti is the son of the former Italian Ambassador to France and Nathalie Coe, the Long Island heiress, and a nephew of Robert Coe, ex-U.S. Envoy to Denmark. Educated in England, he works in Rome, adores fast-driving cars, is a big catch for any girl.

Tom and Tommy

Thomas Schippers, the Adonis-like able conductor (his profile has often been compared to that of Michelangelo's David), is the pride and joy of Kalamazoo, Michigan, where he was born. Discovered by Gian Carlo Menotti, he now leads the New York Philharmonic, the Metropolitan Opera orchestra, and many others. He usually spends his vacations in Corfu, and because of his marriage to Nonie Phipps, his name is always coming up in exclusive Palm Beach and Long Island drawing rooms.

Thomas Bancroft, Sr., and his son **Thomas Jr.,** are major figures in the U circles of Long Island and Manhattan. The latter, whose mother was Edith Woodward, was first married to the current Princess Charles d'Arenberg and is now wedded to the lovely Melissa Weston. Handsome and full of humor, he is ever drawn into society, although he resists it as much as he can, preferring sports and other diversions.

Tommy Phipps, son of one of the famous Langhorne sisters and therefore a nephew of Lady (Nancy) Astor, is blissfully married to Mary Cheseborough and writes plays (*Four Winds* and *Motel*).

Tom Emery, a member of the famous Cincinnati clan, who recently took on as his third wife the delightful French chanteuse Vicki Autier, is a highly original, offbeat fellow and an enthusiastic chess player. He keeps his European headquarters in Biarritz.

Wherever his wife, Fleur Cowles, leaves a trace, easy-going lumber tycoon **Tom Meyer** has been there too. Guests sleep on foam rubber mattresses in their country home near the British capital.

Tom Kernan is the terribly able editor in chief of *Maison and Jardin.* He used to make monthly trips to Italy to keep an eye on the Condé Nast magazine *Vogue-Novita.* He is a *cordon bleu* cook, and the luncheons in his weekend house at Senlis are Lucullan feasts.

Tom Curtis was for many years the theater critic for the Paris edition of the *Herald-Tribune* before switching to the same assignment for the *New York Times.* He does many interviews with screen stars, and since they all like him, he is always in their midst. Gifted with a prodigious memory, he is a fund of information on the entertainment world.

Tom Keogh, the talented painter and illustrator, was married at one point to Theodora Roosevelt and later escorted Nathalie Philippart, the ballerina, everywhere. He also makes his headquarters in Paris.

Tommy Shevlin is a busy Palm Beach sportsman, who plays golf, swims, bicycles, and takes off with his wife "Durie" on big game hunts in Africa.

Thomas Stewart, a very fine baritone from Texas, has scored notable successes as Amfortas in *Parsifal* at the Bayreuth Festival, as Jokanaan in *Salomé* at the Paris Opera, and in many other roles at the German Opera House in Berlin of which he is a member. He is the husband of Evelyn Lear, another splendid young American singer who is forging a great European career for herself.

Tom Courtenay, a narrow-faced and narrow-hipped British

actor, is much in demand after his smashing performance in *The Loneliness of the Long Distance Runner*. He is all over the place, rushing from Hollywood where he went to appear in *King Rat* to Spain and Finland for the movie *Doctor Zhivago*. A long list of future assignments will keep him spinning.

Thomas Milian, a Cuban exile, not yet thirty, with a wonderfully brooding, handsome face, speaks excellent English and Italian and is kept busy on all sorts of European screen assignments. His base is in Rome, and his new romances provide the Via Veneto with titillating gossip.

Tom Wolfe's staggeringly ironical articles in *Esquire* and the *Herald-Tribune*'s Sunday section on today's manners and morals have made him a No. 1 conversation piece. Outfitted and coiffed in his own special way, this Virginian is contributing much to Manhattan's party circuit.

Tony and Anthony

In England there are many but those who recur most frequently in N.S. talk are:

The Earl of Snowdon, who was catapulted into royal circles by his surprising marriage to the Queen's sister. A pixyish, talented fellow with artistic leanings (his uncle is Oliver Messel), and a difficult position to fill, he has decided to continue his excellent photographic work. Although he always follows his wife, his hands held in the back, in observance of protocol, his is an independent spirit. His photographs appear often in American *Vogue*.

Anthony Sampson, educated at Oxford, is the son of a distinguished research scientist. His uncommon intelligence led him to several important magazine writing assignments, and he has become an authority on Africa where he has spent much time. But it is his brilliant volume *Anatomy of Britain* which has assigned him great stature and entrée all over the world.

Viscount Lambton, a Member of Parliament, is one of the most attractive members of *Debrett's Peerage.* Gifted with six children (five of whom are girls), from his wife, tall, Amazon-like Belinda Bridget, he owns the fine country seat, Flodden Field, in Scotland.

Tony Pawson, whose looks never change, has adorned the jet set for many seasons. Soft-spoken, polite, and gentle, he is a favorite extra man in his incessant wanderings. He has acquired a property near Alicante where he intends to retire a few weeks every year.

Tony Nutting, the dashing former British Cabinet minister, who is equally at home on both sides of the Atlantic, is currently the spouse of ex-model Anne Gunning. They have chosen a location near Tangiers where they have erected a whitewashed villa in which to spend their holidays.

Tony Quinn, now divorced after a long marriage to Katharine de Mille and married to Yolanda Addolori, has the same magnetism for women that his name has for the public when it appears on the marquees. Not socially minded, he never fails to make an impression when he does put in an appearance at parties.

Actor **Tony Perkins** is popular with certain egghead and yé-yé sets. An offbeat operator, he never conforms and therefore his independence is often the source of admiring comments.

Tony Duke, a brother of the American Ambassador to Spain and a son of Mrs. T. Markoe Robertson, is connected with many members of American society. Civic-minded, he is interested in boys' camps and arranges for benefits to pay for some of their expenses. His current wife is Diane Douglas.

Town and Country's editor, **Anthony Mazzola,** is busy covering society all over the world. Since he oozes sex appeal, the girls complain that he is married.

Many who knew **Toni Gardiner** at the time her father was stationed in the Middle East with the British Army still call her by this nickname, even though she is now the consort of King

Hussein of Jordan. This healthy, sporting young woman is officially known as Princess Muna, which in Arabic means Flower of the Desert.

Tony de Bekassy is the son of one of the six marriages contracted by Eleanor Close, Mrs. Marjorie Merriweather Post-Close-Hutton-Davies May's daughter. Currently Mrs. Leon Barzin, she honored him with a magnificent birthday ball at her Chateau in Vaux sur Seine, which was the talk of Paris for weeks.

Violet, Violette

The Countess James de Pourtales and Duchess de Sagan (in her own right), whose mother was the famous Anna Gould, Duchess of Talleyrand, is exquisitely feminine, very blonde, and occupies the superb Chateau du Marais outside Paris.

The Hon. Mrs. Violet Traffusis, a gifted writer and intellectual hostess, has three houses: one in Paris, a country place nearby, and the famous Villa l'Ombrellino in Florence, which she inherited from her mother, Mrs. George Keppel, an historical Edwardian character and beauty.

Mrs. Guy Wyndham, also a good writer and daughter of a famous authoress, Ada Leveson (who befriended Oscar Wilde in his disgrace), is prominent in Lady Diana Cooper's set in London.

Widely admired by such special people as Simone de Beauvoir, Sartre, and Jean Genet is **Violette Leduc,** whose books are always shocking literary sensations (the most recent, *La Batarde,* has stunned even the least squeamish).

Born Lady Violet Asquith close to eighty years ago—her father was Britain's Prime Minister during the First World War—**Baroness Asquith of Yarnbury** is the widow of Mark Bonham Carter. In 1964 she was created a life Peer which gives her a seat in the House of Lords. Her activities and accomplishments, listed in the various *Who's Who,* are enough to make anyone dizzy. Among them is her book on Winston Churchill. Her daughters-in-law are an American, Leslie, whose father was the late Condé Nast, and a Spaniard, Helena, a daughter of Ambassador Eduardo de Callejon.

VIRGINIA

In Washington the most imposing Virginia is **Mrs. Robert L. Bacon,** the last great hostess of the old guard. At one time it was said that the American capital's society was conducted by the three B's; Mrs. Truxton Beale (dead), Mrs. Robert W. Bliss (ailing), and Mrs. Bacon, who is still in there swinging and holding her own despite much recent competition. Because of her many wonderful friendships in all the embassies, she is received everywhere on her trips like a V.I.P.

Manhattan's **Mrs. Byron Foy** (Virginia Peine) is blonde, cozy, humorous, with all sorts of friends along different circuits. She has been married three times previously to men of different backgrounds and interests, including Quentin Reynolds.

Virginia Pope, whose position in the international fashion circles (for many years she was fashion editor for the *New York Times*, currently for *Parade*) has been most eminent, is a civilized lady who speaks admirable French and Italian and who, because of her profession, travels widely.

Mrs. William Hutton is one of the most beautiful and impersonal of the young matrons of New York society, a daughter of Earl E. T. Smith, and related to many prominent American dynasties on the East Coast.

Lady Ogilvy, sister-in-law of Alexandra of Kent, welcomed in the royal enclosures of Britain, is an American heiress in her own right (the late Otto Kahn was her grandfather). Born Virginia Ryan, she is called Ginny.

Lady Sykes is mentioned in worldwide racing society since, her husband Sir Richard Sykes is one of its leading members.

The American-born wife of **"Aubrey" Casardi,** the Italian Ambassador to Japan, was Virginia Harris from St. Louis. An outgoing person, she has been adored everywhere her capable husband has been sent, leaves a host of friends in her path, and is likely to stay with them all over the globe.

Rome's **Donna Virginia Ruspoli** was born to the purpled Patrizi clan and married into an equally radiant one. Because of her young daughter, Patrizia, she is now often on the move.

Mrs. Darryl Zanuck, a well-liked, well-dressed matron, patiently waits on the West Coast for the return of her husband from his interminable, varied film assignments here, there, everywhere.

Mrs. Ambrose Chambers, widow of the renowned American lawyer, has lived in Paris for ages. She is entrenched solidly not only with the passing nomads whom she visits but with the old French guard. Her apartment in the historical Palais Lambert provides a fine frame to her way of life.

In Boston, Cape Cod, St. Moritz, and on many cosmopolitan paths **Mrs. Serge Semenenko,** the former Virginia Boyd, follows in the wake of her husband with a ready smile. To be married to a financial genius (her Russian-born mate has large interests ranging from Tiffany to French and Co., from Warner Bros. to the First National Bank) must not be easy, but she seems to take it all in her stride.

Vittorio

is a popular Christian name in Italy.

If Italy were still a monarchy, **Prince Vittorio Emanuele of Savoy** would be the Crown Prince. Nordic in appearance (his mother is a Belgian Princess with a German mother), tall, slim, and blond, he is younger in looks and manners than his actual age. Friendly with the yé-yé set, he turns up in St. Tropez, Gstaad, and wherever this particular group gathers. A stockbroker, he commutes constantly from Geneva, where he lives, to European capitals. His much-publicized romance with Marina Doria appears to be in drydock.

Count Vittorio Cini, one of Italy's leading industrialists and most public-spirited citizens, has magnificent residences in Venice, Monselice, and Rome. A widower—his wife was Lyda Borelli, one of the great screen vamps of European silent films—he lost his only son, Giorgio, in a tragic airplane accident in 1949 at the Cannes airport, has three daughters, all married, and owns a spectacular collection of great paintings by old masters.

Both **Vittorio de Sica** and **Vittorio Gassman** belong to the world of stage and screen. The second, once wed to Shelley Winters, makes news with his diversified romances. The two of them have a marvelous humor and it is difficult to tell their mots apart.

A new star in N.S. is **Vittorio de Nora,** a southern Italian who has struck it rich and spends his money freely on the amenities of modern life. He and his wife both pilot their two baby jets.

In the palaces of Rome's blackest aristocracy and along the Via Veneto (his tempestuous marriage with British actress Dawn Addams keeps hitting the newspapers for one reason or the other) the name of **Vittorio Massimo,** Prince de Roccasecca dei Volsci, recurs. The wife of his brother, Princess Maria Adelaide di Savoia-Genova, is a member of the Italian Royal Family.

Handsome, blond sportsman **Count Vittorio Camerana,** whose mother was closely related to the Agnellis, holds a fine position with Fiat in New York City. His Belgian wife, Christine, is pretty and well-dressed.

Vittorio Marzotto, one of the leaders of the Liberal Party in Italy, loves racing cars, skiing, and recently took on a second wife. His family owns a great industrial empire, and he roams the Mediterranean on his fine yacht, *Le Roc.*

Walter

Walter Hoving, the suave, capable, President of Tiffany, has been a trend-setter over many decades (he used to be at Lord and Taylor, later Bonwit Teller) and is a polished after-dinner speaker and civic leader. With his wise wife Pauline van den Doort Steese Dresser Rogers (he is her fourth husband), he is a solid pillar of international society.

The **Duke of Buccleuch,** whose sister is the Duchess of Gloucester, has a collection of paintings at his three country seats, Bowhill, Boughton, and Drumlanrig Castle, that make most museums seem pale in comparison. He never stays long anywhere and is ever traveling.

Popular **Major Walter Lees,** ex-attaché at the British Embassy in Paris, ex-aide de camp to Stavros Niarchos, is currently in the employ of Yul Brynner's business ventures with the French capital as a base.

The former Brazilian Ambassador to Washington and Minister of the Brazilian Treasury, **Walter Moreira Sales,** is a trans-Atlantic commuter from his luxurious but unfinished Parisian apartment. He keeps appearing in Portugal where he has acquired a huge peninsula, Troia, south of Lisbon, which he is developing.

Another Walter is an Englishman who answers the description of Major Thompson, the immortal character created by Pierre Daninos. He is **Walter Prettiman,** a substantially wealthy gentleman, who has the good luck to be the mate of the great Brazilian beauty, Vera Sotomayor, who never fails to marry Britishers. Her past husbands have, in fact, included Yvor Bryce and the current Baron Dunsany.

Walter Chiari, the sexy Italian actor and musical comedy star, has never married, but has been off and on one of Ava Gardner's favorite escorts. Occasionally much publicity is devoted to some delightful Miss claiming the baby she has given birth to has been sired by him. Like all good Italians, he may hope it's true, since they believe in the sweet theory that the more children, the better.

Where snobbism for Hollywood is alive, there's **Walter Wanger,** who is a fine producer and good company. He is now related to Long Island society since his daughter Stephanie (a result of his marriage to Joan Bennett) is Mrs. Frederick Guest.

Index

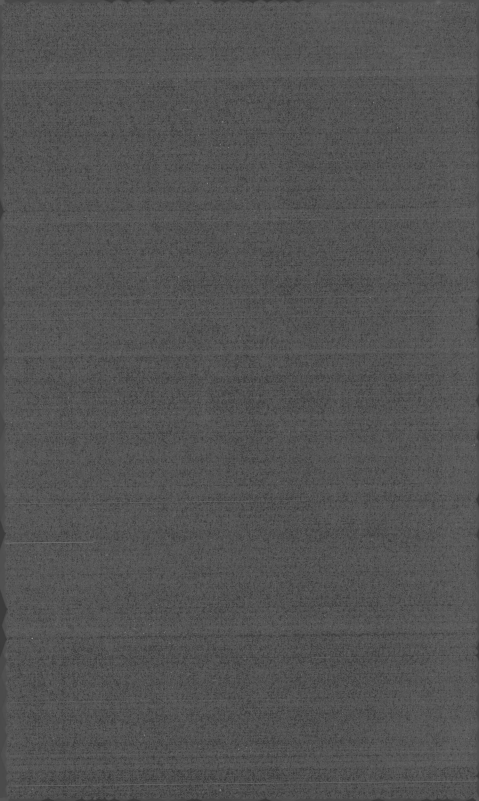